D0160871

INTERNATIONAL
MEDIA RESEARCH

International Media Research offers a rigorous and critical review of key approaches and concerns that have recently defined the field of media research. The contributors to this volume analyse and reflect upon dominant themes and debates that have made media research an increasingly important element of political, social and cultural enquiry. The book opens with an introduction which surveys the current state of the field, and continues with a critical evaluation of the work of the leading media scholar, Elihu Katz. It goes on to explore the relationship between media studies and adjacent fields: cultural studies and new work on gender and sexuality.

Contributors drawn from the UK, USA, Canada and Belgium consider the relationships between media research and media policy in different national and international contexts. Focusing on the European Union, East-Central Europe, North America and Latin America, these chapters assess the impact of social, economic and political circumstances on policy debates and the shaping of a research agenda. The final chapter adopts a transatlantic perspective in tracing and analysing the history of the media's role in reporting war.

This major survey firmly places media research in the wider context of political and social change and its analysis, and provides a defining but also questioning perspective on its achievements.

Contributors: Jean-Claude Burgelman, Peter Dahlgren, Elizabeth Fox, Daniel C. Hallin, Joke Hermes, Sonia Livingstone, Vincent Mosco, Vanda Rideout, Colin Sparks.

Editors: John Corner is Professor in the School of Politics and Communication Studies, University of Liverpool. Philip Schlesinger is Professor of Film and Media Studies, University of Stirling and the Director of the Stirling Media Research Institute. Roger Silverstone is Professor of Media and Communications at the London School of Economics and Political Science.

INTERNATIONAL MEDIA RESEARCH

A critical survey

*Edited by John Corner,
Philip Schlesinger and
Roger Silverstone*

London and New York

First published 1997
by Routledge
11 New Fetter Lane, London EC4P 4EE

Simultaneously published in the USA and Canada
by Routledge
29 West 35th Street, New York, NY 10001

First published in paperback 1998

The authors have asserted their moral rights in accordance with
the Copyright, Designs and Patents Act 1988.

© 1997 The editors; individual chapters © the contributors

Typeset in Times by
Ponting–Green Publishing Services, Chesham, Buckinghamshire
Printed and bound in Great Britain by
Redwood Books, Trowbridge, Wilts

All rights reserved. No part of this book may be
reprinted or reproduced or utilized in any form or by
any electronic, mechanical, or other means, now
known or hereafter invented, including photocopying
and recording, or in any information storage or
retrieval system, without permission in writing
from the publishers.

British Library Cataloguing in Publication Data
A catalogue record for this book is available from the
British Library

Library of Congress Cataloguing in Publication Data
International media research: a critical survey / edited by John
Corner, Philip Schlesinger and Roger Silverstone.
p.   cm.
Includes bibliographical references and index.
(alk. paper)
1. Mass media–Research.   2. Mass media and culture.
3. Mass media policy.   I. Corner, John, 1943–   .
II. Schlesinger, Philip, 1948-   .   III. Silverstone, Roger.
P91.3.I56   1997
302.23–dc20   96–17635

ISBN 0–415–09035–0 (hbk)
ISBN 0–415–18496–7 (pbk)

CONTENTS

CONTRIBUTORS

Jean-Claude Burgelman is currently Associate Professor at the National Fund of Scientific Research, University of Brussels, Belgium, where he formerly worked as a full-time researcher. He is Director of the research centre for the Study of New Media, Information and Telecommunication (SMIT), which is dedicated to long-term research into the societal aspects of communication technologies and services.

John Corner is Professor in the School of Politics and Communication Studies at the University of Liverpool. He has written extensively on broadcast journalism, media audiences and cultural analysis. His books include the edited collections, *Documentary and the Mass Media* (1986), *Popular Television in Britain* (1991), the co-authored study *Nuclear Reactions* (1990) and the monographs *Television Form and Public Address* (1995) and *The Art of Record: Critical Studies in Documentary* (1996).

Peter Dahlgren is Professor of Media and Communication Studies, Lund University, Sweden. His research and his teaching emphasize social and cultural theory, television analysis, journalism and the public sphere, qualitative methods, and philosophy of science. He has authored a number of articles and published *Television and the Public Sphere* (1995). He has also edited two volumes with Colin Sparks: *Journalism and Popular Culture* (1992) and *Communication and Citizenship* (1991).

Elizabeth Fox has an internationally recognized record of achievements in the field of Latin American communications. She has worked as a journalist, directed international aid programmes, designed and conducted multi-country development research on communication issues, and managed an office of strategic planning for a US government agency. Dr Fox has written numerous books, articles and manuals on Latin American development, communications, and health promotion. She presently directs the communications programme for Latin America for the BASICS Partnership for Child Survival.

Daniel C. Hallin is Professor of Communication at the University of California at San Diego, and holds a Ph.D. in Political Science from the University of

California, Berkeley. He is author of *The 'Uncensored War': the Media and Vietnam*, and has written on coverage of Central America and on the Gulf War.

Joke Hermes is a lecturer in Media Studies at the University of Amsterdam. She has contributed theoretical and substantive work to a number of books and journals, including James Curran and Michael Gurevitch's collection *Mass Media and Society* (1991) and the *European Journal of Communication*. Her study of readership, *Reading Women's Magazines*, was published in 1995.

Sonia Livingstone is Programme Director of the M.Sc. in Media and Communications at the London School of Economics. Her research interests focus on the media audience, particularly the audience for such television genres as the soap opera, crime shows, talk shows and children's media. She is author of *Making Sense of Television* (1995) and co-author (with P. Lunt) of *Mass Consumption and Personal Identity* (1992) and *Talk on Television* (1994).

Vincent Mosco is Professor in the School of Journalism and Communication at Carleton University, Ottawa, Canada. He received his Ph.D. from Harvard where he currently holds a research position with the Program on Information Resources Policy. His most recent book is *The Political Economy of Communication: Rethinking and Renewal* (1996) and he is a member of the editorial boards of academic journals in the USA, Canada, England and Spain.

Vanda Rideout is completing her doctoral dissertation in Sociology at Carleton University. Recent publications with V. Mosco, include, 'Communication policy in the United States' in M. Bailie, D. Winseck, S.H. Yoon (eds) *Democratizing Communication? Comparative Perspectives in Information and Power* (forthcoming), and 'Telecommunication policy for whom?', in *Alternate Routes* (1993).

Philip Schlesinger is Professor and Director of the Stirling Media Research Institute at the University of Stirling, Scotland. He is also a Professor of Media and Communication at the University of Oslo and is presently engaged in research on political communication and democracy and on Europeanization and national identity. Among his recent books are *Media, State and Nation* (1991), and the co-authored studies *Women Viewing Violence* (1992) and *Reporting Crime* (1994). He is an editor of the journal *Media, Culture and Society*.

Roger Silverstone is Professor of Media and Communications at the London School of Economics and Political Science. He is the author of *The Message of Television: Myth and Narrative in Contemporary Culture* (1981); *Framing Science: the Making of a BBC Documentary* (1985); *Television and Everyday Life* (1994); and is the editor of *Consuming Technologies: Media and Information in Domestic Spaces* (with Eric Hirsch) (1992); *Communication by Design: the Politics of Information and Communication Technology* (with Robin Mansell) (1996); and *Visions of Suburbia* (1996).

Colin Sparks works at the Centre for Communication and Information Studies of the University of Westminster. His current research is concerned with the restructuring of the media, particularly television, in the former communist countries. He has published widely on this subject, on the UK press and television industries, and on cultural theories. He is a member of the editorial board of *Media, Culture and Society*, and a director of the European Institute for Communication and Culture.

ACKNOWLEDGEMENTS

This book began in discussions between the editors following an approach by Routledge to produce a reference work for media research. We felt that the appropriate response should not be an encyclopaedia but a book, or a series of volumes, which would aim to provide authoritative reviews of recent developments in key areas: to report, to reflect and to comment. This is the outcome.

The fact that the editing of this volume has been demanding could no doubt be warmly testified to by our authors. Despite having experienced a detailed level of editorial intervention, they have been patient and cooperative in reworking their material. Indeed the complexity of the editorial process only gradually emerged as we realized that, in trying to define the standards that might be attained by a book of this kind, we were asking more of our contributors than was perhaps customary.

For each of the chapters we have sought comprehensiveness and clarity. At the same time, we have not asked authors to write to a formula. We have encouraged them to speak with a distinctive voice regarding their objects of analysis and to bring a balanced assessment to bear so that the reader would come away from any given contribution with a good sense of a range of approaches and findings. Most of the essays are followed by annotated bibliographies intended to highlight the key works for those who wish to study further the themes covered. Occasionally, the individual writer has done the essential bibliographical work in the chapter itself, and in those cases we have judged it unnecessary to carry a separate bibliographical section. It is our intention that the book will be used both by media researchers and teachers in higher education institutions internationally, offering some authoritative reviews of the literature which are at the same time strongly personal statements of what is important in the areas selected.

We have chosen our authors with care. Each of them is an established and accomplished scholar in the field and together they provide a broad and, above all, an international array of perspectives on some of the key areas of recent and contemporary media research.

We would like, finally, to record our thanks to the two associate editors, Marjorie Ferguson and Jérôme Bourdon, and to our editor at Routledge, Rebecca Barden, each for their patience and their help.

1

EDITORS' INTRODUCTION

John Corner, Philip Schlesinger
and Roger Silverstone

PURPOSE AND SCOPE

In recent years, media research has enjoyed explosive growth as the centrality of the media to contemporary societies has increasingly imposed itself on our consciousness. It has become more and more obvious that, with the internationalization of media institutions, products and consumption, media research cannot be limited to what happens within given, national frontiers; at the same time, the rapidly expansive nature of recent academic investigation, while most often still profoundly steeped in national traditions, has been on an increasingly international scale as the field entrenches itself more widely in all continents.

The pace of work has been such as to allow little time for reflection within the research community on the factors that have shaped specific areas of investigation, and in particular, those where we have shed most light, and those patches of darkness that still remain. Despite the plethora of monographs, edited collections and journals that have appeared, there has been much less by way of considered assessment of overall findings in the most densely researched areas than might be expected. The conventional forms of publishing have simply not provided sufficient space for extended analysis on the scope and limitations of existing achievements. Bearing this perspective in mind, the present collection is the beginning of an attempt to provide the necessary elbow-room for a wide-ranging set of individual explorations.

So this book responds to our sense that it is now time for a deeper evaluation of the present state of media research than is customary. We think of this collection of lengthy essays not as complete in itself but rather as the first of several such surveys of the field over the coming years, and ask our readers to interpret it in that light. Clearly, therefore, we do not intend the book to be taken as an exhaustive account of the present state of play but rather to be read as a contribution that will both illustrate and illuminate several major themes judged to be both of interest and importance for those engaged in media scholarship.

In this introductory chapter we want to look, first, at some features of the field as it has been constituted historically, noting not only the difficulties in achieving a coherent intellectual and academic identity but also the continuities with current concerns. We then want to comment briefly on three themes that we identify as of particular significance and which are developed in different ways throughout this book. These are: the comparison between circumstances in North America and Europe; the changing form of the linkage between states, markets and media systems; and the perennial question of the relationship between research and policy. In a final section we look at some prospects (and some problems) for future enquiry before introducing the chapters themselves.

THE HISTORICAL FORMATION OF THE RESEARCH FIELD

As John Durham Peters has recently remarked, 'the future of the field depends in many ways on coming to terms with the past of the field'. This is a past not only of routes taken but of routes ignored and, indeed, sometimes of routes actively discouraged. Towards the end of this introduction we look at the present shape of media research, but it may be useful here to reflect briefly on key elements in its making.

There is a sense in which 'mass communication' (or more recently 'media research') is, internationally, a project which has been in a sometimes precarious state of formation for over fifty years. Its history is far less a matter of tracing a narrow, continuous strand of specialized enquiry than of looking at a rather disparate and still not fully documented succession of theoretical projects, empirical engagements and often heated debates. Right from the start, in the separate kinds of intellectual response in Europe and North America to the emergence of modernity, public communication and 'mass culture', the field has never consolidated itself fully as an international academic enterprise.

The separate national and historical contexts occasioned by, for instance, the propaganda campaigns of 1930s European fascism, by American preoccupations post-World War II, both with public opinion and with the world's most aggressive young advertising industry, and by the longstanding concern of the British literary intelligentsia about declining cultural values, produced radically different starting points for enquiry. We may note, however, that some form of anxiety about some form of influence was a factor held in common across the diversity and it is only recently, as we shall discuss later, that this has become less so.

Even in the United States, where from the 1930s onwards the most sustained and ambitious programmes of research into 'mass communication' were undertaken from within the social sciences, there was a running anxiety about the coherence of the field, related to an eagerness (which has continued through to this day) to spot 'convergence' wherever it showed itself. So much so that Bernard Berelson, albeit with polemical intent, was able to offer an obituary for the entire enterprise in his famous *Public Opinion Quarterly* essay of 1959, 'The state of communication research'. He argued that the main problem was excessive fragmentation combined with a perceived absence of significant new ideas after the developments of the previous decades (for instance, the work of Lazarsfeld *et al.* on mediated influence, and of Hovland on persuasion). However, as many

2

commentators have since pointed out, Berelson painted a more gloomy picture than was perhaps justified by exaggerating the number of relevant 'bits' that ought to cohere.

In 1950, the publication of the volume which he edited with Morris Janowitz, *A Reader in Public Opinion and Communication*, had signalled a major point in the emergence of an interdisciplinary project. As well as the roll call of North-American-based pioneers – Lasswell, Blumer, Katz, Cantril, Lazarsfeld, Lippmann, Hovland, Löwenthal among them – the collection drew extensively from the work of writers who would not easily have recognized themselves as researching from 'within' its ostensible boundaries. *Post-facto* recruitment of 'outside' researchers is still, of course, an important way in which the field reconfigures and develops. It is worth noting here just how important certain anthologies have been, as acts of attempted consolidation. Twenty years later in Britain, Jeremy Tunstall's *Media Sociology* (1970) performed a rather similar function, as did Denis McQuail's *Sociology of Mass Communication* (1972), the latter indicating at its margins the arrival of 'new' critical and cultural theory to supplement, and at times to contest, the social science emphasis.

Such a tradition of concern over shape and direction, divergence and convergence, should not be seen simply as the 'failure' of a research specialism to establish itself properly. It is a reflection both of the increasing centrality of media-related issues to a whole range of studies in the social sciences (and latterly, in the humanities too) and also of the way in which study of the media has a tendency, because of the interconnections between questions of structure and agency, process and meaning, to draw attention to the limitations of particular theories and methods which are applied to it. In doing so, it acts to ferment both dissent and development, pulling in new ideas and new approaches to the perennial question 'What is it important to look at and how should we look at it?' with the same energy as it rejects others. The very dynamics of media developments themselves – the rate and scope of change across the technological, institutional and cultural realms – have in a sense determined the awkward character of media research's lineage. Our chapter assessing the work of Elihu Katz (chapter 2) brings out well some of the detail of this in the course of plotting one highly distinguished career.

In nearly every national academic system, media research has been an interdisciplinary or multi-disciplinary endeavour (only quite recently with any roots in significant undergraduate teaching) and thus has never really acquired an institutional identity strong enough to keep its boundaries tidy. One might argue that such an ambition, were it to develop, would be self-defeating anyway.

Thanks largely to Paul Lazarsfeld's perceptive – but by no means disinterested account, one aspect of earlier conflict has attained widely recognized status internationally – namely, the division between 'critical' and 'administrative' research. This dichotomy, essentially one between a European-influenced commitment to placing media processes within a framework of political scepticism and critique and a dominant (but by no means exclusive) tendency towards assessing the functionality of media systems within 'given' policy parameters in the USA, has been revisited many times. It has been variously revised and refuted, although its continuing use as a reference point must indicate a certain suggestiveness. Allowing for the simplistic nature of the division, it is certainly not hard to see on which side the greater possibilities for research funding lie. With this come greater opportunities for at least some form of sustained investigative relationship with institutional practices and processes. We consider the question of the relationship between media policy and media research a little later.

So even the briefest of genealogical sketches produces a rather turbulent picture, though a fascinating and valuable one for intellectual history, in which continuities are less apparent than differences and disjunctions at each new stage in the development of media technologies. Although media research has always been overdetermined by the interplay between the different economic and political perspectives on modernity, in its analyses and enquiries over the years it has engaged with an astonishing range of conceptual shifts and methodological reappraisals. In the last two decades, perhaps the most important of these have concerned the re-positioning of many strands of research within a larger project investigating the changing shape of late modern 'culture'. The European contribution here, theoretical and empirical, has been stronger in determining the general character of the field than at any previous stage in its development. A number of our contributions connect with this point and we return to it ourselves below.

THREE THEMES

Making comparisons

When we were considering the overall design of this book, we were concerned to ensure that a comparative element was built into it. This was not a quest for individual essays that engaged in formal comparison so much as for the collection as a whole to provide sufficient diversity of content to bring into relief international similarities and differences both in the style of media research and in its objects of study.

The reader cannot fail to be struck by two broad sets of comparisons that inform almost all of the essays. One grand line of distinction concerns Europe and the Americas. And there is a further division within each of these broad geographical categories: first, our contributions cover both North America (with its own significant fissure between the USA and Canada) and then Latin America; they also deal with the 'advanced' Europe centred upon the European Union and with part of the post-communist Europe that awaits entry to the EU. Each of these areas is characterized by distinctive relations between the national state, the market, and the media, in which the historical weight of inherited institutional patterns, political and economic practices and cultural norms should not be underestimated. And it is this matrix of relations which holds the interpretive key to the developments that are assessed in these pages.

As we noted earlier, the United States has been the first and foremost locus of media research in historical terms. The USA has also made the running in the reshaping of the media environment, most notably in terms of technological advance and deregulatory policies whose impact has been felt both in the Americas and also across the Atlantic, as well as further afield. Despite its proximity to the United States, Canada's federal government has striven to use media and cultural policies to shore up the state's distinctiveness. Hence, the theme of politico-cultural power relations, and how these are underpinned by media economics, is a central issue for debate. But this question traverses all the Americas and resonates far beyond, as the stand-off between the European Union and the USA over GATT in late 1993 showed. That said, proximity to the USA produces an especially sharp reaction to the question of cultural sovereignty. Much media development and policy-making in Latin America has been shaped by the pattern of US investment and cultural exports to that continent and this has interacted with indigenous factors to produce some unique results.

In the European Union and its member states, so far as questions of media and cultural policy are concerned, the USA has been both a model at times to be emulated and at others to be rejected. On the European continent itself, the expanding European Union has provided an aspirational model for the transitional national states of the post-communist era. For such aspirant outsiders the EU signifies modernization, the market economy and pluralistic democracy. Looked at from within, however, the drive to integration has hardly been without contradictions between the economy and culture, and institutional differences rooted in the distinctive histories of the member national states continue to hold sway over the Union's development. These differences are manifest in the field of media policy and will continue to be so. One way of looking at this is to say that there is therefore no single 'European' model for the media, as the weight of the national state remains decisive in the shaping of media institutions. Nevertheless, by comparison with the United States, there is still a different range of possibilities in Europe for the relations between state, market and media. Hence, moving from the west of the continent to its centre, it is apparent that the post-communist states are being profoundly shaped in their development patterns by 'European' constraints and possibilities.

Media, state and market

A further theme which is addressed at several points, sometimes directly and sometimes only through its bearing on other factors, is the positioning of media systems in relation both to the organizations of the state and to the mechanisms of the market. Media systems have an important public role both in information provision and also in offering a forum for debate and space for a public to recognize itself as such. Thus, media systems are necessary institutions to any form of civil society. This perspective emphasizes output which is broadly journalistic over that which is offered primarily as entertainment, but there is by no means a sharp division here and there are grounds for seeing many kinds of dramatic material, serious and popular, as having a public function too.

The notion of the 'public' has been a troubled term in contemporary political analysis, indicating a degree of autonomy both from direct state intervention and from the realm of market structures and corporate influence. In Britain and other European countries, for instance, there has been a tendency for the tradition of 'public' broadcasting to become too closely linked with the interests of the state (thereby allowing more recent commercial initiatives to project themselves as democratic and liberatory). In many other countries, however, notably the United States, 'public' broadcasting exists only in a marginal form where it exists at all, even though national regulation has produced a pattern of provision which is by no means a simple reflection of private imperatives.

Systems of funding are a major factor, of course, but they are not the only one, since requirements of 'public' responsibility have regularly been made of 'privately owned' media and this looks likely to become the dominant mode by which any public requirements upon the media might now conceivably be made. Such sanctions have either been implemented through bureaucratic oversight over commercial activities (as in the case of the British Independent Television Commission) or through the 'softer' mechanisms of bodies of public appeal (as in Press Complaints Boards). An additional problem in the regulation of public media systems is that notions of 'the public' have often tended towards an emphatically unitary idea, and consequent unwillingness to register multiplicity and variety; this has also occasionally led to countenancing imposed homogeneity. Reappraisal on this point, retaining a principle of cohesion but discarding neat unities, is clearly a prerequisite of any cogent policy in the future, whatever national historical differences obtain.

But how might media systems gain the maximum space for independent information-gathering analysis and debate, with the consequent expectation of 'public' value, and also have viable and stable funding? This has been the problem, variously posed, for the critical review of media systems internationally, and it has increasingly become precisely an international issue because to address it in the terms solely of a national media economy has become either impossible or imprudent. It is not suprising that the 'solutions' variously arrived at, often carrying strong historical legacies, have so often been one form or other of accommodation to the international media market. As our three chapters on policy shifts show, the intensified round of deregulation in western Europe (where the United States model has been influential though not decisive) has been joined by the wholesale deconstruction and reconstruction of media systems, and media–politics relations, within the former communist countries. Here, the swing from state to market has been most dramatic (notwithstanding concealed continuities), carrying an impetus which has had, so far, little time for that 'intermediate' category of the public that has been the focus for so much liberal democratic debate.

Yet, despite the widespread consolidation of market models, linked to new technologies of production and distribution and variously pledged (or not) to the observance of 'public' principles, state and supra-state organizations (for instance, the EU) still exert a measure of regulatory influence over the media as an industry and over certain forms of public representation. Governmental effectiveness in the former area is determined by the particular forms of economic control which specific states operate, namely the larger settlements made in any given polity between the 'state' and the 'market'. Their function as regulators of content depends in some measure on the strength of 'public feeling' upon which they can draw (and also orchestrate) concerning specific notions of cultural nationalism and morality as well as broader rights of citizenship. That the state could, and should, intervene to protect citizenship against erosion through the unchecked promotionalism, selectivity and inequalities of markets – thereby paradoxically regulating for freedom against neo-liberal constraint – should be an established principle of any self-aware democratic politics. But the protection of state interests against those of public knowledge is, of course, still a major cause of actual intervention in many countries. Moreover, the possibilities of certain kinds of state interest being well served by market interests, to the general detriment of the broader public interest, are considerable. It is how to initiate cogent policy in this complex configuration, rather than any single alignment with either side of the state/market relation, which now represents the greatest problem for ensuring the democratic character of press and broadcasting.

All of the above means that, outside of improbable schemes for wholly alternative funding, the products of mass media systems will have an increasingly commodified character as the exchange-value of media products extends to areas where it has so far been resisted and intensifies in areas (e.g. globally marketed entertainment) where it has always been present. It is thus very hard to resist the view that a global economic squeeze on public culture is occurring. Assessing just how and to what degree 'public' values are sustainable or not in the face of this underlying pattern of commodification and how states might act in the public interest to check and contest a thoroughgoing privatization of citizenship is therefore a more important task for international media research than either of the two rather 'diversionary' paths which offer themselves – the search for non-commodified alternatives or the repetitive denunciation of commodification *per se*.

Research and policy

The well-established, though contentious, distinction between critical and administrative research mentioned earlier emerges in a newer form in a number of the chapters that follow. Colin Sparks, Jean-Claude Burgelman, Vincent Mosco and Vanda Rideout and Elizabeth Fox, in their various ways, explore the relationship between media research and media policy. One way of understanding that relationship is to suggest that the funding crisis in scientific research in almost all the developed countries has created a situation in which media research is increasingly being constrained, if not determined, by the perceived needs of government and industry. This results, it can be argued, in a profound skewing of the research agenda to issues defined as more or less exclusively relevant to the management of the polity and the economy. In turn, media research, like so many other areas of social science, is increasingly condemned to short-termism and pragmatism both in the selection of research areas and the approaches that are taken. And this can lead not only to a narrowing and skewing of the research focus, but also to a weakening of an alternative, humanist and critical tradition, which is left to scrabble at the margins of media research and scholarship. The increasing emphasis on the involvement of what in the UK's particular jargon are research's 'end-users', an emphasis which has now been enshrined in the basic agenda of the research infrastructure and has been incorporated into the two major programmes of media research funded by the British Economic and Social Research Council over recent years, can be seen to embody this trend towards 'relevance' most clearly.

However, the increasing relevance of media (especially, of course, the converging technologies of television and telecommunications) in the formation of national policy, and the increasing success of media researchers in persuading policy-makers and funders at all levels that there is indeed a social agenda to be pursued here, produce something of a double-edged sword. It can lead, reactively, to the reinforcement of extraneously defined political and economic priorities at the core of media research.

Two factors complicate matters further. The first is the argument that media research has an obligation to engage in public policy, but to do so with the aim of actually shifting the policy agenda. In addressing issues of political communication and of representation (in both senses of the word) as well as those of the regulation and consumption of new information and communication technologies, media research should be seen to be involved in a constant debate with those who, by virtue of ownership or election, have the power to steer media culture. The second complicating factor, and this comes through particularly in the contributions of Fox and Sparks, is the variation in the relationship between research and policy, geographically and historically. In both Latin America and in post-Soviet Central and Eastern Europe changing state–media relations and the relations between states and wider sets of regional or global forces have both defined and legitimated a necessarily shifting relationship between research and policy.

Substantial links between research and policy therefore seem to be inescapable, though experience suggests that they are by no means non-negotiable. If the research community acknowledges and accepts a responsibility for the ways in which media figure in contemporary society, then that still begs the question as how best, in specific circumstances, to honour that role.

There is a danger when discussing the relationship between research and policy that the differences as well as the links between different policy arenas will go unacknowledged. It is in the nature of things that media will intrude into economic, political and cultural policy-making at every social level, from the supra-national (as in Europe) to the national as well as at the local. And of course media policy research impacts on wider questions of citizenship and democratic participation as well as on the regulation or deregulation of markets in telecommunications, broadcasting or electronic networks. It can also shape policies regarding aesthetic strategies in broadcasting or software design as well as those concerning gender or ethnic participation in media industries. There is, further, a danger that we may underestimate the significance of the different approaches that media policy research might take with respect to each of these different domains. Convergence in the world may or may not be matched by convergence in theory and approach, but what is obviously signalled is the need for media policy research to be newly sensitive to the rapid and often strategic changes in the world which it addresses, as well as to be continuously reflexive about its own presuppositions and agendas.

Two final points might be worth making. Media research often emerges at the interface of the humanities and the social sciences. It is clear from the policy research chapters in this volume that the dominant voices, perhaps inevitably and necessarily, come from within the latter. In almost all the cases discussed, cultural policy as such, and the media's role in its development, tends to get overlooked in favour of more narrowly conceived political, social and economic objectives, as it does more generally in the literature. This issue might be addressed in future work, especially since questions of particular form and content remain central and media analysis itself increasingly has to take into account the inseparability of medium and message. Second, and more controversially, it is possible to argue that, given the challenges of the intellectual agenda, research specifically oriented to policy is the last thing that media researchers should be undertaking; that they should be committed, rather, to more fundamental and unconstrained enquiries into the political, social and cultural processes of mediation.

FUTURES

Media research since the mid-1980s has seen shifts, both voluntary and reactive, in a field which in many respects has struggled to keep up with the rapid pace of change in public media culture. During this period it is not just that media have become ever more ingrained into the fabric of contemporary society, but as we have already suggested, it is now impossible to consider either public or private life without taking the media's central role into account. We have become increasingly dependent on media systems that are extending well beyond the relative simplicities of broadcasting. Media space is becoming fragmented and diverse, but it is also becoming more intense, more pervasive. It is, of course, both global and local, public and private. However both the global and the local and the public and private are imprecise and inaccurate as descriptors of the complex realities that are now emerging. The postmodernist fancies of hyper-realities, virtual communities and electronic hearths and democracies, of cyber-worlds universally accessible through the flick of a switch, or the click of a mouse, are often too easily claimed but they can also be too easily denied Perhaps the researcher's role is now becoming one in which a degree of informed imagination – an ability to engage with the speculative and not simply being content to limit attention to actual circumstances – will be a more important element than it has been hitherto.

It is not our intention to try and predict what the next few years will bring in the field, though certain new trends are beginning to emerge and some questions are beginning to become more insistent. Indeed looking ahead, perhaps, to the next volume of this survey, we can point to a number of key issues where there might be some significant movement. We have just signalled the first of these. The 'convergence' much noted in media is all at once a technological, an industrial and a social process. As computers, telephones and television sets connect more tightly together, as we move inexorably towards an interactive screen-based culture of potentially infinite reach and probable information overload, we will have to attend not just to the ways in which changes are managed in public and private space, but to the profound contradictions that they will surely throw up. In many respects we will be confronted by old problems in new clothes: problems of media access and media influence; problems of ownership and control; problems of citizenship; and problems of disentangling the social and the psychological dimensions of media use. Yet the relative decline not just of public service broadcasting in its historic forms, but also of broadcasting as such, is already placing large question marks alongside many of the received wisdoms. So too is the relative weakening of what once, albeit rather briefly as now transpires, may have been national broadcast cultures. In an age of fragmenting and conflicting cultural and individual identities, there may be persuasive grounds for thinking that the new media and the patterns of use, communication and dependence that they engender could conceivably themselves become the cores around which old identities reconfigure and new ones form. At all events, this is an issue that will surely be pursued.

All this has profound implications for our work. There is the relationship between the 'discipline' of media studies and adjacent disciplines and discourses, related to which are issues concerning methodology and the kinds of question we choose to ask. The various dimensions of convergence are going to require both new methods and a greater reflexivity in our use of existing ones. They also are likely to require an even greater openness to approaches being developed in fields alongside our own, principally it might appear, in the sociology and philosophy of technology, in cultural anthropology, in psychology and indeed in cybernetics. Interactivity, multimediation, new forms of textuality and different relationships, both cultural and political, between receivers and senders, as well as the blurring of boundaries between otherwise discrete categories and processes of information and communication, are together likely to pose new challenges which existing approaches may well be hard pushed to address.

The capacity to grapple with this rapidly but unevenly changing media world will place a premium on our capacity to think innovatively. If we were asked to be more specific about the issues and questions that need attention, either by way of opening up new approaches or revising old ones, we would identify ideas of 'influence', the bearing of the media on questions of 'identity' and the cultural relations of technology as three areas around which new work is required.

Influence of one form or another remains the primary (if undeclared) premise upon which most international media research operates. A longstanding concern with the range of effects that might be exerted on directly political perceptions has been joined in many countries by anxieties about depictions of violence, pornography and the bearing which a wider range of mediated imagery has on social consciousness. However, many strands of research have become justifiably wary of strong causal theses, placing the emphasis on multiple variables and the acute problems of measurement which 'influence' poses. There is no doubt that the more recent emphasis on 'interpretation' has worked, whether intentionally or not, as a counter to many (in some cases, to *any*) ideas of textual controls and effects. Yet, despite the mood of conceptual and methodological scepticism, there is still much nervous ambivalence (and indeed straight inconsistency) on the question of the media's functions in the shaping of 'public' and 'private' perceptions and values, an ambivalence which exists alongside continuing political and public concern. One task for future research is to be clearer in the way it conceptualizes influence, distancing itself both from unwelcome behaviourist legacies and also from the more functionalist variants of 'ideology'. It might then move to a more reconstructive phase, going beyond critique and 'retreat' towards a more adequate if necessarily tentative, exploration of the kinds of constitutive dynamics that may be variously at work.

This clearly relates to the present high level of research interest in 'identity politics'. The question of whether or not the media have maintained the social order and social solidarity or have undermined them is a core issue here, despite the fact that much discussion of 'media and identity' has proceeded as if links with the older, 'influence' agenda are non-existent. We can be confident that what now amounts to an obsession with the relations between media and various collectivities (national, ethno-cultural, sexual) will continue. This complicates the picture that we have of how media interact with collectivities at each level. The explorations that are needed are various. It is often too easily assumed that media are importantly constitutive of the wider cultures sustaining particular collectivities. But what, for instance, are the limits of public policy in sustaining a national group's sense of itself by supporting indigenous media production? Pose this question and you are obliged to confront the transnational flow of cultural products. How can national cultures be sustained and at the same time significant differences be accommodated? More fundamentally still, what is the weight of history and the role of collective memory in constructing a sense of 'collective self'? As in many areas on the research agenda, extra-mediatic factors need to be more fully considered in any assessment.

Finally, a concern with the specific characteristics of media as technology, a concern repressed by the emphasis on textuality and reception, has once again re-emerged in the field. Indeed, McLuhan has become something of a guru to the cyber-generation, in their eyes arguing correctly for the profound and direct effects of new media upon the human sensorium. As we have already noted, any research agenda which seeks to take the issue of technology seriously is faced with a complex array of questions. Technological convergence is a matter of industrial restructuring, horizontal and vertical integration, increasingly conducted on a global scale and increasingly requiring new approaches to policy and regulation. The whole media environment changes as a result, with developments in textual form that threaten the existing assumptions of media aesthetics and of reception theory. The problem, identified clearly by Raymond Williams in the 1970s, is how to confront these issues without falling into the traps either of technological determinism or the kind of social reductionism which often ensnares those working on technology/society relations. Existing studies in the sociology of technology, as well as some areas of current work in cognitive science, might well be useful in enhancing the capacity of media research to make progress here.

Central to enquiry in all these areas are issues of representation, in its dual sense, and of the interaction between institution, medium, text and interpretation. The media's construction of images, both literally and metaphorically, always has a pre-given political significance. And within the politics of media imaging there is also (however minimal it may sometimes be) a politics of access, of visibility, of criticism and of contestation through which media intervene in, and help to shape, the wider political process. Just how this is done and how it might vary for the better or worse have always been core issues in media research and they are likely to remain so as we approach the millennium.

A last point might be made about the need for future work to resist the temptation towards a division of the field into specialist sub-areas that increasingly run the risk of conducting their enquiries in relative ignorance of each other. So, for instance, much policy research proceeds unaware of what is going on in audience analysis; textual scholars find the investigation of the social context of their objects of enquiry a dispensable extra; studies of production are undertaken which show no interest in the symbolic complexity of what is produced. Of course, academic specialization has a certain irresistible impetus and a researcher who tries to be all-encompassing risks superficiality; but too sharp a segmentation of interests will merely increase the chance of research 'missing' the real relationships and consequences, the real points of movement. More studies that try to develop links across commonly unconnected bodies of work would, we think, be welcome.

THE CONTENTS: AN OUTLINE

Each of the chapters that follows addresses the relationship between media research and adjacent projects in distinct ways, focusing either on the discourses of interweaving disciplines or on the relationship between a media research agenda that emerges from the academy and one defined by policy-makers in government or elsewhere.

Indeed, this shifting context is embodied in the career of Elihu Katz, whose forty years in media research is sympathetically but critically reviewed by Sonia Livingstone as she traces both consistencies and inconsistencies in a lifetime devoted to empirical study, central to which has been the careful attention paid to the problems of media effects and media audiences. From his early work with Paul Lazarsfeld in the now classic *Personal Influence* (1955), she suggests that Katz has pursued questions of influence from within a multidisciplinary perspective, though one firmly grounded within a social psychological tradition. Katz's concerns have ranged from the role of the primary group and interpersonal networks in mediating media influence, to the attempt to make sense of the mechanisms of public opinion formation, and more recently to the cultural and subcultural factors affecting media response. His work has shifted, though by no single or uniform route, from a social psychology of uses and gratifications to a characterization of media process within a complex cultural and technological environment. As a result, Livingstone notes that Katz has refused to adjudicate on the question of the 'active' or 'passive' audience as this has become a prominent (and frequently a radically over-simplified) theme in research, insisting rather on the need to be sensitive both to the context in which reception takes place and to the kind of communication under study.

Livingstone stresses Katz's commitment to making media research relevant, and to do so in a way that bridges the gap between administrative and critical approaches. Katz's concern with the politics of media research has evolved without his having articulated an explicit political agenda of his own, but Livingstone argues that his fundamental contribution to the field has been both through his rigorous attention to evidence, his refusal to accept a singular or closed definition of media effects, and his capacity to incorporate throughout his work a sensitivity to both social and psychological processes. The chapter as a whole charts the career of one of the most influential media researchers of his generation.

The two chapters which follow review recent developments at the interface of media research and other perspectives involved in the interpretation of contemporary culture. In the first of these, Peter Dahlgren considers Cultural Studies as a way of enquiring into media processes that employs a distinctive, if eclectic, cluster of concepts and methods. This approach has quite recently seen remarkable growth in North America. Much of Dahlgren's chapter is taken up with identifying the elements that make up the 'theoretical landscape' of work in this area and then with identifying the tensions and uncertainties which have made it so intensively polemical. He shows how, by organizing itself around ideas of 'culture', the approach has been sensitive to meanings and values, and to the complexity of informational and affective processes in ways that other traditions of enquiry often fail to display. Dahlgren believes that, given the direction taken by new media technologies and uses, this alertness will be increasingly valuable, although he also points to problems of conceptual messiness (particularly those around the politics of culture and cultural power) which have so far tended to reduce the clarity and import of many studies. As well as being established as a discrete area of enquiry, Cultural Studies has increasingly influenced the development of other arts and social science disciplines interested in the media (for instance, political science, urban geography, linguistics and sociology). Dahlgren finishes by considering what the future shape of Cultural Studies might be, as its institutional consolidation occurs simultaneously with a wide dispersal of many of its guiding ideas across other areas of work.

Joke Hermes, in her own words, attempts to offer a 'sexing' of media studies, one which entails a hard questioning of the theories of society and theories of subjectivity presently implicit in much media research. She organizes the main strand of her discussion around the idea, first picked up on and then criticized, that media enquiry is split between a 'public knowledge' project and a 'popular culture' project. Hermes moves in and out from this central line of discussion to engage with a wide range of current writing and research, sometimes offering concise reviews of key publications which seem to her either to have advanced or retarded the development of debates about gender. Her assessment involves attention to how at least some parts of media studies are caught awkwardly between a critical revision of 'modernist' concepts and a sometimes nervous recognition of the possibilities and benefits of 'postmodern' perspectives. This provides her with a route into examining recent debates both about the changing character of the 'public sphere' and about the revised terms on which the 'political' and the 'public' should now be defined and discussed. She concludes with a section on the idea of 'cultural citizenship', seeking here to link a radical (and largely optimistic) account of social identity, and its constituent factors of sexuality and of social performance, with the changing nature of media texts and forms of address.

We have already drawn attention to the increasing importance in media research of coming to terms with changing political contexts that affect both institutional and representational processes. In presenting critical reflections on those relationships in the next four chapters we are also addressing the international dimension of media research. Arguments about globalization tend to mask the significant differences in media cultures around the world. Those cultures have emerged as a result of the complex interrelationships between media institutions with different funding and regulatory systems as they have struggled with the distinct politics and policies of state and region.

Colin Sparks's chapter provides a theoretical framework for understanding media policy change in several European post-communist states. He argues for a theory of transition to capitalism that points significantly to continuities in the relation between the state and the media, broadcasting in particular. The post-1989 'revolution', he argues, has overturned idealistic expectations of the emergence of a fully democratized civil society, resulting rather in the dominance of economics over social relations. Many of the intellectual visionaries of yesteryear have entered the structures of political power, thus having an unusual weight in the determination of media policy. The rapid changes have seen the integration of the former communist states of Europe into the world market-place. And the structure of ownership and control of media in the countries of East-Central Europe examined (the Czech Republic, Hungary, Poland, Slovakia) has begun to converge with the various ruling models of Western Europe, especially those in which party-political power over broadcasting remains strong and unmediated. Rather than engaging in a deep democratization of broadcasting institutions, considerable political control has remained in the hands of governments.

The political culture that has sustained the public service broadcasting model in various west European countries is absent in the post-communist world, and the importation of the institutional forms of public service plainly do not in themselves offer a guarantee of a serious measure of autonomy for producers. Moreover, there has been an overarching nationalist dynamic in the region, which, despite its different negotiations in each case, has resulted in media policy being heavily linked to attempts to defend the national culture. This has been least successful in the case of the film industry, and whereas the press has been most open to international ownership, it is in broadcasting that the stakes remain the highest. But, nonetheless, as the post-communist states move towards a 'European' norm, the interplay between the national and global will continue to shape significantly the evolution of the media. As we have noted earlier, it is also clear that the process of marketization will, in one form or another, regulate the precise terms of this evolution.

Jean-Claude Burgelman considers the implications of the rapid changes in the technological and regulatory environments of both broadcasting and telecommunications for the pursuit of an effective media policy in Europe and also for the formation of an effective media policy research strategy. In particular, he argues, media policy research has failed to recognize both the diversity and complexity of Europe as a media environment, and it has also failed to acknowledge the convergence presently taking place between hitherto quite discrete media and communication technologies and the organizations that own and control them. The dilemmas posed for broadcasting policy, for example, in the withering away of the national state's capacity to regulate its own broadcasting culture, the contradictions faced by public service broadcasting in an increasingly market-oriented and fragmented environment, and the internal confusions of EU policy on indigenous media production as it affects, especially, the small countries of the Union, are matched by similar dilemmas in the field of telecommunications. Here the hype around the information superhighway reflects both a utopian vision of the possibilities for European cultural integration and a fundamental misreading of the dynamics of social, technological and economic changes as they affect media innovation. The inability to comprehend the significance of the inelasticities of demand and the actualities of media and communication technology use in everyday life are consistently undermining the formation of viable policy.

Media policy research, Burgelman suggests, is therefore in danger of simply replicating this lack of vision. He argues that the multiple convergence of technology and policy (especially media, telecommunications and market policies) requires an equivalent convergent response in research. This will need to move away from a predominantly media and technology-centric perspective in order to take due account of the specificities of history, the complexities of state–market relations, the subtleties surrounding the definition of public and universal service and the non-uniqueness of the European experience. He presents media research with a formidable challenge, one which in his own argument requires a move towards 'grand theory' that others might contest, but one which in any event needs to be taken seriously if work in the field stands any chance of being heard and acted upon outside the confines of the academy.

Vincent Mosco and Vanda Rideout concern themselves with recent media policy in North America. Like the other policy articles, their survey attempts to chart the shifts in academic and political ideas about policy as well as instancing the more significant policy changes themselves. They see a broad division between pluralist, managerialist and class power perspectives as the most useful way of interpreting policy formation and they offer clear and extensive synopses of just what each perspective involves, in the process addressing the extent to which there can be said to be convergence between them. They note particularly the way in which the more structural approaches to policy analysis from the class-power position have registered tensions and mediating factors often overlooked in earlier work.

In the second half of the chapter, the authors provide a schematic account of current tendencies in policy, noting shifts (such as deregulation, privatization and internationalization) upon which debate has focused. They trace the most recent shifts in policy back to a central and pressing economic imperative – the requirement of the capital accumulation process, as it globally reconstructs, to commodify the expanding communications sector for maximum profit. The section concludes with an endorsement of the value of a class-power assessment, together with a critically pessimistic sense of the possibilities for change.

In her contribution, Elizabeth Fox ranges over a significant part of the post-war development of Latin American research into media and popular culture. She charts how the research agenda across the entire continent has been shaped by changing relations between the state and the media, and how the state's policies have been profoundly influenced by global forces. Latin American research, she clearly shows, has gone through distinct phases: a predominant concern with development communication giving way to an analysis of dependency, and then a focus on national communication policies decentering into the study of popular culture and a slowly growing interest in questions of new media technology and regulation. What is especially striking is that there are concerns that traverse the entire continent of Latin America, despite the large number of diverse states there.

Behind these developments lies the positioning of Latin America in the global economy, and its relations, above all, with the United States. The drive towards the free market, and the continental shift from authoritarian regimes to the widespread installation of democracies, have been the grand structural factors affecting the field of media and cultural research. The agenda of the researchers – a stratum of the intellectuals of Latin American society – has been moving along

16

with their own shifting perceptions of change and the kind of research both permitted and demanded by the institutional spaces available for conducting it. The issues faced by researchers in Latin America have something in common with those addressed in Europe and North America. But the relations between media, state and nation are decidedly different in each context and therefore the impact of global change has a distinctive impact in each continent. This is also clearly evident from our other contributors' work.

The last chapter of this first volume preserves the above-mentioned themes but does so within a different optic, focusing on a specific site where media–state relations interact. In his chapter on war and the media, Dan Hallin places the more specific analysis of news coverage of some major conflicts in the broader context of social and cultural theory and historiography. He argues that in order to understand how wars are covered and affect public opinion we need to take a long-term view of the evolution of relations between media and states, bearing in mind how these differ from case to case. We also should think about war and its place in the broader national culture, not least in how it interacts both with previous experience of armed conflict in a given society and the ways in which it relates to questions of gender difference. War exposes the modes of control exercised over the public sphere and reveals processes of social mobilization against external threat.

Many of the fundamental parameters of war reporting and government control presently affecting us were established well before the Second World War and have centred on the balance drawn in particular situations between the accreditation of reporting and censorship of coverage. Since the Second World War, the crucial shift, it is argued, has been from total war to partial engagements. Most Anglo-American research has concentrated on limited conflicts involving the USA and the UK and consequently the most developed body of work deals successively with the Vietnam War, the Falklands/Malvinas, Panama and Grenada conflicts, and the Gulf War. In the latter case, in particular, the globalization of television news coverage came to the fore, raising new issues about effective censorship at the level of the nation-state. This should be weighed against the broad finding that the national news media do play a largely patriotic role, whatever their differences with political and military elites. As the research agenda has been crucially shaped by the given circumstances of each war, media research has tended to be discontinuous. Hence, Hallin argues, our understanding of wartime communication and its place in society needs to be addressed much more systematically in future.

2

THE WORK OF ELIHU KATZ: CONCEPTUALIZING MEDIA EFFECTS IN CONTEXT[1]

Sonia Livingstone

INTRODUCTION: THEMES AND DEBATES IN MEDIA RESEARCH

Over the past four decades, Elihu Katz has made a major contribution to our understanding of the workings of mass communication by analysing mass media institutions, contents, processes and effects in their social and political contexts. Katz has taken an interdisciplinary and original approach, conducting influential research on an interconnected set of issues which have strongly influenced the agenda for media research, such as relations between individuals, groups and media institutions, the selective and active television viewer, the diffusion of innovation, media effects and media imperialism, among others.

This chapter offers a critical reading of Katz's work, locating it as part of the shifting set of debates which constitute the culture of mass communications research. My aim is to illuminate Katz's work and its continuing relevance to the field and to read his work as symptomatic of developments and problematics in mass communications research over the past forty years. Many aspects of Katz's work merit a chapter to themselves, both because of the diversity of his interests and because his key ideas have each generated considerable bodies of work. My main focus will be on the contribution to audience research of Katz's key articles on media theory and of his most influential books, for each of these presents an empirical project which illuminates the intersection of several significant theoretical issues. For an overview of his main works, I refer the reader to the primary sources at the end of this chapter.[2]

Throughout his career, Katz has developed several 'middle range' theories, each of which has made a significant contribution to the course of media research. Furthermore, Katz has always actively participated in research debates, reflecting his continuing interest in the possible convergence of different approaches to media research. To understand Katz's contribution, therefore, I will locate my interpretation of his work within the debates of the field. I would note, however, that it is difficult to do justice to a researcher who has sustained his contribution to these debates over the forty years which also includes most of the history of television and of modern communications research.

I will organize my reading of Katz's work both historically and thematically. The historical narrative traces his developing theories and empirical research, as marked by the key contributions of *Personal Influence* in 1955, the two diffusion books of 1966 and 1969 – *Medical Innovation* and *The Politics of Community Conflict*, *The Uses of Mass Communications* in 1974, *The Export of Meaning* in 1990 and *Media Events* in 1992 (although the work for both these two last books was begun during the early 1980s). I will map this narrative onto three themes underlying Katz's work. First, at the level of social problems which invite social scientific research, Katz has always been concerned with the question of media effects. Second, on a more conceptual level, Katz's work can be seen to further, in various ways, our understanding of the complex relations between public opinion, media and social interaction. Third, at a metatheoretical level, Katz has persuasively advanced an agenda of convergence – among issues, methods, political positions, academic disciplines and research traditions.

Taking these themes in reverse order, Katz's metatheoretical agenda has been to negotiate a convergence in approaches to the study of media processes among different disciplinary orientations. As the new discipline of mass communications emerged as part of the academic expansion of the post-war era, Katz and others drew upon social psychology and sociology to conceptualize the audience, albeit rather differently in his different works. Then and later, Katz has also been interested in the relationship between the now-established discipline of mass communications and other disciplines, particularly the humanities.[3] Recently, the approach to audience research exemplified by *The Export of Meaning* has raised the possibility of convergence between so-called administrative and critical schools of mass communications research,[4] itself part of a broader debate over epistemology and the politics of research. For Katz, concerned with establishing the field of mass communications, his emphasis on convergence reflects a conviction that ideas evolve best through responding to the challenge of alternative positions, that they become vulgar versions of themselves if they remain within hermetically sealed traditions (he has been critical of uses and gratifications research in this respect), and that mass communications will develop more productively if divergent tendencies and hostilities are countered.

As regards the conceptual agenda, many of Katz's works reflect different permutations of his long-term fascination with the relations between three domains: media (institutional contexts); public opinion (democratic processes); conversation (interpersonal networks). A significant aspect of Katz's contribution is the way in which his various works represent different explorations of this conceptual agenda, emphasizing a range of ways in which mass media processes are anchored in their psychological, social and political contexts in such a way as still to leave room for manoeuvre for the active audience. Thus *Personal Influence* conceives of the active audience as firmly located in local groups and communities. In *The Uses of Mass Communications* the active viewer is conceptualized primarily in terms of the individual needs which motivate selective exposure.[5] The viewers in *The Export of Meaning* are engaged in divergent reception according to their cultural backgrounds. And in *Media Events* the viewer is participating in domestic conversation as part of the new global public sphere.

Lastly, the focus on media effects is, in one sense, obvious, and reflects one of Katz's central concerns, namely to legitimate the value of academic research for policy purposes. Broadcasters, government bodies and the public have a long-standing anxiety about possible effects of the media and have often found the conclusions of social scientists to be unsatisfactory. Katz has tried to categorize the findings of media effects research in policy-relevant ways, although at the same time he recognizes the complex and contingent nature of the findings. He has addressed the question of effects in diverse ways, from analysing the social responsibility of broadcasters and the institutional determinants of production to studies of, typically, indirect effects and sources of audience invulnerability.

Katz's concern with media effects is also central to his work in a more complex sense than that of meeting the demands which the public place on social science. Katz began his career during the heyday of the 'minimal effects' approach which argued that social scientific research had largely failed to provide evidence for substantial effects of the media on a vulnerable mass audience, and indeed his work contributed significantly towards establishing this approach. However, forty years ago also saw significant optimism about both social science and the mass media as forces which, if used appropriately, could further the project of the enlightenment, educating the public towards being rational, informed citizens participating in a democratic society. The task, then, was to redirect mass communications research in a more productive direction.

In this context, Katz's work represents an attempt to reframe the problem of media effects, separating it from both the hegemony thesis of critical scholars, for whom audiences are far from active participants and by whom empirical social scientific investigation of actual audiences was rejected, and from the mechanistic, individualistic approach of experimentally based effects theorists for whom, similarly, audiences were passive and vulnerable and by whom the social group was underestimated. Katz has consistently suggested that media effects should be (re)contextualized if we are to appreciate the role of active, empowered audiences within social structures. He thus tries to clear a space within which we can rethink the problem of media effects by drawing particularly on analyses of the activities of the primary group and of everyday contexts of conversation, for these complicate any linear causal theories and posit more complex patterns of audience involvement with the mass media.

His reluctance to restrict this diversity of everyday contexts, social factors, and modes of audience involvement which research should consider, leads Katz to engage with broader debates about the contexts and processes of everyday life within which the media operate. These centre on the long-standing and hotly contested debate between critical and administrative schools of mass communication. These two schools of thought both conceive of this multiplicity of processes in different ways and, moreover, each emphasizes some aspects to the neglect of others. Consequently, an account of these debates and of Katz's own role in attempting to bring these schools to a point of convergence or agreement regarding appropriate ways to investigate the mass media, is central to understanding Katz's broader project regarding the contextualizing of media effects, as I elaborate in the next section.

In addition to effects, the other major question policy-makers ask of research concerns public opinion, and Katz's commitment to an integration of academia and policy can also be seen in his substantial body of work on public opinion and attitudes in Israel, as particularly developed through his direction of the Israel Institute of Applied Social Research. Here too, his aim has been to produce high quality social science research which establishes the practical value of good quality academic work over 'quick and dirty', non-theoretical research. It is no mean achievement to sustain credible conversations with both the academic community and decision-makers in government and media organizations. In answer to the question of how one can demonstrate the usefulness of academic research in addressing rather than merely complicating policy questions, and of how one can further interdisciplinary convergences in the new discipline of mass communications, Katz's approach has been to produce convincing and methodologically rigorous empirical work rather than to offer 'his' articulated media theory which engages directly with the sociological theory on which his insights so productively draw.

In Katz's work, each substantive empirical demonstration stands alone: from *Personal Influence* to *Media Events*, each study is a one-off, offered as a convincing advocate of Katz's views on both audiences and the conduct of audience research, as I shall elaborate in this chapter. By inspiring others to follow where he has begun, Katz's contribution to the field can be valued for showing a way forward for media research at key points in its history. As noted above, a common thread clearly runs through all his work: this concerns the conversation–opinion–media nexus which, as Peters (1989) has observed, reflects Katz's commitment to using research to further the democratic project. Yet this thread remains largely implicit in Katz's work, with a few exceptions, and is not, for example, referred to in the field as 'Katz's theory'. But while some might regret that he has not also offered more theoretical development and engagement with those theories on which he draws, Katz himself would probably see this as an intellectual sophistication likely to undermine rather than promote the confidence of policy-makers in the usefulness of academic media research.

EARLY DEBATES IN MASS COMMUNICATIONS RESEARCH AS BACKGROUND TO KATZ'S WORK

Katz is still most cited for his early collaboration with Paul Lazarsfeld. Sills (1981) identifies the three major features of Lazarsfeld's research style as being collaboration with others, creation of research institutes, and the search for a convergence between different intellectual traditions;[6] all of these feature strongly in Katz's own work. Moreover, as for Lazarsfeld, Katz's own history and work reflect the complex relationship between so-called critical and administrative or positivist mass communications. Despite being a beneficiary, broadly speaking, of the American government's post-war policy of funding mass communications research useful to the administration, and despite his consistent attack on the Frankfurt School approach to the media, Katz was directly connected to the Frankfurt School tradition via Lowenthal[7] and he inherited Lazarsfeld's interest in integrating critical and administrative schools of mass communications.

Horkheimer's (1972) essay on traditional and critical theory, published in 1937, set out the epistemological and political framework for the critical theory of the Frankfurt School. In contrast, Lazarsfeld (1941) specified the parameters of administrative (or positivist) research on mass communications, as research which 'is carried through in the service of some kind of administrative agency of public or private character' (p. 8). In relation to audience research, critical researchers 'construe audience members as embodying larger social and political structures . . . [while administrative researchers] embrace the liberal–pluralist ideal of democratic life . . . [which regards individuals as] potential sites of creativity, novelty, independence, and autonomy' (Swanson, 1992: 322). Yet at the same time as distinguishing between these approaches, during the late 1930s Paul Lazarsfeld, as director of the Princeton Office of Radio Research (later the Columbia Bureau of Applied Social Research[8]), attempted 'to explain the "critical approach" sympathetically to an American audience' (1941: 325). He argued that critical research could contribute challenging problems, new concepts, useful interpretations and new data. He saw it to be the task of administrative research to translate these into empirical studies. Yet, in this task, Lazarsfeld saw himself as having failed; certainly this early attempt to integrate critical and administrative research was largely unsuccessful (Jay, 1973; Lazarsfeld, 1969).

At the time, Adorno (1969) favoured the link between critical ideas and empirical research, noting 'one of the most important justifications for empirical research – that virtually all findings can be explained theoretically once they are in hand, but not conversely' (p. 364). Yet he clearly found Lazarsfeld's approach frustrating: 'I considered it to be my fitting and objectively proffered assignment to *interpret* phenomena – not to ascertain, sift, and classify facts and make them available as information' (Adorno, 1969: 339), particularly as the Rockefeller Foundation had ruled out the analysis of 'the system itself, its cultural and sociological consequences and its social and economic presuppositions' (p. 343) when funding the Princeton radio project.[9] Adorno was also concerned about relying on self-report data (recent developments in audience reception research are consistent with this concern in trying to link audience's subjective reactions to both text and context). Thus in his audience research, Katz echoes Adorno's recognition that 'it would be naive to take for granted an identity between the social implications to be discerned in the stimuli and those embodied in the "responses"' (1969: 353) when he says that 'I insist on the confrontation of the latent-message analysis with the question of what gets through to the viewer' (Katz, 1978b: 137).

In his memoirs, Lowenthal, one of the founder members of the Frankfurt Institute of Social Research, discusses how he found it easier than Adorno 'to combine the theoretical and historical outlook with the empirical requisites of sociological research' (Jay, 1987: 140), although he also gives examples of how Lazarsfeld 'failed to see the political and analytical meaning of my study [of biographies]' (Jay, 1987: 132). He adds, 'finally I also learned – it wasn't particularly difficult – to assert my own individuality as a sociologist, while at the same time familiarizing myself with what seemed to be significant and important in American social research. Later I attempted to convey this synthesis to my students' (p. 141) – of whom Katz was one.

Maybe the separation of administrative and critical mass communications research has in the past been to the advantage of both schools, for each developed its own strengths. However, recently many, particularly those in audience research, have declared this a stale, even a false, dichotomy – to be transcended rather than perpetuated[10] – thus agreeing at last with Katz who has consistently argued for convergence. Katz wrote his first bridge-building article in 1959 when mass communications was being formed into a discipline: it reads today with a strikingly modern feel, yet only now have media researchers caught up with Katz's early vision for the field and begun to overcome their mutual ignorance and hostility (Fejes, 1984). Although Katz's empirical work has mainly contributed to administrative, or functionalist, mass communications,[11] in his more theoretical works, Katz has always looked more broadly.

If we put together Katz's apparent resistance to developing theory with his emphasis on the illustrative empirical study and his informed use of theories from other disciplines, one might infer that Katz regards mass communications as a set of problematics, not as a discipline in its own right, an approach with which I am sympathetic. Katz's work makes a strong case for the importance of drawing on diverse established disciplines to study mass communication processes in context. However, his career spans the period in which mass communications has attempted to establish itself as a separate discipline – founding new departments, institutes, doctoral programmes and journals of mass communication, and so is taken to support this move.

PERSONAL INFLUENCE: ON DEVELOPING NEW THEORETICAL FRAMEWORKS FOR MASS COMMUNICATIONS

Let us consider Katz's first significant publication. In *Personal Influence*, Katz and Lazarsfeld significantly amend Lasswell's classic question for mass communication research, 'who says what to whom with what content on what channel?', by demonstrating that the hitherto 'direct' flow of mass media influence was fundamentally mediated by pre-existing patterns of interpersonal communication in local communities. The innovative concept of the two-step flow challenged the popularity of the direct effects model, the separate study of mass and interpersonal communications, and the image of the viewer and listener as part of a mindless, homogeneous mass. As a result, *Personal Influence* has generated a research tradition which extends the theory in many new directions. It is also significant for establishing the mould for media research which many have followed as the field has expanded.

At several points, Katz has advocated the social theorist, Tarde, as 'the social theorist of diffusion *par excellence*' (Katz *et al.*, 1966: 156). Tarde argued for the rationality of public opinion as contrasted with the mindlessness of the masses; Katz sees him as the originator of the active/passive voter/viewer debate and observes similarities between Lazarsfeld's proposal of the two-step flow (Lazarsfeld and Gaudet, 1944) and Tarde's social psychological essay of 1898, 'La conversation' (Katz, 1992b). It is significant for Katz that Tarde's theory may be studied empirically: 'I . . . am prepared to wager that Tarde's formulations probably lend themselves more readily than the others to strict, and testable formulation' (Katz, 1992b: 82). In this, Katz echoes the aims of Lazarsfeld before him to base mass communications theory on the assumptions and methods of an empirical science.[12] As regards the substance of the two-step theory, Katz notes that:

> ironically, Tarde's hypothesis anticipates the *revision* that the two-step hypothesis has undergone (and is still undergoing), in its current emphasis on the flow of influence not the flow of information; on the group as a unit of analysis, not the individual; and on the mutuality of conversation, not the relay from leaders.
>
> (Katz, 1992b: 81)

This revision may be seen, in part, as response to the criticisms directed towards the theory (Gitlin, 1978). The theory, it was suggested, advocated minimal effects only because it studied short-term over long-term effects and behavioural over ideological effects. The problem, Gitlin argued, was that Katz and Lazarsfeld only considered effects that could be measured quantitatively and thus neglected the long-term consequences of the media and the possibility of non-change as a media effect, both of which have been hypothesized by ideological traditions of media studies[13]. Methodologically too, criticisms have been made of aspects of the design of the Decatur study and of the limitations imposed by the historical context in which the study was conducted and which restrict the generality of its findings. Katz and Lazarsfeld's particular approach to empirical research, namely strict quantification and coding, short-term effects, a marketing orientation, a claim to scientific objectivity and political neutrality, itself derived from their grounding in functionalist sociology.

Merton's (1955) description of the emerging field of the sociology of knowledge, when applied to media research, captures the 'Columbia School' framework within which Katz has worked:

> searching out such variations in effective audiences, exploring their distinctive criteria of significant and valid knowledge, relating these to their position within the society and examining the socio-psychological processes through

24

which these operate to constrain certain modes of thought constitutes a procedure which promises to take research in the sociology of knowledge from the plane of general imputation to testable empirical enquiry.

(p. 510)

Katz defines this functionalist approach as one which 'argues that people bend the media to their needs more readily than the media overpower them; that the media are at least as much agents of diversion and entertainment as of information and influence. It argues, moreover, that the selection of media and content, and the uses to which they are put, are considerably influenced by social role and psychological predisposition' (Katz, 1973: 164–5). As a model for processes of diffusion of innovation and of audience activity, this approach lays out a clear research programme, although the stress on 'testable empirical inquiry' is a double-edged tool. It poses a challenge to those who develop theory without testing it against real-world processes, and yet it imposes limitations on the scope of theoretical enquiry as certain questions are more 'testable' than others.

This functionalist perspective supports the democratic or pluralist political agenda which for Peters (1989) underpins *Personal Influence*. Peters suggests that 'much of the history of American mass communication theory and research is an attempt to carry out a political project without being articulate about that project' (p. 199), and that discussion of media effects is really a discussion of 'the perils and possibilities of democracy' (p. 200), of 'how to conceive of the public sphere in an age of mass media' (p. 212). The underlying debate, therefore, concerns mass society, a debate 'which turns on the question of the viability of democracy in an age of media and bureaucracy' (p. 216). Mendelsohn (1989) concurs: 'this limited effects paradigm is deeply embedded in the theory of action that was first promulgated as a rationale for basing new 18th- and 19th-century democratic governance on public opinion and popular will' (p. 819). Katz's work typifies this broadly normative tradition, examining issues of media effects, bureaucracy, voters, public opinion, and so forth, in order to emphasize (and protect) the self-determining potential of the individual against the power of the mass media and to promote a professional-client model of producer–audience relations (e.g. Katz, 1978a, 1992a, 1992b). Yet Katz rarely presents an explicitly political agenda beyond expressing his broad interest in the relation between media, public opinion, citizenship and conversation.[14]

Peters argues that 'the genius of *Personal Influence* was to rescue the public sphere from the media' (1989: 215) and thereby to resolve the crisis of participatory democracy in a media age. Yet he, like others, is sceptical of the argument that the mass media, far from being usurpers of public space are, instead, supporters of it through the medium of active debate within primary groups. Just as Schiller (1989), commenting on *The Export of Meaning*, questions whether divergent and resistant interpretations among audiences have any actual effect on established power structures, Peters asks whether the interpersonal step of the two-step flow has any identifiable effect in shaping collective understandings or ordering social worlds.[15] Maybe these questions remain for future research: the significance of Katz's work lies partly in keeping open the possibility of an empowered audience and a more participatory democracy. And while his optimism may be questioned, it provides a counterposition to the prevailing pessimism, thereby keeping the debate alive.

AUDIENCES, EFFECTS AND THE POLITICS OF MEDIA RESEARCH

Personal Influence was highly significant in the early history of media research as the originator of the theoretical shift from direct effects to indirect effects which depend on the mediating role of interpersonal relations. The theory of opinion leadership and the two-step flow of communications has been developed in numerous studies of consumer research (Feick and Higie, 1986), public opinion (Black, 1982), survey methodology (Weimann, 1991) and mass communications (Rogers and Shoemaker, 1971). However, like his uses and gratifications research (see below), it is often cited by his critics for representing, as it was intended to, the way forward for administrative research. By endorsing the problematic (though still commonplace) transmission model of the media (Carey, 1975) and by emphasizing the value of empirical social scientific methods over high theory, it took mass communication research firmly in an 'administrative' direction, divorcing it from the emerging school of critical mass communications. For Sproule (1989), Katz and Lazarsfeld (1955) played a key role in (re)writing research history to create 'the magic bullet myth' of direct media effects in order to demonstrate the success of the Columbia approach in putting media research on a scientific footing.[16]

Consequently, the main criticisms of *Personal Influence* addressed the meta-theoretical rather than the substantive agenda, arguing against the received version of *Personal Influence* as a standard work which established a way forward for administrative research, rather than against a research monograph intended as one contribution among many to a diverse and continuing programme of media research. Gitlin claims that '*Personal Influence* can be read as the founding document of an entire field of inquiry' (1978: 208) and criticizes it as an approach which itself criticizes the analyses of power, influence and ideology advocated by critical mass communications.[17] From a different theoretical position, but also concerned about the reading of *Personal Influence* which lets the media off the hook, Lang and Lang (1983) attack administrative research for its 'downgrading of the mass media *vis-à-vis* personal influence' (p. 134). Like Gitlin, they too see the minimal effects paradigm, significantly established by *Personal Influence*, to be a consequence of the methodological approach taken to empirical research by the Columbia researchers.

There is a certain irony in the criticisms of the politics of administrative researchers, for example, for developing psychological propaganda and persuasion research as, supposedly, a means of helping governments to manipulate the people. Originally, Lazarsfeld and others were motivated to conduct propaganda research because, as members of the Socialist Student Movement, they were concerned that their propaganda was unsuccessful in the face of that of the growing nationalist movement of Vienna in the 1920s. Indeed, when discussing the earlier Marienthal study in Vienna, which linked social stratification and social psychology, Lazarsfeld (1969) claims that his work 'had a visible Marxist tinge' (p. 278), and he recalls the almost accidental way in which he happened upon market research methods (and funding) when empirical research techniques were otherwise lacking to pursue these ends.[18] Subsequently, much administrative research has been conducted with a liberal rather than manipulative intent, whatever the purposes to which it is subsequently put (Rossi, 1980, comments on the pitfalls of applied research). In his defence, Katz points out the contradiction in attacking 'the "administrative" orientation for providing powerful tools of persuasion to the marketers, politicians, etc. while arguing that the effects of such persuasive attempts are invisible in the short run' (1987: 30). Lang and Lang (1983) concur, arguing that administrative research contains 'much that is critical of existing institutional arrangements and practices' (pp. 131–2) and that 'empirical research can be used by any group, including crusaders against the status quo' (p. 132).

Katz (1978b) notes further that contemporary critical media studies also 'betray[s] an interest in affecting policy' (p. 135): indeed, present political and economic conditions increasingly mean that policy-relevant research findings, which Katz has always aimed to provide, are demanded of us all. It seems to me that the possibility of research being 'co-opted' is making present critical researchers cautious about making claims beyond those of complexity and context-dependency. Katz would be impatient with this and expect media research to offer clear answers to the why and how questions which in any case implicitly underpin all research.

THE USES AND ABUSES OF USES AND GRATIFICATIONS THEORY: A SOCIAL PSYCHOLOGICAL APPROACH TO THE ACTIVE AUDIENCE

In the 1940s and 1950s, mass communications research was closely entwined with social psychology and sociology. In *Personal Influence* (1955), the social psychology of the group is used to account for the diffusion of media effects, and links between interpersonal and mass communications, often neglected in subsequent research, were central.[19] Although since then, mass communications has become a more-or-less distinct discipline, Katz has always drawn upon these other disciplines to develop a more complex approach to mass communication processes. Over this same period, sociology and sociological forms of social psychology became increasingly separate from psychology and psychological forms of social psychology.[20] Katz drew more upon the former and yet valued the psychological for emphasizing the autonomy of the individual and as a corrective against sociological reductionism. Consequently, his is a more social constructionist account of the active audience compared, say, to the experimental approach of the Yale school (Hovland, Janis and Kelley, 1953), for Katz consistently locates cognitive and motivational accounts of audience activity in the context of the primary group and social networks.

The roots of the disputes in media theory about the contribution of social psychology can be traced back to the 1920s and 1930s. Adorno's (1969) understanding of social psychology drew more on psychoanalysis, influenced by Fromm's work at the (Frankfurt) Institute of Social Research, than on the embryonic tradition of positivist social psychology. For researchers at the Institute before the Second World War, it was their explicit aim to develop a critical social psychology (Bronner and Kellner, 1989) 'to explain the *processes* through which individual consciousness was adjusted to the functional requirements of the system, in which a monopolistic economy and an authoritarian state had coalesced' (Habermas, 1989: 293). This approach contrasts with the largely individualistic social psychology which developed in America. Smith (1983) misidentifies Katz as part of this latter tradition, failing to see the significance of a more sociologically grounded mass communications for social psychology.[21] While Adorno's *The Authoritarian Personality* was seen to offer 'a potential model for large-scale, theoretically guided programmatic research using sophisticated empirical methods and bearing on an important social problem seen in its historical social context' (Smith, 1983: 173), the unresolved problems with this project contributed to the individualizing of the social in social psychology (Farr, 1991),[22] resulting in an 'experimental social psychology [with] its ahistorical, narrowly natural-science-oriented ways' (Smith, 1983: 173). Consequently, Katz's and others' (Ball–Rokeach and DeFleur, 1976) advocacy of the potential contribution of (sociological) social psychology for mass communications is insufficiently recognized.

It is typical of Katz that he advanced his argument for drawing on social psychology in media research through innovative empirical work. Katz and Foulkes (1962) argued that, given the demise of the early effects or campaign approach to the mass media ('what do the media do to the people'), there were two routes open for continued work on the mass media – studying the diffusion of new ideas and its relation to social and technical change, and studying media uses and gratifications ('what do people do with the media?'). For Katz, the two key mediating variables derive from the Columbia Bureau of Applied Social Research's persuasion model during the 1940s and 1950s, namely interpersonal relations – leading to diffusion of innovation, and selectivity – leading to uses and gratifications. Of these two routes, Katz and his colleagues investigated first the former (Coleman, Katz and Menzel, 1966; Crain, Katz and Rosenthal, 1969; Katz *et al.*, 1963), and then the latter (Blumler and Katz, 1974; Blumler *et al.*, 1985; Katz *et al.*, 1973). As work on the two-step flow and on diffusion of innovation (Rogers, 1983) has shown, interpersonal relations provide networks of communication (channels of information for the diffusion of innovation), pressure to conform (group dynamics and social normativity) and sources of social support (and social identity), each of which affects the individual decision-making upon which diffusion depends. Selectivity, the belief 'that individuals seek information that will support their beliefs and practices and avoid information that challenges them' (Katz, 1968: 795), is understood both as a cognitive defence against media power and positively as the interests of the active viewer which 'impress the media into the service of individual needs and values' (Katz, 1979a: 75). Contemporary extensions of this research draw on theories of social cognition to elaborate how and why viewers selectively and constructively make sense of television (Hawkins, et al., 1988; Livingstone, 1990).

The sociological diffusion research (Katz et al., 1966) can be contrasted with the more psychological uses and gratifications approach (see Blumler and Katz, 1974), in terms of their starting point (text/message versus audience need), context (social structure and culture versus individual habits), and effect (acceptance of intended message versus need gratifications). However, in both these approaches the mass media are seen as plural (different channels, different genres), as are the audience (diverse individuals, groups, etc.), and the socio-cognitive processes of media influence are foregrounded (acceptance, expectations). Thus throughout his work, Katz has argued against a view of mass society comprised of monolithic and homogeneous media and a mass audience of defenceless viewers.

Critics note that Katz's concept of selectivity focuses more on motivation than meaning, and so tends to view the text as an inkblot of which viewers can make any use they wish. Symptomatic of contemporary uses and gratifications, the typology of the active viewer proposed by Levy and Windahl (1985) mis-understands the hermeneutic nature of meaning creation, seeing it rather as gaining 'a more or less clear understanding of the structure of the message' (p. 115), and Rubin (1985) and Palmgreen et al. (1985) assume the text to be a source of given and obvious messages. Yet for Katz 'activity inheres in the creative translation of media messages by individuals in the process of perceiving and attributing meanings' (Katz, 1979a: 75). Blumler, Katz and Gurevitch (1985) see this creative process of meaning negotiation as a route 'to build the bridge we have been hoping might arise between gratifications studies and cultural studies' (Katz, 1979a: 75).[23] In studying audience reception of *Dallas* (Liebes and Katz, 1990), Katz took uses and gratifications in this new direction, but has been less successful in taking uses and gratifications theory with him.

Ironically, just as uses and gratifications theory is criticized for regarding the text as open to any readings or uses which viewers find gratifying, these same critics tend to use uses and gratifications theory for everything and anything, routinely citing its limitations in order to critique (a stereotype of) the social psychological tradition, and hence to demarcate critical mass media research.[24] Thus, in criticizing uses and gratifications theory for being mentalistic and individualistic, Elliot (1974) neglects the discussion in the introduction to *The Uses of Mass Communications* (see also Katz et al., 1973; Katz and Adoni, 1973) of the ways in which needs are seen as having socio-structural rather than individual psychological origins and as being subject to social, cultural and historical influences. This discussion was far from incidental, having developed from Katz's interest in social groups (cf. *Personal Influence*), although admittedly this aspect of the theory has been insufficiently developed (Wright, 1974).[25]

Notwithstanding such criticisms, vigorous and interesting empirical research has followed in the footsteps of Katz, Blumler and Gurevitch as part of the active audience tradition. Swanson (1992) suggests that the main discoveries are 'that gratification-seeking mediates between content and effect and may result in consequences not obvious from manifest content' (p. 309), and 'that the seeking of gratifications is one of the influences that shape people's exposure to mass media' (p. 311). Hence uses and gratifications theory undermines extrapolations about use from content and represents a new, contextualized, way of approaching media effects. Since its initial exposition in *The Uses of Mass Communications*, the theory has developed fruitful integration with other theories of use, reception and effect (Rosengren, Wenner and Palmgreen, 1985). In its emphasis on active audiences, the social contexts of use and different motivations for using different media or different contents, recent work on audience ethnography (Bausinger, 1984; Seiter *et al.*, 1989; Silverstone and Hirsch, 1992) echoes uses and gratifications research, particularly the work of Katz *et al.* (1973).

AUDIENCE RECEPTION: TOWARDS AN INTEGRATED CONCEPTION OF THE AUDIENCE ACROSS SOCIAL SCIENCE AND THE HUMANITIES

Katz and Foulkes (1962) suggest that:

> the uses and gratifications approach represents a bridge to the theorists of popular culture – the group of humanists, psychoanalysts, reformers, etc., who have been speculatively analyzing the mass media and mass society. Until very recently, they have been paid no heed by the empirically oriented mass media researcher and have returned the compliment.
>
> (p. 379; see also Katz, 1959)

However, the basis on which such bridge building is to occur remains unelaborated, although from a brief comment in Katz and Foulkes (1962), it seems that common ground is to be found in the fact that while popular culture theorists are, ultimately, concerned with questions of effect, they, like uses and gratificationists, approach the issue the other way around, asking what people do with the media – focusing on escapism and fantasy – rather than vice versa.

The Export of Meaning, an empirical study of the cross-cultural reception of *Dallas*, integrates Katz's work on uses and gratifications with that on diffusion and social networks, resulting in the emphasis on subcultural and family decodings. Liebes and Katz offer a reading of the primordial themes of the prime-time American soap opera and relate these themes to the diverse processes of audience reception in different cultures. The book thus furthers the debate over cultural imperialism[26] by revealing the resistance of local cultures to an American product, not through rejection or avoidance (except in the case of Japan) but through (sub)cultural renegotiations of the programme.[27] In addition to this substantive value, this book is at least as significant for illustrating the viability of a convergent approach to audience research. *The Export of Meaning* integrates different disciplines (literary theory, linguistics, sociology, mass communications), approaches (administrative, critical), communication foci (audience, text, context), and methods (qualitative and quantitative audience research, textual analysis), resulting in a productive conceptualization of the active viewer. While these convergences have been most successful in relation to the soap opera (Livingstone, 1990), the insights thereby derived are currently being extended to other television genres.

Katz sees these convergences regarding audience reception research as stemming directly from uses and gratifications research, claiming that 'gratifications research begat audience decoding' (Katz, 1987: S37).[28] This is contentious, for uses and gratifications is not known as an innovative research domain. The most cited work on audience decoding, Morley's *The Nationwide Audience*, opens with an attack on uses and gratifications as the tradition against which this work is to be understood.[29] Instead, critical researchers see audience reception research as motivated primarily by political arguments about the heterogeneity of the audience (or the problems of assuming homogeneity among audiences and a privileged status for the textual analyst). They have been concerned to 'focus almost exclusively on disempowered groups within the mass audience and endeavour to gauge how, through acts of interpretation, members of such groups resist dominance' (Swanson, 1992: 322). Reception research is also rooted in epistemological arguments about polysemy and the context-dependency of meaning. Finally, through the ethnographic turn, audience reception research represents an attempt to rescue empirical research for the critical tradition (Seiter *et al.*, 1989). Katz's appropriation of reception research to the administrative tradition is too imperialistic a move. However, the coincidence of developments in administrative and critical schools which led both to acknowledge the limitations of textual interpretation, of inferring effect from content, and of failing to place viewers in a sociocultural context, was clearly responsible for the enthusiastic support for reception research during the 1980s and 1990s.[30]

But a moment of coincidence may not herald a future of convergence. What is more likely to undermine old oppositions (Livingstone, 1993) is the broader crisis in the social sciences of established disciplinary boundaries, of methodological certainty and of political commitment.[31] For Ang (1994) and some others, any convergence between social science and humanities approaches to audience response is more apparent than real.[32] Particularly, Ang challenges the frequent, often implicit, assumption that diversity of interpretation – as demonstrated, for example, in *The Export of Meaning* – is evidence of audience autonomy or freedom from media power. She argues that such an assumption only makes sense in relation to the closed-circuit, transmission model of communication advocated by liberal–pluralist researchers which assumes that there is a trade-off between locating power in the sender or the receiver of a message.[33]

From a rather different position, in *Media Events* Katz and Dayan also challenge the opposition of broadcasters/text and audiences which has tried to apportion more or less power to each side. They undermine any simple opposition of media and audience, not by advocating the interpretive relation between text and reader (as in *The Export of Meaning*), although this idea is central to *Media Events*, but by focusing on the institutional arrangements and social interconnections which link media and audience. *Media Events* shows the complex interplay among diverse participants involved in the new genre of 'media events': the broadcasters, marketers, diplomats, journalists, public relations experts, viewers, fans, contestants, experts, technicians, managers, and so forth. In this way, Dayan and Katz take further earlier work on diffusion of innovation, showing the constructive role of media and audiences in an ever more complex set of relations between public opinion, everyday conversation and media representation and participation. These complexities are such that, it is suggested, the rhetorical, symbolic, narrative, and ritual structures of this new genre take over the construction and outcome of cultural and political events, transforming them first and foremost into media events.

Media events represent both the opportunities and dangers of a media-dominated democracy. Television enfranchises: media events create a national or even international sense of occasion – liminal moments for society which reflect, idealize, and at the same time, authenticate a vision of society for the public. Yet if these liminal moments substitute for political participation and political change, then their reactionary, manipulative or narcotizing effects should be at the forefront of our concern. Certainly, Dayan and Katz claim a wide range of effects for media events – on participants and on institutions, at the time of the event and subsequently, including the ways in which live broadcasting confers legitimacy and charisma on the 'celebrities' involved, the interruption of everyday routines which casts viewers into roles proposed by the script of the ceremony, effects on the climate of opinion by encouraging or inhibiting the expression of certain beliefs, changes to the organization of politics and political campaigning, and instances of direct political or social change resulting from a media event. While the link between the theory and data is weakest in relation to these claims of effects, it is likely that Katz's theoretical direction (and, indeed, the complexity of the actual cultural/political links between media and everyday life) has taken him beyond the possibility of readily 'testable empirical inquiry'.

ON THE CONTINUING QUESTION OF MEDIA EFFECTS

A central focus of Katz's work has been on the effects of the mass media. In his description of the history of mass communications as an oscillation between conceptions of active and passive viewers – and hence between minimal effects and powerful media (e.g. Katz, 1980b, 1987), Katz offers his vision of the field, classifying media research by research tradition, by research centre, by decade.

Although this classification is inevitably oversimplified, Katz's aim is the vital one of recontextualizing our notion of effects. Some twenty years ago, Katz welcomed the early signs of this: 'the study of mass media "effects", with its primarily psychological bias, is now broadening to take account of the *social* processes involved in the spread of influence and innovation' (Katz *et al.*, 1966: 154). Looking back some years later, Katz welcomes as fruitful rather than regrets as unfocused the diverse conceptions of media effects which resulted from this broadening of approach: 'shifting from one to another definition of effect has released the field from the morass of persuasive effects. Shifting from individual to societal effects has released the field from psychologism and refocused it on *sociology* and politics' (1981: 267).

His work has played a substantial role in effecting this shift in the field. From the addition of interpersonal communication to the influence of the media in the 1950s to the selective and motivated viewer of *The Uses of Mass Communications* (1974) in the 1970s and the interpretive, culturally grounded viewer of the late 1980s and early 1990s, Katz has consistently argued for a socio-psychological, selective viewer, although – interestingly – conceived in different ways as media theory has developed. Thus for Katz, 'the effects of the media are mitigated by the processes of selectivity in attention, perception, and recall, and ... these, in turn, are a function of predispositional and situational variables such as age, family history, political affiliation, and so on' (Katz, 1987: S26), and research must map these processes of selectivity and their dependence on social context. Here is the context for his view that 'what deserves emphasis, however, is that these studies of media "uses and gratifications" are not only interesting in themselves; but they are, ultimately, an effort to understand "effects"' (Katz *et al.*, 1973: 164). By *The Export of Meaning* (1990), he and Tamar Liebes saw the process of cross-cultural reception as being so complex that 'effects', the classic social psychological question, have become almost too difficult to address.[34] Yet *Media Events* with Daniel Dayan (1992) attempts directly to rethink effects by taking a more complex social semiotic, anthropological, critical approach. The media are, in this book, connected with broader public debates about changing relations between society, technology, citizenship, identity and democracy.

Yet Katz's writings on effects have sometimes been misunderstood, particularly the common identification of *Personal Influence* with the claim of minimal effects. Certainly, because straightforward evidence for powerful media has not been forthcoming, Katz has always argued against those who, from whatever perspective, *claim* powerful media effects (e.g. Hall, Gitlin, Noelle-Neumann and Gerbner). And equally certain, *Personal Influence* argued against strong effects, although not for null effects. The point was that Katz and Lazarsfeld felt themselves led by the *data* to emphasize the mediating, but not wholly undermining, role of the social and communicative context in processes of effect. In terms of research strategy, Katz argues against the kind of broad theorizing which results in what he sees as the untestable or at least typically untested theories of hegemony and ideology (Fejes, 1984). Boudon (1991) discusses Katz and

Lazarsfeld's two-step flow theory as an example of Merton's middle-range theory, where middle-range theories attempt to integrate relevant hypotheses and empirical regularities but assume that 'it is hopeless and quixotic to try to determine the overarching independent variable that would operate in all social processes' (p. 519).

The two-step flow of media influence, the uses and gratifications tradition, the concern with cultural imperialism in the reception of *Dallas* and with media events, have all been taken as different kinds of arguments against effects or for 'audience autonomy'. Yet for Katz, these represent instead different and creative attempts to rethink the central problem of effects by both avoiding advocacy of a major ideological position and by moving beyond the impasse of methodological difficulties towards exploring the social and contextual factors which circumscribe, mediate or facilitate media effects. Katz's interest in people's everyday lives, their motivations and understandings, and their location in local networks, suggests that he would never have expected to find clear evidence for a single process whereby the media affects a vulnerable audience. His continuing focus on the influence of the media has required him to seek an alternative and more complicated route to tracing its diverse and indirect processes. Yet, a careful meta-analysis which seeks patterns among studies of these multiple and context-dependent processes remains to be conducted: only then can we assess whether Katz's recontextualizing approach is more successful than those of others who seek a grand, unifying theory (Livingstone, 1996).

In *Media Events*, Katz tries to show what a more contextualized notion of effects would look like, for a major claim of the book is that the whole question of effects, whether conceived in terms of political effects on public opinion or ideological effects in maintaining the status quo, should be rethought using an anthropological perspective on the media which emphasizes ceremony, symbolic community, ritual and liminality. Katz and Dayan use the phenomenon of media events to demonstrate the inextricable interconnections between everyday conversations, media processes and public opinion, arguing that these diverse, particular and located processes provide the context for understanding media effects. *Media Events* also pushes forward Katz's metatheoretical agenda of convergence among disciplines by studying active viewers in global/local and community/domestic contexts as a way of gaining a broader conception of media effects. Now that the primary group is increasingly an imagined rather than an actual community, and that the media are inextricably integrated into everyday life, this kind of multifaceted analysis of a genre may be a more sophisticated way, if not the only way, of addressing the question of effects.

On the level of middle-range theory, Katz appears to have shifted his position. Yet, a continuity is apparent in the claim that 'the entire genre of media events deals with the relationships among elites, broadcasters, and audience' (Dayan and Katz, 1992: 225), for this is also true of his earlier work on the relations between bureaucracies and clients, or the study of journalist ethics, public opinion and election campaigns, public service broadcasting and the research agenda, or the two-step flow of media influence. In each case, including that of the academic's own relation to funders, Katz hopes to work out how these relations can be framed by a public service rather than a market model. It is partly for this reason that social science method becomes central, as an important means of providing accountability, within a framework in which research is motivated less by the specifics of developing theoretical axioms than by the broad democratic aim of improving the quality of administrative decision-making and, as a consequence, enhancing the public good.[35]

CONCLUSIONS

In a moment of disillusion, Katz concludes that 'we teeter back and forth between paradigms, without getting very far. We need to perform some crucial experiments and to agree on appropriate research methods rather than just storing a treasury of contradictory bibliographical references in our memory banks' (Katz, 1992b: 85).[36] Such a conclusion depends on Katz's characterization of media research history in terms of an oscillation between powerful media and powerful audiences (Katz, 1980b; see also Mendelsohn, 1989). This oscillation can itself be seen as stemming from the contradictions within the liberal–pluralist approach to media research, which sees the audience both as public and as mass (Livingstone and Lunt, 1994), although often at different times. Yet, as the debate itself becomes a self-conscious one, I would suggest that we cannot return to the days when one side was advanced over the other. Media researchers are now irrevocably aware of the debates which structure their field, together with the epistemological and political origins which motivate them, and so must surely progress beyond the oscillation which has structured the field hitherto. Katz played a key role in keeping the active viewer side of the debate alive; now we must move beyond the active versus passive conception of the viewer altogether (Livingstone, 1993).

I suggest that, when we look back over the last half century of media research, Katz should precisely not be criticized for that for which he has sometimes been criticized, namely the methodological, political and epistemological arguments about the conduct and purpose of media research. In this respect, Katz's contribution has been vital – keeping alive a series of debates in which, especially among many British researchers, the odds have been against him. For these debates have been highly productive for the field, as I have tried to show in this chapter, although ironically, we are now more than ever in need of the synthetic skills of researchers like Katz in defining the future of the field. Despite, or even in his case because of, his positive response to the inevitable critical commentary surrounding new developments in a field, Katz's contributions have stood the test of time: the work on personal influence and diffusion established the mediating role of social groups in processes of media effects; no new genre or form of media can be studied without asking what uses and gratifications it provides for its audience; the work on *Dallas* is still one of a few studies linking audience reception to cultural context and processes of media imperialism; and so forth.

However, having been original in so many areas, Katz's work is vulnerable to the charge that he opens up new areas for research but offers little development of them, maybe because his valuing of collaboration takes him in ever-new directions while others are inspired to undertake this development of his key ideas. Yet perhaps in consequence, much of Katz's underlying, integrative, conceptual agenda remains implicit. Interestingly, while this agenda has remained remarkably constant over forty years, the different ways in which Katz has pursued it are testimony to the different assumptions and priorities of different decades of media research. To elaborate this, either as an account of a constant theoretical framework or as a narrative of research development, would require an engagement with the intellectual currents of social theory on which Katz perceptively draws but to which his work does not contribute substantially. Perhaps his recent advocacy of Tarde as the integrating theorist for media research reflects his awareness of this lack. Of course, such a criticism could be made of most other media researchers, and in this respect, media research is still a domain, a set of problematics, rather than a discipline. To the extent that media researchers believe that the media are central to social, cultural and political developments, the case still needs to be made convincingly to those outside, with empirical demonstrations and middle range theories providing the (vital and necessary) starting point for such a case. It remains a challenge for media research to transcend its tendency to regard intellectual engagement with high theory as a complication rather than an enhancement of the quality and direction of useful research.

For the present, it would be fair to conclude that media research has successfully established Schramm's (1961) claim that the media affect some of the people some of the time (Livingstone, 1996). The question for the future concerns the meaning and consequences of this statement – the kinds of effects, the diverse kinds of power relations between media and audiences, the contexts within which the media is influential, and the relation between effects, however reconceived, and pleasure, identity, everyday practices, citizenship. Katz has long argued for exactly this contextualizing of media effects, and his work encompasses a broad range of stimulating and productive approaches whose implications merit further exploration. He has given us many characters and plots to play with in the never-ending soap opera of media research; promoting a continuing debate between social science and humanities, establishing new models for media effects research, generating a diversified and theoretically challenging agenda for audience research, recognizing as vital the link between research and policy, and insisting on conceptualizing key constructs in terms of the complexities and particularities of their real-world context.

NOTES

1 I would like to thank Jay Blumler, Rob Farr, Michael Gurevitch, Elihu Katz, Tamar Liebes, Rodney Livingstone, Peter Lunt and the editors of this volume for their help with sources and their constructive criticism of earlier drafts of this chapter.

2 As the present chapter concerns Katz's work rather than offering an account of his career, I here summarize the latter: Ph.D. (1956) in sociology at Columbia University; Research Associate at the Bureau of Applied Social Research, Columbia University; Lecturer at Columbia, then Chicago and Jerusalem; founding Director, Israel Television (1967–9); presently Emeritus Professor of Sociology and Communications at the Hebrew University of Jerusalem, Trustee Professor at the Annenberg School for Communications, University of Pennsylvania, and Scientific Director of the Israel Institute of Applied Social Research, Jerusalem; has held various additional profess-ional affiliations and offices, and received a number of prestigious awards and honours.

3 Katz's commitment to interdisciplinarity has led him to draw in his research on linguistics, anthropology, semiotics, political science and literary theory, as well as social psychology and sociology.

4 For example, see the special issues, 'Ferment in the field', 1983, and 'Future of the field', 1993, of the *Journal of Communication*.

5 This book contributes rather less to the conceptual agenda as it does not address conversation and social interaction.

6 This concern with convergence might be traced back to Lazarsfeld's time at the Vienna Psychological Institute in the 1920s, when the director, Karl Buhler, 'attacked all narrowly based "schools" of psychology ... and tried to develop a point of view that could unite them' (Ash, 1989: 148), taking an interdisciplinary approach theoretically and integrating qualitative and quantitative methods (Jahoda, 1983).

7 When at Columbia University Bureau of Applied Social Research, Katz wrote his master's thesis (1950), supervised by Leo Lowenthal, on radio fanmail on the subject of 'happiness'.

8 The aim of the Bureau of Applied Social Research was to use empirical methods to combine social psychology and sociology in order to understand what broadcasting means in the lives of its listeners and viewers.

9 Katz (personal communication) suggests that for Lazarsfeld administrative research takes the client's problem as given while critical research asks whether the client may be part of the problem. The distinction does not map in any simple way onto others such as theoretical/empirical or quantitative/qualitative.

10 See discussions in Livingstone (1990), Lindlof (1991), Seiter *et al.* (1989), Morley (1992), Silverstone (1994).

11 This is less true of his later works, especially *Media Events*.

12 The notion that social psychological questions – concerning social identity, com-munication and meaning, influence, interpersonal and intergroup relations etc. – are especially amenable to empirical test is contestable (Harré and Secord, 1972); the epistemological problems of effects and reception research might suggest the opposite.

13 In fact, Lazarsfeld was relatively uninterested in mass communications, simply using media research to develop new social science methodologies (Morrison, 1978); yet the approach he developed had long-term effects on mass communications research.

14 In an article on political communication, Katz (1971b: 304) argues that 'election campaigns, for all their faults, may be the major learning experience of democratic polities. They deserve, therefore, to be better designed.'

15 Empirical research conducted in the tradition of Social Representations Theory (Farr and Moscovici, 1984) would support Katz here, for this too regards spontaneous conversations in primary groups as the locus for generating considered public opinion which influences decision-makers and which diffuses throughout, or marks differences among, the general public.

16 Similarly, while political and epistemological debates dominated critical social science through the 1970s and 1980s, they tend not to form part of Katz's retelling of media research history (e.g. the conclusion of Katz, 1987).

17 Katz notes in his review of *Inside Prime Time* (1985) that Gitlin does not always meet these critical standards in his own work.

18 A similar justification might be offered for the contemporary use of focus groups in audience research (Lunt and Livingstone, 1996).

19 At a time when the interpenetration of the mass media into everyday life was less marked than today, theorizing the relations between mass and interpersonal communication was challenging (Berger and Chaffee, 1988; Cathcart and Gumpert, 1983; Hawkins, Wiemann and Pingree, 1988; Rubin and Rubin, 1985).

20 See Farr (1991) on the historical separation of psychological from sociological forms of social psychology.

21 It is typical of (psychological) social psychology that The Yale Program of Hovland *et al.* (1953) is seen as studies in persuasive rather than mass communication.

22 Recently, a more critical social psychology has developed (Billig, 1991; Farr and Moscovici, 1984; Gergen, 1982; Himmelweit and Gaskell, 1990; Shotter, 1993).

23 Katz is unusual when he suggests that 'some of us are still trying' (1987: 30) to build bridges between approaches, for 'there is no history of a systematic acknowledgement of Marxist scholarship by traditional communications research in the United States' (Hardt, 1992: 236).

24 See, for example, Morley's introduction to *The Nationwide Audience* (1980), work which, ironically, Katz and Liebes develop in *The Export of Meaning*. Although social psychology might seem an appropriate field with which to theorize the active viewer, critical audience research has tended to mark its distance from social psychology, and the term is often used pejoratively to signify administrative, reductionist or positivist research (Livingstone, 1990).

25 Silverstone (1994) defends Katz and Lazarsfeld, noting the primacy of the concept of sociability in their work. Rubin and Windahl (1986) and Ball-Rokeach and DeFleur (1976) have responded to the individualistic criticism of uses and gratifications by considering the sociostructural conditions of media dependency. However, such criticisms of uses and gratifications theory hinge on whether the theory is taken to draw on and refer to a more sociological or psychological form of social psychology; Katz would locate his work within the former tradition, although some other uses and gratificationists are better located within the latter.

26 Katz and his colleagues also address the theme of cultural imperialism in *Broadcasting in the Third World* and *Media Events*.

27 Schiller (1989) criticizes *The Export of Meaning* for creating the straw person – the passive, *tabula rasa* of mass audiences – against which the active viewer concept is seen as progress: who, he asks, as does Morley (1991), would have expected audiences around the world to simply absorb American cultural imperialism? Katz might answer that in fact many have feared just this.

28 Swanson (1992) also sees audience reception research as the way in which uses and gratifications has attempted to answer its critics regarding the problem of interpretation and the role of the text. Katz claims 'audience "decoding" as steps towards a better understanding of uses and effects . . . decoding is now conceptualized as a social psychological process via which viewers enter into "negotiation" with a text' (Katz, 1987: 38).

29 Curran (1990) criticizes the supposed innovativeness of critical audience studies, describing the recent turn to audience reception as 'the new revisionism', and noting that the now-derided effects tradition first documented 'the multiple meanings generated by texts, the active and creative role of audiences and the ways in which different social and discourse positions encourage different readings' (pp. 149–59). Maybe one could read *Personal Influence*, albeit against the grain, as a contribution to cultural studies, for it shows how interpretative communities, according to their own subcultural characteristics, resist or conform to the ideological meanings of the media.

30 Research on audience resistance offers 'recovery from the excesses of manipulation models of Frankfurt inspiration' (Gitlin, 1990: 191) as well as from the supposed hypodermic model of effects (Katz, 1980b). However, Schiller points out that 'where this resistance and subversion of the audience lead and what effects they have on the existing structure of power remain a mystery' (1989: 149). Morgenstern (1992) notes that audiences are considered duped by the media when they express opinions in favour of the status quo and resistant to the media when they express contrary opinions: the empirical test is not whether they are affected by the media, but whether they endorse an implicit theory of the left!

31 Ang (1994) argues that 'critical theory has changed because the structure of the global capitalist order has changed' (p. 202). Consequently, convergence among critical and positivist researchers is also a matter of contention for the Frankfurt School. Lowenthal still insists on the continued, even increasing, necessity for ideology critique (Jay, 1987: 239) while Habermas argues for the 'ambivalent potential of mass communications' (Habermas, 1989: 302). Given 'the steady advance of pluralist themes within the radical tradition' (Curran, 1990: 157), Habermas cites Katz and Lazarsfeld (1955) among other works when arguing that empirical media research reveals how popular culture may contain critical messages, how 'ideological messages miss their audience because the intended meaning is turned into its opposite under conditions of being received against a certain subcultural background' (Habermas, 1989: 304) and how 'the inner logic of everyday communicative practice sets up defenses against the direct manipulative intervention of the mass media' (p. 304).

32 Hardt (1992) suggests that the recent administrative versus critical debate (as in the *Journal of Communication*, 1993) represents 'Goffmanesque example[s] of impression management rather than a substantive debate among several different theoretical positions. In fact, notions of compromise or friendly accommodation in the spirit of common interests clouded the potential for the emergence of real differences and radical changes on this occasion' (p. 21).

33 Ang (1994) suggests starting from the assumption that: 'the potential infinitude of semiosis [is] corroborated by the principle of indeterminacy of meaning ... [so that] any containment of variation and difference within a limited universe of diversity is always-already the product of a determinate ordering by a structuring, hegemonizing power, not, as the functionalist discourse of liberal pluralism would have it, evidence of a lack of order, absence of power' (p. 204).

34 Schiller notes a contradiction between the increasing global penetration of mass media into politics, culture and daily life, and the revival of the limited effects paradigm in the active audience literature.

35 For example, see Katz (1971b, 1977).

36 Unfortunately, there can be no definitive experiment or agreed methodology which resolves all debate, for on the contrary, the more crucial the experiment the more heated the debate it generates (consider the famous case of Milgram's experiments on obedience to authority).

37 Katz (personal communication) notes that he was recruited by Lazarsfeld to 'save' the study that became *Personal Influence*.

38 Elihu Katz is author of well over 100 articles. For reasons of space, I have selected those of particular theoretical significance to the development of media theory, with a focus on the audience. I have also omitted those articles whose content overlaps with Katz's books, and those which address issues outside the scope of this paper (e.g. problems in journalism, elections studies, public opinion, religious behaviour, and the reporting of the Arab-Israeli conflict and peace process; see, for example, Katz and Feldman, 1962, Katz *et al.*, 1969, Katz and Parness, 1977; Katz, 1989; Katz and Levinsohn, 1989; Katz, 1992a).

SONIA LIVINGSTONE

PRIMARY SOURCES

Books by Elihu Katz (complete list)

Katz, E. and Lazarsfeld, P.F. (1955) *Personal Influence: the Part Played by People in the Flow of Mass Communication*, Glencoe, Ill.: The Free Press of Glencoe. Translations into Japanese (1960), German (1962), Italian (1968). Presents the 'two-step flow' theory of mass communication influence, in which opinion leaders seek out mass media messages relevant to their expertise and disseminate these through vertical or horizontal flows in their local community, especially during periods of uncertainty, resulting in a selective transmission process (which resists or facilitates social change) mediated by inter-personal relations in primary groups. The book develops the idea of the opinion leader (from Lazarsfeld's *The People's Choice*[37]), describes the 'Decatur' study which traced actual channels of communication (for opinions on shopping, fashion, films and politics) in an 'average' American city, and discusses the role of the small group, with its norms and networks, in analysing the interpersonal mediation of mass communication processes.

Coleman, J.S., Katz, E. and Menzel, H. (1966) *Medical Innovation: a Diffusion Study*, Indianapolis: Bobbs-Merrill. An analysis of the social psychological factors – individual, interpersonal and institutional – affecting decision-making in the medical profession. The case study explores the role of innovation in social change by examining the diffusion and adoption of a new drug in four communities. The medical decisions of individual doctors are shown to depend on the social and professional networks of relationships – local patterns of communication and influence – among doctors. See also Katz, E. (1961) 'The social itinerary of technical change: two studies on the diffusion of innovation', *Human Organization*, 20(2): 70–81.

Crain, R.L., Katz, E. and Rosenthal, D. (1969) *The Politics of Community Conflict: the Fluoridation Decision*, Indianapolis: Bobbs-Merrill. Applies theories of diffusion of innovations, community conflict and alienation to the problem of resistance to fluoridation. From their study of the process of decision-making in several hundred communities, the authors conclude that none of these theories are appropriate as the decision is primarily political and its outcome is largely, and in a counter-intuitive manner, determined by the differing democratic structures (elite or participatory) of local governments.

Katz, E. and Danet, B. (eds) (1973) *Bureaucracy and the Public: a Reader in Official–Client Relations*, New York: Basic Books. An edited volume addressing bureaucracy as a problem for sociology and society, focusing on the interaction between clients and officials in formal organizations, and including articles on culture and community aspects of bureaucracy, the influence of organizational structure, situational influences and strategies for innovation and change. The volume combines critical and social scientific approaches to bureaucracy, and raises issues of the individual in society (or group), agency and structure, meaning and function, stability and change. Katz's articles in the volume examine the response of Israeli organizations to new immigrants and the rhetoric of clients' persuasive appeals to officials. See also Katz, E. and Danet, B. (1966) 'Petitions and persuasive appeals: a study of official–client relations', *American Sociological Review* 31(6): 811–22. Katz, E., Gurevitch, M., Danet, B. and Peled, T. (1969) 'Petitions and prayers: a method for the content analysis of persuasive appeals', *Social Forces* 47(4): 447–63.

Blumler, J. G. and Katz, E. (eds) (1974) *The Uses of Mass Communications: Current Perspectives on Gratification Research*, Beverly Hills, CA: Sage. An edited volume which includes the theory and evidence for the 'uses and gratifications' paradigm together with its major criticisms. It is generally taken as the definitive statement of this

40

approach. In the first chapter, which summarizes the past, present and potential of uses and gratifications, Katz *et al.* define the approach as the study of '(1) the social and psychological origins of (2) needs, which generate (3) expectations of (4) the mass media or other sources, which lead to (5) differential patterns of media exposure (or engagement in other activities), resulting in (6) need gratifications and (7) other consequences, perhaps mostly unintended ones' (p. 20).

Katz, E. and Gurevitch, M. (1976) *The Secularization of Leisure: Culture and Communication in Israel*, London: Faber & Faber; and Cambridge, MA: Harvard University Press. Also in Hebrew, *Tarbut Hapnai Be Yisrael* (*The Uses of Leisure in Israel*), Tel Aviv: Am Oved (1974). Presents an empirical audit of the uses of leisure, culture and communication in Israel following the introduction of television in 1970. It adopts a broadly social psychological perspective, charting the changing consumption patterns of the public in public and private forms of elite and popular cultural activities, as related to national and subcultural contexts. It broadens the functionalist perspective of the uses and gratifications approach to include all forms of leisure, and adds a policy orientation. See also Katz, E., and Adoni, H. (1973) 'Functions of the book for society and self', *Diogenes* 81: 106–21.

Katz, E. and Wedell, E.G. (1977) *Broadcasting in the Third World: Promise and Performance*, Cambridge, MA: Harvard University Press; and London: Macmillan. Analyses the ways in which broadcasting institutions have been introduced into developing countries, showing the social, political and cultural conditions and constraints which resulted in a significant discrepancy between the promise of modernization – of transferring technology, knowledge and investment from the West to the Third World – and the actual performance (and unintended side-effects) of broadcasting in developing countries. The book draws on original research in eleven countries to emphasize the complex processes of institutional and cultural change across diverse national contexts. See also Katz, E. (1979b) 'With what effect? The lessons from international communications research', in J.S. Coleman and R. Merton (eds) *Qualitative and Quantitative Social Research*, New York: Free Press.

Katz, E. (1977) *Social Research on Broadcasting: Proposals for Further Development. A Report to the British Broadcasting Corporation*, London: British Broadcasting Corporation. Katz's response to the BBC's invitation to prepare 'an agenda for new projects of social research in the field of broadcasting', based on extensive interviews with broadcasters and researchers. The report discusses three kinds of research: evaluative (effects and functions), critical (organizations and output) and diagnostic (policy-related), and considers what broadcasters want to know about audiences, what social research can and cannot do, the often problematic broadcaster-researcher relationship, and outlines a wide-ranging research agenda. See also Katz, E. (1978a) 'Looking for trouble', *Journal of Communication* 28(2): 90–5.

Roeh, I., Katz, E., Cohen, A. and Zelizer, B. (1980) *Almost Midnight: Reforming the Late Night News*, Beverly Hills, CA: Sage. An account which integrates the broadcaster's and academic's, or insider's and outsider's, perspective on the shaping of a new nightly news show which set out to rethink the standard news format by inviting an informal, intimate relationship between viewers and presenter. The book details a model for innovation within a broadcasting bureaucracy, through a (sometimes problematic) collaboration between researchers and broadcasters, with the joint ideal of improving the news and gratifying unmet audience needs.

Katz, E. and Szecsko, T. (eds)(1981) *Mass Media and Social Change*, London: Sage. An edited volume containing the diverse but individually significant papers presented to the symposium on Mass Communication and Social Change at the 9th World Congress of Sociology. The papers discuss the central issue of whether the mass media should be conceptualized as agents of social change or reinforcers of the status quo, generally disagreeing with the view of the media as disembodied agents of persuasion, instead locating the media firmly within a context of social, cultural and political institutions.

Liebes, T. and Katz, E. (1990) *The Export of Meaning: Cross-Cultural Readings of Dallas*, New York: Oxford University Press. Reprinted by Polity Press, Cambridge (1994). A study of the active reception of television by audiences to examine notions of cultural imperialism and the global village. The social–semiotic meanings of the highly successful American soap opera, *Dallas*, are analysed using themes of primordiality and seriality, and related to the ways that specific subcultures accept, resist or renegotiate the ideological messages of the text. Israel is used as a microcosm of global cultural and ethnic differences in order to compare reception processes among Moroccan settlers, Israeli Arabs, newly arrived Russian Jews and kibbutz members in Israel, and American and Japanese viewers in their own countries. Focus group discussions show viewers, through the group's negotiation of meaning, using diverse cultural resources to interpret the drama according to different frameworks, and making referential readings (interpreting the drama as a window on the world) or critical readings (critiquing the drama as a cultural and technical product) of the text. See also Katz, E. and Liebes, T. (1986) 'Mutual aid in the decoding of *Dallas*: preliminary notes from a cross–cultural study', in P. Drummond and R. Paterson (eds) *Television in Transition*, London: British Film Institute. Liebes, T. and Katz, E. (1986) 'Patterns of involvement in television fiction: a comparative analysis', *European Journal of Communication* 1(2): 151–72. Liebes, T. and Katz, E. (1988) '*Dallas* and Genesis: primordiality and seriality in popular culture' in J.W. Carey (ed.) *Media, Myths, and Narratives: Television and the Press*, Newbury Park, CA: Sage. Liebes, T. and Katz, E. (1989) 'On the critical abilities of television viewers', in Seiter, E. *et al.* (eds) *Remote Control: Television, Audience, and Cultural Power*, London: Routledge.

Dayan, D. and Katz, E. (1992). *Media Events: the Live Broadcasting of History*, Cambridge: Harvard University Press. Reprinted by Harvard University Press (1994). Translated into Italian and French (forthcoming). Applies an anthropological framework to understanding the meaning of the new phenomenon of 'media events' – the live broadcasting of 'historic' events around the world (e.g. the Olympic Games, Kennedy's funeral, the British royal wedding). The celebration of media events in the living room, the experience of 'not being there', is analysed as a new and potentially transformative ritual whose form and significance must be negotiated among organizers, broadcasters and audiences. The events themselves can be seen as scripted – as contest (e.g. the Olympic Games, the Senate Watergate hearings), conquest (e.g. Sadat's visit to Jerusalem, the Pope's visit to Poland) or coronation (e.g. the royal wedding, the mourning following Kennedy's assassination) – and the aesthetics, functions and effects of this genre are traced. See also Katz, E. (1980a) 'Media events: the sense of occasion', *Studies in Visual Anthropology* 6: 84–9. Katz, E., Dayan, D. and Motyl, P. (1981) 'Communications in the 21st century: in defense of media events', *Organizational Dynamics* 10: 68–80. Katz, E. and Dayan, D. (1985) 'Media events: on the experience of not being there', *Religion*: 305–14. Katz, E. and Dayan, D. (1986) 'Contests, conquests, coronations: on media events and their heroes', in C.F. Graumann and S. Moscovici (eds) *Changing Conceptions of Leadership*, New York: Springer. Dayan, D. and Katz, E. (1987) 'Performing media events', in J. Curran, A. Smith and P. Wingate (eds), *Impacts and Influences*, London: Methuen.

Selected key articles by Elihu Katz[38]

Katz, E. (1957) 'The two-step flow of communication: an up-to-date report on an hypothesis', *Public Opinion Quarterly* 21: 61–78. Reviews solutions 'to the problem of how to take account of interpersonal relations in the traditional design of survey research' (p. 61), and locates the Decatur study (Katz and Lazarsfeld, 1955) and the drug diffusion study (Coleman, Katz and Menzel, 1966) in the context of related research, reflecting on the conceptual and methodological issues which arise.

Katz, E. (1959) 'Mass communications research and the study of popular culture: an editorial note on a possible future for this journal', *Studies in Public Communication* 2: 1–6. Agrees that while the study of short-term media effects is 'dead', research should now address not what the media do to people but what people do with the media (i.e. uses and gratifications) and thereby aim for a more complex link to effects and also build a bridge to the humanist tradition of studying popular culture.

Katz, E. (1960) 'Communication research and the image of society: convergence of two traditions', *American Journal of Sociology* 65(5): 435–40. Argues for a convergence between the persuasion model of (urban) mass communications with studies of community, diffusion and interpersonal relations in rural sociology.

Katz, E. and Foulkes, D. (1962) 'On the use of the mass media as "escape": clarification of a concept', *Public Opinion Quarterly* 26(3): 377–88. A discussion of the commonly used but little analysed concept of escapism, showing how uses and gratifications provides a useful framework to separate the alienated desire for escape (use) from escapist media content (gratification), and offering an analysis of the social context, psychological process and consequences of media exposure.

Katz, E., Hamilton, H. and Levin, M. L. (1963) 'Traditions of research on the diffusion of innovation', *American Sociological Review* 28: 237–52. Reprinted in C.W. Backman and P.F. Secord (eds) (1966) *Problems in Social Psychology: Selected Readings*, New York: McGraw-Hill. Multidisciplinary research on the process of diffusion of innovation is reviewed as it relates to the following aspects of diffusion: the (1) *acceptance*, (2) over *time*, (3) of some specific *item* – an idea or practice, (4) by individuals, groups or other *adopting units*, linked (5) to specific *channels* of communication, (6) to a *social structure*, and (7) to a given system of values, or *culture* (1966, p. 156).

Katz, E. (1968) 'On reopening the question of selectivity in exposure to mass communications', in R.P. Abelson *et al.* (eds) *Theories of Cognitive Consistency: A Sourcebook*, Chicago: Rand McNally and Co. Argues for the notion of selectivity as central in explaining the power of the audience to minimize media effects. Examines whether selectivity can be shown to involve motivated choice associated with the quest for reinforcement, and thus distinguished from the mere expression of interest or utility or from de facto selectivity whereby social circumstances expose people to congenial communications.

Katz, E. (1971a) 'Television comes to the people of the book', In I.L. Horowitz (ed.) *The Use and Abuse of Social Science*, New Brunswick, New Jersey: Transaction Books. An autobiographical and sociological account of the founding of Israel Television by its Director, 1967–9.

Katz, E. (1973) 'Television as a horseless carriage', in G. Gerbner *et al.* (eds) *Communications Technology and Social Policy*, New York: Wiley. Draws on an analysis of the television's introduction in developing countries to argue for the runaway character of the medium, against those who consider it controlled by national and international interests.

Katz, E., Gurevitch, M. and Hass, H. (1973) 'On the use of the mass media for important things', *American Sociological Review* 38(2): 164–81. An empirical study of the different uses and gratifications which audiences derive from books, television, radio, newspapers, cinema and interpersonal communication.

Katz, E. (1978b) 'Of mutual interest', *Journal of Communication* 28(2): 133–41. Katz responds to critics of *Social Research on Broadcasting* that he colludes with broadcasters, is atheoretical, identifies professionalism with public service and is selective.

Katz, E. (1979a) 'The uses of Becker, Blumler and Swanson', *Communication Research*

6(1): 74–83. A defence against critics of uses and gratifications theory in which Katz uses the criticisms to aid theory development.

Katz, E. (1980b) 'On conceptualising media effects', *Studies in Communication* 1: 119–41. Argues that 'the history of empirical work on the effects of mass communications can be written in terms of two concepts: selectivity and interpersonal relations' (p. 119), so that 'the "power" of the media rises and falls, conceptually, as a function of the importance attributed to the intervening processes of selectivity and interpersonal relations' (p. 120), an importance which he shows oscillates over the past six decades of research. See also Katz, E. (1988b) 'On conceptualizing media effects: another look', in S. Oskamp (ed.) *Television as a Social Issue*, Newbury Park, CA: Sage.

Katz, E. (1981) 'Publicity and pluralistic ignorance: notes on "The spiral of silence"', in Baier, Kepplinger and Reumann (eds), *Public Opinion and Social Change*, Opladen: Westdeutscher Verlag. Motivated by his concern over the (problematically absent) relation between theory and research on public opinion and on mass communication, Katz critiques Noelle-Neumann's theory of the spiral of silence and locates it in the context of other theories of powerful effects.

Katz, E. (1983) 'The return of the humanities and sociology', *Journal of Communication* 33: 51–2. Attributes the ferment in the field to the reunion of the social sciences with the humanities, an interdisciplinarity which is resulting in a productive broadening of research questions away from short-term effects to include media history, genre and more long-term, subtle effects.

Blumler, J.G., Gurevitch, M. and Katz, E. (1985) 'REACHING OUT: a future for gratifications research', in K.E. Rosengren, L.A. Wenner and P. Palmgreen (eds) *Media Gratifications Research: Current Perspectives*, Beverly Hills, CA: Sage. Reflects on the last ten years of uses and gratifications research, acknowledging the limitations of 'vulgar gratificationism' with its 'audience imperialism' and 'disappearing message', supporting audience reception research, and advocating cross-cultural comparisons and improved links between micro and macro-level analyses.

Katz, E. (1987) 'Communications research since Lazarsfeld', *Public Opinion Quarterly* 51: 25–45. Argues that the minimal effects paradigm of Lazarsfeld's Bureau of Applied Social Research can deal with subsequent criticisms from the institutional, critical and technological paradigms of media research.

Katz, E. (1988a) 'Disintermediation: cutting out the middle man', *Inter Media* 16(2): 30–1. Diverse bodies use the mass media to communicate directly to the public, cutting out traditional intermediary institutions, and thereby introducing technological and institutional determination.

Katz, E. (1990) 'Viewers' work: the Wilbur Schramm Memorial Lecture', presented to the University of Illinois, Urbana, 6 September. Reconsiders Schramm's distinction between reality and fantasy television (and active and passive viewers) in relation to current audience research, and argues that different approaches could be reconciled, given agreed rules of evidence and good research, so as to understand better the nature of the work viewers do when watching television.

Katz, E. (1992b) 'On parenting a paradigm: Gabriel Tarde's agenda for opinion and communication research', *International Journal of Public Opinion Research* 4(1): 80–6. Traces Lazarsfeld's approach to the relation between conversation, public opinion and media influence back to Tarde, and asks how much of Tarde's agenda has been accomplished one hundred years later.

Katz, E. and Haas, H. (1994) 'Twenty years of television in Israel: are there long-run effects on values and cultural practices?', manuscript. Replicates the leisure survey of Katz and Gurevitch (1974) and charts the changes. While acknowledging the problems of causal inference, Katz suggests some effects of both medium and message which, while sometimes contradictory, have generally slowed, but may facilitate, the change from collective to individualistic values.

REFERENCES

Adorno, T.W. (1969) 'Scientific experiences of a European scholar in America', in D. Fleming and B. Bailyn (eds) *The Intellectual Migration: Europe and America, 1930–1960*, Cambridge: Cambridge University Press.

Ang, I. (1994) 'In the realm of uncertainty: the global village and capitalist postmodernity', in D. Mitchell and D. Crowley (eds) *Communication Theory Today*, Cambridge: Polity Press.

Ash, M.G. (1989) 'Psychology and politics in interwar Vienna: the Vienna Psychological Institute, 1922–1942, in M.G. Ash and W.R. Woodward (eds) *Psychology in Twentieth-century Thought and Society*, Cambridge: Cambridge University Press.

Ball–Rokeach, S.J., and DeFleur, M.L. (1976) 'A dependency model of mass–media effects', *Communication Research* 3: 3–21.

Bausinger, H. (1984) 'Media, technology and daily life', *Media, Culture and Society* 6: 343–51.

Berger, C.R. and Chaffee, S.H. (1988) 'On bridging the communication gap', *Human Communication Research* 15(2): 311–18.

Billig, M. (1991) *Ideology and Opinions*, Sage: London.

Black, J.S. (1982) 'Opinion leaders: is anyone following?', *Public Opinion Quarterly* 46: 169–76.

Boudon, R. (1991) 'What middle–range theories are', *Contemporary Social Psychology* 20(4): 519–24.

Bronner, S.E. and Kellner, D.M. (1989) 'Introduction', in S.E. Bronner and D.M. Kellner (eds) *Critical Theory and Society: a Reader*, New York: Routledge, 1–21.

Carey, J.W. (1975) 'Communication and culture', *Communication Research* 2: 173–91.

Cathcart, R. and Gumpert, G. (1983) 'Mediated interpersonal communication: toward a new typology', *Quarterly Journal of Speech* 69(3): 267–77.

Curran, J. (1990) 'The new revisionism in mass communication research', *European Journal of Communication* 5(2–3): 135–64.

Elliott, P. (1974) 'Uses and gratifications research: a critique and a sociological alternative', in J.G. Blumler and E. Katz (eds) *The Uses of Mass Communications: Current Perspectives on Gratifications Research*, Beverly Hills, CA: Sage.

Farr, R.M. (1991) 'The long past and the short history of social psychology', *European Journal of Social Psychology* 21(5): 371–80.

Farr, R.M. and Moscovici, S. (ed.) (1984) *Social Representations*, Cambridge: Cambridge University Press.

Feick, L.F. and Higie, R.A. (1986) 'People who use people: the other side of opinion leadership', *Advances in Consumer Research* 13: 301–5.

Fejes, F. (1984) 'Critical mass communications research and media effects: the problem of the disappearing audience', *Media, Culture and Society* 6(3): 219–32.

Gergen, K.J. (1982) *Toward Transformation in Social Knowledge*, New York: Springer-Verlag.

Gitlin, T. (1978) 'Media sociology: the dominant paradigm', *Theory and Society* 6: 205–53.

Gitlin, T. (1990) 'Who communicates what to whom, in what voice and why: about the study of mass communication', *Critical Studies in Mass Communication* 7(2): 185–96.

Habermas, J. (1989) 'The tasks of a critical theory of society', in S.E. Bronner and D.M. Kellner (eds) *Critical Theory and Society: A Reader*, New York: Routledge, 292–312.

Hardt, H. (1992) *Critical Communication Studies: Communication, History and Theory in America*, London: Routledge.

Harré, R. and Secord, P. (1972) *The Explanation of Social Behaviour*, Blackwell: Oxford.

Hawkins, R.P., Wiemann, J. and Pingree, S. (ed.) (1988) *Advancing Communication Science: Merging Mass and Interpersonal Processes*, Newbury Park, CA: Sage.

Himmelweit, H. and Gaskell, G. (eds) (1990) *Societal Psychology*, Newbury Park, CA: Sage.

Horkheimer, M. (1972) 'Traditional and critical theory', in M. Horkheimer (ed.) *Critical Theory: Selected Essays*, New York: The Seabury Press.

Hovland, C., Janis, I. and Kelley, H.H. (1953) *Communication and Persuasion*, New Haven: Yale University Press.

Jahoda, M. (1983) 'The emergence of social psychology in Vienna: an exercise in longterm memory', *British Journal of Social Psychology* 22(4): 343–9.

Jay, M. (1973) *The Dialectical Imagination: a History of the Frankfurt School and the Institute of Social Research, 1923–1950*, London: Heinemann Educational Books.

Jay, M. (ed.) (1987) *An Unmastered Past: the Autobiographical Reflections of Leo Lowenthal*, Berkeley, CA: University of California Press.

Katz, E. (1971b) 'Platforms and windows: broadcasting's role in election campaigns', *Journalism Quarterly* 48 (summer): 304–14.

Katz, E. (1985) 'Review of *Inside Prime Time*', T. Gitlin, 1983, New York: Pantheon Books. *American Journal of Sociology* 90(6), 1371–4.

Katz, E. (1989) 'Journalists as scientists', *American Behavioral Scientist* 33(2): 238–46.

Katz, E. (1992a) 'The end of journalism? Notes on watching the war', *Journal of Communication*, 42(3): 5–13.

Katz, E. and Feldman, J.J. (1962) 'The Kennedy–Nixon debates: a survey of surveys', *Studies in Public Communication* 4: 127–63.

Katz, E. and Levinsohn, H. (1989) 'Too good to be true: notes on the Israel elections of 1988', *International Journal of Public Opinion Research* 1:(2), 111–22.

Katz, E. and Parness, P. (1977) 'Remembering the news: what the picture adds to recall', *Journalism Quarterly* 54: 231–9.

Katz, E., Gurevitch, M., Danet, B. and Peled, T. (1969) 'Petition and prayers: a method for the content analysis of persuasive appeals', *Social Forces* 47(4): 447–63.

Lang, K. and Lang, G.E. (1983) 'The new rhetoric of mass communication research: a longer view', *Journal of Communication* 33(3).

Lazarsfeld, P.F. (1941) 'Remarks on administrative and critical communications research', *Studies in Philosophy and Science* 9: 3–16.

Lazarsfeld, P.F. (1969) 'An episode in the history of social research: a memoir', in D. Fleming and B. Bailyn (eds) *The Intellectual Migration: Europe and America, 1930–1960*, Cambridge: Cambridge University Press.

Lazarsfeld, P.F. and Gaudet, H. (1944) *The People's Choice*, New York: Duell, Sloan and Pearce.

Levy, M.R. and Windahl, S. (1985) 'The concept of audience activity', in K.E. Rosengren, L.A. Wenner and P. Palmgreen (eds) *Media Gratifications Research*, Beverly Hills, CA: Sage.

Lindlof, T.R. (1991) 'The qualitative study of media audiences', *Journal of Broadcasting and Electronic Media* 35(1): 23–42.

Livingstone, S. (1990) *Making Sense of Television: the Psychology of Audience Interpretation*, Oxford: Pergamon.

Livingstone, S. (1993) 'The rise and fall of audience research: an old story with a new ending', *Journal of Communication, Special Issue, 'The future of the field'* 43(4): 5–12.

Livingstone, S. and Lunt, P. (1994) *Talk on Television: the Critical Reception of Audience Discussion Programmes*, London: Routledge.

Livingstone, S. (1996) 'On the continuing problem of media effects', in J. Curran and M. Gurevitch (eds) *Mass Media and Society*, London: Edward Arnold.

Lunt, P. and Livingstone, S. (1995) 'The focus group in media and communications research: the critical interpretation of public discussion', *Journal of Communication* 46(2): 79–98.

Mendelsohn, H., (1989) 'Socio–psychological construction and the mass communication effects dialectic', *Communication Research* 16(6): 813–23.

Merton, R.K. (1955) 'A paradigm for the study of the sociology of knowledge', in P.F. Lazarsfeld and M. Rosenberg (eds) *The Language of Social Research: a Reader in the Methodology of Social Research*, New York: The Free Press, 498–510.

Morgenstern, S. (1992) 'The epistemic autonomy of mass media audiences', *Critical Studies in Mass Communications* 9: 293–310.

Morley, D. (1980) *The Nationwide Audience: Structure and Decoding*, London: British Film Institute.

Morley, D. (1991) 'The consumption of media: review of the export of meaning', *Journal of Communication* 41(2): 202–4.

Morley, D. (1992) *Television, Audiences and Cultural Studies*, London: Routledge.

Morrison, D. (1978) 'The beginning of modern mass communication research', *European Journal of Sociology* 19(1): 347–59.

Palmgreen, P., Wenner, L.A. and Rosengren, K.E. (1985) 'Uses and gratifications research: the past ten years', in K.E. Rosengren, L. A. Wenner and P. Palmgreen (eds) *Media Gratifications Research: Current Perspectives*, Beverly Hills, CA: Sage.

Peters, J.D. (1989), 'Democracy and American mass communication theory: Dewey, Lippman, Lazarsfeld', *Communication* 11: 199–220.

Rogers, E. and Shoemaker, F.F. (1971) *Communication of Innovations: a Cross–cultural Approach*, New York: Free Press.

Rogers, E.M. (1983) *Diffusion of Innovations*, New York: The Free Press.

Rosengren, K.E., Wenner, L.A. and Palmgreen, P. (eds) (1985) *Media Gratifications Research: Current Perspectives*, Beverly Hills, CA: Sage.

Rossi, P.H. (1980) 'The presidential address: the challenge and opportunities of applied social research', *American Sociological Review* 45(6): 889–904.

Rubin, A.M. (1985) 'Uses of daytime television soap operas by college students', *Journal of Broadcasting and Electronic Media* 29(3): 241–58.

Rubin, A.M. and Rubin, R.B. (1985) 'Interface of personal and mediated communication: a research agenda', *Critical Studies in Mass Communication* 2: 36–53.

Rubin, A.M. and Windahl, S. (1986) 'The uses and dependency model of mass communication', *Critical Studies in Mass Communication* 3(2): 184–99.

Schiller, H.I. (1989) *Culture Inc.: the Corporate Takeover of Public Expression*, New York: Oxford University Press.

Schramm, W., Lyle, J. and Parker, E.B. (1961) *Television in the Lives of Our Children*, Stanford, CA: Stanford University Press.

Seiter, E., Borchers, H., Kreutzner, G. and Warth, E.-M. (1989) *Remote Control: Television Audiences and Cultural Power*, London: Routledge.

Shotter, J. (1993), *Cultural Politics of Everyday Life*, Buckingham: Open University Press.

Sills, D.L. (1981) 'Surrogates, institutes, and the search for convergences: the research style of Paul F. Lazarsfeld', *Contemporary Sociology*, 10 (May): 351–61.

Silverstone, R. (1994) *Television and Everyday Life*, London: Routledge.

Silverstone, R. and Hirsch, E. (eds) (1992) *Consuming Technologies*, London: Routledge.

Smith, M.B. (1983) 'The shaping of American social psychology: a personal perspective from the periphery', *Personality and Social Psychology Bulletin* 9(2): 165–80.

Sproule, J.M. (1989) 'Progressive propaganda critics and the magic bullet myth', *Critical Studies in Mass Communication* 6(3): 225–46.

Swanson, D.L. (1992) 'Understanding audiences: continuing contributions of gratifications research', *Poetics* 21(4): 305–28.

Weimann, G. (1991). 'The influentials: back to the concept of opinion leaders?' *Public Opinion Quarterly* 55: 267–79.

Wright, C.R. (1974) 'Functional analysis and mass communication revisited', in J.G. Blumler and E. Katz (eds) *The Uses of Mass Communications: Current Perspectives on Gratifications Research*, Beverly Hills, CA: Sage, 197–212.

3

CULTURAL STUDIES AS A RESEARCH PERSPECTIVE: THEMES AND TENSIONS

Peter Dahlgren

How is it possible to understand soap operas as cultural practices without studying the broadcasting institutions that produce and distribute them, and in part create the audiences?

(Garnham, 1995: 71)

Cultural studies did not reject political economy *per se*, discussions of capitalism have always figured centrally in its work; rather it rejected the way certain political economists practice political economy.

(Grossberg, 1995: 72)

The cultural studies literature plays much with the word 'power'. The problem is that the source of this power remains, in general, opaque. And this vagueness about power and the structures and practices of domination allows a similar vagueness about resistance.. . . . Can we not admit that there are extremely constrained and impoverished cultural practices that contribute nothing to social change?

(Garnham, 1995: 69)

Cultural studies believes that culture matters and that it cannot be simply treated (or dismissed) as the transparent, at least to the critic, public face of dominative and manipulative capitalists. Cultural studies emphasizes the complexity and contradictions, not only within culture, but in the relations between people, culture, and power.

(Grossberg, 1995: 76)

Critical political economy is at its strongest in explaining who gets to speak to whom and what forms these symbolic encounters take in the major spaces of public culture. But cultural studies, at its best, has much of value to say about . . . how discourse and imagery are organized in complex and shifting patterns of meaning and how these meanings are reproduced, negotiated, and struggled over in the flow and flux of everyday life.

(Murdock, 1995: 94)

These short excerpts from a recent polemical exchange about Cultural Studies demonstrate that work defined under this heading is still highly controversial. The quotations cited above reflect on the tensions between the perspectives of Cultural Studies and of Political Economy, with each side tending to depict the other as an inadequate framework for the analysis of culture and the media. Other debates around Cultural Studies are aligned differently, as we shall see below. Cultural Studies is currently the subject of contending claims which are often also of significance for media studies more generally. For even if the definitive attributes of Cultural Studies as a distinctive field refuse to be fixed, culture as an analytic theme and as a perspective on the media (and social life generally) continues to grow in prominence. And while there are a number of differing approaches to culture within the human sciences, today it requires a significant feat of evasion to take a cultural perspective on the media without in some way coming to terms with the literature of Cultural Studies and its existence as an established, and rapidly growing, academic project.

Cultural Studies is notoriously heterogeneous. Its diversity makes any attempt to offer a synoptic account of it precarious. However, this caveat does not alter my argument in this chapter, which is that there is an intellectual vitality, a set of concerns, and an array of theoretical and empirical orientations within Cultural Studies from which media research greatly benefits.

I shall argue as a media researcher who identifies considerably with the Cultural Studies project, who has been inspired by it, but can also see some of its limitations. While much of the work of Cultural Studies in its formative years dealt with the media, today media enquiry is only a relatively small part of its interests. However, what Cultural Studies at its best has to offer has less to do with specific topic areas and more to do with the kinds of perspective that it has developed, its modes of theorizing and its methodological innovations.

I begin with some reflections on the radical heterogeneity of media research quite independent of its linkage with Cultural Studies. Then I offer a snapshot account of the evolution of the latter, before turning to a discussion of what I take to be its core theoretical elements. These cluster around three themes: culture, meaning and power. I follow that discussion with some reflections on critical theory and postmodernism and then address major dilemmas and tensions, concluding with some brief pointers about what Cultural Studies might offer media research in the future.

THE MULTIPLICITY OF MEDIA RESEARCH

For media research, the focus of analysis is an array of topics which can be grouped according to the classic steps of the communication chain: 'senders' and the circumstances of production, forms and contents of the output, and the processes and impact of reception/consumption. However, such categorization becomes increasingly awkward at a time when the media are becoming so pervasive and so integrated – both institutionally and experientially – with the social world. It becomes quite difficult within late modern society to distinguish, for example, lived, everyday cultures from ubiquitous and highly intertextual media cultures. Institutionally, the media are becoming ever more entwined in global, corporate configurations. Media research has tried to capture these developments and to emphasize the interfacing of media structures and processes within changing contexts. Thus, for example, we have had 'waves' of research linking media with a new international information order, with the political economy of media technology, with the fall and rise of social formations, with the transformations of political cultures and the emergence of social movements, with the micro-settings of everyday life, and with young people's use of popular media in shaping their identities.

The intellectual horizons informing contemporary media research are also diverse. Here, strands of enquiry deriving from the established social scientific traditions of sociology, psychology, social psychology, and political science (which can still manifest versions of positivist thinking) are to be found alongside the more interpretive currents inspired by anthropology, literature and film studies. There is now a whole alignment of post-positivist trajectories, including critical theory, hermeneutics, feminism, and poststructuralism. Any effort to try to impose a unity on media research, to transform it from a loose field into a 'discipline', is thus flawed.

CULTURAL STUDIES, A SPRAWLING EVOLUTION

With these points about the diverse character of media research in mind, I want to note some key moments in the evolution of Cultural Studies and briefly to identify some of its main concerns. The aim here is largely descriptive, to convey a sense of the increasingly wide range of topics with which Cultural Studies engages (see, for example, Brantlinger, 1990; Turner, 1990; Hall, 1992; Mc-Guigan, 1992; Harris, 1992; Grossberg, 1993).

The conventional beginning is Britain in the late 1950s, when the New Left emerged as a political grouping. This political element is crucial and not merely circumstantial. As Hall (1992) recounts, the New Left was involved in a strenuous dialogue with Marxism, rejecting the dogmatism of the British Communist Party and the Soviet Union, yet trying to extract a viable analytic framework from the Marxian tradition in order to understand and to confront contemporary economy and society. The origins of Cultural Studies are therefore to be found primarily in the attempt to develop a critical political practice. Most histories of Cultural Studies also mention in particular three key authors and their landmark works: Richard Hoggart's *The Uses of Literacy* (1957), Raymond Williams's *Culture and Society* (1958), and E.P. Thompson's *The Making of the English Working Class* (1963). All, in very different ways, contributed to the conceptualizing of culture as a feature of the lived practices of everyday life, which needed to be understood in political terms. I will return to this point below.

The formation of the Centre for Contemporary Cultural Studies in 1963 at the University of Birmingham, first under Hoggart, then with Stuart Hall as the leading figure, constitutes another decisive stage. The decade of the 1970s at the Centre is often seen as a sort of 'golden age' of Cultural Studies, where much ground-breaking work was done. There are accounts of the various theoretical conflicts which were generated while wrestling with different versions of Marxian theory (in particular Althusser's and Gramsci's). The efforts to develop a Marxist theory of ideology based in class analysis, were interrupted, first by feminism (see Franklin *et al.*, 1991) and then by questions of race (e.g. Centre for Contemporary Cultural Studies 1982). Other theoretical influences were incorporated, chief among them a linguistic turn which continued to foster semiotic approaches to meaning. The broad range of work undertaken in the Centre during the period is usefully summarized in Hall *et al.* (1980). For a recent collection of texts centring on Hall's contribution to Cultural Studies and its encounters with Marxism, postmodernism, race and other topics, see Morley and Chen (1996).

Much of the theoretical development in the early years proceeded by encounters with media structures and processes: Hall's classic article on 'Encoding/decoding' (in Hall *et al.*, 1980) is a case in point. Cultural theory was brought in from anthropology, especially via Lévi-Strauss, and ethnographic methods were utilized in several projects, among them two well known books by Willis (1977) and Hebdige (1979). Both not only made use of Gramscian hegemony theory, but also thematized the notion of everyday resistance. Together with other texts they are evidence of the weight given to the theme of subcultures. Morley's (1980) study of the sense-making processes around current affairs television also made use of ethnographic methods. This book not only was of more direct pertinence for media research, it also signalled the major ethnographic turn to qualitative audience research which rose to prominence in the 1980s (see also Morley, 1992). The processes of reception, the contextually situated production of meaning by media audiences, was now seen as an empirical social question which could not be answered by merely specifying the ideological dimensions of media output through the use of a critical semiotics.

During the 1980s, Cultural Studies became not only increasingly theoretically diverse, but also increasingly institutionalized. While the centre at Birmingham was subject to financial cutbacks and some staff left for other positions in Britain and beyond, Cultural Studies as an academic field was beginning to establish itself. New courses were launched, notably the innovative one on popular culture at the Open University (see Miller, 1994), which greatly helped to spread the work of the Centre. (Several important texts with a media focus derived from this course, for example Bennett *et al.*, 1986). In Britain, Cultural Studies continued to draw from and to influence literary studies (see Easthope, 1991), as well as cinema studies, resulting in new and productive approaches to film and television (see MacCabe, 1986).

But Cultural Studies was also beginning to move overseas, particularly to Australia (cf. Fiske *et al.*, 1987; Frow and Morris, 1993), Canada (cf. Blundell *et al.*, 1993) and the United States, losing its uniquely British profile (Schwarz, 1994). Especially in the United States, Cultural Studies began to get a firm foothold within the university sector (for a British Cultural Studies encounter with America, see Clarke, 1991). This development was not without problems, to which I will return. The theoretical eclecticism continued to grow, within an increasingly geographically dispersed Cultural Studies. By now the theme of popular pleasure was finding a more central place (see Harris, 1992), as much new writing focused on various aspects of popular culture, for instance TV soap operas (Ang, 1985; Hobson, 1982), romance novels (Radway, 1984), and feminist analysis of popular media (Modleski, 1984).

In the United States, Cultural Studies was taken up partly by media researchers, but also by people working in literature departments. Cultural Studies here not surprisingly shed much of its Marxist legacy, and instead became the ground on which many approaches could meet: concern with feminism, race and ethnicity, and with postmodernity in its various guises, made their way into its 'core'. The Cultural Studies of the 1990s shows the prevalence of discourse analysis and poststructuralism; it also displays a strong focus on identity politics, post-colonialism, globalization, multiculturalism and national identity – the latter theme more evident in Europe, Canada and Australia than in the United States. The journal *Cultural Studies* was launched in the latter part of the 1980s. Though now based in America (initially, it was edited from Australia), in its pages one finds ample evidence of Cultural Studies' transnational character; for example, the May, 1994 issue was devoted to Nordic research. In 1990 a major conference was held at the University of Illinois Urbana-Champaign, which resulted in a collection of forty papers (Grossberg *et al.*, 1992). From its financially modest but intellectually ambitious origins in Birmingham in the 1960s and 1970s, Cultural Studies had arrived as an established academic field. This is apparent from the large number of textbooks and anthologies aimed at the student market (e.g. Barker and Beezer, 1992; During, 1993; Gray and McGuigan, 1993; Inglis, 1993).

From this brief overview, I want now to go back and look in more detail at some central theoretical strands.

THEORETICAL LANDSCAPES: CULTURE, MEANING, POWER

Cultural Studies' core concern is with culture as a key concept for understanding features of our contemporary historical situation. In recent decades there has also been a deep-rooted concern with culture outside of Cultural Studies, a culturo-logical 'turn' in social theory more generally, upon which Cultural Studies has drawn (cf. Chaney, 1994; Alexander and Siedman, 1990; *The Polity Reader*, 1994). I cannot, of course, retrace all the debates that were generated around the concept of culture, but I do want to highlight a number of interrelated core themes.

The first has to do with culture as an aesthetic versus a sociological–anthropological issue. Certainly within the traditions of literary and artistic humanism, culture – often with an implied capital C – has been seen as something produced by artists and writers, to be analysed aesthetically. From the standpoint of Cultural Studies, it was particularly the work of Raymond Williams which helped extract culture from the literary–aesthetic ghetto and make it a concern for social analysis as well as significantly broadening the range of things which could be regarded as 'cultural'. Williams and the tradition of British cultural materialism which he represents (see Milner, 1993, for a discussion of the role of cultural materialism in the development of Cultural Studies) took the important step of treating culture as a part of lived experience in society, and not just as a body of texts or as art. This does not mean that the aesthetic dimension became irrelevant. On the contrary, Cultural Studies has paid considerable attention to aesthetic questions, for instance, in respect of popular music, styles of dress, television programmes and film. But the point is that these analyses are placed in socio-historical contexts in such a manner that aesthetics becomes a tool for illuminating aspects of the social.

Cultural Studies also increasingly came to challenge the traditional distinction between high, or elite culture, and low, or popular culture. The challenge did not consist in simply dismissing any differences between these categories, but rather in arguing that the distinctions could not be understood purely in aesthetic terms. What is deemed high or low culture is always in part a question of power relations within society. Incorporating the work of sociologists of culture, chiefly Bourdieu (1984), Cultural Studies could argue that taste is never merely a question of individual preference, but is socially located in complex hierarchies and the identifications they mobilize. Cultural Studies does not follow the line of argument about 'mass culture' developed by the Frankfurt School, which saw popular culture as inexorably tied to the commodification of consciousness under capitalism. Likewise, Cultural Studies rejected the American-derived idea of mass culture as an expression of cultural democracy. Popular culture came to be taken seriously for its potentially conservative, ideological dimensions, but also for its meanings, pleasures and practices. The very notion of popular culture raises the issue of the popular and 'the people', long a central topic of debate within Marxism and Cultural Studies (for a succinct survey of the debates around the concept of popular culture, see Storey, 1993).

The above two themes come together in the opposition between idealist and materialist understandings of culture. This polarity poses the question of whether culture should be seen as separate from, and by implication superior to, the world of the social, or as derived from and helping constitute the social. In support of the latter view, there is an array of positions within social theory (including Marxism), various strands of anthropology, and sociologies of culture. The Marxism of Gramsci, with its emphasis on practice, social consciousness and everyday life, became a central point of reference. By contrast, the sociologies of Durkheim, which makes use of an idealist conception of collective consciousness, or that of Parsons, which sees culture basically as an integrating, stabilizing system, have found no place in Cultural Studies.

Cultural Studies' materialism takes a constructivist and dialectical perspective on culture, that is to say its premise is that people and social institutions in specific historical circumstances produce culture, which in turn helps to produce and reproduce society. In this perspective, culture also consists of the circulation of values, and, more generally, meaning. A major step in the advance of cultural theory within Cultural Studies was the incorporation of elements of semiotics during the 1970s. The names of Roland Barthes, and, to a lesser extent, Umberto Eco, both of whom build upon the work of de Saussure, figure prominently here. One could argue that what began to emerge was a communications perspective on culture, a perspective particularly applicable to the study of the mass media, though it was also utilized in the study of communication within other social settings.

In its initial phase, this semiotic turn had a quasi-objectivist character. The semiotic conceptual toolbox, including signs, signifiers, signifieds, codes, and conventions, was mobilized to illuminate specific processes of sociocultural signification. This approach to semiotics emphasized the structural quality of signification: the meaning actually communicated could be elucidated by examining semiotic structures. These semiotic structures were linked to social structures, and therefore to the realm of power and ideology. But it can be noted here that this structuralist rendering of culture and meaning, greatly influenced by the appropriation of Althusser's Marxism, was visibly in tension with more 'culturalist' readings, as Hall (1980) noted in a seminal article. The culturalist orientation, especially associated with Williams and E.P. Thompson, emphasized agency and experience. In other words, culture and meaning are in part constituted by people's subjectivities and cannot simply be equated with, and read off from, cultural texts. Debates on these issues became very intricate, but it is fair to say that the theoretical polarity between structure and agency remains crucial, not only within Cultural Studies and theories of signification, but also within Marxist theory and sociological approaches to the social order more generally.

This brings me to the key theme within Cultural Studies' concept of culture, namely that culture is a bearer of social power. This is not to say that Cultural Studies merely reduces culture to power, nor does it reduce meaning to ideology, but rather that it sharply refutes the dominant theoretical traditions which have kept culture immune from questions of power. Culture, as a materialist category, embodied in social institutions and practices, shapes subjectivity and social relations. Social relations are 'always already' the embodiment of power relations. Orginally Cultural Studies emphasized class antagonisms, but, as mentioned above, feminism raised questions about patriarchy and social order. Race and ethnicity were also increasingly highlighted: one of the Centre's landmark works in the 1970s (Hall *et al.*, 1978) was a study of how the media portrayal of mugging in Britain, as a crime wave basically perpetrated by blacks, played into the hands of state power.

The theme of power within Cultural Studies was largely cast in terms of Gramsci's much-cited notion of hegemony, which was an attempt to conceptualize how the powerful in society elicit support and consent from subordinate groups. With this move, Cultural Studies could link together a materialist understanding of culture and signification with a non-determinist view of power and ideology: ideology is not merely given, an essentialist feature of late capitalist life, but rather an accomplishment, an achievement which has to be continuously re-made because it is contestable. Neo-Gramscian hegemony theory thus keeps the door open for the possibility of resistance to ideology. If ideology is seen as consisting of processes of meaning that support social relations of domination, those meanings can potentially always be challenged and redefined. As a theoretical orientation, this emphasis on challenge and resistance focuses precisely on the interconnections between human agency and socioeconomic structure. Culture, particularly popular culture, can be treated as a plane of ideological struggle.

Yet as the quotations at the start of this chapter suggest, Cultural Studies continues to have a polemical relationship with political economic conceptions of power. From the perspective of political economy, the 'objective' circumstances of social existence have more explanatory power than the 'subjective' factors of ideology. While this is an issue for Cultural Studies, it is also a question of which version of political economy is being put forward. Few accounts would opt for a fully deterministic and reductionist brand, seeing culture as a mere epiphenomenon of the 'genuine reality' formed by economic dynamics. At the same time, few cultural theorists would deny that the logic of capital and its institutional manifestations contribute to shaping social power. It is between these extremes that many positions have been articulated, with differing conceptions of how much independence can be accorded to cultural phenomena in explaining the reproduction of, and levels of resistance to, dominant power.

For example, is social class to be seen as the fundamental variable of domination, shaping social location, subjectivity and identity, or is it merely one of several factors to be weighed, along with gender, ethnicity and other categories? My own judgement is that while class is a central and indispensable category, there can be no fixed gauge as to its relative weight in all situations; context and articulation become paramount. The political economy of class must be set in relation to other concrete forms of domination in specific instances; in some cases it will have more bearing, in others, less. Certainly the feminist movement and the struggles of oppressed people of colour have demonstrated that gender and racial subordination are not merely a function of social class. At the same time, class can intertwine with these other forms of domination. There are few practitioners of Cultural Studies or Political Economy who argue that there is an irresolvable incompatibility between these different forms of categorization and attributed relations. Most will acknowledge the possibility of complementarity. In practice, however, research has not often demonstrated this.

A good deal of Cultural Studies' research during the 1980s centred upon the notion of resistance. This was conceptually expanded beyond the work of the Centre by a number of authors (e.g. Fiske, 1989) and put into theoretical frameworks which downplayed the role of social structure and power. The argument was that if meaning is fundamentally polysemic and can thus never be fully stabilized, and, further, if meaning is socially negotiated, then media audiences have much greater interpretive freedom than traditional critiques of ideology give them credit for. The image of the powerful media gave way to an image of powerful audiences, who could make sense of media output in virtually unlimited ways. Structure, many commentators pointed out, had all but been replaced by agency.

This view gained momentum, with 'resistance' to hegemony being seen as enacted by 'active' audiences who interpreted media, especially popular entertainment, in alternative and oppositional ways. Even the gaining of pleasure from media artefacts was in some cases heralded, in and of itself, as evidence of resistance. The excesses of this particular Cultural Studies wave eventually evoked critical responses, both from within Cultural Studies (cf. Morris, 1990) and from the wider field of media research. Curran (1990), for example, saw it as part of a 'new revisionism', conceptually situated close to the traditional liberal views emphasizing individual choice in a setting devoid of structural domination.

JUXTAPOSITIONS: POSTMODERNISM, POLITICAL ECONOMY AND CRITICAL THEORY

Cultural Studies is close to the centre of that movement towards greater self-reflection prevalent in academic life today. Within Cultural Studies we find the various claims and debates of feminism, psychoanalysis and, not least, postmodernism. This open-ended and agonistic dimension is an important feature of Cultural Studies, and has led to some important modifications in its view of what culture is. Thus, within the original, Raymond Williams-inspired, notion of culture was the idea that it pointed to 'the whole way of life' of a society. This totalizing perspective was of course already called into question by the study of subcultures. Moreover, with the increasing influence of the poststructural and postmodern theory produced by a number of largely French theorists (Foucault, Derrida, the later Barthes, Baudrillard and Lyotard), the tendency to think in terms of the unity of culture began to give more and more ground to the theme of heterology. Culture was conceived increasingly as a myriad of partially overlapping systems of value and meaning in a society; while national cultures could not be dismissed, attention to the details of the cultures of specific groups grew. 'Difference' became a pervasive concept.

It is important to emphasize that changes in the view of culture are embedded in a shift in theory which exceeds even the wide parameters of Cultural Studies. I referred above to poststructural views of signification, in which meaning is seen as radically contingent. These views became an important building block of the postmodern perspective. Subjectivity, too, came to be cast in terms of contingency and multiplicity: particularly through the influence of Lacanian psychoanalysis: the human subject is seen as decentred, fragmented, never fully at one with itself, but always in the process of struggling for wholeness, desiring that which it lacks. Perhaps most fundamentally, knowledge itself, as understood in the Enlightenment tradition, is increasingly problematized. The claims of knowledge and science to rest on firm foundations have been confronted; universalist representations of knowledge have not only been historicized or treated as contingent to social circumstances, but also seen as ultimately inseparable from power. While such ideas have evolved over the course of the past century, the critical and relativist view of knowledge was given a strong push in the 1970s and 1980s through the works of 'neo-Nietzschean' writers such as Foucault and Lyotard. Again, these developments signal not a collapse of the possibilities of knowledge according to the Enlightenment, but rather a deep modification of our understanding of its limits.

For Cultural Studies, the incorporation of postmodern thought had major consequences. Research began to thematize the heterogeneity of culture. Hebdige's (1988) essays marked an important step in Cultural Studies' use of postmodern thought while retaining a critical perspective. Further, the theoretical portrait of the dispersed, nomadic subject helped make identity work and identity politics a focus of its concern. This was linked with feminist analyses of gendered identity, specifying how specific groups learn to become male or female and what these distinctions mean in different contexts. Baudrillard's work on simulation and simulacra (for instance, Baudrillard, 1983) helped foster a strand within Cultural Studies which underscored the collapse of the distinctions between 'the real world' and the cultural forms which express, stage, and enact it. Many currents within postmodern thought, with its radical questioning of representation, were readily applicable to the media (see, for instance, Mellancamp's (1990) collection on television).

And it is especially here, at the border crossing between postmodernism and the critical tradition, where significant theoretical developements have occurred. The principal issues can be formulated thus: given the massive dose of relativism which postmodernism injects into our understanding of knowledge, of representation, and of the self, on what grounds can one speak of domination and subjugation? On the basis of what intellectual foundation can one specify something else as ideological? How does one formulate an emancipatory vision in the wake of heterology? Such questions emerge not only within Cultural Studies, but also within critical, or Western Marxism, which has had increasing difficulties since the 1970s in offering a full and compelling account of the sociohistorical world. Singled out by postmodernism as one of the main 'grand narratives' of the Enlightenment legacy, the theoretically totalizing tendencies of Marxism, with their anchoring in class analysis, have fallen on bad times in an increasingly fragmented social world.

However, it is my contention that both within and beyond Cultural Studies, postmodernism offers opportunities for reconstruction of the critical tradition. This tradition, through Kant, Hegel and Marx, all the way to the Frankfurt School, psychoanalysis and feminism – has emphasized the critique of domination and of unnecessary constraints on human freedom. It is very much a child of the Enlightenment. The encounter with postmodernism, far from acting as an obstacle or a diversion, can help further to develop and enhance the liberatory project, adapting it to newer social conditions (see Pieterse, 1992). It is to Cultural Studies' credit that it has provided space for this theoretical encounter.

PETER DAHLGREN

AXES OF TENSION

As should be evident from this brief and selective overview, Cultural Studies embodies both conceptual and institutional dilemmas. In this section, I will briefly call attention to some major difficulties, organizing the presentation around four sets of polarities – all closely related and criss-crossing at several points.

The first tension concerns the issue of a fluid versus fixed identity for Cultural Studies, which is continuously poised between the need to define its turf and a desire to keep its boundaries permeable. Obviously any field or discipline must be somewhat fluid if it is not to atrophy. It must evolve across time. But what are the definitive elements? In the case of Cultural Studies, the answer remains somewhat in doubt. Certainly there are implicit boundaries; for example, the journal *Cultural Studies* includes specific kinds of article but not others. Yet, when a field gets as heterogeneous as Cultural Studies, the very label becomes too elastic.

A second tension concerns the principles of selection by which Cultural Studies has drawn on other traditions of enquiry. Cultural Studies is paradoxically both broad, drawing upon many different intellectual currents, yet narrow in the sense that it tends systematically to isolate itself from certain kinds of analytic approach altogether. With its emphasis on culture, meaning, subjectivity, etc., it generally avoids using and testing itself against such strands as macro-sociology (population profiles, systematic accounts of social stratification, migration, etc.), the sociology of culture-producing institutions and the political economy of cultural industries. This is unfortunate since interconnections would be mutually beneficial. (See Golding and Murdock, 1991, for such a discussion from the perspective of political economy.)

Thirdly, there is the continuing issue of Cultural Studies as a political versus academic enterprise. It is not impossible to do politically relevant work in academic settings, but one must acknowledge the real hindrances involved. As it becomes entrenched in the university, Cultural Studies becomes subject to all the institutional pressures of academic life: the need for standardized syllabuses and textbooks, the financial imperative to attract students, the gamesmanship of getting research grants, career strategies for obtaining and holding academic jobs. The 'market strategy' of Cultural Studies at the university often seems to result in a tendency to equate the popular with youth culture, leading to a constricted sociological horizon, not to mention a displacement of political perspectives. The larger critical perspectives on the social order tend to be replaced by celebratory accounts of the popular. There are, of course, genuine efforts to maintain a political focus in the research, and to treat teaching reflexively as a critical practice (see Giroux, 1994). Cultural Studies' self-proclaimed political identity is nevertheless difficult to maintain in an academic setting. The social situation of critical or leftist academics and intellectuals *vis-à-vis* the majority of the population, especially oppressed groups, has often been ambiguous. There is an understandable sensitivity to the social hierarchy involved; Left academics want to avoid elitism. With regard to the mass media and popular culture, this expresses itself in a reluctance to take a critical position on questions of value. No doubt fuelled by the relativism of the postmodern wave, we have witnessed a rise of what McGuigan (1992) terms 'cultural populism', where academics, not wanting to disparage the experiences of ordinary people, may celebrate popular culture as an expression of solidarity. (For a vehement rebuttal of this trend, see Berman, 1991; the issue is also addressed in Modleski, 1986). The perspective of the Frankfurt School on popular culture has come to represent for some people in Cultural Studies the paradigmatic elitist and 'politically incorrect' attitude to take. Significantly, many people now working in Cultural Studies are personally involved in the pleasures of popular culture; an involvement which Adorno and Horkheimer most emphatically did not share. Acknowledging or even experiencing the pleasures while at the same time keeping political horizons in view can be difficult.

A fourth tension lies in the relationship between textual and socio-institutional analysis, and is closely related to that between the humanities and the social sciences within Cultural Studies. For a variety of reasons, including the fact that texts are easier to work with, both in the classroom and as research objects, and also because many scholars in Cultural Studies come from the humanities and have backgrounds in literature and film, Cultural Studies is coloured by humanities-inspired textual research. There is a social scientific strand within it, largely represented by ethnographic and other forms of qualitative research but certain modes of social science tend to be selectively avoided. Thus, Cultural Studies tends to produce a skewed body of knowledge, quite often ignoring the macro-institutional settings in which cultural texts are produced, circulated and experienced.

Like the critical theory of the Frankfurt School, the political thrust of Cultural Studies includes, at the theoretical level, a transdisciplinary response, a dialogical and critical encounter with its contemporary disciplinary 'others'. For critical theory, this was chiefly mainstream sociology and psychology, as well as orthodox Marxism. For Cultural Studies, it is a whole range of disciplines in the humanities and social sciences. Both critical theory and Cultural Studies are historically situated. Both begin to lose their efficacy as critical interventions when subjected to extensive systematization and codification. Yet, at the same time, those committed to the critical project must understand the conditions and limits of critique as a form of knowledge, even in its most efficacious renderings.

Critique as such is but one moment or phase of the knowledge process; the critical project more generally also needs 'positive knowledge', a key theme in Habermas's attempts to reconstruct historical materialism and ground the human sciences. The larger emancipatory and reconstructive visions and their projects also need useful knowledge on which to base decisions and practices. The questions are of course, what kind of knowledge this is, for whom, and for what purpose? The answers are always contingent. Yet such positive knowledge must be formulated in ways that make it relevant for the critical enterprise (for a concise programmatic statement on critical media research from a Cultural Studies perspective, see Hall, 1989).

As the previous sections of this article have indicated, there are tensions within the diverse menu of the Cultural Studies tradition, as well as some notable absences on the terrain which it has defined for itself. It cannot simply be incorporated as a self-defined domain within the pluralistic landscape of media research. Indeed, many of the traditional perspectives and issues within media research will continue to be compelling, without their giving any thought to Cultural Studies. The very hetereogenity of the field speaks strongly for this.

But as the media become all the more central to the organization and experience of social life, as our everyday culture increasingly becomes a media culture, media research will continue to find the strands of work in Cultural Studies a valuable source of ideas. Along with shifts in the scale and cultural reach of the media will also go shifts in their nature. The indications are that they will become less obviously and directly 'mass' and more specialized, personalized and interactive, decreasingly phenomena for which one is only an audience. As a widely varying range of resources for cultural practice, they will be important constituents of cultural change, of new forms of cultural stratification and perhaps of a reconfiguration of cultural power.

Throughout this chapter I have claimed that Cultural Studies' efforts to explore and develop ideas about meaning, the theoretical import it gives to subjectivity and, most fundamentally, the primacy it accords to the power dimensions of culture, constitute an achievement with increasing relevance to contemporary social analysis. This, despite the problems and the evasions which are documentable too. I would speculate that while the basic contours which dominate in media research today will continue to do so for a number of years to come, we will see an increase in activity on the 'margins'. In these margins, we will find different strands of interpretative and critical work being generated, with Cultural Studies playing a pivotal role in their formation and development and in mediating their relationship with core concerns and perspectives. With the development of work on a distinctive methodology for researching culture, for giving cultural analysis a stronger and more comprehensive empirical dimension (see Alasuutari, 1995), the interconnections possible at this level should become more extensive and productive too.

Finally, I have stressed the importance of Cultural Studies' openness to intellectual developments in philosophy and social theory. The current turbulence within the philosophy of knowledge and science is something which, far from avoiding, it has fully engaged with. This is important for the long-term development of media research: like classic critical social theory, Cultural Studies continues to confront scientistic self-delusion. It is not impossible that we might do media research which is theoretically and methodologically sound, socially useful, politically provocative and yet which is constantly aware of its provisionality and limits. Indeed, the field of research as a whole should not place lesser demands on itself.

PRIMARY SOURCES

The literature of Cultural Studies is immense, especially if one includes texts from cultural theory, postmodernism, feminism, multiculturalism, and other related areas. I wish to highlight here a few key texts on the media which will be helpful to those not familiar with work in the area.

The collection by Stuart Hall *et al.* (1980) not only provides a summary overview of the kind of empirical work carried out at the Centre for Contemporary Cultural Studies in Birmingham during the 1970s, but also gives a sense of the range of theoretical work which early British Cultural Studies drew on.

During the 1980s, a number of books appeared which were to become 'classics'. There are five that I would mention here, in alphabetical order. Ien Ang's (1985) study on how viewers experience the TV programme *Dallas* was based on letters written by viewers rather than ethnographic observation but it opened up a number of important themes in reception studies and issues of meaning production. Dick Hebdige (1988) makes use of the critical essay – a prevalent form within Cultural Studies – to address a wide range of topics within popular culture, mobilizing important themes from postmodern thought. Tanya Modleski (1984) analyses popular women's fiction and TV soap operas to develop a more nuanced understanding of the relationship between women's fantasies and popular culture. Janice Radway (1984) interviewed readers of popular women's fiction, and in a work often noted for both its methodological and theoretical innovation, illuminated the meanings such literature can have within the context of the women's everyday life circumstances. Finally, while David Morley's first major ethnographic study (1980) has earned a place in the history of both media research and Cultural Studies. His collection of articles (1992) not only summarizes his early efforts and presents important later work, but also offers discussions of the methodological issues and debates that occurred in the 1980s over ethnographic audience studies.

Two interpretive histories of Cultural Studies are found in Brantlinger (1990) and Turner (1990). While Turner follows more closely the unfolding of Cultural Studies, the former is more intellectually ambitious. Brantlinger engages in extensive conceptual exposition and situates the development of the area, in both the United States as well as Britain, within contemporary thought. James Carey (1989) has long espoused the idea of Cultural Studies and his post-positivistic approaches to media research represent an important American strand of work.

Popular music is a subfield of Cultural Studies as well as of media research and is often linked to analysis of youth culture. Simon Frith is a key figure here, and of his many publications, *Sound Effects* (1981–3) is particularly notable. Frith is exemplary in his attempt to combine political economic and cultural enquiry. The more recent collection on music video by Frith *et al.* (1993) is an excellent source. Closer to home, I can also mention that in Sweden in recent years there has been enormous activity in the area of youth culture, focusing on style, music, entertainment and modernity. The English-language collection by Johan Fornäs and Göran Bolin (1994) provides an overview of this work.

As I mentioned early in this chapter, there are a number of anthologies which offer overviews of Cultural Studies, and these can be very helpful sources. The ones by Simon During (1993) and Ann Gray and Jim McGuigan (1993) are careful selections including both theoretical and empirical case studies. The large collection by Lawrence Grossberg *et al.* (1992) reflects the diversity that often arises from conference-based anthologies, yet at the same time it can be seen as a report on the current pluralization of Cultural Studies. The recent collection by Morley and Chen (1996) is particularly useful in that it traces Stuart Hall's intellectual and political development in several areas, illuminating important steps in the development of the whole field. This anthology includes several pieces by, and interviews with, Hali.

REFERENCES

Agger, B. (1992) *Cultural Studies as Critical Theory*, London: Falmer Press.

Alasuutari, P. (1995) *Researching Culture: Qualitative Method and Cultural Studies*, London: Sage.

Alexander, J. and Siedman, S. (eds) (1990) *Culture and Society: Contemporary Debates*, Cambridge: Cambridge University Press.

Allen, R.C. (1992) *Channels of Discourse, Reassembled*, London: Routledge.

Ang, I. (1985) *Watching Dallas*, New York: Methuen.

Barker, M. and Beezer, A. (eds) (1992) *Reading Into Cultural Studies*, London: Routledge.

Baudrillard, J. (1983) *Simulations*, New York: Semiotext(e).

Bennett, T., Mercer, C. and Woollacott, J.. (eds) (1986) *Popular Culture and Social Relations*, Milton Keynes: Open University Press.

Berman, R. (1991) 'Popular culture and populist culture', *Telos* 87 (Spring): 59–70.

Blundell, V., Shepherd, J. and Taylor, I. (eds) (1993) *Relocating Cultural Studies*, London: Routledge.

Bourdieu, P. (1984) *Distinction: a Social Critique of the Judgement of Taste*, London: Routledge.

Brantlinger, P. (1990) *Crusoe's Footprints*, London: Routledge.

Carey, J.W. (1989) *Communication as Culture*, London: Unwin.

Centre for Contemporary Cultural Studies (1982) *The Empire Strikes Back: Race and Racism in 70's Britain*, London: Hutchinson.

Chaney. D. (1994) *The Cultural Turn*, London: Routledge.

Clarke, J. (1991) *New Times, Old Enemies*, London: HarperCollins.

Curran, J. (1990) 'The new revisionism in mass communication research: a reappraisal', *European Journal of Communication* 5(2/3):135–64.

During, S. (ed.) (1993) *The Cultural Studies Reader*, London: Routledge.

Easthope, A. (1991) *Literary into Cultural Studies*, London: Routledge.

Featherstone, M. (1991) *Consumer Culture and Postmodernism*, London: Sage.

Fiske, J. (1989) *Understanding Popular Culture*, London: Unwin Hyman.

Fiske, J., Hodge, R. and Turner, G. (eds) (1987) *Myths of Oz: Readings in Australian Popular Culture*, Sydney: Allen & Unwin.

Fornas, J. and Bolin, G. (eds) (1994) *Youth Culture in Late Modernity*, London: Sage.

Franklin, S., Lury, C. and Stacey, J. (eds) (1991) *Off-Centre: Feminism and Cultural Studies*, London: Unwin Hyman.

Frith, S., Goodwin, A. and Grossberg, L. (1993) *Sound and Vision: the Music-Video Reader*, London: Routledge.

Frow, J. and Morris, M. (eds) (1993) *Australian Cultural Studies: A Reader*, St Leonards: Allen & Unwin.

Garnham, N. (1995) 'Political economy and cultural studies: reconciliation or divorce?', *Critical Studies in Mass Communication* 12: 62–71.

Giroux, H.A. (1994) *Disturbing Pleasures: Learning Popular Culture*, London: Routledge.

Golding, P. and Murdock, G. (1991) 'Culture, communication and political economy' in J. Curran and M. Gurevitch, (eds) *Mass Media and Society*, London: Edward Arnold.

Gray, A. and McGuigan, J. (eds) (1993) *Studying Culture: an Introductory Reader*, London: Edward Arnold.

Grossberg, L. (1993) 'The formation of cultural studies: an American in Birmingham', in V. Blundell *et al.* (eds) *Relocating Cultural Studies*, London: Routledge.

Grossberg, L. (1995) 'Cultural studies vs. political economy: is anyone else bored with this debate?', *Critical Studies in Mass Communication* 12: 72–81.

Grossberg, L., Nelson, C. and Treichler, P. (eds) (1992) *Cultural Studies*, London: Routledge.

Hall, S. (1980) 'Cultural studies: two paradigms', *Media, Culture and Society* 2(1): 57–72.

Hall, S. (1989) 'Ideology and communication theory' in B. Dervin (ed.) *Rethinking Communication*, London: Sage.

Hall, S. (1992) 'Cultural studies and its theoretical legacies' in L. Grossberg *et al.* (eds) *Cultural Studies*, London: Routledge.

Hall, S., Critcher, C. Jefferson, T., Clarke, J. and Roberts, B. (1978) *Policing the Crisis: Mugging, the State, and Law and Order*, London: Macmillan.

Hall, S. *et al.* (eds) (1980) *Culture, Media, Language*, London: Hutchinson.

Harris, D. (1992) *From Class Struggle to the Politics of Pleasure*, London: Routledge.

Hebdige, D. (1979) *Subculture: the Meaning of Style*, London: Routledge.

Hebdige, D. (1988) *Hiding in the Light: on Images and Things*, London: Comedia.

Hobson, D. (1982) *Crossroads: the Drama of a Soap Opera*, London: Methuen.

Inglis, F. (1993) *Cultural Studies*, Oxford: Blackwell.

Jensen, K.B. and Jankowski (eds) (1991) *A Handbook in Mass Communication Research*, London: Routledge.

Kellner, D. (1990) *Television and the Crisis of Democracy*, Boulder: Westview Press.

Kellner, D. (1995) *Media Culture*, London: Routledge.

MacCabe, C. (ed.) (1986) *High Theory/Low Culture: Analyzing Popular Television and Film*, Manchester: Manchester University Press.

McGuigan, J. (1992) *Cultural Populism*, London: Routledge.

McRobbie, A. (1994) *Postmodernism and Popular Culture*, London: Routledge.

Mellancamp, P. (ed.) (1990) *Logics of Television*, Bloomington: Indiana University Press; and London: BFI.

Miller, R.E. (1994) 'A moment of profound danger: British cultural studies away from the Centre', *Cultural Studies* 8(3): 417–37.

Milner, A. (1993) *Cultural Materialism*, Melbourne: Melbourne University Press.

Modleski, T. (1984) *Loving with a Vengeance: Mass Produced Fantasies for Women*, London: Methuen.

Modleski, T. (ed.) (1986) *Studies in Entertainment*, Bloomington: Indiana University Press.

Morley, D. (1980) *The 'Nationwide' Audience*, London: BFI.

Morley, D. (1992) *Television Audiences and Cultural Studies*, London: Routledge.

Morley, D. and Chen, K.S. (eds) (1996) *Stuart Hall: Critical Dialogues in Cultural Studies*, London: Routledge.

Morris, M. (1990) 'Banality in cultural studies' in P. Mellancamp (ed.) *Logics of Television*, Bloomington: Indiana University Press; and London: BFI.

Murdock, G. (1995) 'Across the great divide: cultural analysis and the condition of democracy', *Critical Studies in Mass Communication* 12: 89–100.

Pieterse, J.N. (ed.) (1992) *Emancipations, Modern and Postmodern*, London: Sage.

The Polity Reader in Cultural Theory (1994) Cambridge: Polity Press.

Radway, J. (1984) *Reading the Romance*, Chapel Hill: University of North Carolina Press.

Schudson, M. (1991) 'The sociology of news production revisited', in J. Curran and M. Gurevitch (eds) *Mass Media and Society*, London: Edward Arnold.

Schwarz, B. (1994) 'Where is Cultural Studies?', *Cultural Studies* 8(3).

Storey, J. (1993) *Cultural Theory and Popular Culture*, Hemel Hempstead: Harvester Wheatsheaf.

Turner, G. (1990) *British Cultural Studies*, London: Unwin Hyman.

Willis, P. (1977) *Learning to Labour*, New York: Columbia University Press.

4

GENDER AND MEDIA STUDIES: NO WOMAN, NO CRY[1]

Joke Hermes

Gender is less and less a 'fashionable' academic subject. To focus on gender means paying insufficient attention to ethnicity or to sexuality, which will lead to an inadequate theorization of social and discursive practices and structures. Or it means focusing on women or femininity, whereas men and masculinity have until recently escaped critical attention. In general 'gender' has become a theoretical tool that is almost impossible to wield. More the pity for interdisciplinary fields such as media and communication studies, in which gender has hardly been given the theoretical attention it deserves. In this chapter I will try to defy the odds and present a summary overview of how gender has its place in media and communication studies debates. To make room for my particular interpretation of gender's place in this field, I will mix that old-fashioned noun and its reified sound with adjectives and verb forms such as 'gendered' and 'gendering'. At the risk of sounding obtuse, what I hope to accomplish is a 'sexing' of media studies to paraphrase Elspeth Probyn's (1993) title for her exposé of gendered positions in cultural studies, which in turn paraphrased the novelist Jeanette Winterson.

My 'sexing' of media studies will focus on those areas in media research that, as a political scientist turned cultural theorist, I am most familiar with. At one end of this trajectory are the media as an integral part and co-producer of the public sphere, at the other end is popular culture. A huge gulf would appear to separate the two, not least in terms of the place accorded to theoretical reflection on the genderedness of, say, citizenship and journalism on the one hand and of media consumption on the other. In an article on what he calls the New Audience Research, John Corner (1991) subsumes my personal trajectory under two 'projects': the public knowledge project and the popular culture project. In my understanding they are largely separate domains in one of which gender is relatively unimportant, while it is a major research interest in the other. I will briefly summarize Corner's points on this distinction because I have used it to structure my discussion here into two large sections devoted to the two projects. In the third section, the conclusion, I will try to bring the two projects together, in the interest of finding new ways to understand and theorize questions of gender in media studies. To bridge the two projects, I will develop the notion of cultural citizenship.

Gender has not been considered to be very important in what Corner calls the 'public knowledge project '. This project focuses on news and current affairs, and the politics of information in general. The viewer/reader is seen as citizen (Corner, 1991: 268). Much more attention has been given to gender and gender-related issues in the 'popular culture project', which is primarily concerned with 'the implications for social consciousness of the media as a source of entertainment' (ibid.). In this domain, according to Corner, questions of 'taste' and pleasure within industrialized popular culture take predominance. The viewer/reader is seen as a consumer. My symptomatic reading is concerned with how media consumption has invited gender theorization, while the politics of media, information, education and citizenship have not. The divide between 'public knowledge' and 'popular culture' would seem to echo other divisions such as between 'serious business' and 'pleasure', between 'production' and 'consumption', and thus between what in a highly conservative vocabulary would be seen as men's business and women's pastimes.

A brief initial glimpse at the public knowledge domain, to appropriate and broaden Corner's heuristic term, with its focus on news values, news production, broadcasting and broadcasting policy, confirms its idealization of the viewer/ reader as citizen and its abhorrence of what is seen as a development towards commercialization and consumerism. A collection edited by Jay Blumler on public broadcast television makes this abundantly clear (Blumler, 1992). The popular culture project on the other hand has focused on fictional genres rather than news media, and gender and gender-related issues come high on its research agenda. Pleasure and (everyday) meaning production are key interests. Feminism has been and is a source of innovation and critical thought, even if credit has not always been given where it was due (Drotner, 1993). Both projects are considered by their practitioners to be 'political' enterprises. What is meant by 'political' is vastly different however. The politics of citizenship and the politics of pleasure belong to different planets altogether.

James Curran, in a review of developments in mass communication research, decries popular culture research as 'revisionist' and narcissistic. Referring to Janice Radway's study of romance reading and Swedish research on teenage rock groups, Curran writes that Radway's (1984) *tour de force* fails because it may offer 'an account of romance addicts in relation to patriarchy but not to their flesh and blood husbands' (1990: 154). The Swedish research finds even less grace in Curran's eyes because it is 'engaged in analysing cultural consumption and identity formation almost as an end in itself. It belongs to the literature on socialization within the pluralist tradition rather than to the radical tradition of cultural studies' (ibid.). Clearly Curran can see no viable political agenda of any kind emanating from this type of research, either it remains too abstract or it is too meticulous. Many feminists and popular culture researchers would disagree. His position typifies modernist media criticism whereas Radway's (1984) romance study can be seen as one of the founding texts for postmodern media research.

The public knowledge project and the popular culture project represent forms of media research based on totally different assumptions. It is especially the modernist/postmodernist difference that I wish to use as an entry for my symptomatic reading. Whereas gender is the dreaded Other in the one project, an unspoken ghost definitely of the female sex, it has tended to be conflated with women and femininity in the other project while masculinity was allowed to go unresearched and, in a sense, unchallenged as the norm, as that from which femininity deviates (Coward, 1983). Both projects could do with a flavouring of the type of politics the other project champions. The modernist citizenship jargon (whether in its pluralist or in its Marxist version) would be much more appealing were it infused with a notion of pleasure. The postmodern politics of pleasure could do worse than to take seriously the criticism of overly celebratory views of everyday media use as practices of resistance. In the sections dealing with modernism and the public knowledge project and with postmodernism and the popular culture project these issues will return. Although my use of terms such as modernism and postmodernism will largely explain itself below, a brief pre-liminary comment might be in order, as might a short discussion of what is meant by 'gender'.

I take modernism to refer to the Enlightenment, to belief in progress, in rationality and the individual. Postmodernism I see as the radical questioning of Enlightenment values: such as the autonomy of individual subjects and gender or ethnicity as their fixed properties (see Flax, 1990). Both terms are labels for forms and styles of (academic) reasoning. Both relate to modernity as a situated historical period (Hall, 1992), today being 'high modernity' or 'late modernity' (Huyssen, 1990; Murdock, 1993). Gender, not unlike modernism and postmodernism, only exists in our use of the term to invoke sexed realities. It certainly is not a natural consequence of sexual difference, as Ien Ang and I have argued earlier (Ang and Hermes, 1991). Gender is socially constructed in the form of gender definitions, gender positionings and gender identifications. A wide array of social practices and discourses, among which is media consumption, produce gender through these modalities (Ang and Hermes, 1991: 316). Gender thus exists as (practices of) gendering and attains reality in the effects of these practices. Sex is often misread as the ultimate 'natural' basis for gender difference but is in fact as much a construction as 'gender' is. Both gender and sex are, in Judith Butler's words, the sedimented effect of reiterative or ritual practice (1993: 10). It is the performativity of gender, or the power of discourse to produce gender and genderedness through reiteration, that I am interested in here (Butler, 1993: 20).

For too long in mass communication research when gender was the focus (and this was strictly the province of a small group of women researchers) it was used to debate sex-role stereotyping and unequal professional access (Tuchman, 1973; Gallagher, 1980; Baehr, 1981; Creedon, 1989). It became conflated with indi-viduals' biological sex. In media and cultural studies gender was conceptualized as femininity. This held the essentialism at bay, although no reader of, for example, Angela McRobbie's research on the teenager magazine *Jackie* would have believed that the codes McRobbie reconstructs were relevant to the femininity of anyone else but young women (see McRobbie, 1991. The research was conducted at the end of the 1970s and early 1980s). Stereotypical portrayal of men has never been a source of concern, while recently we have seen an increasing interest in the construction of masculinity (Craig, 1992; Easthope, 1990; Hearn, 1992).

Optimists need to beware, however. Even those theorists who speak of the genderedness of media texts, such as John Fiske (1987), when he introduces the concept of 'gendered television', recognizing that there are both feminine and masculine forms of gendered television, equate this genderedness with highly stereotypical feminine and masculine attributes (see also Brown, 1990 and 1994, on soap opera and the feminine aesthetic). The result is neither highly flattering for women nor very desirable from a feminist point of view. As Elspeth Probyn remarks: 'Strangely enough, given his aspirations for resistance, Fiske's segregation of genres into masculine and feminine actually works against crediting women's intelligence and skill as television viewers. In constructing these texts as quintessential feminine narratives he downplays the ability of women as readers to find 'feminine' meanings in the face of texts that are not specifically women's genres (1993: 53). Women who enjoy men's genres, lesbians who enjoy traditional women's genres, men who read women's magazines, these cannot be issues for mass communication research as it stands now because, apart from a small number of exceptions, there is no adequate theoretical assimilation of gender in media theory, either at the level of social research itself or in reflection on the direction the field has taken as a whole. Gender, femininity and masculinity, continue to be seen in an overly essentialist manner which effectively blocks further enquiry. Generally speaking, mass communication research needs to be dislodged both from its reductionist view of gender. which is expressed through its preoccupation with women and the feminine in the popular culture project, and from the collective delusion that gender is something that only occurs out there and not in the heart of research practice itself (which is the idle hope of the public knowledge project).

MODERNISM AND THE PUBLIC KNOWLEDGE PROJECT

Gender has a marginal place in the public knowledge project. Often, discussions of media and the public sphere tend to speak of neutral species, such as citizens, who hardly have a gender. Voet opens her overview of feminism and citizenship by stating that, '(u)ntil recently, feminism was the wrong topic for citizenship theorists and citizenship was the wrong topic for feminists' (1995: 1). She quotes Carole Pateman, one of the few feminist theorists who wrote about women and citizenship before the late 1980s, as remarking that 'citizenship has always been a paradox for women: women were excluded as women in past citizenship, and included as citizens, but not recognized as women, in modern citizenship' (in Voet, 1995: 5). In recent years there has been an increase in feminist studies of citizenship, democracy and the public sphere, but neither Pateman's work (1989, 1992) nor the work of other feminist theorists of the public sphere (Elshtain, 1981; Dietz, 1985; Fraser, 1989; Mouffe, 1992) has held any interest for those in public knowledge-related research in media and communication studies. To be fair, nor have other theorists of citizenship (see Turner, 1993, 1994; van Steenbergen, 1994) taken up issues posed by feminism either. One of the few links between the theorization of gender, the public sphere, citizenship and the media is provided by Nancy Fraser (1987, 1989, 1990). Her critical reading of Habermas has been read as possibly providing a starting-point for a feminist media theory of the public sphere.

One of the main theorists of the public knowledge project is Jürgen Habermas, as even a cursory look at the literature, for instance the 'Recent social theory' issue of *Media, Culture and Society* (October 1993) will reveal. Habermas's 'Strukturwandel der Öffentlichkeit' (1962), translated in 1989 as 'Structural transformation of the public sphere', has of late captured the English-speaking academic audience. In its initial reception by Continental European audiences (able to read German) it was primarily seen as a historical account of the constitution of the bourgeois or civil public sphere in the mid-eighteenth century. Its late 1980s reception also focuses on its properties as a theorization of the problems of late modern societies in which citizenship has ceased to hold the place it had in (nostalgic renderings of) earlier historical periods and is seen as besieged by commercialism and consumer materialism. In his later work, the theory of communicative action, Habermas subsumes commercialism and consumer materialism conceptually under the 'colonization' of the life world. The capitalist state and economy infringe on the integrity of social interaction in the life world. Strategic motives replace communicative action (Habermas, 1981: (2) 525–32). Whereas the consumer role was initially a compensation for the effects of class positions, it turns into a form of colonization because the so-called subsystems of state and economy can only use 'the media' that are appropriate to their own functioning, money and power. Under these circumstances, how can the *Öffentlichkeit*, or the public sphere (literally 'openness') be revitalized?

In a lucid account of Habermas's *Structural Transformation* text and his *chef d'oeuvre, The Theory of Communicative Action*, John Durham Peters (1993) shows how Habermas is a true 'Frankfurter', who both distrusts manipulative, commercial media and sees them as a potentially liberating power (see also Honneth, 1985 and Jensen, 1990). The *Structural Transformation* text is one that Peters deems promising for the analysis of public communication in late modern societies, as an archaeology of the ideas and ideologies that inform current practices and policies of the mass media (1993: 542). The central tension is that today 'the mass media are, in general, just splendid for representation but horrid for participation' (1993: 566). The original liberal bourgeois public sphere would seem to be a far cry from today's politics which are characterized as a mere matter of voting and of show and entertainment. Peters is critical of such an idealist form of criticism and counsels that a 'more catholic conception of (mass) communication, appreciative of its gloriously raucous as well as soberly inform-ative qualities' would make Habermas's theory, focused resolutely on plain speech as the centre of democratic life, even more useful (1993: 567).

Evidently, Habermas's work both offers useful insights and has its drawbacks in respect of the central questions of the public knowledge project in media studies. The most important limitation, from my perspective, is that it is highly problematic to try to theorize the role of mass communication today from the position of a fierce dislike of its popular entertainment aspects, especially given the fact that popular entertainment is one link in a chain of signifiers that connects popular culture, passivity and femininity. From a gendered perspective there is also a second major drawback to (using) Habermas's influential theoretical project, which is its extreme gender-blindness. His theory of communicative action is based on the distinction between system and lifeworld, both of which have a public and a private side. The system functions through power (the state) and money (the economy), the lifeworld consists of the public sphere and the family, which function through generalized forms of communication. Both the social domain that Habermas names the 'system' and the one he calls the lifeworld have been criticized by feminists for their specific forms of gender inequality and the exclusion of women. In fact, Habermas's idealized rendering of the public sphere ignores gender, class, ethnicity or popular culture, which he himself has admitted (Habermas in McLaughlin, 1993: 603). The question is whether Habermas's huge theoretical enterprise is amenable to feminist claims and criticism. Nancy Fraser in particular (1987, 1989, 1990) has taken on the project of using Habermas's theoretical work for feminist ends.

Fraser holds that the blind spots in Habermas's theory are traceable to his categorical opposition between system and lifeworld institutions which obscures other potentially more critical elements of his work (1987: 55–6). This opposition derives ultimately from Habermas's distinction between symbolic and material reproduction. Fraser argues that childrearing for example is typically a 'dual-aspect' activity (1987: 34) which is both symbolic and material reproduction. In the Habermassian scheme of things there is no place for such activities. Likewise, Habermas sees the family as a place of socially integrated, symbolic reproduction and the paid workplace, on the other hand, as a system-integrated material reproduction domain. Given the impressive body of socialist–feminist theory and research (see Barrett, 1980 or Segal, 1987), one is easily convinced by Fraser's argument that, of course, the household, like the paid workplace, is also a site of labour and a site of power. She describes what she terms 'families' (rather than households) as 'sites of egocentric, strategic and instrumental calculation as well as sites of usually exploitative exchanges of services, labor, cash and sex, not to mention, frequently, sites of coercion and violence' (1987: 37). In media and cultural studies, research such as Ann Gray's (Gray, 1992) on the place and use of the videorecorder in households from her female informants' point of view, has shown how important it is to recognize, to put it mildly, that for women the home is a place of work, whereas for men it is a place of leisure. Such a recognition is necessary in order to understand their different relationships to media technology and, partly as a consequence of this, to media texts (see also Gray, 1988 and Morley, 1986).

Fraser attempts to put Habermas's theoretical notions to use by overruling the categorical distinction between system and lifeworld and by showing how, for example, the roles through which mediation between the household (or the family) and the official economy and the state are channelled, are gendered roles. Habermas only recognizes the roles of the worker, the consumer, the citizen and the client. The exclusiveness of this set of roles takes us to the heart of modernist theory where we find that it is based on a categorical distinction between the feminine and the masculine, whether it concerns spheres or roles. Icons such as the worker and the citizen are clearly masculine, whereas the consumer and the client are feminine roles. Fraser refers to the history of advertising for consumer-goods which has always interpellated its subject as feminine, to underscore this point (1987: 43). She suggests adding the role of child-rearer in order to explicitly gender all the roles and transform them and the institutions they mediate.

I applaud this type of demystifying strategy, as will become clear below. There is, however, a catch in the particular strategy Fraser suggests. The child-rearer role Fraser proposes to use as lever is so obviously a woman's role, that her theorization of gender unfortunately comes to echo what has been called feminine ethics or mothering theory by McNay (1992) or maternalist feminism by Dietz (1992), famous spokeswomen of which are Ruddick (1980) and Gilligan (1982). Dietz suggests appreciating maternalist feminism for making citizenship a feminist concern and for broadening our view of political morality (1992: 73) but also the need to recognize that mothering is not of the same order as political bonding. Fraser is not a maternalist although she comes close to such a position in her (implicit) claim that motherhood or child-rearing should provide the model or the starting point for a new type of citizenhip. To make such a claim is to misunderstand how feminism should deal with the public–private distinction. Rather than reject it, we should find new ways of understanding the nature of the private and of the public, as well as a different mode of articulation between them (Mouffe, 1992: 9). Such a new understanding hinges crucially on a non-essentialist understanding of (gender) identity as well as on a recognition of existing gender connotations.

In Fraser's work, gender appears to be strictly coupled to 'manhood' or 'womanhood' as exclusive options for individuals. In order to provide the much-needed opening up of the unspoken gender dimension in Habermas's work that Fraser is in favour of, her criticism needs to go beyond the experiential claim on which it is based. Fraser's feminist criticism of Habermas's work then is highly necessary but by no means enough, nor, regrettably, does it address the media or media theory. However, her work has been used to formulate starting points for a feminist media theory as part of the public sphere debate, for instance by Lisa McLaughlin (1993).

McLaughlin regrets the absence of a feminist media theory that recognizes the

71

need to engage with current theorization of the public sphere. She follows Fraser's view of the women's movement and sees it as both a place of withdrawal into specific oppositional identities and as a public actor directing oppositional claims and agitational activities through the media and other channels towards wider publics (1993: 600). She is, however, also critical of Fraser's idealized conception of the women's movement's shared oppositional identity, important though women's (alternative) media are (see Steiner, 1992 for an overview). Inspired by, but critical of, Fraser's work, McLaughlin tries to extend it to the media. She restricts herself to drawing the outlines of such a feminist media theory. On the one hand, a viable feminist media theory should keep feminism from remaining a 'counterpublic' (see Negt and Kluge 1993 [1972]). The mass media today offer too much potential for oppositional causes to ignore them. The Internet is but one example for multigendered or non-gendered subjectivities and citizenship (Baym 1995: 154; Haraway, 1985). On the other hand, argues McLaughlin, a viable feminist media theory should also help feminism to refrain from taking on the appeal of the mass media. The last position is scorned by McLaughlin as a recuperative and conservative feminism, one that retreats into 'private practices' (1993: 614).

Although McLaughlin makes perfectly clear that feminist media theory has far too little addressed questions of the public sphere, democracy and citizenship, it does not become quite clear *how* we should continue this project. Regretfully, McLaughlin does not go very far in developing the feminist media theory for which she sees a need. A highly instrumental vision of the media characterizes her point of view. Nor does she engage with the fact that feminism has problematized gender and the position of women. Gender is not recognized 'in its particularity', as she urges us to do with feminism (recognizing its white, middle-class background), and could easily be exchanged with ethnicity or age, which is to ignore fatally gender's central position in the modernist public knowledge debate. Moreover, her modernist rejection of the popular and popular pleasure precludes her from formulating a criticism that will go to the heart of the public knowledge project's gender bias, which can be understood as a gendered subtext. Like Fraser, McLaughlin is unable to expel or come to terms with the gender ghost in the modernist media debate, which I am sure will continue to haunt this discussion if it is not properly attended to.

The yield of my discussion of Habermas and his feminist critics, and their contribution to a gendered media debate within the confines of the public knowledge domain, is decidedly meagre. Gender is not theorized other than as the positions of women and men in the public sphere, on top of which the feminist point of view is either to make room for one of women's most conservative roles (child-rearing) or to bypass the specificity and the wide-ranging influence of gender(ed) stereotypes altogether. There are, to my mind, more useful ways of – symptomatically – reading Habermas and key texts in the modernist media debate, which do more justice to my concern over the gendered character of central notions in the public knowledge debate. Habermas's distrust of commercial media (a distrust clearly shared by McLaughlin among others) and the value he appears to set on plain speech, point to this other type of gender criticism of modernist media theory.

Women are not really the problem as far as modernist media theory is concerned, as long as they behave like men. The news, for instance is open to them as a profession, or as a text to be consumed. Not that they will necessarily be taken seriously as media producers or consumers. Klaus Bruhn Jensen's decision not to interview women for his study of how the news is interpreted is a case in point. He did not 'consider the gender variable' in order to focus the analysis, he argues (Jensen, 1990: 59). We might wonder what it is about gender that it may 'unfocus' an analysis. I contend that the problem for modernist media theory is not gender as such but rather the association femininity has in modernist thought, especially when it concerns the media and mass culture. Women are not the problem but their close association with femininity is. (Modernist thought, of course, has shown itself singularly unable to see social subjects other than as chained to their supposedly unequivocally interpretable biological sex). Modernism's associations with femininity are predominantly negative: passivity, emotionalism, irrationality, gullibility, consumerism. All those things in fact that are considered to clash with honest politics and upright citizenship and that can be characterized as deviations from the male norm (Chapman and Rutherford, 1988; Craig, 1992: 1). Debate about the future of public service broadcasting, at first sight little gendered, provides a good illustration of how gender stereotypes lurk beneath the terms used to condemn or show concern, in this case over the growing commercialization of (European) broadcasting.

The spectre of commercialization motivates a collection edited by Jay Blumler, *Television and the Public Interest. Vulnerable Values in West European Broadcasting* (1992). It consists of a number of case studies dealing with particular west European countries, preceded by theoretical articles and concluded by two evaluative chapters. In his 'Introduction' Blumler casts off by stating that the breakup of the old public service monopoly is coterminous with the loss of consensus over the purposes that broadcasting should serve (1992: 2). Obviously such a state of affairs encourages the renewed stating of goals and for the purpose of this article the rhetoric employed by Blumler does not leave all that much to be imagined. The 'commercial deluge', as he calls it, is clearly a danger. Producers will only focus on ratings, broadcasting will not be able to fulfil its role in encouraging 'reasoned argument in civic and electoral choice ' (1992: 203) any longer.

Though not uncritical of public service broadcasting itself, Blumler and other contributors to the collection lament the advent of commercial television as the downfall of the public broadcasting system, which will 'shift the emphasis from a principled to a pragmatic pluralism, yielding only that amount and those forms of diversity that are likely to pay' (Blumler in Blumler, 1992: 32). The result of this will be a 'bland and homogeneous international media culture' (1992: 34). No less than the integrity of civic communication is threatened. Gloomily Blumler forecasts that the priorities of providers and viewers alike could shift from information towards entertainment. Current affairs programmes will cater more for viewers' spectator interests than their citizen roles. He speaks of a horse race model, of soundbites over substance, information and dialogue (1992: 36). Obviously his arguments are paternalistic (which is not always entirely a bad thing, though it is a dangerous rhetoric), less obviously they also continue a masculine-biased view of media and communications.

The values that Blumler deems vulnerable are quality, innovation, professionalism, standards, social relevance, serving a variety of interests and cultural self-determination (1992: 206). They stand for the 'integrity of civic communication' which Blumler sees as based on 'established requirements of impartiality, objectivity and non-editorializing' (1992: 35). These requirements can be contrasted with involvement, partiality, subjectivity and connectedness; values that women cherish according to common sense but also according to the afore-mentioned proponents of feminine ethics and mothering theory such as Carol Gilligan (1982). Mary Field Belenky et al.'s (1986) interesting research on women's epistemological development found some of the same characteristics. I am no fan of essentialist theories such as Gilligan's but want to offer the specific 'feminine' qualities they discover as a contrast to what Blumler regards as the foundation of European democracy. From such a point of view, it becomes clear that the neutrality of the public sphere, so valued by modern critics, is actually a bias. Mothering ethics has a valid point of criticism when it argues that feminine qualities are excluded from public life, and that the particularistic type of moral reasoning Gilligan (1982) found among women is not an accepted form of reasoning in politics at all. The implicit gender dimension of the terms Blumler uses are of course not intended to criticize what according to some are women's moral standards. Although connectedness is not easy to conceptualize within theories of citizenship as they stand, that should not prove impossible. No, the terms Blumler uses are common enough in modernist debate. Historically, however, the central imperative of modernist discourse is to ward off the implications and attractions of the feminine and of femininization. The feminine and by association commercial and consumerist goals are dangerously attractive, they ensnare and then, if we may believe earlier, more outspoken modernist discourses, like vines, they strangle what they grow on.

Modernism, or Enlightenment discourse has a dual structure – an optimistic view of history, of the rationality of human beings, of our capabilities to know and recognize truth, set off against a dark vision of the irrationality and dangerous emotionalism of the masses, of the possibility of progress and history turning against itself. Modern masculinity can be seen to be constructed as a defence against these 'dark forces' and their feminine connotations (for a fascinating account see Theweleit, 1980). As a consequence the feminine has to be guarded against and women can only be allowed into masculine domains as honorary men, described, for example by former news editor and bureau chief Deborah Howell in *True Confessions – My Life as a White Male* (1993). She recounts her luck in finding a woman as boss in her first job. 'My boss was a woman (an incredible oddity then) and didn't see anything wrong with sending me to cover murders, fires, courts and cops and city hall and natural disasters. Bless her. She gave me guy lessons' (1993: 198–9). (See also Van Zoonen, 1994: 57 on women journalists and professional socialization.)

Women (without a capital) may cope and even make careers in male domains but 'Woman', according to Andreas Huyssen (1986), should be seen as modernism's Other. This is not to say that male modernist authors have not flirted with femininity. Indeed, Huyssen quotes Flaubert's famous claim 'Madame Bovary, c'est moi.' He then goes on to show how the imaginary femininity of these authors went hand in hand with the exclusion of women from the literary enterprise and with the misogyny of bourgeois patriarchy (1986: 45). Rosi Braidotti (1991) has put forward a similar argument concerning the work of Derrida and Deleuze and the 'becoming-woman' of philosophy. She wonders how 'the feminine as the "dark side" of Western theoretical discourse relates to the speech, the intelligence and the discursivity of real-life women?' (1991: 106), and concludes that both Derridean and Deleuzean philosophy should be met with suspicion because, respectively, of their anti-feminism and their overlooking of the claims put forward by the women's movement to control our own bodies and sexuality, and to be autonomous social agents (1991: 119).

'Woman' or 'the feminine' is not entirely absent from modern thought then but she is no more than a place of inscription, a blankness, a void. In the mass culture debate she has been inscribed, according to Huyssen (1986) 'as reader of inferior literature – subjective, emotional and passive – while man (Flaubert) emerges as writer of genuine, authentic literature – objective, ironic, and in control of his aesthetic means' (1986: 46). The aesthetic means of modernism can be read as a warding off, a protection against *Trivialliteratur* and the banalities of everyday life, of the domain of women, the private sphere. Huyssen goes on to argue that from the second half of the nineteenth century there is a 'chain effect of signification: from the obsessively argued inferiority of woman as artist . . . to the association of woman with mass culture . . . to the identification of woman with the masses as political threat' (1986: 50). A historical reconstruction of the place of woman and the feminine in modernist ideology presents us, then, with an intricate web of meanings, all of which have been snowed under in the liberal rhetoric of contemporary modernist political thought. Clearly, that which is associated with the feminine bears not much good and since these genderings of mass culture and of consumption and emotion usually remain implicit, it is all the more difficult to formulate a sensitive criticism in terms that are meaningful within modernist political debate.

A critical gendered media theory has two formidable tasks. To paraphrase Tania Modleski's critical deconstruction of key texts in literary criticism, it has to expose 'the masculinist bias' of media criticism that adopts metaphors of production and integrity as opposed to shallowness and consumption in order to differentiate between progressive and regressive (see Modleski, 1986: 42). But critical gendered media theory ideally does more. It should try to offer concepts and metaphors that will open up current modernist media theory. Although I feel more connected with postmodern feminist media criticism, which at certain points has progressed beyond an exclusively binary view of gender, inspiring and inspired by queer theorists such as Kosofsky Sedgwick (1990) and Butler (1990, 1993), I also recognize the need to continue theorizing the political in a more narrow sense than is usual in postmodern theory and in popular culture research especially. Modernist media theory is certainly one forum in which such a task is usefully undertaken. This is not only because it stores extensive knowledge and insight in political debate on media institutions but also, surely, because it would be worthwhile to bring a feminist awareness of a different order than that which focuses exclusively on women as a social group (important though that is) – which we might call a gendered awareness – to this part of the field of communication research.

Which concepts and metaphors should be introduced to the modernist media debate in particular? My preference would be for a renewed notion of citizenship and a multi-faceted view of the media consumer. Blumler, for example, recognizes that the public broadcasting system he reveres, did tend to neglect the audience in that it was based on a bond broadcasters *felt* with their audiences, one which they could *imagine* to be reciprocated (1992: 17, my emphasis). Later on in his text Blumler distinguishes between viewers' spectator interests and their citizen roles (1992: 36). We might wonder whether we should not try theoretically to integrate these two aspects of modern-day subjectivity somewhat more, rather than conceptualize them as completely separate. The integration of spectator interests and citizen roles could perhaps take place under the insignia of 'cultural citizenship', a term I borrow from Martin Allor and Michelle Gagnon (1994), in their study of the coming-into-being of an independent Quebecois public culture from the early 1960s. Quebecois emergent state practices involved the 'production of the field of *la citoyenneté culturelle*; a field of distinction of the citizen as both the social subject, the sovereign subject of a nation, and as the object of new forms of political power linking the distinctive traits of the citizen with those of the cultural producer and consumer' (1994: 26). I would propose that one strategy to gender modernist media criticism would be to exploit fully a notion such as 'cultural citizenship' and to contemplate how, for example, we could recognize both the social position of concrete groups of romance readers and the political dimension of their claim that they also learn from that genre, or the feeling of women's magazine readers that, at their best, women's magazines may be enlightening texts (Radway, 1984: 107; Hermes, 1995).

Obviously such genres as women's magazines or romances produce particular types of subjectivity and (self)knowledge. Rather than take these to be of no consequence for the political and for citizenship in the public sphere, we might wonder whether an opening up of public debate to the particular types of argumentation audience research has found, would not restore some lost vitality to the public sphere. The consumption of popular culture always also entails the production of hopes, fantasies and utopias. To my mind, they therefore could and should be part of politics and of citizenship in its (ideal) sense as deliberation about what for most of us would be the best kind of life. Such a renewed political debate would not, as is the case now, recognize only rational argumentation as valid. Cultural citizenship entails that rational and moral argumentation needs to be extended to encompass aesthetic and emotional claims. It is in this respect that we can use part of Habermas's theory of communicative action. The three types of claims we make in communicative action relate to three different kinds of rationality. Some of our claims are cognitive–instrumental, others are normative and practical and a third set are aesthetic and practical (Habermas, 1981: (1) 326). The third set of claims is the most problematical in Habermas's writing. It relates to the inner world (as opposed to 'the objective world' and 'the social world') and its claims are elsewhere described as claims of authenticity and integrity (Habermas, 1984: 439–40). In the normal course of events these claims are not disputed. The theory of communicative action presupposes, however, that all claims are open to dispute in specialized discourses. Both political theory and practice would therefore, in an ideal world, have to be open to such specialized discourses. For the time being modernist media studies should recognize that its own jargon is based on the exclusion of the feminine, which entails a far too narrow conception of (public) knowledge and politics and a much too judgemental stance concerning all that is deemed feminine. What exactly is it that makes enjoying popular literature, a tabloid or commercial television programmes so bad for democracy? And how can anyone guarantee that 'serious' news media are not secretly consumed as if they were the equivalent of a sports match?

Peter Dahlgren and Colin Sparks's two edited collections (*Communication and Citizenship. Journalism and the Public Sphere* (1991) and *Journalism and Popular Culture* (1992)) provide space for questions such as these to be entertained. Most interesting are those contributions that not only signal the interwovenness of public and private life but try to make theoretical sense of it. From such a perspective the media can be seen as a starting point that may prove to be the lever needed to pry open the public sphere and citizenship debate. Such a rewriting could start, for example, from the conclusions Ann Crigler and Klaus Bruhn Jensen (1991) draw from their two audience studies about how people make sense of politics. They state that 'the interesting common feature of the samples is the nature of the themes, which are at once generalized yet concrete, practice-based concepts that appear to derive from everyday experience' (1991: 180). They also conclude that the 'fictional genres of mass communication and the stories and jokes of interpersonal communication may have been under-researched as aspects of political communication and understanding' (1991: 191). Through audience studies, then, the everyday, domain of the feminine *par excellence*, may yet find its place in political theory in other than the paternalist derogatory sense of a domain in which the people need continual education and control.

The gendering of media studies should result in removing impediments for equal cultural citizenship, which is a task that has been undertaken since the beginning of second-wave feminism and which has only gained importance with the realization that the multicultural society is here to stay. It consists of an ongoing critique of how minorities are represented in the media, a task that remains well within the limits of the modernism of the public knowledge project but is nonetheless important (see Gross, 1989; H. Gray, 1992). Part of this task is to expose too the mythology surrounding women and minorities in media texts and the media industry. Rivers (1993) suggests that the media are tuned in to a long tradition that foregrounds female evil, weakness, untrustworthiness, emotionalism and unreliability, just as Said (1987) exposes how orientalism is at the heart of western discourse about its own identity. These myths and discourses are partly constitutive of the public sphere as we recognize it. Gendering media studies is therefore also a task connected with cultural citizenship in that citizenship needs to supersede the binary distinction between reason and affect (Young, 1987); between the West and the Rest (Hall, 1992); between self and Other, between quality and trash, between information and entertainment.

In a critique of Habermas's notion of civic society, Young (1987) argues the case for respecting instead of denying difference, for not opposing reason to desire and affect, and for allowing a little wildness and playfulness in our conceptual-ization and practice of public life. This entails creating an image of a more differentiated public, a process started by the new social movements (Young, 1987: 75). Rather than see this new public sphere as a collection of special interest groups, who need to represent their unique individuality, which is the basis of the claim to citizenship of maternalist feminism, or mothering ethics, the ultimate goal needs to be a citizenship independent of ethnic, religious or gender identities (Mouffe, 1992: 9). Mouffe argues that a 'non-gendered' conception of citizenship is possible but that it 'requires a non-essentialist framework, which implies that there is no fixed identity corresponding to men *as* men or to women *as* women' (1992: 10). In fact, we need to wonder whether 'identity' should be the focus of debate about citizenship and the public sphere at all. Would 'activity' not be a much better starting point, one that would allow for the incorporation of a whole range of activities (such as watching popular television) that now fall outside the public knowledge project?

Media theorists need to extend a non-essentialist view of identity, or perhaps 'activity', to the point of a self-reflective criticism of the gender stereotypes encapsulated in the terms of the debate itself. They also need to extend it to the realization that a plethora of different media, commercial and public-service, capitalist and sponsored are here to stay. Our hybrid contemporary media saturate our everyday lives with a mass of conflicting images, that offer many shades of sexism but also of emancipation and occasionally of feminist femininity and masculinity. The current modernist canon needs radical revision to provide the possibility of dealing adequately with issues of gender and media. Stereotypical portrayals of women, or under-representation of women in the media are hardly the main problem from a theoretical perspective. Inscribing popular culture and pleasure in the domain of quality and citizenship, however, can only be successful when it slays (i.e. 'demythologizes') the monster of the feminine lurking behind the grim holding on to neutrality, impartiality and non-commercialism in the guise of the popular. A second major strategy to provide a place for gender (as well as for ethnicity or sexuality) in the public knowledge project is to understand identity as partial, temporary and as a choice (albeit that such choices may be negative choices or the result of silence implying consent) and as less important than the actual activities involved in media use and citizenship.

POSTMODERNISM AND THE POPULAR CULTURE PROJECT

At first sight, the popular culture project would appear to be much more emancipated than the public knowledge project. Gender is often thematized, an impressive number of feminists are working in this field. Ien Ang and I have argued (1991), however, that research on media consumption, an important domain within the popular culture project, has hardly offered theoretically sensitive tools to deal with questions of gender. The debate has been about women and the construction of femininity rather than about how women and men take up temporary gender identities that do not necessarily correspond to their sex. It has essentialized and reified gender identity. Briefly, our argument runs as follows.

Early 1970s feminist media criticism tended to focus on what was felt to be media texts' unrealistic and dangerous depiction of women. Sustaining these accounts was the assumption that media images carry transparent, straightforward meanings, and the further assumption that women as viewers passively absorbed these messages and would act accordingly (e.g. Brownmiller, 1984; Friedan, [1963] 1974; Greer, 1971). These modernist accounts were countered by feminist scholars who used structuralist, semiotic and psycho-analytic frameworks. They stressed that the media construct meanings and identities that serve as subject positions from which texts become meaningful and pleasurable (e.g. Kuhn, 1982; Modleski, [1982] 1984; Doane, 1987; Gamman and Marshment, 1988). These authors, in their turn were criticized for their textual determinism by a third generation of postmodern–feminist media researchers who argued that texts become meaningful in particular, local contexts, and that ethnography or in-depth interviewing were essential to a reconstruction of meanings.

Modleski's research on soap opera (1984), for example, resulted in her description of the 'ideal mother' position as a near inescapable point of identi-fication for viewers. Seiter et al.(1989), in an audience ethnography, found otherwise. The textual position of the ideal mother, according to them, is not easily accessible to working-class women (1989: 241). Neither did Seiter et al.'s informants hate 'the villainess' who features in Modleski's analysis as the character we are allowed to hate unreservedly and who is the negative image of the spectator's ideal self (1984: 94). On the contrary, Seiter et al.'s informants hated 'the whiners', with whom they were supposed to empathize. It seems fair to conclude that textual analysis cannot predict or determine the actual meanings and pleasures media texts have for audiences. A second conclusion following discussion over Modleski's chapter on soap opera, is that gender is not a unified concept. Class, for instance, cuts through the presumed category of 'women'. A comparison of Andrea Press's (1990) research on *Dynasty* with Seiter *et al.*'s research confirms this. Whereas Seiter *et al.* found working-class women to be the more critical viewers, Press found exactly the opposite. While working-class women speak very little to differences between the *Dynasty* characters and themselves – which in Press's view indicates their acceptance of the realism of the *Dynasty* text – middle-class viewers 'consciously refuse to be taken in by the conventions of realism which characterise this, like virtually all prime-time shows' (1990: 178).

This briefest of overviews of debate in the popular culture project exemplifies three characteristics of how gender is discussed. It is feminist debate and women researchers who have predominantly taken up issues of gender. They do not, second, so much discuss gender (femininity and masculinity), as women and femininity. Men and masculinity were, until very recently, conspicuously absent. In as far as gender presented a problem, it was a problem of women, the defined sex, rather than of men. Masculinity, after all, is the norm (Coward, 1983). The third point is the development in feminist/popular culture research towards poststructuralist and postmodern points of view. The current predominance of a postmodern perspective in feminist popular culture research has much to do with the near incompatability of a strict modernism with feminism. This becomes clear when one takes a closer look at classic feminist texts on popular culture.

Friedan's (1963[1974]) concern over women's magazine readers with whom she strongly identifies; Greer's (1971) cynical evocation of herself as a young girl swooning over romances, both show how the feminist author was always too close to 'ordinary women' to argue convincingly the case of the false consciousness of all those women reading women's magazines and romances. Psycho-analytical conceptualization of the subject as split provided a welcome way out of the untenable position feminism's modernist/Marxist inheritance had wrought. The faultline between modernist and postmodernist thought in feminism is therefore marked by the confession. I am a feminist but I also happen to love reading . . . romances, lesbian pulps, *The Thorn Birds*, or watching soap opera (see, for example, Kaplan, 1986; Ang, 1985, 1990a). From a feminist perspective, identity, one can understand Kaplan and Ang as saying, is more productively seen as partial and constructed, involving fantasy scenarios, political criticism, dealing with oppression, hardship and disappointment as well as with building a sense of mattering to the world at large. If that is the case for feminist intellectuals then why should it not be the case for feminism's (potential) constituency, 'ordinary women'?

Postmodernism, therefore, for many feminist cultural critics and media theorists was a logical choice. While the term 'postmodernism' was claimed by theoreticians such as Lyotard (1979) and Jameson (1983, 1984), who effectively declared the bankruptcy of 'Grand Narratives' and introduced radical relativist epistemology, feminist popular culture research fuelled a political line of reasoning within postmodernism. Feminists' involvement in questions of how the media could provide women viewers and readers so much pleasure, while they offered such patently distorted representations of women, was a strong incentive to theorize gender in relation to particular (groups of) women and to distrust the universalism of grand theory, as suggested by postmodernists. Feminism's own 'grand narrative' of women's emancipation, based on the presumed universality of women's oppression and the idea that essentially there was something uniquely feminine that all women shared, broke into pieces over the contradictory feelings theorists themselves had over specific media genres. Nor was it tenable to see one locus of power producing what was soon recognized to be a wide range of feminine consciousnesses. Discourse analysis, inspired especially by the work of Michel Foucault (1979, 1980), reconstructed different and competing versions of femininity. Black feminists and lesbian feminists wreaked havoc politically with any unitary feminist programme (see hooks, 1989; Echols, 1984), which they claimed to be white, middle-class, and 'hetero-sexist'. As a result, in as far as one can speak of a feminist programme, singular, since the late 1980s it needs to be seen as a programme that advocates respect for difference and diversity.

Though initially not deliberately postmodern, feminist poststructuralism started to merge with and enrich the political strand of postmodernism, as opposed to its textual twin (Baudrillard, 1983, 1988; see also Best and Kellner, 1991; Kellner, 1995). It is formulated as a critique of Enlightenment values (Flax, 1990) or as a blueprint for a politics of difference, particularity, locality and respect (Haraway, 1988; Young 1987, 1990; Fraser and Nicholson, 1990). Although feminist postmodernism does not consist of a concrete programme (pace McNay, 1992: 121 who is critical about using the term), and never completely breaks its link with a modernist metanarrative of (personal) emancipation (McNay, 1992: 123), it is a useful label to denote feminism's investment in social relations at the micro-level, as well as on a more abstract level, and its investigation of the personal as (part of) the political. Regrettably, the fact that the politics of the personal or the micro-analysis of everyday life are as much political as macro-analysis, escapes many critics. Drotner (1993) chastises Corner (1991) for letting the distinction between macro and micro levels' analysis, distinctive of respectively the public knowledge project and the popular culture project, slide into a discussion of political hierarchies in which 'macro-analysis per definition seems to be more political in nature' (1993: 34). Drotner counters that the analysis of viewing relations is not less political but that it may involve a different kind of politics.

This raises the question of what kind of politics is involved in popular culture research? Generally, popular culture research has come to focus more and more on media reception, as part of the postmodern feminist interest in the local and the everyday and in how women and men 'actively and creatively make their own meanings and create their own culture' (Ang, 1990b: 242). Because of its open research structure, its lengthy contact with media users and its interest in how culture is actually made, this type of reception analysis has been given the label 'media ethnography'. The type of ethnography used is inspired by interpretive ethnography (Clifford and Marcus, 1986; Marcus and Fischer, 1986), by the political dimension of this research practice in general and its relation to informants in particular. Marcus and Fischer (1986) understand ethnography to be a critical practice in itself that should be aimed at giving a voice to other groups and other cultures. Fieldwork accounts should ideally have the form of dialogues or even polylogues (see also Clifford, 1988). A first political aspect, then, is giving voice to those who are usually silenced by the dominant culture. Second, interpretive ethnography questions the position and authority of the researcher her or himself and urges her or him to be self-reflective to a much higher degree than mainstream social research would ask for. How, for example, does one's ethnicity, gender or age matter (see Warren, 1985)? But also, as Probyn puts it: 'in acknowledging our own particularities, we are forced to approach those of others with care and always remember that our stories and our bodies, can displace others, that as we speak we may be perpetuating the conditions that silence the subaltern' (1992: 96).

The third form politics takes in the popular culture project is the politics of (everyday) resistance as given form in and through media consumption. John Fiske (1987) is probably the best-known spokesman for the theoretical position that our pleasure in popular culture, and especially in popular television, comes not only from recognition and identification but especially from playing with and exploring the rules and limits of popular television texts. He argues that television in a way 'delegates' the production of meaning and pleasure to its viewers, which makes television a 'semiotic democracy' (1987: 236). Popular pleasure, like carnival, is based on a refusal of control, of the social identities proposed by the dominant ideology (1987: 240–1). Discussing quiz shows, for example, Fiske points out two forms of liberation involved in viewing these programmes, contrary to the dominant view that watching quiz shows is a form of incorporation in dominant capitalist or patriarchal norms. '(T)he first is to give public, noisy acclaim to skills that are ordinarily silenced; the second is simply to be 'noisy' in public, to escape from demure respectability, from the confines of good sense that patriarchy has constructed as necessary qualities for "the feminine"'(1990: 136).

Fiske's position, based on the work of de Certeau's view of everyday resistance as the tactics of the subordinate versus the strategies, the rules and the marked places of the powerful (de Certeau, 1988), is intriguing and suggestive. However, de Certeau is rather romantic about everyday life, and tends to understand the tactics of everyday life solely as means of escape from obligations and the dominant order, whereas many forms of escape are in line with, rather than opposed to the overarching structure of people's lives (Radway, 1988: 366). De Certeau's romanticism is reflected in Fiske's work which has been criticized on the same grounds for its exaggeration of the resistant qualities of the pleasures of media consumption (see Ang, 1990b; Gitlin, 1991; Morris, 1988). Despite the sometimes critical reception of his work, Fiske's writings can be seen as a strong example of the politics of media ethnography. In my own work on how women's magazines are read, like Fiske I invoke the concept of 'empowerment' to show

how reading magazines may, from time to time, strengthen readers' identities in the form of fantasies of ideal selves. However, especially in the case of a mundane, everyday medium such as women's magazines, which tend to take second place to other media and other (daily) activities, empowerment needs to be seen in combination with the criticism of, and disappointment in the magazines, positions which readers voiced strongly (Hermes, 1995: 48–51). I suspect that for most media it is the balance between audience empowerment and this kind of criticism (or disappointment) that is important to understanding their appeal and their resistant qualities. Such a starting point would be in line with what Ien Ang has called 'a more thoroughly *cultural* approach to reception' (1990b: 244) which would not stop at the 'pseudo-intimate moment of the media/audience encounter, but should addresses the differentiated meaning and significance of specific reception patterns in articulating more general social relations of power' (ibid.). Although the politics of popular culture research centrally addresses issues of pleasure, this is more than a liberal defence of these pleasures. Rather, ideally, they constitute a cultural critique from the point of view of active audiences, one that recognizes the local and contradictory nature of everyday meaning-making.

Back now to the politics of gender in the popular culture project, and in particular to masculinity. It is not strictly speaking true that masculinity has only recently become a research interest in the popular culture project. Bennett and Woollacott's (1987) intertextual analysis of James Bond perpetuates a tradition of literary analysis of male genres and/or male heroes (cf. Cawelti, 1976; Berger, 1992). However, the male heroes are usually not analysed from a gender perspective. That has until recently been reserved for women and femininity. Recurrent themes in genre analyses of male heroes focus on their professional identities and on how the text works against homo-erotic identification. Work, or a profession, after all, are what makes a man a man (Tolson, 1978; Seidler, 1991; Segal, 1990). And a real man cannot be gay (cf. Wernick's (1991) analysis of advertising aimed at men).

The call to analyse masculinity in terms of gender is new, though not unproblematical. Often, there is a suggestion that it is time for a simple redressing of the balance: we have concentrated so much on women, let's now take a closer look at men. Implicitly, it is stated that femininity and masculinity are on a par and that the same set of tools would enable the critic to deconstruct either or both. In fact, this amounts to a perpetuation of an essentialist view of gender, which not only suggests a symmetry between masculinity and femininity (and between women and men) but also a more or less direct relationship between men and masculinity, and women and femininity. For example, a collection published not long ago was entitled *Men, Masculinity and the Media* (Craig, 1992).

Studies that deconstruct masculinity as object for the female gaze are exceptional and groundbreaking. Heroes in action and adventure genres such as *Magnum P.I.* (Flitterman, 1985) or *Miami Vice* (King, 1990) are widely on display. One may wonder with Fiske (1987: 257) whether the masculine is becoming both the object and the subject of the look, which exscribes the feminine from the narrative. Arguably, in the case of *Miami Vice*, the designer wardrobe of Crockett and Tubbs can be seen as a masculine appropriation of a feminine language and pleasure (ibid.). The masculinity of both detectives is not in question however, according to Fiske. He reads the style of both men, as well as their possessions (such as the Ferrari), as markers of the masculine popular hero (1987: 258–9). King (1990) disagrees. 'Sonny is "feminized" by his objectification; the cultural gender confusion over the prominence of a *male* model manifests itself physically in Sonny's trademark stubble, which serves to remind us that this pretty displayed human is, counter to our expectations, a man' (1990: 283). King goes on to argue that it is not just the homo-erotic implications of the male model as object of the male and the female gaze that is unsettling about *Miami Vice*, but also the 'feminine' position of the male character. Sonny Crockett is a consumer, surrounded by consumer goods (even though, remarks King, there has yet to be an episode in which Sonny shops, 1990: 285); he is often shown being unable to perform his job (criminals get away in Miami Vice). The postmodern gender confusion *Miami Vice* gives rise to, is directly a result of its play with fundamental gendered categories: to consume is associated with femininity; to produce or to work with masculinity (Modleski, 1984, 1986). The deep divide in modernism is visited upon its postmodern stepchild. King's argument runs along the same lines as my critique of the modernist public knowledge project. He is convinced that '(g)ender still remains obscured as an explicit issue within the postmodern debate, a structuring absence that can only be implicitly read into the masculine and feminine assignments given to categories of postmodernism like surface, consumption and work' (1990: 290). I cannot but agree with his conclusion that what I have called the textual or aesthetic strain of postmodernism has few ties with feminist postmodernism.

In the Craig collection *Men, Masculinity and the Media* (1992) most of the articles reiterate the points of view referred to above, such as the identification of maleness with work (Strate, 1992); or the warding off of homo-erotic implications when the male body is on display (Steinman, 1992: 203). What is most intriguing about this collection, however, is that it becomes clear that masculinity should not be thought of in binary terms (Fiske, 1987: 203), clarifying though that may be, but as the uniform norm for all (see Fiske, 1987: 200–1; Root, 1984: 16). Just as women may participate in the public sphere as long as they assent to being 'one of the boys', maleness can actually incorporate the feminine and the spectacular to an extent that is not usually obvious. Denski and Sholle's case study of Heavy Metal bands makes this quite clear. They wonder how 'young, heterosexual, white boys come to identify with performers who border on transvestism?' (1992: 53). The feminized appearance of the band is analysed as an attempt at flamboyance and rebellion against societal and parental rules. But also as a response to feminine power. 'By taking the feminine into itself, heavy metal disavows the need for women, thus overcoming the fear of exercising desire' (1992: 55).

Masculinity, then, is both the norm for men and women and can incorporate masculinity and femininity in a multitude of ways. Postmodern culture, according to some, can be recognized by its gender bending at a textual level, which should not be misread as a reaching out to feminism or to women. Boscagli (1992) argues that the display of emotion on television by men, including by US Army General Schwartzkopf, is no more than a ploy by patriarchy to control both ends of the gender spectrum. Just as femininity is related to but not identitical with woman, modernism's Other, masculinity is the norm, not identitical with but related to almost all imaginable categories, encompassing feminity, ethnicity, age and so on under the icon of the all-powerful male. In the modernist public knowledge project it is more usual for masculinity-as-norm to be displaced onto other categories, whereas it would seem to be less veiled in the postmodern popular culture project. But there too man (i.e. heterosexual, white, middle-class, healthy masculinity) is like a fun-house mirror, though there is not much to laugh about, in which others (women, blacks, gays, the physically disabled) see themselves reflected as deviant, lacking. Individual men do not control man-as-mirror, just as individual women are not a real blankness or void in the public sphere. The distance between social subjects, producers of culture/producers of meaning and discursive identities cannot be stressed enough if.we are to understand how gender works, and if we are to formulate a feminist agenda that makes sense of gender in a new way, whether it concerns the public sphere debate or how we make sense of popular culture. Partly these tensions can be resolved by appealing to a broad notion of cultural citizenship. Such a notion can only be successful if it gets thoroughly dis-embodied, if it can be taken to refer to practices and activities rather than to groups of sexed individuals. Again, the main issue is to recognize the power relations inherent in how media theory implicitly links the self and society, and in how the binary character of the various versions of gender definitions used all work towards a continuous reinscription of those power relations.

CONCLUSION: ON CULTURAL CITIZENSHIP

Reviewing how gender has been thought of in media studies, I found that gender has meaning in reference to concretely sexed bodies (rather than partial identities or activities), as a mythology of the dangers of the feminine, and, of course, as a marker of genres. A stereotypical view of genre would suggest that media texts are easily assigned to either the public sphere and beneficial to matters of citizenship and democracy, or to the realm of the popular, which is read as a danger zone either because the popular is connoted as consumptive, passive and commercial or because the popular is coded as a domain of counter-strategies. Gender in media studies is thus intimately related to how we think of society as fundamentally split. Instead of a one-way division between the public and the private, or the public and the popular, I would be in favour of recognizing the many divisions in social life, and do away with this particular mystifying division. Cultural citizenship, as a concept, could be a tool in such a strategy. To substantiate cultural citizenship, we need to demythologize the popular and accord it meaning as one of many inputs for governmental politics. Not, I might add, as a source of panic and regulation but rather as one of the many fora of public discussion. For that to be possible, the logics particular to popular media need to be recognized as valid.

The linchpin of theories of the public sphere is reason. Citizenship is thought of as reasonable. Habermas's ideal-speech situation, likewise, is eminently rational. If anything, popular culture research (guided by postmodern and feminist theory) has argued that emotion and feeling are just as important to our (everyday) lives. If democracy can be said to be deliberation among the many about how to attain the best life possible for as many as possible, then it makes no sense to set such exclusive store by reasoned argument in our theorization of it. To rethink citizenship as cultural citizenship means to accept that those who inhabit mass democracies use many different logics to shape their lives and to deliberate what for them personally or as a group is the best life possible. These different logics are based on emotion and experiential knowledge, just as much as on rational thought. Ideally, political debate should take into account the constraints of its own rule system (which disallows theatricality to a large extent, and does not explicitly recognize emotions as a ground for political decision-making), and its underlying sources. Instead of governmental politics that rely strongly on convention, on advisory bodies and on dealing in percentages, we could have political debate that does recognize the impossibility of deciding on certain subjects, that makes a determined effort to be close to the forms political debate currently takes, which include the new popular infotainment genres.

This may seem a rather roundabout route to a gendering of media (studies) and to changing the status of the feminine. However, the mid-1990s wave of infotainment and reality TV programmes should alert us to the sliding of the distinction between the public sphere and the popular, not only in feminist–theoretical terms but also and especially in everyday practice. Different authors have opened up debate about these new genres in various contexts. Corner (1995) seeks to understand television's new forms and genres in the framework of arguments about 'quality', thereby largely leaving behind the distinction, grate-fully used in this article, between the public and the popular. Others have focused on public debate in the domain of infotainment (Livingstone and Lunt, 1994), sometimes focusing on gender (Livingstone, 1994; Masciarotte, 1991).

Livingstone (1994) understands the talk show to be a moral genre in which concrete individuality is grounded in the domain of television discourse (1994: 438). Using interview material, she analyses how women and men are audience members of talk shows. She defines gender difference in terms of Carol Gilligan's theory of women's ethical reasoning, which has been criticized for its essentialism. With some effort, Livingstone is able to link statistically characteristics of the talk show as genre to gender difference. Women are less likely to find talk show debate messy or chaotic, or to side with the experts. Livingstone bypasses the fact that the talk show is as much gendered at the level of cultural practice as it is in terms of the two sexes of audience members. Regrettably, she does not address the difference between fans and non-fans, which according to her (Livingstone, 1994:

444) was more important. Focusing on such a difference can tell us much more about how popular, everyday forms of talk are woven into the domain of the public thereby changing the character of public debate.

Masciarotte (1991), on the other hand, understands Oprah Winfrey, *prima inter pares* among talk show hosts, to be moderator and embodiment for public feminine authority, which she sees as a discursive position, not by definition tied to the feminine body. The disruptive effect of talk show talking, irritating as it is by conventional public sphere standards (showing participatory chaos and spectacular emotionalism; allowing for multiple points of view, rather than arguments pro or contra; deferring solutions or closure), according to Masciarotte, in fact moves the feminine 'away from the essentialist, and even culturalist, strategies of speaking from the margins and/or under repression' (1991: 98). The individual speaking as a voice from the mass exposes what Masciarotte calls the bourgeois illusion of the distinction between public and private (ibid.).

The ordinary person, rather than the expert, is the emblem of new media genres. But rather than understand these new media genres as introducing a 'feminin- ization' of television, a first order or classic feminist strategy of gendering, we should employ a second order or postmodern feminist strategy of gendering – linked to a 'culturalization of citizenship' – which understands feminization as disruption of the system, rather than as tied to individual women. Nevertheless, it is gratifying to see the most popular of media giving more space for individual women. If academic research is to provide an incentive for the emancipation of women and other minority groups, we had best deploy our talents at the level of second-order strategies, given that our strategies for documenting (hetero)sexism (and racism) ultimately legitimize the very categories and boundaries on which the power relations are built that we aim to attack and dissolve. Therefore, I would have liked Livingstone's analysis much better if she had not taken a rather tortured route to proving that there are statistically measurable, though small, differences between women and men as audiences but if she had concentrated on how fans (men and women) make sense of the programme as opposed to those who are critical. That would enable us to follow how the gendering of a genre takes place and concomitantly how a genre is assigned cultural and political value. It would also be fascinating to see whether there are differences between women and men as audience members, and whether there are different styles of engaging with talk shows related to notions of femininity and masculinity which can be interpreted as partial identities developed across gender lines. Such a strategy could de- mythologize issues of quality and cultural value in the privately used public fora that are the media.

From a more conventionally political point of view, I see three 'steps' for a gendering of media studies. First, we need a renewed conceptualization of identity, as I have argued above. It does not pay to argue endlessly over the extent to which identities are malleable or flexible. It would make much more sense to better understand how identities are lodged in practices (which usually have a certain amount of fixity in any social subject's life, even if they do not define a person from the cradle to the grave). From a theoretical notion of practice, it is but a short step to understand gendering in terms of cultural quality rather than in terms of a sexed body. It is much easier to argue for a revaluation of practices, such as to define what is meant by good versus bad (or boring) popular television, than for a revaluation of identities. Cultural citizenship would then encompass differently gendered activities, which could be discussed in terms of their overt or covert gendering, as I have tried to do here. Presumably other dimensions than the gender dimension would often take precedence, demythologizing that very same dimension. For example, in interviews with viewers of the Norwegian news programme *Dagsrevyen* Hagen (1994) found that a dominant opposition in which *Dagsrevyen* became meaningful, was between one's duty as a citizen versus boredom rather than between feminine and masculine viewing styles.

Second, cultural citizenship would not only function as a crowbar to pry apart practices and identities, or as a means to mix together issues of pleasure with issues of politics, it could help redefine the boundaries of the public and the private in a firm insistence on how both are articulated at the level of the everyday and are reciprocally involved in how we constitute ourselves in relation to society. The public knowledge project has, of course, tended to keep the public and the private too far apart (fearing the intrusion of the one upon the other); whereas the popular culture project has tended to conflate the two too easily. Neither has given due to the interplay between each. Ideal versions of the public sphere often entail visions of a range of many different spheres or debates (Murdock, 1993: 523) alongside each other, having a plural and decentred rather than a privileged character (McLaughlin, 1993: 606). The relation between these different debates, practices and discussions is provided by the cultural, by shared, common frames of reference. In that sense politics in a broad sense cannot do without the cultural.

The third step comes after reconceptualizing identity, and after theoretically recognizing the interwovenness of the public and the popular. It is to envisage a new *Öffentlichkeit* in all its constructedness. Such a new, ideal public space would provide room for what Negt and Kluge called 'counterpublics', which rather than 'communities' firmly stresses the *mediated* character of collective experiences of marginalization and expropriation. As Hansen (1993: 207) points out, using the example of African-American and of the (in her words) gay/lesbian/queer movement, the counterpublic effectiveness of 'community language' depends on two factors: 'the extent to which it knows itself as rhetoric, as a trope of impossible authenticity, reinventing the promise of community through synthetic and syncret-istic images; and two, to the extent to which it admits difference and differentiation within its own borders, is capable of accepting multiply determined sexual–social identities and identifications'.

Insofar as cultural citizenship is to be related to individual social subjects, it can be understood as what Grossberg (1992: 57) has called 'mattering maps' on which our affective investments get charted. But it is the performance, the practice of living, making, forming these investments, the gendering that matters, not their relation to any pre-given category. If we are to understand what some women like about men's genres, how lesbians enjoy traditional women's genres, or how men read women's magazines, we cannot but let go of the idea that identities are fixed, and of the idea that gender actually refers to people.

NOTE

1 I would like to thank John Corner, Marty Allor, Mariette van Staveren and Pieter Hilhorst.

PRIMARY SOURCES

Ien Ang and Joke Hermes (1991) in 'Gender and/in media consumption' provide a theoretically original overview of how gender has been thought in feminist research. The piece concentrates on media consumption but holds a strong, more general argument about gender as constructed rather than given.

Mary Ellen Brown (1990) edited a wide-ranging collection on television and women's culture, which focuses on popular culture. As a whole it is a good introduction to postmodern popular culture research.

Carol Clover (1992) in *Men, Women and Chain Saws* provides the opposite of an overview. By concentrating on different horror subgenres she offers intriguing arguments about the fluidity and constructedness of gender positions. For instance, how and why do young male audiences identify with the female heroines of films like *The Texas Chain Saw Massacre*, or *Carrie*? Or even more intriguing, why do they like rape-revenge horror movies (the title of the subgenre may be taken literally). One of the most fascinating accounts about gender (involving masculinity as well as femininity) and media genres.

Among other things, Michele Wallace writes about media texts in *Invisibility Blues* (1990). Her highly personal and direct style of writing introduce a set of issues to do with the combination of gender, ethnicity and media texts and practices. Her precise deconstructions offer considerable food for thought.

Suzanna Danuta Walters's (1995) *Material Girls. Making Sense of Feminist Cultural Criticism* is one of the few book-length studies that deal with gender and media. Its central argument offers two different traditions of feminist thought (a more sociological 'images of women' approach versus a structuralist and semiotic 'woman as image' or 'signification' perspective).

Feminist Media Studies (1994) by Liesbet van Zoonen uses Stuart Hall's encoding/decoding model as a guide to discuss a wide range of feminist research organized by topic. Contrary to the other texts mentioned here, it also deals with public sphere and 'encoding' issues, such as women in journalism.

REFERENCES

Allor, M. and Gagnon, M. (1994) *L'etat de culture. Généalogie discursive des politiques culturelles Québécoises*, Montreal: Grecc (Concordia University/Université de Montréal).
Ang, I. (1985) *Watching Dallas: Soap Opera and the Melodramatic Imagination*, London and New York: Methuen.
Ang, I. (1990a) 'Melodramatic identifications: television fiction and women's fantasy', in M.E. Brown (ed) *Television and Women's Culture. The Politics of the Popular*, London, Newbury Park: Sage, 75–88.

Ang, I. (1990b) 'Culture and communication. Towards an ethnographic critique of media consumption in the transnational media system' *European Journal of Communication* 5(2/3): 239–60.

Ang, I. and Hermes, J. (1991) 'Gender and/in media consumption', in J. Curran and M. Gurevitch (eds) *Mass Media and Society*, London and New York: Edward Arnold, 307–28.

Baehr, H. (1981) 'Women's employment in British television', *Media, Culture and Society* 3(2): 125–34.

Barrett, M. (1980) *Women's Oppression Today*, London: Verso.

Baudrillard, J. (1983) *Simulations*, New York: Semiotext(e).

Baudrillard, J. (1988) *The Ecstacy of Communication*, New York: Semiotext(e).

Baym, N. (1995) 'The emergence of community in computer-mediated communication', in S.G. Jones (ed) *CyberSociety. Computer-mediated Communication and Community*, Thousand Oaks, London: Sage, 138–63.

Bennett, T. and Woollacott, J. (1987) *Bond and Beyond. The Political Career of a Popular Hero*, Houndmills, Basingstoke and London: Macmillan.

Berger, A.A. (1992) *Popular Culture Genres*, London: Sage.

Best, S. and Kellner, D. (1991) *Postmodern Theory. Critical Interrogations*, Houndmills, Basingstoke and London: Macmillan.

Blumler, J. (ed) (1992) *Television and the Public Interest. Vulnerable Values in West European Broadcasting*, London, Newbury Park: Sage.

Boscagli, A. (1992) 'A moving story. Masculine tears and the humanity of televised emotions', *Discourse* 15(2): 64–79.

Braidotti, Rosi (1991) *Patterns of Dissonance. A Study of Women in Contemporary Philosophy*, Cambridge: Polity Press, translated by Elizabeth Guild.

Brown, M.E. (1990) 'Motley moments. Soap opera, carnival, gossip and the power of the utterance', in M.E. Brown (ed.) *Television and Women's Culture. The Politics of the Popular*, London, Newbury Park: Sage, 183–200.

Brown, M.E. (1994) *Soap Opera and Women's Talk. The Pleasure of Resistance*, Thousand Oaks, London: Sage.

Brownmiller, S. (1984) *Femininity*, New York: Fawcett Columbine.

Butler, J. (1990) *Gender Trouble. Feminism and the Subversion of Identity*, London, New York: Routledge.

Butler, J. (1993) *Bodies That Matter. On the Discursive Limits of 'Sex'*, London and New York: Routledge.

Cawelti, J. (1976) *Adventure, Mystery and Romance. Formula Stories as Art and Popular Culture*, Chicago: University of Chicago Press.

Certeau, M. de (1988) *The Practice of Everyday Life*, Berkeley: University of California Press, translated by Steven Randall.

Chapman, R. and Rutherford, J. (1988) *Male Order. Unwrapping Masculinity*, London: Lawrence & Wishart.

Clifford, J. (1988) *The Predicament of Culture. Twentieth Century Ethnography, Literature and Art*, Cambridge, MA and London: Harvard University Press.

Clifford, J. and Marcus, G. (1986) *Writing Culture. The Politics and Poetics of Ethnography*, Berkeley: University of California Press.

Clover, Carol, J. (1992) *Men, Women and Chain Saws. Gender in the Modern Horror Film*, London: British Film Institute.

Corner, J. (1991) 'Meaning, genre and context: the problematics of "public knowledge" in the New Audience Studies', in J. Curran and M. Gurevitch (eds) *Mass Media and Society*, London and New York: Edward Arnold, 267–84.

Corner, J. (1995) *Television Form and Public Address*, London and New York: Edward Arnold.

Coward, R. (1983) *Patriarchal Precedents: Sexuality and Social Relations*, London: Routledge & Kegan Paul.

Craig, S. (ed.) (1992) *Men, Masculinity and the Media*, Newbury Park, London: Sage.

Creedon, P. (ed.) (1989) *Women in Mass Communication: Challenging Gender Values*, Beverly Hills, London: Sage.

Crigler, A.N. and Jensen, K.B. (1991) 'Discourses on politics: talking about public issues in the United States and Denmark', in Peter Dahlgren and Colin Sparks (eds) *Communication and Citizenship. Journalism and the Public Sphere*, London and New York: Routledge, 176–92.

Curran, J. (1990) 'The new revisionism in mass communication research: a reappraisal', *European Journal of Communication* 5(2/3): 135–64.

Dahlgren, Peter and Sparks, Colin (eds) (1991) *Communication and Citizenship. Journalism and the Public Sphere*, London and New York: Routledge.

Dahlgren, Peter and Sparks, Colin (eds) (1992) *Journalism and Popular Culture*, London, Newbury Park: Sage.

Denski, S. and Sholle, D. (1992) 'Metal man and glamour boys: gender performance in heavy metal', in S. Craig (ed.) *Men, Masculinity and the Media*, Newbury Park, London: Sage, 41–60.

Dietz, M. (1985) 'Citizenship with a feminist face. The problem with maternal thinking', *Political Theory* 13(1): 19–39.

Dietz, M. (1992) 'Context is all: feminism and theories of citizenship', in C. Mouffe (ed.) *Dimensions of Radical Democracy. Pluralism, Citizenship, Community*, London and New York: Verso, 63–85.

Doane, M.A. (1987) *The Desire to Desire. The Woman's Film of the 1940s*, London: MacMillan.

Drotner, K. (1993) 'Media ethnography: an other story?', in U. Carlsson (ed) *Nordisk forskning om kvinnor och medier*, Göteborg: Nordicom, 25–40.

Easthope, A. (1990) *What a Man's Gotta Do. The Masculine Myth in Popular Culture*, London: Paladin.

Echols, A. (1984) 'The taming of the id: feminist sexual politics, 1968–83', in C.S. Vance (ed.) *Pleasure and Danger. Exploring Female Sexuality*, Boston, London: Routledge & Kegan Paul, 50–72.

Elshtain, J.B. (1981) *Public Man, Private Women. Woman in Social and Political Thought*, Princeton: Princeton University Press.

Field, Belenky, M., McVicker, B., Rule Goldberger, N. and Mattuck Tarule, J. (1986) *Women's Ways of Knowing. The Development of Self, Voice and Mind*, New York: Basic Books.

Fiske, J. (1987) *Television Culture*, London and New York: Methuen.

Fiske, J. (1990) 'Women and quiz shows: consumerism, patriarchy and resisting pleasures', in M.E. Brown (ed.) *Television and Women's Culture. The Politics of the Popular*, London, Newbury Park: Sage, 134–43.

Flax, J. (1990) 'Postmodernism and gender relations in feminist theory', in L.J. Nicholson (ed.) *Feminism/Postmodernism*, New York and London: Routledge, 39–62.

Flitterman, S. (1985) 'Thighs and whiskers, the fascination of *Magnum P.I.*', *Screen* 26(2), 42–58.

Foucault, M. (1979) *Discipline and Punish. The Birth of the Prison*, New York: Vintage Books/Random House, translated by Alan Sheridan.

Foucault, M. (1980) *The History of Sexuality. Volume I: An Introduction*, New York: Vintage Books/Random House, translated by Robert Hurley.

Fraser, Nancy (1987) 'What's critical about critical theory? The case of Habermas and gender', in Seyla Benhabib and Drucilla Cornell (eds) *Feminism as Critique. Essays on the Politics of Gender in Late-Capitalist Societies*, Cambridge: Polity Press, 31–55.

Fraser, Nancy (1989) *Unruly practices. Power, discourse and gender in contemporary social theory*, Minneapolis: University of Minnesota Press.

Fraser, Nancy (1990) 'Rethinking the public sphere. A contribution to the critique of actually existing democracy', *Social Text* 25(6): 56–80.

Fraser, N. and Nicholson, L. (1990) 'Social criticism without philosophy. An encounter between feminism and postmodernism', in L.J. Nicholson (ed.) *Feminism/Postmodernism*, New York and London: Routledge, 19–38.

Friedan, B. (1974) *The Feminine Mystique*, New York: Dell. Originally published in 1963

Gallagher, M. (1980) *Unequal Opportunities. The Case of Women and the Media*, Paris: Unesco.

Gamman, L. and Marshment, M. (eds) (1988) *The Female Gaze. Women as Viewers of Popular Culture*, London: The Women's Press.

Gilligan, C. (1982) *In a Different Voice. Psychological Theory and Women's Development* Cambridge, MA: Harvard University Press.

Gitlin, T. (1991) 'The politics of communication and the communication of politics', in J. Curran and M. Gurevitch (eds) *Mass Media and Society*, London, New York: Edward Arnold, 329–41.

Gray, A. (1988) 'Behind closed doors. Video recorders in the home', in H. Baehr and G. Dyer (eds) *Boxed In. Women and Television*, New York and London: Pandora Press, 38–54.

Gray, A. (1992) *Video Playtime. The Gendering of a Leisure Technology*, London: Comedia/Routledge.

Gray H. (1992) 'Television, black Americans and the American dream', in R.K. Avery and D. Eason (eds) *Critical Perspectives on Media and Society*, New York and London: Guildford Press, 294–305.

Greer, G. (1971) *The Female Eunuch*, London: Paladin.

Gross, L. (1989) 'Out of the mainstream. Sexual minorities and the mass media', in E. Seiter, H. Borchers, G. Kreutzner and E.M. Warth (eds) *Remote Control. Television, Audiences and Cultural Power*, London and New York: Routledge, 130–49.

Grossberg, L. (1992) 'Is there a fan in the house?: the affective sensibility of fandom', in L.A. Lewis (ed.) *The Adoring Audience. Fan Culture and Popular Media*, London and New York: Routledge, 50–65.

Habermas, Jürgen. (1962) *Strukturwandel der Öffentlichkeit*, Frankfurt a.M.: Suhrkamp Verlag.

Habermas, Jürgen (1981) *Theorie des kommunikativen Handelns*, 1& 2 Frankfurt a.M.: Suhrkamp Verlag.

Habermas, Jürgen (1984) *Vorstudien und Ergänzungen zur Theorie des kommunikativen Handelns*, Frankfurt a. M.: Suhrkamp Verlag

Hagen, I. (1994) 'The ambivalence of TV news viewing: between ideals and everyday practices', *European Journal of Communication* 9: 193–220.

Hall, S. (1992) 'The question of cultural identity' in S. Hall, D. Held and T. McGrew (eds) *Modernity and its Futures*, Cambridge: Polity Press, 273–325.

Hansen, M. (1993) 'Unstable mixtures, dilated spheres: Negt and Kluge's *The Public Sphere and Experience*, twenty years later', *Public Culture* 5(2): 179–212.

Haraway, D. (1985) 'A manifesto for cyborgs. Science technology and socialist feminism in the 1980s', *Socialist Review* 15(80): 65–107.

Haraway, D. (1988) 'Situated knowledges: the science question in feminism and the privilege of partial perspective', *Feminist Studies* 14(3): 575–99.

Hearn, J. (1992) *Men in the Public Eye*, London and New York: Routledge.

Hermes, J. (1995) *Reading Women's Magazines: An Analysis of Everyday Media Use*, Cambridge: Polity Press.

Honneth, A. (1985) *Kritik der Macht. Reflexionsstufen einer kritischen Gesellschaftstheorie*, Frankfurt a.M.: Suhrkamp.

hooks, b. (1989) *Feminist Theory: From Margin to Center*, Boston, MA: South End P

Howell, Deborah (1993) 'True Confessions – My Life as a White Male', *Media Stu Journal* 7(1/2): 197–204.

Huyssen, A. (1986) 'Mass culture as woman. Modernism's other' in A. Huyssen, *Afte Great Divide. Modernism, Mass Culture, Postmodernism*, Bloomington and Indianap Indiana University Press, 44–62.

Huyssen, A. (1990) 'Mapping the postmodern' in L.J. Nicholson (ed.) *Femin Postmodernism*, New York and London: Routledge, 234–80.

Jameson, F. (1983) 'Postmodernism and consumer society' in Hal Foster (ed.) *The ι aesthetic. Essays on Postmodern Culture*, Port Townsend, Washington: Bay P 111–25.

Jameson, F. (1984) 'Postmodernism, or the cultural logic of late capitalism', in *New Review* 146: 53–93.

Jensen, J. (1990) *Redeeming Modernity. Contradictions in Media Criticism*, Newbury F London: Sage.

Jensen, K.B. (1986) *Making Sense of the News*, Aarhus: The University Press

Jensen, K.B. (1990) 'The politics of polysemy: television news, everyday conscious and political action', *Media, Culture and Society* 12(1): 57–77.

Kaplan, C. (1986) '*The Thorn Birds*: fiction, fantasy, femininity', *Sea Changes*, Lon Verso, 117–46.

Kellner, D. (1995) *Media Culture. Cultural Studies, Identity and Politics between Modern and the Postmodern*, London and New York: Routledge.

King, B.S. (1990) 'Sonny's virtues: the gender negotiations of *Miami Vice*', *Screen* 3 281–95.

Kosofsky Sedgwick, E. (1990) *Epistemology of the Closet*, Berkeley: Universit California Press.

Kuhn, A. (1982) *Women's Pictures. Feminism and Cinema*, London: Routledge & K Paul.

Livingstone, S. (1994) 'Watching talk: gender and engagement in the viewing of audi discussion programmes', *Media, Culture and Society* 16: 429–47.

Livingstone, S. and P. Lunt (1994) *Talk on Television. Audience Participation and Pι Debate*, London and New York: Routledge.

Lyotard, J.-F. (1979) *La condition post-moderne. Rapport sur le savoir*, Paris: Editior Minuit.

Marcus, G.E. and Fischer, M.M.J. (1986) *Anthropology as Cultural Critique. Experimental Moment in the Human Sciences*, Chicago and London: Universit Chicago Press.

Masciarotte, G.-J. (1991) 'C'mon Girl: Oprah Winfrey and the discourse of feminine t *Discourse* 11: 81–110.

McLaughlin, Lisa (1993) 'Feminism, the public sphere, media and democracy', *Mε Culture and Society* 15(4): October: 599–620.

McNay, L. (1992) *Foucault and Feminism, Power, Gender and the Self*, Cambridge: P Press.

McRobbie, A. (1991) *Feminism and Youth Culture: from 'Jackie' to 'Just Sevent* Basingstoke: MacMillan.

Modleski, T, (1984) *Loving with a Vengeance. Mass-produced Fantasies for Women*, York and London: Methuen. Originally published in 1982.

Modleski, T. (1986) 'Femininity as mascquerades: a femininist approach to ι culture', in C. MacCabe (ed) *High Theory, Low Culture*. Manchester, Manchε University Press.

Morley, D. (1986) *Family Television. Cultural Power and Domestic Leisure*, Lon Comedia.

Morris, M. (1988) 'Banality in cultural studies', *Block* 14: 15–26.

Mouffe, C. (1992) 'Preface. Democratic politics today', in C. Mouffe (ed.) *Dimensions of Radical Democracy. Pluralism, Citizenship, Community*, London and New York: Verso, 1–14.

Murdock, G. (1993) 'Communications and the constitution of Modernity', *Media, Culture and Society* 15(4): 521–39.

Negt, Oskar and Kluge, Alexander (1993) *The Public Sphere and Experience*, Minneapolis: University of Minnesota Press. Translated by Peter Labanyi, Jamie Daniel and Assenka Oksiloff, published originally in 1972.

Pateman, C. (1989) *The Disorder of Women. Democracy, Feminism and Political Theory*, Cambridge: Polity Press.

Pateman, C. (1992) 'Equality, difference, subordination: the politics of motherhood and women's citizenship', in G. Bock and S. James (eds) *Beyond Equality and Difference. Citizenship, Feminist Politics, Female Subjectivity*, London and New York: Routledge, 17–31.

Peters, J.D. (1993) 'Distrust of representation: Habermas on the public sphere', *Media, Culture and Society* 15(4): 541–71.

Press, A. (1990) 'Class, gender and the female viewer: Women's responses to *Dynasty*', in M.E. Brown (ed.) *Television and Women's Culture. The Politics of the Popular*, London, Newbury Park: Sage, 158–82.

Probyn, E. (1992) 'Theorizing through the body' in L. Rakow (ed.) *Women Making Meaning. New Feminist Directions in Communication*, New York and London: Routledge, 83–99.

Probyn, E. (1993) *Sexing the Self. Gendered Positions in Cultural Studies*, London and New York: Routledge.

Radway, J. (1984) *Reading the Romance. Women, Patriarchy and Popular Literature*, Chapel Hill, NC: University of North Carolina Press (an English edition was published in 1987 by Verso, London).

Radway, J. (1988) 'Reception study. Ethnography and the problems of dispersed audiences and nomadic subjects', *Cultural Studies* 2(3): 359–76.

Rivers, Caryl (1993) 'Bandwagons, women and cultural mythology', *Media Studies Journal* 7(1/2): 1–18.

Root, J. (1984) *Pictures of Women. Sexuality*, London: Pandora Press.

Ruddick, S. (1980) 'Maternal thinking', *Feminist Studies* 6(2): 342–67.

Said, E.W. (1987) *Orientalism*, New York: Random House/Vintage Books.

Segal, L. (1987) *Is the Future Female? Troubled Thoughts on Contemporary Feminism*, London: Virago.

Segal, L. (1990) *Slow Motion: Changing Men, Changing Masculinities*, London: Virago.

Seidler, V. (1989) *Rediscovering Masculinity. Reason, Language and Sexuality*, London and New York: Routledge.

Seidler, V. (1991) *Recreating Sexual Politics: Men, Feminism and Politics*, London and New York: Routledge.

Seiter, E., Borchers, H., Kreutzner, G. and Warth, E.M. (1989) 'Don't treat us like we're so stupid and naive', in E. Seiter *et al.* (eds) *Remote Control. Television, Audiences and Cultural Power*, London and New York: Routledge, 223–47.

Steenbergen, B. van (1994) 'The condition of citizenship. An introduction', in B. van Steenbergen (ed.) *The Condition of Citizenship*, London, Thousand Oaks: Sage, 1–9.

Steiner, Linda (1992) 'The history and structure of women's alternative media', in Lana Rakow (ed.) *Women Making Meaning. New Feminist Directions in Communication*, New York and London: Routledge, 121–43.

Steinman, C. (1992) 'Gaze out of bounds: men watching men on television', in S. Craig (ed.) *Men, Masculinity and the Media*, Newbury Park, London: Sage, 199–214.

Strate, L. (1992) 'Beer commercials: a manual on masculinity', in S. Craig (ed.) *Men, Masculinity and the Media*, Newbury Park, London: Sage, 78–92.

Theweleit, Klaus (1980) *Männerphantasien*, Reinbek bei Hamburg: Rowohlt.

Tolson, A. (1978) *The Limits of Masculinity*, London: Tavistock.

Tuchman, G. (1973) 'The symbolic annihilation of women by the mass media', in G. Tuchman, K. Daniels and J. Benét (eds) *Hearth and Home. Images of Women in the Mass Media*, New York: Oxford University Press, 3–38.

Turner, B.S. (ed) (1993) *Citizenship and Social Theory*, London, Newbury Park: Sage.

Turner, B.S. (1994) 'Postmodern culture/modern citizens', in B. van Steenbergen (ed.) *The Condition of Citizenship*, London, Thousand Oaks: Sage, 153–68.

Voet, R. (1995) Feminism and citizenship. Feminist critiques of the concept of social–liberal citizenship, University of Leiden, dissertation.

Wallace, M. (1990) *Invisibility Blues. From Pop to Theory*, London: Verso.

Walters, S.D. (1995) *Material Girls. Making Sense of Feminist Cultural Theory*, Berkeley, Los Angeles: University of California Press.

Warren, C.A.B. (1985) *Gender Issues in Field Research*, Qualitative Research series, 9, Newbury Park: Sage.

Wernick, A. (1991) *Promotional Culture. Advertising, Ideology and Symbolic Expression*, London, Newbury Park: Sage.

Young, I.M. (1987) 'Impartiality and the civic public. Some implications of feminist critiques of moral and political theory', in S. Benhabib and D. Cornell (eds) *Feminism as Critique. Essays on the Politics of Gender in Late-Capitalist Societies*, Cambridge: Polity Press, 56–76.

Young, I.M. (1990) 'The ideal of community and the politics of difference', in Linda J. Nicholson (ed.) *Feminism/Postmodernism*, London and New York: Routledge, 300–23.

Zoonen, L. van (1994) *Feminist Media Studies*, London: Sage.

5

POST-COMMUNIST MEDIA IN TRANSITION

Colin Sparks

INTRODUCTION

The collapse of communism has had a major impact both on the mass media in the countries involved and on aspects of media theory. Writing on this subject has advantages as well as difficulties. The chief advantage is that there has been a close relation between theories of the media and the practical implementation of policies. In many cases, the marginal oppositionists of 1988 were at the centre of government in 1990. The ideas they espoused in opposition were tested against the real world in a way that has eluded many Western intellectuals.

The disadvantages are numerous. The first is the variety of post-communisms. Here, only the European examples are considered, but these provide a range of cases. It is difficult to find a common thread between the extreme government control of the mass media in Serbia and Croatia and the relative freedom and democracy of Slovenia (Thompson, 1994; Splichal, 1993). The media of the former German Democratic Republic (DDR) were absorbed into an already existing capitalist media system (Boyle, 1994). In Bulgaria and Romania the process of reform is very far from complete (Iordanova, 1995; Marinescu, 1995; Raycheva, 1995). In the largest European post-communist experiment of all, the territory of the former USSR, we have a combination of state disintegration, a variety of successor state-forms and an uneven process of marketization which often seems to take a completely unregulated form (McNair, 1994).

This chapter concentrates on the most stable examples of change: the four countries of the Visegrad group. Poland, Hungary, the Czech Republic and Slovakia display important differences, but they have enough in common to be considered as a group. Examples from other states are used when they illustrate particularly clearly the points at issue, but the main focus of this chapter is upon those four countries.

The processes of change in these cases have been what may be termed 'normal' ones. These states have not been absorbed into another state. Internal forces hostile to change have not been able to enforce relative inertia. They have not been gripped by the horrors of ethnic strife and war. National separation and the formation of new states were achieved relatively amicably. There have been external influences upon these countries but the main contours of change have been decided by internal political forces. They have mostly reached decisions without recourse to violence and by means which are recognizably democratic. The changes effected there are, in their character, direction and limitations, clear examples of attempts to follow the two axes of integration into the world market and democratization which are common features of the whole post-communist epoch.

The second major problem is the relative scarcity of scholarly writing in the area. It is only a few years since the decisive events took place, and academics notoriously work to slower timetables than that. An additional complication is that many of the people who played a key role in writing about the mass media in these countries when they were communist have, since 1989, been propelled into other spheres of life. In fact, there has been little that one can call 'media policy' or a discourse about media policy. Political decisions have been taken. Directions of development have been laid down. Commentaries, not to mention polemics, on these developments abound. Taken overall, however, the press of events and the conflicts of transition have been so intense that it is premature to speak of policy in the same way as it is possible in, say, the USA or the EU.

The third area of difficulty concerns terminology. The questions discussed here, in particular democracy and communism, are finally inextricable from their ideological and political contexts. A simple expedient is adopted: the common description of the states of central and eastern Europe is accepted. Before 1989, the states were called 'communist'. This term, and associated derivatives like 'post-communist', are used without any evaluative content whatsoever.

The problems associated with the term 'democracy' admit of no such simple solution. Many contemporary texts on democracy manage to consider this question without any serious discussion of the mass media (Bobbio, 1989). Those which do often seem to regard democracy as something outside of the media themselves, to which they are more or less desirable additions (Keane, 1991: 179). One major exception is that provided by the Italian theorist Zolo (Zolo, 1992). In this chapter, it is argued that only in and through the mass media in a contemporary large scale society can representative democracy be constituted. The quantity and variety of information, and the range of views represented, in the mass media are at least as much indices of democracy as are electoral systems. This chapter, therefore, examines the extent to which the promises of the democratic revolutions of 1989 have actually been realized.

A second theme sometimes provides a strong contrast to the first. These experiments in the construction of media systems are being undertaken alongside a substantial shift in the form of property ownership from a collective state to a private individual mode. All of the economies of the region are moving from centrally directed command models to market-driven ones. This marketization is also taking place in the mass media, and the interplay between that dynamic and the democratic imperative is important.

Throughout, the focus of attention is on broadcasting, and in particular television. This is partly because, as will become apparent below, developments in the press proceeded almost without any conscious policy whatsoever. There have certainly been major changes in the press scene, but these have been the result of more or less spontaneous actions rather than deliberate policies.

The shape of this chapter is determined by the above concerns. The theme of the constitution of democratic life through the mass media is used as an optic to view five aspects of thinking and research. These are: theories of the nature of the mass media in communist societies; theories about the nature of the transition from communism to post-communism; theories of civil society; the problem of public service broadcasting; issues of national identity in an increasingly marketized media system. Finally, suggestions as to what will be central issues for theory and research now that the period of immediate post-communism is past are presented.

THE COMMUNIST MEDIA

The first question to resolve is the nature of the communist media systems. The social systems themselves were not static and evolved over time. The same was true of the media systems, which on the eve of the fall of communism were diverse (Jakubowicz, 1990).

In some cases, Romania for example, it seems that the classical model of Stalinism persisted (Gross, 1990: 102). At the other extreme, the People's Republic of China still retains communist political control of the media system, but there has been a massive development of commercial media in the last two decades. The media system is already very far from any classic communist model (Huang, 1994).

The majority of communist countries seems to have been situated somewhere between these two extremes. If there was a period when the media system approximated closely to the classic model, this was long past by 1989. In the case of Poland, for example, the decay of the purely communist system dates from the 1950s, and by the 1980s the media system was relatively diverse (Goban-Klas, 1994). In the press there was a range of permitted publications (Kowalski, 1988). In television, strict party control was more or less confined to news and current affairs programmes. Entertainment programming was often purchased directly from the west (Jakubowicz, 1989). The situation had reached a stage in which one prominent commentator argued that, in place of the uniform and passive mass opinion allegedly produced by the communist media system, there were three distinct but overlapping 'public spheres'. One was the official discourse of the communist media. The second was that of the church media. The, third that of the enormous quantity of illegal and semi-legal oppositional literature, mostly deriving from Solidarity (Jakubowicz, 1991).

Two important Central European exceptions to the trend towards much looser media systems were Czechoslovakia and the DDR. In the former, there had been a long-term process of relaxation of control over the media, which culminated in the late 1960s with the Prague Spring. One of the direct consequences of the Russian invasion of 1968 was the installation of an extremely rigid media system. By the 1980s, although there had been some degree of integration into the world market in terms of sources of imported programming, the system remained tightly controlled compared with its neighbours.

The regime in the DDR had long had to contend with the fact that its population shared a common language with the continent's most successful capitalist state, and many of the inhabitants could receive terrestrial signals from the West. Late in the life of the DDR, one expert wrote that while 'in the GDR "media pluralism" in the bourgeois sense does not exist and is not wanted', nevertheless 'the decisive feature with regard to communication culture in the GDR is that two opposed media systems are in operation' (Hanke, 1990: 185). One was that of the DDR, the other that of the capitalist Federal Republic.

The evidence of this brief review suggests that there was no fixed and rigid 'Soviet media model' of the kind beloved by cold warriors of either side. The systems displayed a degree of diversity and were responsive to different political and economic pressures. They were capable of considerable modification and adaptation in different circumstances. In particular, the degree of 'openness' of the systems to different perspectives varied quite widely. There was, except in moments of extreme crisis and system disintegration, quite tight control of the news and current affairs output. The less directly political material, especially the entertainment material, was often acquired from outside the communist world and thus tended to embody quite different value systems to those officially espoused and promoted by the system itself.

While the systems were capable of modification, it is important to recognize that they were nevertheless incapable of self-transformation and remained recognizably different from that prevailing in the more optimistic interpretations of Western experience (Mrozowski, 1990: 214). The nature of the media systems in the 1980s was part of a more general combination of a holding exercise by the communist leadership against internal opposition and a partial accommodation to the capitalist world market. The attempt to engineer the emotional landscape of the audience through the construction of serious dramatic material became relatively unimportant compared with the mass of imported capitalist series. Even the news changed its character from an assertion of the values of the communist system to a crude restatement of its unchallengeable presence.

There is no evidence whatsoever that in any country any significant section of the ruling elite, or even the leading figures of the media systems, had any thought of transforming the systems towards anything remotely resembling a democratic one. Although the media systems did not much resemble the Western caricatures produced in the epoch of high cold war, they remained essentially different from those prevailing in capitalist democracies.

THE NATURE OF THE TRANSITION

The fact that the media systems of the communist countries did not correspond to popularly held Western views suggests that some of the more common theories about the end of communism require revision. In particular, theories about the nature of the process of transition itself require examination.

General theories of communism are often presented as abstract social theory, but they lead logically to accounts of the ways in which the societies themselves changed, and to ways in which the media were implicated in those changes. It is possible to review the range of accounts, and group them in three classes of theory. The common-sense view of this change is that it is simply one of a transition from socialist totalitarianism to capitalist democracy. The best known exponent of this is Fukuyama. According to him, the fall of communism represents the final triumph of liberal capitalism over all other ways of organizing human relations. While he acknowledges the difficulties which still remain in the way of the total Americanization of the world, he claims that it is no longer possible to put forward any coherent alternative view of society and claim that it represents a better and superior mode of life. This, of course, is a theorization of the dominant mood amongst Western governments and publicists in the immediate aftermath of 1989 and as such may be taken to be almost the official view of our times (Fukuyama, 1992).

An important variation on this theme is advanced by Bauman. In his account, the fall of communism represents the final defeat of modernity. This is less obviously and rosily optimistic than the official version, but it contains the same view of a total and irreversible transformation. According to Bauman, the project of modernity was an attempt to subordinate the material world, including the unruly human part of it, to the dictates of reason. Communism represented the logical extreme of this project, attempting to totalize rational control of human experience and to plan every aspect of human life in accordance with the dictates of reason. Since this has now demonstrably failed, there can be no question but that we are living in a postmodern world in which chance and the non-rational are recognized to play a central role in human affairs. This may well lead to a riskier and more threatening world, but it will also be a richer one, since the attempt by modernity to overcome the uncertainties inherent in being was a denial of the human condition (Bauman, 1992).

A second group of theorists argue that a less profound change has taken place. Many of the exponents of this current of thinking are Western non- and anti-Stalinist left-wing writers. For them, societies like the Soviet Union were profoundly contradictory. On the one hand, they displayed economic structures which were non-capitalist. They had state plans, state control of heavy industry and a state monopoly of foreign trade. Even if they were not pure examples of socialist production and distribution, they were certainly some kind of transitional society. On the other hand, they were characterized by the domination of a bureaucratic elite which monopolized political power and which maintained its rule by means of varying degrees of terror (Miliband, 1991; Hobsbawm, 1994).

In this view, the establishment of capitalist property relations is the decisive feature of 1989. The social meaning of the process is that the bureaucratic elite are establishing themselves as private capitalists in a market economy. The political conditions which follow from this are indeterminate. It is likely that at least in the short term the resulting political systems will be vulnerable to dictatorial pressures.

While this position is most often associated with the left, similar arguments are put forward by writers with a different approach. One example is the analysis of the 'condition of post-communism' advanced by George Schöpflin. He argues that the total character of communism meant that opposition often took an extremely simplified and often moralistic form unsuitable for the exercise of democratic political power. While, in the aftermath of 1989, liberal democratic forms have been adopted everywhere, both the psychic attitudes of the population and the ideologies of the former opposition mean that the substance of political life has often departed from these forms. Despite these limits, however, there was a fundamental break with communist economic life. Thus, while we may expect the classic economic benefits of liberal capitalism like choice and the satisfaction of individual aspirations, there is a much greater question mark over the extent to which the collective aspiration towards democracy will easily be achieved (Schöpflin, 1993: 300).

The final group of theorists argues that changes have taken place primarily at the political level. Most of the proponents of such views argue that the bureaucracy formed a ruling class rather than an elite. The revolutions of 1989 were above all political events, involving a radical change in the way that the societies were governed. While they permitted and legitimized a change from state property to private property, they were a mechanism by which the bureaucracy attempted to preserve its power by means of economic self-renewal.

In one version, the bureaucracy constituted a state capitalist class, holding productive property in common and collectively confronting proletariat and peasantry in the same manner as do individual capitalists. A major feature of these systems was their attempt at autarchic national development. By the 1980s this had reached stagnation. The peculiarity of state capitalism as a system is that it fuses political and economic power and is thus much less able to adapt easily to changing circumstances. The state capitalist class needed political democracy in order to transform itself into a private capitalist class and reintegrate into the world economy (Callinicos, 1991).

Another version of this theory argues that the bureaucracy constitutes a 'new class' in both Western and communist societies. The processes at work were the same in the West and in communism: 'What has led to the recent demise of communist people's democracies is but an extremely exaggerated manifestation of similar problems with Western representative democracies' (*Telos* Staff, 1991: 7–8). The best outcome of the shift from communism to capitalism would be a shift from a society in which the New Class was the unchallenged dominant group in society to one in which it was only the most important. The other possible outcome would be a collapse and decline into chaos (Piccone, 1990).

The third group is thus unified in the belief that there is, at the level of the basic structures of society, a degree of continuity and that the transformation essentially affects the political forms. This version of change tends to minimize the degree of change involved in the ending of communist rule.

One major test of any social theory is how well it corresponds with actual developments. We can apply such a test to theories of the end of communism with relatively little difficulty. Six years after the events of 1989, most of the societies display striking continuities with the past. This is nowhere more obvious than in broadcasting, and it provides powerful evidence that the revolutions, while real, were limited and political in character (Sparks and Reading, 1994).

Examination of the events reveals important variations upon the general theme of a political revolution. These may be considered as a series of gradations of completeness along an axis provided by the willingness or otherwise of the ruling group to engage in political reform.

The first, and most obvious, variation is that, in a number of communist countries, there has not yet been a political revolution. Examples of this group are China, North Korea and Cuba. In these cases there is no sign of a serious readiness to undertake any transformation of the political system even though there is often a real readiness to undertake extensive economic change. The second variant is those countries in which the bureaucracy has managed to establish more or less complete control of the process of change and where the political quarrels have been contained within the bureaucracy itself. Examples of this group are the former USSR, Romania and Bulgaria. The third group is countries in which the reform wing of the bureaucracy was able to negotiate the transfer of power to the more respectable elements of the opposition. The clearest examples of this are Poland and Hungary. The final group is those countries in which the bureaucracy lost control, even if very briefly, of the process of change. The two examples of this are the velvet revolution in Czechoslovakia and the collapse of the DDR.

All but the last group have in common the fact that the shift towards a new media order was an orderly process controlled by the elite. While there were changes at the very top level, the bulk of the media professionals remained in post and the structures established by the communist regimes experienced the revolution as an important but not fundamentally disruptive event. Media policy and changes to the mass media were worked out as the result of negotiations between competing elite groups without any serious participation on the part of the mass of population.

The final group is interesting because it provides a glimpse of the possibility of a different kind of media policy: one articulated by media workers and by the mass of the population. In the case of the events in Prague, the duration was extremely brief and, in the absence of any thorough study, known only to have restricted itself to opposition to the control of the old stalinist bureaucrats (Smid, 1992: 2–3). The strike in Czechoslovak television in protest against the refusal of the communist management to cover the protest demonstrations in Wenceslas Square escalated into a takeover of television by the strike committee. Although it lasted only a few weeks, during this period control of television slipped out of the hands of the bureaucracy.

The case of the DDR was far richer and longer and its main aspects are much better known (Boyle, 1994). The collapse of party control of the media was accompanied by an attempt to organize a new constitutional framework for social communication at the level of the state. This involved both media workers and representatives of oppositional groups. In the first months after the collapse of the communist regime there was a serious effort to construct a form of 'communicative democracy' which would have gone some way towards empowering ordinary citizens. On 5 February 1990, the *Volkskammer* (Parliament of the DDR), at the instigation of the 'Round Table' founded by the Citizens' Movement, adopted a Resolution on the Media which, among other things: guaranteed freedom of conscience for journalists; obliged 'the mass media to give unhindered public access to a diversity of opinions; set up a Media Control Council, whose membership included members of the Citizens' Movement, elected politicians and religious groupings, in order to oversee radio and television' (Boyle, 1994: 210–13).

None of this survived unification. The unification treaty established that broadcasting would be run along West German lines, with each Land having an important role to play. A West German broadcaster, Rudolf Mühlfenzl, with strong links to the ruling CDU, was appointed as interim commissioner responsible for winding up the DDR institutions and planning the new services. He was assisted by an advisory council, of whose 18 members only two were not representatives of political parties. Mühlfenzl took the lead in ensuring that all of the attempts at media democracy which had been instigated in the early period were crushed. Journalists were subjected to rigorous political screening. The leading positions in the new broadcasting stations were overwhelmingly filled by party loyalists from the West.

In the press, the picture was much simpler, in that many of the east German papers were taken over directly by Western publishers and established Western publications entered the new market. Control in the newsroom reverted to the owner and publishers, through their agents the editors. All of the attempts to protect the journalists from editorial pressure and the efforts to establish channels through which all citizens could both receive reliable and impartial information and express their own views on matters of public interest were extinguished.

In creating a space for public involvement, however brief, the DDR provides a unique case in the former communist countries. What was snuffed out by the imposition of the norms of media life of the West in eastern Germany hardly appeared in most of the other countries in which the communist regimes collapsed during 1989–91.

In all of these cases the key feature of the transition was a managed and negotiated transfer of power between the existing elite and the oppositional elite. In some case, like Romania and Bulgaria, these were basically constituted by different factions of the *nomenklatura*. In other cases, notably Poland, the deal was struck between the reform wing of the Communist party and an opposition which had fought it in one form or another since at least 1956. To say that the process of change was negotiated does not imply that it was easy or painless, or that it did not involve the clash of real social forces.

The evidence from the development of the mass media suggests that theories which stress the limited character of the revolutions and the strong elements of continuity between one stage and the next provide the best explanation for the general processes. There is little evidence for any total and rapid transformation of every area of social life such as would be required to provide empirical support for the contentions of the most dramatic theories like the one advanced by Fukuyama. Nor, on the other hand, is there evidence that the revolutions were simply confined to the economic level. In television, the continuities were sufficiently strong as to suggest this view was at the very best a gross over-simplification. In the case of the press, there is stronger evidence for the 'restoration of capitalism', but on closer examination this is revealed as often consisting of sections of the bureaucracy seizing state property for themselves and completing the transformation from collective to private capitalists in a wild and uncoordinated fashion.

The best known case, that of the party-owned regional media in Hungary, is not at all atypical. Although in a number of cases the staff enforced the retirement of particularly hard-line chief editors inherited from the communist regime, the replacement was usually from the senior staff of the paper in question. The representatives of the staff then negotiated deals with Western media companies, ceding ownership of the papers in return for the funding and training needed to ensure the continuation of the paper (Giorgi, 1995: 44–6). In these cases as in others, some individual members of the old regimes were sacrificed, but the structures remained, albeit with a new, and much closer, relationship with the world market. There is no evidence that in doing this those who seized the press had to engage in a serious social struggle to transform the relations of production in the industry.

THE DEBATE OVER CIVIL SOCIETY

The controlled nature of the transformations has produced a problem for some of the leading theories of democratization and the media. In particular the idea of constructing a 'civil society' has become very problematic.

Civil society was one of the most important ideas of the opposition. Its provenance is usually dated to an essay by the Polish oppositionist Adam Michnik, written in the mid-1970s. This essay, or at least its English translation, does not actually employ the term 'civil society' but it clearly anticipates the central strategies of those who came to employ it. Michnik rejected both of the existing strategies of opposition to the communist regime: that of attempting to influence the party leadership in desirable directions with a hope of reforming the system into democratic socialism; and that of attempting to organize the overthrow of the system and its replacement by some other form of social organization. Michnik proposed an attempt to build alternative structures – associational groups, publishing enterprises, and so on – outside the official mass organizations of communist society.

In the short term, this perspective did not command much support, at least in Poland. Michnik and his interlocutors belonged to the intelligentsia and the dominant Polish tradition of opposition comprised large-scale proletarian protests like strikes and battles with the riot police. These, in the early 1980s, led to a massive strike wave and the foundation of Solidarity. At the high point of the union there were proposals for immediate and radical changes in society. These included a radical restructuring and democratization of the mass media. The intention was to free the media from the power of the Communist party, to enable the citizens to receive accurate opinion and information, and to empower them to articulate their views and opinions. In terms of the governance of radio and television, for example, these proposals involved the construction of a body of lay citizens to oversee their workings (Reading, 1994).

After the imposition of martial law in December 1981, the opportunity for mass involvement in political life was destroyed. In its place, there was an enormous effort at the construction of underground and church-sponsored groups, meetings, publications and so on. The idea of the importance of building civil society gradually came to gain support. The foundations of civil society were already being laid in the web of illegal and semi-legal organizations, and these could continue to be expanded until such point as the regime was prepared to negotiate terms.

So long as the regimes were not prepared to negotiate in any serious way, the idea of constructing civil society stood for a general range of oppositional activities, none of which could claim any particular priority or importance over the others. Within the unity of opposition, however, there were different interpretations of what this new strategy might actually mean in practice.

In modern usage, it is possible to detect three mutations of the classical formulation of civil society as the site of economic life and the pursuit of individual interest. The first of these is the one closest to the original in that it retains the tripartite structure of the original. On this account, the problem with communist societies is that the state has swallowed the family and civil society. The programme which follows from that is simple: the sphere of the state must be reduced and the family and civil society must be resurrected. In economic terms, the state should be stripped of as much as possible of its economic role and the various activities privatized. In social terms, the family must once again become the centre of emotional and reproductive life. As has been pointed out by critics and proclaimed by some of its adherents, this was essentially a 'Thatcherite' programme for the urgent construction of private capitalism (Meiksins Wood, 1990). This 'materialist' interpretation was probably the most widespread view in Eastern European countries (Ost, 1989: 78).

Not all of the oppositionists in the communist countries were entirely happy with the prospect of overthrowing communism in order to build capitalism. Instead, they looked to a third way, which would encourage a benign form of civil society. The theoretical result of this was a revision of the classical model into new, 'idealistic' forms. The state remained but it was joined by the economy. On the other hand there was the separate and distinct realm of civil society. This latter consisted of voluntary organizations, associations, the family and so on (Arato and Cohen, 1990).

Even this, however, did not quite satisfy all of the proponents of the term, since civil society in this formulation remains a category which could contain negative social forces and organizations as much as positive ones. The final reformulation was to define civil society in terms of purely positive elements. In this version, the category effectively consists not of the activity of all people associated outside of the sphere of the state and the economy but only of the activity of nice, educated, concerned, professional people associated outside of the sphere of the state and the economy (Benda *et al.*, 1988: 231).

From these different theoretical conceptions of the nature of civil society flowed different strategies for the organization of the mass media. In the case of the 'Thatcherite' example, represented most clearly in media terms by the Belorussian writer Oleg Manaev, the mass media are no different from any other part of the economy. State ownership necessarily means dictatorship over the media and is incompatible with democratic political life. Following Hayek, Manaev argues that in any society there are active elements, called 'subjects', and those who are acted upon ('objects'). In a state directed system only the state itself is a subject (Manaev, 1993: 120). The best way to break this is to privatize as much of the mass media as quickly as possible. The existence of private media means that at the very least the views of several different social subjects are available to the mass of the population (Manaev, 1993: 147–8).

Representatives of the other interpretations tend to stress the ways in which the relaxation of party control over the media allows the representation of previously silenced voices and the empowerment of the citizens against large social organizations (Fedorowicz, 1990: 83). The general hope was that all of this activity which developed underground in the years of opposition and which flourished as the systems entered terminal collapse would continue to provide the guiding principle for social communication in the new liberated environment.

The negotiated character of the revolutions of 1989 meant that none of the concerns of the more idealistic interpretations of civil society as a political programme for reconstructing society were realized in practice. The case of television we will consider at length below. In the press, there was certainly an explosion of publications, but the dominant move was towards marketization and commercialization. In terms of ownership, there were three different tendencies. Very many new publications were founded, ranging from the voices of newly legalized political parties through to pornography. Some of the former dissident publications, most notably *Gazeta Wyborca* Poland and *Lidove Noviny* in the Czech Republic, survived and became major papers, although very often their staff was now quite different from what it had been in opposition (Spindler-Brown, 1994). In most countries, the effective ownership of existing communist titles was seized by their own journalists, usually with real power residing in the hands of the senior journalists. In Poland, on the other hand, there was a controlled process of selling off the property of the state publisher (RSW) to various parties. There was an attempt to ensure that the journalists had the option of setting up cooperatives to run papers. Some papers were thus transferred into the hands of their employees. Everywhere, however, the new owners were often so short of capital that they were soon forced to find foreign partners. The best known examples of this tendency are those from Hungary cited above, in which the editors of the local communist press seized control of the communist papers and sold them off, on the grounds that this was the only viable strategy for their continuation, to the West German Springer group. Elsewhere, the process has not usually been so dramatic and rapid, but over time in a wide range of countries foreign owners have come to hold major investments in the press (Jakubowicz, 1993; Goban-Klas, 1994).

What is common to all of these situations is that there was no noticeable attempt to implement any democratic empowerment of the citizens. There seems to have been no attempt to initiate support for minority publications, to empower citizens' associations to supervise the editorial performance of the press, to protect journalists from pressure from owners and editors, or to ensure that the press covered all points of view. The version of civil society which emerged into the reality of post-communism as a successful and viable social theory giving some purchase upon concrete social reality was the economistic one. The major way in which this theory is problematic is in its easy assumption that the dominance of civil society necessarily implies democratic political life.

Reality in the former communist countries has proved far less simple. The former proponents of civil society have found that the state, now under their control, is not quite the incubus that they imagined it to be when they were in opposition. They now discover that it has a function in maintaining forms of social cohesion of which they approve and of representing the unifying national spirit in the face of the splitting tendencies of civil society. They discover that left to itself civil society cannot be trusted to deliver the kinds of media enterprise that they wish to see develop.

The mass media continue to suffer from the effects of an over-powerful state inherited from the communist epoch and at the same time the beginnings of the worst aspects of marketization (Splichal, 1994: 127–48). The governments tend to see broadcasting as their own property. The press, on the other hand, is closely tied either to political parties or to an increasing desire to attract advertising revenue. There is no attempt to establish a media system that responds to the needs and wishes of the citizens of the state.

The idealistic version of civil society is once again as marginal in the former communist countries as it was before 1989 and has always been in the Western capitalist countries. Civil society, in so far as it is a useful concept in social theory, is one which refers to those human activities which are structured and placed by the workings of the capitalist market economy. In contemporary conditions, civil society is the sphere dominated by big capital. It follows that the attempt to build a media system based on civil society is in reality to hand over power to large media corporations. In retrospect the last days of the DDR stand out as a beacon of possibility: there for the briefest of times there was the beginning of the sort of empowerment that the idealistic version of civil society wished to see come to pass.

RESTRUCTURING BROADCASTING

The collapse of communist systems seemed to mark the end of the trajectory of state intervention in the economy. In media theory the policy of complete marketization was at least tacitly endorsed by authors of reports funded by the US Department of State, a major US newspaper chain, and the Soros Foundation (Dougan, 1990; Dennis and Van Den Heuval, 1990; Webster, 1994). These views were not universally shared in the former communist countries, where a 'Swedish' model of the future found considerable support. In broadcasting, advisers from the European Broadcasting Union and the Council of Europe, sympathetic to the idea of a state presence in broadcasting through the mediation of public service broadcasting organizations, often received a favourable hearing.

A further major complication was that the new governments, particularly those with a strong sense of national mission, thought that considerations of economic efficiency and social liberty were properly secondary to the imperatives of political and cultural survival. They therefore tended to have a preference for forms of media, television in particular, over which they could exert direct control. One of the obvious ways in which this could be ensured was through the continuation of direct state ownership of the major television channels.

The future of the structure of broadcasting thus became a site upon which different social philosophies were argued out in concrete terms. The idea of adopting a US-style broadcasting system, in which the main channels are commercialized and public service obligations discharged by a minor complementary organization, has nowhere found favour. Overall, the main debate has been within the European tradition of broadcasting.

This tradition includes both broadcasters whose claims to embody public service values rest upon a real political distance from the government of the day and those who are more or less directly its mouthpiece. The debate in the former communist countries has reproduced these differences. It has mostly been over how far, and in what ways, broadcasters whose ultimate owner is the state can be made independent of the immediate political and economic pressures of the government, and how far privately owned broadcasters can be obliged to behave in publicly responsible ways.

Most of the broadcasting laws establishing the new systems paid homage to the idea of public service broadcasting (Kleinwächter, 1993). Broadcasters were enjoined to cover the entire national territory, to present news and current affairs fairly and impartially, to represent the views of minority groups, to carry out educational tasks, and so on. The laws also, in general, constructed systems of indirect control which distanced the broadcasters from the government. This usually involved a Broadcasting Council charged with overseeing the whole system and administering the granting of licences. There was also, often, a television and a radio council which were charged with the more detailed control of the state broadcasters.

In their inspiration, these plans were admirable attempts to copy the positive feature of political independence which is supposed to be a general characteristic of public service broadcasting in western Europe, and is certainly present in some of the systems some of the time.

It is important to note that in most of these laws there was no attempt whatsoever to empower 'civil society', understood as the representatives of the informal associations of citizens which had been such an important feature of oppositional writing. Mostly, the new political elite has established arrangements which allow it to appoint, and to supervise the work of, their own nominees.

The privatization of sections of broadcasting demonstrated very clearly the extent to which the post-communist governments saw the restructuring as a mechanism for empowering the political elite rather than establishing the control of civil society over society. Two issues were present here: whether to privatize any section of broadcasting, particularly television, and who should be granted the franchises.

The tenor of political life in the post-communist period meant that it was generally accepted in theory and legislation that there should be some degree of privatization, but the new, fervently anti-communist, governments of the region found that it was both convenient and possible to have their own government television stations. There was therefore very often a reluctance actually to award any private franchises.

When franchises for commercial broadcasting have been awarded, they have often been the subject of political contention. Many of the nationals with the skills and contacts adequate to put together credible bids for commercial franchises have political records and political contacts. In some cases, the people inspiring the most credible bids were ones who had only recently been driven out of public television because of their differences with the government of the time. Thus governments which had struggled to exert control over state television were reluctant to allow their erstwhile opponents a franchise which would give them control of a private television channel.

The second major problem was that many of the new governments have a strong nationalist streak in their political ideology and are committed to propagating their version of the national culture. Television is seen to have a central role in sustaining and developing that national culture. While a compliant state owned broadcaster may be forced to carry out this role rather easily, private companies present greater problems. We shall look at some of the ways that problem has been addressed in the next section. Here we need only note that raising the capital for a credible bid for a private franchise has often proved difficult for local entrepreneurs and they have frequently formed alliances with foreign sources of capital. This risk of direct or indirect foreign ownership of commercial television channels has been a factor which has led governments to oppose the award of franchises to particular candidates.

In both Poland and the Czech Republic, the award of the commercial television franchises provoked the ruling parties to attempt to secure parliamentary rejection of the annual reports of the Broadcasting Councils. Had they been successful in this, the Broadcasting Councils would have been obliged to resign. In fact, in both cases, they survived, largely due to the support of the former communists. In Slovakia, on the other hand, the nationalist government was able to sack the Broadcasting Council as a result of a dispute over who should receive the first terrestrial licence.

The outcome so far has been that broadcasting in most of the former communist countries has been highly politicized. There has been, it is important to recall, a major relaxation of some of the formal mechanisms of control, most notably censorship. This was so much the symbol of the old communist order that it was in most countries completely indefensible. That is not to say that the sort of freedom of expression characteristic of capitalist democracies like the USA or Sweden were immediately and everywhere established by law and enshrined in practice. On the contrary, in those countries with strong nationalist or religious influences, various new types of restriction were implemented. Serbia and Croatia, the two sides in the first round of the Balkan tragedy, have both continued to have strong and direct control over the mass media in what the politicians see as their respective national interests. Television has been particularly strongly affected by this, but the main printed media have also fallen under control of the ruling party (Thompson, 1994).

The most frequent form of political intervention has been through government pressure on the broadcasters, the removal of unreliable figures and the appointment of pliant political supporters to key posts. In these aspects, the new governments have continued many of the practices of the communist regimes they replaced.

The best known, and most dramatic, of these pressures were the series of episodes known as the Hungarian Media Wars, in which the Hungarian Democratic Forum (MDF) government tried, between 1991 and mid-1994, to ensure that state radio and television (MTV) provide uncritical coverage of their activities and campaign for their re-election. It is worth briefly recounting the highlights of this struggle in order to illustrate the kind of situation which prevailed (Cunningham, 1994).

The origins of MDF discontent appear to have been in the fact that they perceived that the majority of the newly freed, and often foreign owned, press were extremely hostile to their actions. To remedy this, they turned to the broadcasting organizations. These, however, were headed by individuals who had been appointed after the collapse of the old communist regime largely because they were proponents of independent broadcasting. The broadcasters refused to deliver the kinds of coverage the government wanted. In response, the MDF mobilized demonstrations against the broadcasters, sometimes using extremely ugly anti-Semitism in their propaganda against the alleged betrayal of genuinely Hungarian national interests. The supporters of the broadcasters organized counter-demonstrations. The government suspended the subsidy from the state treasury to the broadcasters. In response, MTV in particular embarked on an aggressive campaign to raise its advertising revenue. The government attempted to sack the heads of radio and television, but the president of the republic and the courts refused to sanction the dismissals. The government accused the head of MTV and his closest supporters of financial mismanagement and forced their resignation. The government appointed its own supporters to the posts of temporary heads and they sacked a large number of journalists and other broadcasters. By the 1994 elections, Hungarian radio and television were producing coverage which was completely supportive of the MDF. In the end, all of this effort proved fruitless and the MDF was heavily defeated in the election.

In summary, our review of the experience of the former communist countries suggests that it is difficult to found public service broadcasting organizations in the present epoch. The reason for this is of more general import. It is often argued that the well-known, if exaggerated, crisis of public service broadcasting is due to a combination of the commercialization and internationalization of the media and a concomitant collapse in the legitimating ideology of public service. The experience of the former communist countries suggests that these are not adequate explanations for the crisis.

Commercial pressures are not yet seriously present in these countries, although they certainly will develop in the near future. There was also a cadre of experts and broadcasters with a wide knowledge of the nature of public service organizations in the capitalist countries, and of their commercial rivals. These people were, and some still are, strongly committed to the attempt to build public service systems out of the communist state broadcasters. Many of the people involved were extremely talented and their proposals took account of the obvious problems which have beset Western public service broadcasters. A variety of technical procedures were proposed, and sometimes even adopted, in order to ensure the independence of the broadcasters from government and political pressure.

The largely negative balance sheet of the attempt to establish public service broadcasters in these countries was not the result of inadequate legal formulations or commercial pressures. The root cause of this failure was the absence of the kind of political culture necessary for any public service broadcaster to survive. This highlights a problem often overlooked in the Western analyses of public service. In its purest form, most obviously with the BBC, the condition for the realization of public service has been a political culture in which the main parties have been prepared to allow a real measure of freedom and independence to the broadcasters, provided they remained more or less within the bounds of the parliamentary consensus. The politicians have always possessed the instruments, formal and informal, to override that independence if they so wished. They have used them relatively sparingly in the past because of the general agreement amongst political leaders and broadcasters that it was in their mutual interest to allow a certain degree of flexibility. Such a political culture does not exist in any of the former communist countries. Governments, even the government of the newly unified Germany, have not been prepared to permit any serious deviation from their own line. It is that political will to intervene that has turned potential public service broadcasters into little more than government mouthpieces.

MEDIA IN THE SERVICE OF THE NATIONAL IDEA

Nationalist ideology has played an important part in the life of many, if not all, of the former communist countries. One reason for this is undoubtedly the existence of real national oppression during the communist period. Another reason is that nationalist ideas provide a totalizing alternative to communism and can be used in a similar way to justify sacrifices on the part of the population, whether of personal liberty or material gain. They provide a convenient public discourse for many of the new, and some of the not so new, leaders which allows them to engage with the concerns of their populations.

The media in general provide one of the key sites in which this nationalist ideology is developed and channelled. The character of media nationalism varies from country to country and is complicated by the fact that the population of many if not all of the states in Central and Eastern Europe are ethnically mixed. The debate is most intense with regard to broadcasting. As we have seen, there was little opposition to the large-scale entry of foreign capital into the Hungarian press, and it has been argued by one of the leading experts on the media that it 'played a positive role in the transition' (Gálik, 1995: 5).

We can observe a variety of strategies to deal with these problems. In the Baltic Republics, long denied political independence by the Soviet Union, the winning of statehood was accompanied by a surge of interest in the national media and the national culture and a determination to give them a distinctly ethnic character (Høyer *et al.*, 1993). In some of these states, and in other countries with divided populations like Ukraine, the new broadcasting systems operating in the national mode have had to compete with the official Russian programmes from Moscow for the attention of the minority Russian-speaking populations (Zernetskaya, 1994).

A diametrically different case is that of Hungary. A large proportion of ethnic Hungarians live outside the borders of the Hungarian state. The Hungarians of the neighbouring states, notably Romania, Slovakia and the constituent states of the former Yugoslavia, were and are national minorities and they did, and still in some cases do, suffer very real national oppression.

The MDF government came to power in 1990 on a nationalistic programme. Although only its extreme right wing seriously entertained revanchist dreams, the government committed itself to the task of representing 'all the Hungarians'. In media terms, this meant that they established a satellite channel, Duna TV, owned by a semi-private foundation but financed initially out of the revenues withheld as a subsidy from MTV. This was devoted to the provision of genuinely Hungarian programming for those ethnic Hungarians living outside the state borders.

The fact that state boundaries and ethnic divisions almost nowhere coincide necessarily means that issues such as these are insoluble in media terms. At the horrendous extreme, they have been resolved by the barbarities of 'ethnic cleansing', and the mass media have played a supporting role in these atrocities, too. This has not only been through tight government political control of the news agenda, as most obviously in Croatia and Serbia, but also through other forms of programming. Even in peaceful and relatively democratic Slovenia, nationalist governments have attempted to encourage television programming reflecting their own version of national identity (Basic-Hrvatin, 1994).

Another set of problems returns us to our central theme of the relationship between democratization and the operations of the market and is best illustrated by the example of the cinema. Many communist countries sustained national cinemas during the period before 1989 (Macek, 1994). These were entirely dependent upon state protection and patronage. They remained much more important in cultural and political life than has the cinema in the West and were the site both of government propaganda and of some of the most famous statements of the opposition. The end of communism and of the cultural subsidies has meant that films have to survive on the market, and in these countries the film market is as dominated by Hollywood productions as it is almost anywhere else in the West. Bulgaria and Romania are two cases in point (Lazarova, 1994; Solomon, 1994). These states face a very obvious choice: either they allow the collapse of their national film industries or they find some way of subsidizing them and protecting them from market forces.

The dilemma is repeated in rather different form in the case of television. One of the results of integrating into the world economy should be the removal of barriers both to the ownership of television channels and to the trade in television programmes. In practice, most of the governments of post-communist countries have fought shy of adopting the extreme free market solutions in these matters. While there has been a growth in imported programming even on the state owned channels, and a redirection of sourcing away from the former communist countries towards the USA, there remain restrictions. Many of the Broadcasting Acts carry specifications about the national composition of the ownership of companies which may hold broadcasting licences, both in terms of their capital and of their directors. In addition, most carry prescriptions about the amount of programming on any channel which may be of foreign origin.

One instance where neither of these restrictions apply is the Czech Republic. The Broadcasting Act is silent both on foreign ownership and on specific programme commitments. However, the actual licence to broadcast issued to the first private terrestrial franchisee contains a detailed appendix which specifies a number of things, including a breakdown of the kinds of Czech produced programmes which must be broadcast and a timetable for achieving these quotas.

In the event, Nova TV has built up a large share of the audience by importing

Western series. There is evidence, however, that as in other countries, audiences would prefer national production provided it is of the same quality as the imports. The dilemma is thus obvious. Despite what the laws and regulations may say, the most commercially effective way to secure high quality programmes in a small country is to buy them on the world market and, for a struggling new channel, this is an extremely attractive option. On the other hand, the regulatory framework, the ideology of nationalism, and what is known of audience tastes point towards attempting to produce local programmes of high quality. Integration into the world market and a response to popular tastes point in different directions.

CONCLUSIONS

We may summarize the main conclusions of this chapter very briefly. The first is that the media systems of Central and Eastern Europe displayed considerable variety in their nature by the end of the 1980s. The second is that those theories which best explain change in the media systems of formerly communist countries are those which stress the elements of social continuity in the ruling class and its institutions. The theories which claim to detect some apocalyptic final point in the events of 1989 are unable to produce convincing evidence in their support.

Third, the idea of constructing civil society as the road to democratization proved definitely false. The more 'idealistic' versions of this theory provide no purchase upon what happened in the construction of the new systems. The 'materialistic' version of the theory fares better in that, in identifying civil society with market capitalism, it did indeed describe the tendency of development, but it failed in arguing that this would be necessarily accompanied by democratic life.

The fourth conclusion is that the necessary condition for public service broadcasting is not a set of institutional arrangements but the existence of a certain kind of political culture. The main political forces and the broadcasters need to share at least some fundamental values and to agree between themselves that broadcasting shall maintain a distance from direct political pressure so long as it behaves responsibly. This political culture is fragile and only met with relatively rarely, even in advanced and stable bourgeois democracies and was absent in the formerly communist countries.

The fifth conclusion is that the use of broadcasting to help construct a national identity is extremely difficult to realize in a free market situation. The kinds of films and TV programmes central to the articulation of a living culture tend to be expensive and in a poor broadcasting environment there will be considerable pressure to substitute imports for indigenous production. Unless there is some kind of political restriction upon this tendency to substitution, then it will tend to erode national production.

We may now consider some of the leading issues in the next five years. The first, and most obvious of these, is that the national question will remain important. Attempts to use the mass media for constructing national versions of reality and national cultures will continue to be an issue.

114

The other leading theme is likely to be the working out of the logic of marketization. In the press, this has already meant a reduction in the number of titles from the high points achieved in the aftermath of 1989 and this trend will continue. At the same time, there is likely to be greater penetration of the market by foreign owners as the shift towards an advertising dominated model continues. The same trends are likely to mean that, in the daily newspaper market, there is the same tendency towards the reduction in the range of titles, concentration of ownership and market stratification which is observable in the developed capitalist economies.

In considering these future questions, we are clearly already discussing matters familiar from western European experience. It seems likely therefore that it will make decreasing sense to consider the former communist countries as a special category distinct from other European examples. Certainly, the analogy with Italy has already frequently been drawn in discussions of the future of these media systems.

To conclude by addressing once again our main theme of democratization, we must certainly note that the period has been marked by some very considerable advances in most of the countries under consideration. Nowhere, however, has there been a plain and simple transition from evil totalitarian communism to perfect liberal democracy.

In even the best cases, like Slovenia and the Czech Republic, the new political elite has made vigorous efforts to ensure that as much of the media as possible represent channels of communication through which they address the populace. Those parts of the media system which they do not control are in the grip of the market, which is swiftly manifesting those limitations characteristic of its mature stages.

Any contemporary democratic system is in large measure constituted in and through the structure of its media system. These societies are therefore still very far from complete democracies. In an even clearer form than many Western societies, they remain trapped in the polarities of, on the one hand, political manipulation of information and opinion, and on the other hand, the commercial manipulation of information and opinion.

That this situation is superior as a democratic form to the iron control of all media by a single central power, as was characteristic of the high period of Stalinism, is beyond question. The clashes and splits present in the emerging systems permit much greater space for the formation of independent opinion and for the information upon which it necessarily depends. This, indeed, is the situation which prevails in even the most advanced of the actually existing democracies and it is certainly a real gain and achievement for the mass of the population.

That, however, is not the central question. The people of former communist countries, just like the people of the West, deserve something a little better than the partial democracy that their media systems currently allow them. In that light, the short and marginal experience of the collapse of the DDR represents a tragically lost opportunity. There was, briefly, a period in which the media were independent of the tyranny of politicians and the tyranny of capital. Such glimpses of the potential of freedom should be an inspiration to all democrats.

PRIMARY SOURCES

This list of titles is organized under a series of main headings. I have listed only works available in published editions. This means that some of the more interesting material, including some of those titles cited in this chapter, which appeared only as conference papers, have been omitted since it would be rather difficult for the non-expert reader to gain access to them.

General theories of transition

Bauman, Zygmunt (1992) *Intimations of Postmodernity*, London: Routledge. Argues that Communism constituted an extreme version of a more general modernist project. This sought to plan nature and society in order to eliminate chance and disorder. The collapse of communism is the collapse of the modern project. In the postmodern world we have to come to terms with contingency.

Callinicos, Alexander (1991) *The Revenge of History*, Cambridge: Polity. A prominent philosopher and leading Marxist activist argues that the communist societies were ruled by a bureaucracy which constituted a state capitalist ruling class. The collapse of communism was due to their inability to compete internationally with Western, and particularly US capitalism, in the economic struggle to develop new weapons. One conclusion of this argument is that a left alternative to capitalism remains thinkable.

Fukuyama, Francis (1992) *The End of History and the Last Man*, London: Penguin. A reading of Hegel's *Phenomenology of Mind* by a US foreign policy expert, in which the ability to risk death in the struggle for 'recognition' is taken as the defining characteristic of the true human being. In this light: 'the major historical phenomena of the last several centuries – religion, nationalism, democracy – can be understood in their essence as different manifestations of the struggle for recognition'. Liberal democracy best satisfies this need. With the end of communism, it is no longer possible even to imagine a different and better world than that of liberal capitalism.

Miliband, Ralph (1991) 'What comes after communist regimes?', in Ralph Miliband and Leo Panitch (eds) *Communist Regimes: the Aftermath. Socialist Register 1991*, London: Merlin, 375–89. A distinguished and representative figure of the non-Stalinist left argued that despite its monstrous dictatorial political system, communism issued out of genuine popular struggles and embodied an economic vision which was superior to capitalism in its human consequences. The end of communism means that the shortcomings of capitalism will be introduced into a region in which it is very likely that it will not deliver even the promised degree of political freedom and democracy.

Schöpflin, George (1993) *Politics in Eastern Europe*, Oxford: Basil Blackwell. An attempt by a leading academic expert on the region at an analytic account of the rise and fall of the communist regimes in eastern Europe. The last half of the book deals with the decline and collapse of communism and 'The condition of post-communism'.

Schöpflin, George (1995) 'Post-communism: a Profile', in *Javnost/The Public* (1): 63–74. Argues that the period of transition is over but that the construction of genuine democracy will take a long time. Identifies the main obstacle as lying in those untouched even by communist modernization.

Telos Staff (1991) 'Populism versus the new class', *Telos 88* (Summer): 2–36. The editorial staff of a famous critical journal, now moving to the right, argue that the master contradiction in all contemporary societies is between the class of experts and the people.

Communism was one extreme version of this. Its collapse will not remove the basic contradiction, but may make it more complicated. At worst it will lead to chaos.

The dying days of the communist media

Hanke, Helmut (1990) 'Media culture in the GDR: characteristics, processes and problems', *Media, Culture and Society* 12(2), 175–94.

Jakubowicz, Karol (1989) 'The media: political and economic dimensions of television programme exchange between Poland and Western Europe', in Jorg Becker and Tamas Szecskö (eds) *Europe Speaks to Europe*, Oxford: Pergamon, 147–65. Details changes in the import strategy of Polish television during the 1980s.

Jakubowicz, Karol (1991) 'Musical chairs? The three public spheres in Poland', in Peter Dahlgren and Colin Sparks (eds) *Communication and Citizenship*, London: Routledge, 155–72. Written in 1989, this article argues that in the last period of communism there were three partly-overlapping 'public spheres' in Poland. One was the official media. Another the Catholic media. The third was the Solidarity media.

Jakubowicz, Karol (1993) 'Stuck in a groove: why the 1960s approach to communication democratization will no longer do', in Slavko Splichal and Janet Wasko (eds) *Communication and Democracy*, Norwood, New Jersey: Ablex, 33–54. Written before the collapse of communism, this article argues for a change of focus from what it calls 'direct communicative democracy' to the more modest goals of what it terms 'representative communicative democracy'. A clear statement by a prominent Polish theorist of the retreat by the opposition from the proposals for radical democracy advanced earlier in the decade.

Splichal, Slavko, Hochheimer, John and Jakubowicz, Karol (eds) (1990) *Democratization and the Media: an East–West Dialogue*, Ljubljana: Culture and Communication Colloquia. Papers from a conference held on the very eve of the collapse of communism (and partly financed by Fininvest). Contains a number of papers about the collapsing media systems of the region.

Szekfü, A. (1989) 'Intruders welcome? The beginnings of satellite television in Hungary', *European Journal of Communication*, 2:161–71. An account of the relatively liberal response of the Hungarian authorities to the impact of foreign television signals.

The idea of civil society

Arato, Andrew (1994) 'The rise, decline and reconstruction of the concept of civil society, and directions for future research', *Javnost/The Public*, 1(1–2): 1–2. 45–53. A review of the fate of the concept of civil society by one of its main proponents. Argues that the concept proved inadequate in itself but nevertheless forms part of the necessary apparatus for the construction of democratic society.

Cohen, Jean and Arato, Andrew (1992) *Civil Society and Political Theory*, Cambridge, MA: Massachusetts Institute of Technology. Two of the leading international theorists' extensive attempt to construct an 'idealist' version of civil society, defined as 'a sphere of social interaction between economy and state, composed above all of the intimate sphere (especially the family), the sphere of associations (especially voluntary associations), social movements, and forms of public communication' (p.ix).

Dienstbier, J. (1988) Contribution to Benda, V., Simecka, M, Jirous, I.M., Dienstbier, J. Havel, V., Hejdanek, L. and Simsa, J. (1988) 'Parallel polis, or an independent society in central and eastern Europe: an enquiry', *Social Research* 55(1–2): 211–46. A leading Czechoslovak dissident, and later foreign minister in a free market government, argues for the 'poetic' version of civil society in which it consists simply of positive and democratic activities, largely of a cultural nature, undertaken by voluntary cooperation between citizens.

Keane, John (1988) *Democracy and Civil Society*, London: Verso. A collection of theoretical essays on civil society by a leading political theorist closely associated with the opposition in central Europe. The argument wavers between the 'idealistic' and 'poetic' conceptions of civil society.

Keane, John, (ed.) (1988) *Civil Society and the State*, London: Verso. A collection of essays, some by Havel and other then-dissidents, which argue for either the 'idealistic' or the 'poetic' versions of civil society.

Post-communist media

Boyle, Maryellen (1994) 'Building a communicative democracy; the birth and death of citizen politics in East Germany', *Media, Culture and Society* 16(2): 183–216. The most readily available account of the collapse of the DDR and the attempts at constructing a new and democratic media system. Argues that these were crushed by the CDU-led imposition of western German structures and politics.

Dennis, Everett K. and Van den Heuvel, John (1990) *Emerging Voices: East European Media in Transition: a Gannett Foundation Report*, New York: Gannett Foundation Media Centre (now called 'Freedom Forum'). A semi-journalistic report on developments in the immediate post-communist period, stressing free market development potential.

Dougan, Diana Lady (1990) *Eastern Europe, Please Stand By. Report of the Task Force on Telecommunications and Broadcasting in Eastern Europe*, Washington, DC: US Department of State. An early report on changes in the region. What eastern Europe is standing by for is, according to the author, economic missionaries from the USA.

Fliess, M. (ed.) (1994) *Looking to the Future: a Survey of Journalism Education in Central and Eastern Europe and the Former Soviet Union*, Arlington, Virginia: Freedom Forum. A survey by US experts of the condition of journalism education, and some information about the media systems, in 17 formerly communist countries. Also contains 8 short essays by experts from those countries.

Giorgi, Liana, (1995) *The Post-Socialist Media: What Power the West?*, Aldershot, UK: Avebury. A report of a research project which gathered much useful information on developments in the media, particularly the printed press. The case studies of the Hungarian local media are particularly interesting.

Goban-Klas, Tomasz (1994) *The Orchestration of the Media: the Politics of Mass Communication in Communist Poland and the Aftermath*, Boulder, CO: Westview. Contains a detailed account of the media in Poland from the start of the communist epoch to the date of publication. Records the shifting nature of the media in communist Poland and the problems of the transition.

Goban-Klas, Tomasz (1990) 'Making media policy in Poland', *Journal of Communication* (4): 50–5. A detailed account of the negotiations surrounding the transfer of power in the mass media in Poland.

Hankiss, Elemer (1994) 'The Hungarian media's war of independence' *Media, Culture and Society* 16(2): 293–312. The text of a Stevenson Lecture, delivered in the University of Glasgow in 1992. An account by the former head of MTV of the struggle between the MDF government and the broadcasters over the political independence of radio and television.

Høyer, Svennik, Lauk, Epp and Vilhalemm, Peeter (eds) (1993) *Towards a Civic Society: the Baltic Media's Long Road to Freedom. Perspectives on History, Ethnicity and Journalism*, Tartu: Baltic Association for Media Research. An historical account of the development of the mass media in the Baltic Republics from the earliest days to post-communism. Has a very strong emphasis on the role of the media in establishing ethnic and national identity.

Jakubowicz, Karol (1995) 'Lovebirds? The media, the state and politics in central and eastern Europe', *Javnost/The Public*, 2(1): 75–94. Discusses changes in the nature of the post-communist media throughout the region in the light of Brzezinski's 3-stage, 15-year, programme for the emergence of democracy.

Kleinwächter, Wolfgang (ed.) (1993a) *Broadcasting in Transition: the Changing Legal Framework in the Eastern Part of Europe*, Netcom Papers, 3, Leipzig: Netcom. A collection of essays by experts from the region covering the events of the transition and the legal arrangements emerging in the first years of post-communism.

Kleinwächter, Wolfgang (ed.) (1993b) *Broadcasting Bills in the Eastern Part of Europe*, Netcom Papers, 4, Leipzig: Netcom. A collection of extracts from the broadcasting laws and draft bills of nine countries in the region.

Manaev, Oleg and Priyliuk, Yuri (eds) (1993) *Media in Transition from Totalitarianism to Democracy*, Minsk: Abris. A collection of essays by both Eastern and Western experts on different aspects of democratization. Includes clear statements by the editors of the case for free market media.

Prevratil, R. (1993) *Communication in the Transition to Democracy: Eastern Europe*, London: World Association for Christian Communication. A report of one part of a study comparing the process of democratization process in eastern Europe and in Latin America.

Reading, Anna (1995) 'The presidents' men: television, gender and the public sphere in central and eastern europe', in Farrel Corcoran, and Paschal Preston (eds) *Democracy and Communication in the New Europe*, Cresskill, NJ: Hampton, 175–94. Written from a feminist perspective, this paper demonstrates that the changes following 1989 did nothing to improve the subordinate position of women in television.

Reading, Anna (1994) 'The people v. the king – Polish broadcasting legislation', *Media Law and Practice* 15(1): 7–12. Records the retreat from ideas of a radical extension of the right to communicate in the thinking of the Polish opposition about the mass media.

Sparks, Colin and Reading, Anna (1994) 'Understanding media change in East Central Europe' *Media, Culture and Society* 16(2): 243–70. Present a typology of change in East Central Europe and argues that the evidence suggests that theories which stress the degree of continuity have greater empirical support than those which emphasize rupture.

Splichal, Slavko (1994) *Media Beyond Socialism: Theory and Practice in East-Central Europe*, Boulder, CO: Westview. Reviews both theoretical debates and practical developments in the region. Concludes that the media are still in the phase of 'antisocialism' but that: 'the connection between the media and polity remains very close and similar to that experienced during socialism'.

Splichal, Slavko and Kovats, Ildiko (1993) *Media in Transition: an East–West Dialogue*, Budapest–Ljubljana: Eotvos Lorand University Research Group for Communication Studies. Contains a series of essays issuing from a conference which attempted to compare aspects of media change in Western and Eastern Europe.

REFERENCES

Arato, A. and Cohen, J. (1990) *Civil Society and Political Theory*, Cambridge, MA: MIT Press.

Basic-Hrvatin, S. (1994) 'Television and national/public memory', paper presented to the European Film and Television Studies Conference, London, July.

Bauman, Zygmunt (1992) *Intimations of Postmodernity*, London: Routledge.

Benda V., Simecka, M, Jirous, I.M., Dienstbier, J. Havel, V., Hejdanek, L. and Simsa, J. (1988) 'Parallel polis, or an independent society in central and eastern europe: an enquiry', *Social Research* 55(1–2): 211–46.

Bobbio, N. (1989) *Democracy and Dictatorship*, Cambridge: Polity.

Boyle, M. (1994) 'Building a communicative democracy; the birth and death of citizen politics in East Germany', *Media, Culture and Society* 16(2): 183–216.

Callinicos, A. (1991) *The Revenge of History*, Cambridge: Polity.

Cunningham, J. (1994) 'The "media war" in Hungary', paper presented to the European Film and Television Studies Conference, London, July 1994.

Dennis, E. K. and Van den Heuvel, J. (1990) *Emerging Voices: East European Media in Transition: a Gannett Foundation Report*, New York: Gannett Foundation Media Centre (now called 'Freedom Forum').

Dougan, D.L. (1990) *Eastern Europe, Please Stand By. Report of the Task Force on Telecommunications and Broadcasting in Eastern Europe*, Washington, DC: US Department of State.

Fedorowicz, H. (1990) 'Civil society as a communication project: the polish laboratory for democratization in east central europe', in S. Splichal, J. Hochheimer, and K. Jakubowicz (eds) *Democratization and the Media: an East–West Dialogue*, Ljubljana: Culture and Communication Colloquia, 73–87.

Fukuyama, F. (1992) *The End of History and the Last Man*, London: Penguin.

Gálik, M. (1995). 'Who's afraid of the press market? The case of Hungary', paper presented to the Political Research Section of the IAMCR Conference, Portoroz, Slovenia, 27–30 June.

Giorgi, L. (1995) *The Post-Socialist Media: What Power the West?*, Aldershot, UK: Avebury.

Goban-Klas, T. (1994) *The Orchestration of the Media: the Politics of Mass Communication in Communist Poland and the Aftermath*, Boulder, CO: Westview.

Gross, P. (1990) 'The Soviet communist press theory – Romanian style', in S. Splichal, J. Hochheimer and K. Jakubowicz (eds) *Democratization and the Media: an East–West Dialogue*, Ljubljana: Culture and Communication Colloquia, 94–107.

Hanke, H. (1990) 'Media culture in the GDR: characteristics, processes and problems', *Media, Culture and Society*, 12(2): 175–94.

Hobsbawm, E. (1994) *The Age of Extremes: the Short Twentieth Century*, London: Michael Joseph.

Høyer, S., Lauk, E. and Vilhalemm, P. (eds) (1993) *Towards a Civic Society: the Baltic Media's Long Road to Freedom. Perspectives on History, Ethnicity and Journalism*, Tartu: Baltic Association for Media Research.

Huang, Y. (1994) 'Peaceful evolution: the case of television reform in post-Mao China', *Media, Culture and Society* 16(2): 217–42.

Iordanova, D. (1995) 'Bulgaria. Provisional rules and directional changes: restructuring of national TV', *Javnost/The Public* 2(3) 19–32.

Jakubowicz, K. (1989) 'The media: political and economic dimensions of programme exchange between Poland and western Europe', in J. Becker, and T. Szecskö (eds) *Europe Speaks to Europe*, Oxford: Pergamon, 147–65.

Jakubowicz, K. (1990) 'Between communism and post-communism: how many varieties of Glasnost?', in S. Splichal, J. Hochheimer, and K. Jakubowicz (eds) *Democratization and the Media: an East–West Dialogue*, Ljubljana: Culture and Communication Colloquia, 40–55.

Jakubowicz, K. (1991) 'Musical chairs? The three public spheres in Poland', in P. Dahlgren and C. Sparks (eds) *Communication and Citizenship*, London: Routledge, 155–72.

Jakubowicz, K. (1994) 'Partnership or domination in European communication?', in *The Mass Media in Central and Eastern Europe: Democratization and European Integration*, Warsaw: National Broadcasting Council. Proceedings of a conference organized under the auspices of the Secretary-General of the Council of Europe, Jadswin, Poland, 2–5 July, 27–41.

Keane, J. (1991) *The Media and Democracy*, Cambridge: Polity.

Kilborn, R. (1993) 'Towards Utopia – or another Anschluss? East Germany's transition to a new media system', *European Journal of Communication* 8: 451–70.

Kleinwächter, W. (1993) *Broadcasting Bills in the Eastern Part of Europe*, Netcom Papers, 4, Leipzig: Netcom.

Kowalski, T. (1988) 'Evolution after revolution: the Polish press system in transition', *Media, Culture and Society* 10(2): 183–96.

Lazarova, S. (1994) 'The problems of film production in the new market economy', paper presented to the European Film and Television Studies Conference, London, July.

Macek, V. (1994) 'Looking for the Slovak film industry', paper presented to the European Film and Television Studies Conference, London, July.

McNair, B. (1994) 'Television in post-Soviet Russia: from Monolith to Mafia', paper presented to the European Film and Television Studies Conference, London, July.

Manaev, O. (1993) 'Mass media in the political and economic system of transition society', in O. Manaev, and Y. Priyliuk (eds) *Media in Transition from Totalitarianism to Democracy*, Minsk: Abris.

Marinescu, V. (1995) 'Romania: private versus state television', *Javnost/The Public*, 2(3): 81–95.

Meiksins Wood, E. (1990) 'The uses and abuses of "Civil Society"', in R. Miliband and L. Panitch (eds) *The Retreat of the Intellectuals. Socialist Register 1990*, London: Merlin, 60–84.

Miliband, R. (1991) 'What comes after communist regimes?', in R. Miliband and L. Panitch, (eds) *Communist Regimes: the Aftermath. Socialist Register 1991*, London: Merlin, 375–89.

Mrozowski, M. (1990) 'Television in Poland', *Media, Culture and Society* 12(2): 213–30.

Ost, D. (1989) 'The transformation of Solidarity and the future of central Europe', *Telos* 79 (spring): 69–94.

Piccone, P. (1990) 'Paradoxes of perestroika', *Telos* 84 (summer): 3–32.

Raycheva, L. (1995) 'Bulgarian mass media in transition (1988–1994)', paper presented to the IAMCR Conference, Portoroz, Slovenia, 27–30 June.

Reading, A. (1994) 'The people v. the king – Polish broadcasting legislation', *Media Law and Practice* 15(1): 7–12.

Schöpflin, G. (1993) *Politics in Eastern Europe*, Oxford: Basil Blackwell.

Smid, M. (1992) 'Television after the velvet revolution', paper presented to the Symposium, Restructuring television in east–central Europe, University of Westminster, 4–5 July.

Solomon, A. (1994) 'A blurry portrait of the Romanian film-maker', paper presented to the European Film and Television Studies Conference, London, July.

Sparks, C. and Reading, A. (1994) 'Understanding media change in east central Europe', *Media, Culture and Society* 16(2): 243–70.

Spindler-Brown, A. (1994) 'Post-communist television in transition', paper presented to the European Film and Television Studies Conference, London, July.

Splichal, S. (1993) 'Post-socialism and the media: what kind of transition?', in S. Splichal and I. Kovats, *Media in Transition: an East–West Dialogue*, Budapest–Ljubljana: Eotvos Lorand University Research Group for Communication Studies.

Splichal, Slavko (1994) *Media Beyond Socialism: Theory and Practice in East-Central Europe*, Boulder, CO: Westview.

Telos Staff (1991) 'Populism versus the new class', *Telos 88* summer: 2–36.

Thompson, M. (1994) *Forging War: the Media in Serbia, Croatia and Bosnia–Herzogovina*, London: Article 19.

Webster, D. (1994) 'New broadcasting legislation in central and eastern Europe', in *The Mass Media in Central and Eastern Europe: Democratization and European Integration*, Warsaw: National Broadcasting Council. Proceedings of a conference organized under the auspices of the Secretary-General of the Council of Europe, Jadswin, Poland, 2–5 July, 77–81.

Zernetskaya, O. (1994) 'Democracy and television in the Ukraine', paper presented to the European Film and Television Studies Conference, London, July.

Zolo, D. (1992) *Democracy and Complexity*, Cambridge: Polity.

6

ISSUES AND ASSUMPTIONS IN COMMUNICATIONS POLICY AND RESEARCH IN WESTERN EUROPE: A CRITICAL ANALYSIS

Jean-Claude Burgelman

INTRODUCTION

Broadcasting and telecommunications policies in Western Europe have leap-frogged into the age of high technology and deregulation since the mid-1980s. As a result, their industrial strategies and policy goals have been gradually merging. At the same time media policy research in Western Europe has not kept up with the searing pace of industry. It remains heavily concentrated on broadcasting or national aspects of communication policy.

Indeed it is evident that until the EU presented its plans for a common market in broadcasting and telecommunications, European media policy research as such did not even exist. At the most one could speak of a common intellectual approach in different countries, often based on diverging national interests, to media policy problems. This does not mean, however, that European media policy research has no specific problems to deal with or that these are not intellectually worthy of consideration. On the contrary. There is a 'Euro-specificity' in media policy, though this is mainly due to the existence of the EU as a 'supranational state' and not to some inherent characteristics which European media or telecommunications services might have.

When studying European problems, of course, one has to bear in mind that the EU is the product of an imposed integration process on what has been until recently, and for many hundred of years, competing, isolated and very hetero-geneous regional entities and/or states. There has never been an organic link between, say, Denmark and Portugal. The EU, in its present form, is thus an entirely heterogeneous entity of 13 different cultures in which the German, French and British markets are, by their sheer size, dominant. EU voting power, however, is structured so that even the smallest member states can have important leverage in any policy debate; and this somewhat offsets the economic and political clout of the big member states. In other words, there is no real pan-European democracy at work in Europe, though the powers of the EU, once there is agreement, are very large ('Brussels decides . . .'). This is particularly true since, as a result of the recession of the 1970s, from 1 January 1996 onwards, it was decided to integrate all these nations into one market in which goods, persons and services could move freely. From then on, the dominant discourse in European policy-making has been the credo to do whatever is necessary to create one market. This affects telecommunications and broadcasting in particular as has been reflected in the importance given to these two sectors in the landmark document the EU published with regard to its overall economic and industrial policy (White Paper, 1993). Before that, the Green Papers on television (1984) and on telecommunications (1987) had already changed the European communication policy landscape. Both Green Papers have the same basic message: communication is a good/service and should therefore move, be sold and be purchased freely within the EU.

These three elements – heterogeneous unification, one free market and the superimposition of a supranational authority – generate the specific problems media policy in Europe has to deal with. More precisely, they shape the way world-wide trends such as deregulation, liberalization, globalization, internationalization and integration take the specific form they do in Europe (Dyson and Humphreys, 1990).

The first sections of this chapter will review these trends in European broadcasting and telecommunications. Given the inevitable restrictions on length, the section on telecommunications will be dealt with in the context of the plans to build the European Information Highway (EIH).

It will be shown that, though they are separate empirical realities and though they respond to distinct internal dynamics,[1] both sectors have changed dramatic-ally over a very short period of time. This is due to more or less the same factors: technological innovation making new ways of delivering communication content possible; new user needs as a result of a changing macro-economic climate (post-Fordism and globalization as a result of hyper-capitalism) linked with a changing consumer culture (with an individualizing and 'pay-per' logic) and finally a neo-conservative or ultra-liberal climate of policy-making which is reinforced by a new ideology of super-individualism and postmodernism. These factors have certainly changed the monopolistic broadcasting and telecommunications scene which characterized Europe until the early 1980s.[2]

Both sections of this chapter will pay particular attention to the assumptions of EU policy and research in this field. What will be analysed is how the (utopian) discourse on European integration contradicts the oligopolistic reality of the market (assuming it to be pluralistic); the overstated and overrated demands of the user/consumer/viewer (assuming explosive demand for new services) and the conflicting agendas of different national state politics (assuming them to be common).

What will become clear from this analysis is that there are not only a substantial number of common presuppositions operating within research and policy-making (e.g. the so called dominance of American television products on the European market) but also that some strikingly similar points of theoretical concern can be detected in both domains: for example the question of public or universal service as a valuable regulatory concept; the simplistic use of the categories 'market' and 'state' as regulatory paradigms in policy debates; the degree of autonomy or dominance attributed to the viewer or user; and the dilemma between local and global in communication policy-making.

The theoretical ambition of this chapter is, given this starting point, to make an argument in favour of 'scientific convergence' in communication policy research. However, in order to do that, research in both domains must avoid – and this will be a theme throughout the chapter – two basic pitfalls: on the one hand, manicheistic thinking and a-historicity with regard to regulatory models; and on the other hand technology-driven assumptions as well as post modernist assumptions relating to user demands.

But, as will be discussed in the final section, avoiding these pitfalls is more a question of vision than science.

One last remark. It is impossible to pay attention to all the relevant aspects of policy since the mid-1980s and to mention all the European researchers and research schools working on the issues. Not only is there insufficient space for such comprehensiveness, but language barriers and the Franco- British dominance of the publication field, make it difficult to give a truly representative overview.[3] Just as there is still no single market for communication, there is a very high degree of 'relative isolationism' in European communication research too and common fora for policy research almost do not exist.[4]

TRENDS AND ISSUES IN WEST EUROPEAN MEDIA POLICY: BROADCASTING

Two obvious trends and related issues come to the forefront when studying the developments in European broadcasting since the early 1980s (Charon, 1991; Collins, Garnham and Locksley, 1988; Euromedia Group, 1992; Garnham, 1990a; Kayzer, 1993; McQuail 1990 and 1991; Pauwels, 1995; Sánchez-Tabernero, 1993; Siune and Treutzschler, 1992). On the one hand, since the early 1980s, one can point to the completely changed nature of the European audiovisual landscape and related policy thinking. On the other hand, one can also point to the problematic position of European public service broadcasting organizations, who no longer enjoy their quasi-monopolistic position and hence the dominance of the field which they have enjoyed for more than fifty years

The changed nature of European broadcasting

If one thing is clear from all the changes that have taken place in broadcasting, it is the industrialization of a sector which until the 1980s had largely been dominated by a non-industrial logic. From the 1980s onwards European capital-ism, witnessing the decline of traditional economic sectors, discovered the service sector and started to buy itself into, from its beginnings in the 1920s, what had been mainly a state-controlled sector in which a cultural discourse on high quality and educational needs dominated. This has had dramatic consequences during the last two decades and has meshed perfectly well together with the EU's Green Paper on television of 1984 and subsequent measures that "freed" television from its national boundaries (see Collins, 1994). From this point on, television was mainly looked upon as a product operating in a market, and EU policy mainly concentrated, then as now, on removing the barriers that hindered competition in this field.

This increasingly dominant approach to policy is based on an assumption that broadcasting can be regulated as well as any other economic good and that audience ratings are the best and most reliable indicators of the public's taste and cultural preferences. This assumption is more than sufficiently challenged by political economy (for a stringent analysis, see Garnham, 1994a) and audience research in which it has been noted that one can only speak of homogeneous markets in broadcasting when the cultural proximity of the audiences is extremely close. There is indeed very little common ground between a Spanish audience and a Scandinavian one. And this again underlines the fundamental friction between the policy of a united 'business-Europe' and the continuing constraints of cultural specificity. Ironically the EU itself used these arguments to defend its position during GATT talks. Here the EU tried to take broadcasting out of the GATT discussions and argued that broadcasting has values other than those of a tradeable object. Therefore the EU could not open its markets to the US because, it was argued, the EU, unlike the US, had no unified market.

Internally speaking, however, the EU stands for maximum liberalization and competition. This has resulted in all kinds of vertical and horizontal integration movements in the European broadcasting industry, in the formation of pan-European groups, in the oligopolization of the broadcasting market in Europe and in the transnationalization – economically as well as politically – of the power relations in the European audiovisual sector. Thus a withering away of the nation-state as a politico-geographical entity in which the audiovisual is organized can be observed across Europe.

On the programming side, this has resulted in an explosion of channels, even though very few are truly pan-European. There are now some 96 nationally based channels and 12 pan-European, mostly satellite, channels available. No more than 3 or 4 of them can be considered truly pan-European in the sense of covering most of the EU member states. The deregulation in broadcasting in Europe, though legitimated at the beginning (in the early 1980s) by a discourse on the supposed need for the European viewer to look over his borders and to become part of Europe, clearly had its most important impact at the national level.

Sixty per cent of all available channels are commercial, whereas in the early 1980s less than 5 per cent of all channels were commercial, and from 1989 there were more commercial channels than public service ones. Finally, 65 of these channels broadcast in the language of the main European cultures: English (29),

French (24) or German (12). On the level of content this increase in channels has resulted in an explosion in demand for cheap programmes.[5] The European broadcasting industry can only provide one-third of the programmes needed (especially in fiction, the most competitive programme category). Hence the need for the import of entertainment and drama and the roots of one of the most complicated questions of media policy in Western Europe: the so-called dominance of the US and the endangering of the European audiovisual culture and industry (Biltereyst, 1992).

These arguments tend to assume, of course, that European production is better, because it is not American; a position which palpably ignores the fact that most American media groups, and indeed European groups too, are multinationals. According to 1993 figures, only two Hollywood studios retain majority American ownership (Paramount and Walt Disney) whereas US companies are heavily investing in European media groups like Superchannel (NBC) or SBS (ABC). The arguments also raise the question as to what is so specific about European culture, such that it has to be considered as endangered (Garnham, 1993). This is a vital but extremely complex research question since it is difficult to imagine how this can be operationalized. As a result, European research in this area, which by and large dominates the effort of those concerned with European media problems, makes more or less the same mistakes as those observed in the debate on the New World International Information Order, a mistake which resides in the fact that studies of the origin of a programme (in itself an irrelevant indicator as the example on the American programming industry indicated) are used to presuppose its effects on the audience.

Consequently, European research will have to demonstrate what the specific quality of European culture is, recognizing its very complexity and its dependence on the competing interests involved. Judgements of quality in broadcasting too are complex and variable (Mulgan, 1990) depending as they do on assumptions about the nature of the audience (consumers versus citizens), broadcasting (being a commercial good or not) and the relationship between broadcasting and society. This difficulty explains why the specificity and the quality of the European audiovisual space tends to be defined, in the end, by audience reach; or alternatively side-stepped, in the more postmodern approaches, as irrelevant. In the latter approach quality is what the viewer makes of it. Nevertheless, if one refuses this reductionist approach (the appeal to audience ratings) or the postmodern escape, it is clear that this question of European identity and subsequently its relationship with national identities, is a vital one. Curiously enough, if one considers the huge amount of flow studies and effect essays, only very few works in media studies are beginning to put this on the agenda (Schlesinger, 1992; Wolton, 1992).

This situation in broadcasting and the debates it has generated has particular relevance for the position of the small countries in Europe (Burgelman and Pauwels, 1992; Pauwels, 1995). All the trends mentioned are much more problematic in these countries because their markets are smaller and their cultures are more hermetic and thus not so easily exportable. There seems to be little interest indeed, for a viewer in the south of Europe in watching Scandinavian soap or, indeed, *vice versa*. It is also always much more difficult to realize a return on investment when a programme is made for an audience of 6 million people, in a language that few understand (and thus needs dubbing, extra promotion, etc., to be exported), than when the same is done for an audience of 50 million. What is seen as a low budget production internationally (2.2. million ECU) is a high budget production in most of the small European countries. Current EU funding that is specifically targeted towards the small countries is barely enough to make ten motion pictures a year. The EU is trapped here by its own philosophy: the promotion of competition and the free market as the ultimate *adagio* for the free movement of goods and services within the community is not compatible with any support, based on cultural interests, of the broadcasting industry.

As a consequence, the import rates in smaller countries are not only much higher than in the larger European ones, but the smaller countries also complain about the fact that they are too dependent on their larger European neighbours as well. This came to a head in the quota debates at the end of the 1980s in which it was suggested that in order to protect the European broadcasting industry each country would have to programme more than 50 per cent of European fiction. The small countries argued that this would oblige them to buy expensively within Europe rather than cheaply in the US. The whole debate resulted in the adoption of some very loose EU recommendations that member states should do their best to broadcast as many European programmes as possible. Indeed, if this problematic position of the smaller European countries does not change, it can be expected that it will only reinforce their negative feelings of being part of a larger unity without being heard and of being forced to accept the dominance of the big nations of the union.

The problematic position of the European public service broadcasting organizations

Everywhere in Europe public service broadcasting institutions, seen in the above context as the most appropriate instruments for public policy to counter these supposedly destructive trends, are facing serious problems of survival (Witte, 1994). There are three reasons.

First, there is constant pressure from big commercial groups, in line with the larger economic movement to 'take away' from the state what is profitable. This has resulted in the break-up of all public broadcasting monopolies in Europe and the explosion of commercial channels at the national level. Second, it can be suggested that many public broadcasters abused their monopoly by, among other things, linking themselves too much to the dominant political powers. As a result, many public service broadcasting institutions lack the political (financial) and popular (audience) support they need today to compete with their commercial opponents. Third, everywhere in Europe a new regulatory philosophy on culture in general is replacing the old post-World War II ones, which are judged to be too paternalistic.

The ensuing postmodern regulatory philosophy can be described in terms of the predominance of consumer culture thinking, which sees audience acceptance of a cultural product as the ultimate and exclusive criterion in policy-making. When applied to the economic reality of broadcasting this implies that it is the size of the audience which dictates and defines the legitimate existence of a programme and, by consequence, of a broadcasting organization. Popularity is thereby equated with quality. Hence the main criterion for regulation today, supported by the EU vision that television is a service like any other, is the ability of a broadcasting institution to be competitive by attracting large audiences.

This puts the European public service broadcasting organizations in a Catch-22 situation. For them, the easiest route to competitiveness can be found in the imitation of commercial strategies (attracting publicity, joint ventures with commercial groups and so on) and commercial programming. In fact, this seems to be the *de facto* strategy of most public broadcasters (Achille and Miège, 1994; Blumler 1992a, 1992b). Audience ratings (and income) will then go up and challenge those of the commercial organizations. But at the same time public service broadcasting institutions will be criticized because they are behaving more or less like commercial organizations. So why then should state or licence funding continue the latter, indeed, being a mechanism for enabling what the market does not provide? And why should the state pay for what is already available for free (on the advertising-based commercial channels)? However, if public service broadcasting could opt for the reverse strategy and generate programming oriented to informational, cultural and educational needs, this would most probably not offer the same high audience figures. Hence, the reasoning goes that since audience rates are too low, there is no need to support public service broadcasting anymore.

This Catch-22 is impossible to resolve as long as broadcasting policy thinking accepts the primacy of audience autonomy and market dynamics. Some authors (Burgelman, 1986; Van Cuilenburg and Slaa, 1993) have tried to escape this by advocating a 'filling the gap strategy' for public broadcasters: public broadcasting institutions have to offer what the market does not, and thus legitimate their non-market funding. In turn, this is criticized for reducing public policy to niche marketing (Garnham, 1994a; Witte, 1994) and that it rests on the assumption that niches instead of masses constitute the organizing principle of broadcasting and society. Audience figures, which suggest that indeed the television market tends to be a mass one and that 'niches' are only marginal phenomena, support this. Other critiques of the 'filling the gap' strategy argue that democracy necessitates an alternative to commercial broadcasting since only a public broadcaster can provide the socially integrative function needed (Missaka and Wolton, 1983; Witte, 1994; Wolton, 1990). It therefore seems impossible to escape a normative debate on (public) broadcasting if one wishes to come to an organizing and operational regulatory framework.

The whole debate on the nature of public service broadcasting as opposed to commercial broadcasting rests indeed on two assumptions (Burgelman, 1990). First it is assumed that public broadcasting, unlike commercial broadcasting, has no inherent operational mechanism that determines its management. Public broadcasting is only a concept. And second, and as a result, it is assumed that a public service exploitation model in broadcasting is indeed a distinct organizational way of running a broadcasting institution.

More precisely, it is accepted that public service broadcasting offers a different output in terms of programming than commercial broadcasting (which is the main reason why a public broadcaster is defended) because public service broadcasting is a different way of organizing communication. Very seldom has this specificity of public service broadcasting been challenged. On the contrary, the specific nature of public service broadcasting is almost accepted as an ontological fact, being there from the beginning. As a result one can almost speak of an ideology of public service broadcasting: 'public service broadcasting was and is superior to commercial broadcasting because it is organized in a non-market way'.

If we pursue this and look at how public broadcasters work in practice, this picture becomes even more problematic. First, flow studies and content analysis demonstrate that in terms of programming practice there is no systematic difference between public and commercial broadcasting. Some public broadcasters offer what is considered typical for a public service model, more in-house drama than imported, more information than commercial stations, but others do not. This suggests that offering different outputs is not an intrinsic result of a distinctive mode of organization of a public broadcasting medium. This has led some critics, when public broadcasting has had a monopoly, to the conclusion that it was as functional to capitalism as commercial broadcasting. Second, if one looks at broadcasting from the point of view of management there is a whole body of research demonstrating that public service broadcasting operates and behaves in the same way as a commercial organization (Burgelman, 1990). In other words, the presupposition that public service broadcasting provides an alternative to commercial programming, because it is organized and managed in a different way, is neither systematic nor universally applicable.

This means that having public service output in broadcasting is not by any means solely dependent on the medium's inherent characteristics. In fact, it may be more related to non-media-specific elements, such as political culture and economic policy.

With respect to contemporary regulatory debates, it follows from this non-media centric point of view that the dominant discourse on communication policy, presented as regulating a communication system in a public service way or deregulating it in a commercial way to fit to a given cultural project, may appear to be a false dilemma. Regulation based on the rationale of a public service model, because of its supposed equation of quality, culture or independence, is not the most important reason why such a system was chosen by the policy-makers.

A non-media centred approach indeed also suggests that a public service can also be defended for its conservative, middle of the road or non-critical characteristics, that is exactly those which would otherwise be seen as distinguishing the market approach. Public service should therefore be regarded as a normative and dynamic set of rules which have to be constantly reviewed and redefined (but not reinvented) in relation to the constantly changing nature of power relations and society.

Building Europe on culture?

One can speculate on the degree with which all these changes in European media and broadcasting policy and, most importantly, in the programming philosophies at work, affect West European society and its citizens. However, the growing and widespread opposition to the idea of an integrated European community, as shown by recent European referendums, the fact that more and more, especially small, countries are questioning the superimposition of a European federal state on national boundaries and that nationalism and cultural particularism have become very fashionable as political movements, are all signs that cultural policy in broadcasting should have higher ideals than offering more of the same. What is indeed needed is a pan-European cultural project emanating from the grass roots (Wolton, 1992). Though more and more critics now perceive this as a necessary condition for a European cohesion, one could point to Jean Monnet, one of the founding fathers of the European Commission, when, at the end of his life and with regard to the difficulties of European integration encountered, he remarked that if he were to start afresh in building the European Community he would no longer start with steel but with culture.

Much more attention, financial as well as political, should go into creating a cultural system in which people recognize themselves as part of their own community, being part of a wider multi-cultural and multi-ethnic European community (Schlesinger, 1992, 1994). It follows that there is a need to promote a culture of diversity, not one of uniformity. Since, unfortunately, this is not how a broadcasting market works, it also follows that the most logical thing to do would be a massive restructuring, directly and indirectly, of European public services. This would in turn necessitate a non-media-centric approach, in which case communication policy becomes a normative choice requiring a certain vision of humanity, of culture and of control far removed from the value freedoms of postmodernism.

TRENDS AND ISSUES IN WEST EUROPEAN MEDIA POLICY: TELECOMMUNICATIONS AND THE EUROPEAN INFORMATION HIGHWAY

From the Green Paper to an information society

The developments and the specific problems in the field of telecommunications are more difficult to put into perspective since the whole area, even without its intrinsic complexity, is constantly evolving.

Moreover, research here has not been predominantly on the agenda of what is institutionally regarded as communication or media studies. In fact it had not been on the research agenda at all until deregulation began to be instituted.[6] Though there is a growing body of, largely interdisciplinary (critical) research (Garbe and Lange, 1991; Hills, 1986; Joosten, 1993; Leyten *et al.*, 1991; Mettler-Meiboom, 1986 and 1987; Garnham, 1990a: 136–53; Kubicek and Rolf, 1986; Kubicek, 1992; Mansell, 1993a; Mulgan, 1991) the amount of independent academic work being done in this area is small. Whether this relative absence of (critical) telecommunication research in Western Europe is related to the dominance during the 1980s of the more accessible debate on television is an open question.

The difficulty of mapping this field is certainly not only linked to constant technological innovations in network technology, compression techniques and changing terminal based or network-based software. In fact, as two fine pieces of recent research demonstrate, it is the interplay between economic restructuring and the specific nature of telecommunications technology, on the one hand (Mansell, 1993a), and the coincident restructuring of the telecommunications sector with a partial restructuring of the Fordist economy, a renewed search for profit maximization in the service sector (as in broadcasting) and the trend to internationalization of the Western economy (see Joosten, 1993), on the other, that complicate things.

Change in this field is also being affected by the delay in taking some of the most important decisions in European telecommunications policy. As long as no full competition is allowed at the network infrastructure level and in basic voice telephony, though both are foreseen for January 1998, full liberalization will not exist. It is therefore more difficult than in the case for broadcasting to give a more or less comprehensive overview of the issues at stake. This is not least because what is being discussed here is the future; most of the benefits policy-makers, industrial groups and other interested actors are predicting, are to a very large degree hypothetical. Though some critics may be too sharp – 'billions of ECU's' spent on all kinds of research into broad band, HDTV and so on, 'and not one single consumer in sight', to quote someone who has been in this field right from the beginning (Garnham, 1994b: 47) – it is certainly the case that even today, after some twenty years of talking about the information revolution, more than 80 per cent of all telecommunications traffic is nothing more than plain old conversations over the phone. This might indicate that the time might have come to start some fundamental questioning of this hype. Why do we need an information society anyhow?

The ambitions of the very extensive EU policies in this field are quite easy to synthesize: full liberalization on all levels (infrastructure, services and applications) is necessary to propel Europe into the information society and create all the assumed benefits associated with it. Recent documents of the EU (White Paper, 1993 and the Bangemann report, 1994),[7] restated the principles underlying EU policy since 1987 when the decision was taken to liberalize telecommunications. Interestingly enough, one does not find many references to the concept of the information society in these first documents of the EU. Their main concern was the abolition of the old public telecommunications operators' monopolies, because in the vision of the EU, and indeed many others, these monopolies were seen as a barrier to the revitalization and competitiveness of the European micro-electronics industry. This argument about the inadequacy and inefficiency of the public telephone monopolies (PTTs) was never questioned but instead linked to a discourse that liberalization would force the whole sector to be more inventive and innovative, and to act in a more consumer oriented way.

However, until now not one single piece of research has operationalized this inefficiency empirically nor compared it with the assumed efficiency of a commercial setting. Even though efficiency is as difficult a concept to measure as is quality, most critiques only concentrate on one or two aspects of the old inefficiencies; like slowness of service and the high prices charged to business users (imposed in order to finance a universal service). What the old monopolies meant for the building up of the economy of a country; for the development of R&D in this sector[8] and through universal service for the standards of living of ordinary people (and thus the general welfare of country) – such issues are most often not considered.

On the other hand, the initial rationale behind the EU's plans in tele-communications also stated that to achieve a competitive EU industry in micro-electronics and related industries, a broad band society was necessary. Hence the setting up of large-scale programmes like RACE (R&D in Advanced Communications Technologies for Europe) which proved to be large-scale failures too, not least because they were too technology driven and underestimated the problems of network investment, of the implications of the development of new compression technologies that could easily deliver the same service as broad-band and of the missing demand for new services (Fuchs, 1992; Joosten, 1994).

The American initiative for an NIIA and the surrounding hype on the information society came just in time for the EU to relaunch its ambitions and to legitimate the billions of ECU spent (and planned to be spent) in this area. Indeed the same arguments are still in play in relation to the European Information Highway: not only will European industry desperately lose the battle with the US unless Europe installs as soon as possible its own version of the information infrastructure; there is an explosion of pressing and unfulfilled demand for new services to be expected and this can only be met when there is a fully competitive market as soon as possible.

From the European information highway to the European information hypeway?[9]

The implementation of the European information highway, as a result of the complex European economic, industrial, social and political context, will have to confront five major problems.

First, it is very likely that a substantial convergence of the European tele-communications and media sector will indeed take place. A pan-Europeanization of the communications industry, with a global outlook and oligopolistic tendencies (Mansell, 1993a), out of which the existing telecommunications operators will appear as amongst the strongest actors looks very likely to emerge (Noam and Kramer, 1994).

Since it is difficult to determine the real cost of both infrastructure and service provision, no single actor will take the risk of being downgraded to carrier status alone[10]. Therefore all potential actors will move into horizontal as well as vertical differentiation. Inevitably telecommunications, cable, software, consumer electronics and content producers will become interlinked. Consequently we can point to the likely emergence of European-wide conglomerates in which the 'rich' telecommunications companies will certainly dominate other possible actors (media industries, software companies, and so on).

Moreover, to be competitive in an environment of service convergence regardless of the nature of the network (cable or telecommunications) and of increasing multi-media applications, a corporate actor must control as much as possible of the different domains of the communications process: production, distribution of both hardware and software (including content). This will again stimulate the formation of pan-European groups and will raise specific questions with regard to legitimating a specific policy on pluralism and diversity.

A second problem area is the likeliness of far-reaching regulatory difficulties with regard to this convergence of broadcasting and telecommunications (Bustamente *et al.* 1993; Garnham and Mulgan, 1991; Slaa and Burgelman, 1994). Broadcasting and telecommunications are indeed two of the main actors which are already merging. As a consequence, the regulatory principles of both actors, based on their mechanisms and patterns of distribution, will no longer be adequate and will need to be re-conceptualized. What is indeed the nature of a telecommunications-delivered medium? Is a porno database delivered by a telecommunications operator subject to the normal rules of media control or to those of telecommunications (where there has been little or no content control)? If a racist party starts a closed-user broadcast channel, can it be held accountable for it or not (as under media law)?

More generally speaking 'how will broadcasting regulation based upon the concept of general public reception and the protection of cultural and political values be reconciled with telecommunication regulations based upon the regulation of message carriage but not content?' (Garnham, 1990b: 11). These are highly complex and yet unanswered questions, especially if one takes into account that, historically, the different nations of Europe, have highly differentiated traditions in the regulations of cultural and economic matters.

So if one wants to regulate, a new definition of these mass media being delivered in a telecommunications way will be needed. Does a medium become a mass medium when it hits potentially more than 1, 2 or more than 20 per cent of the audience? Or is it when it is offered for free? New techniques will also blur the distinction between closed-user television (more typical of telecommunications) and subscription television. What are the implications here? In any case, these examples make it clear that regulatory definitions of mass media will have to be looked for in a non-media-centred way since their physical or technical appearances will no longer be a valid way to classify them.

A third problem area related to building up the EIH is the uncertainty with regard to the demand for new services for which these networks are necessary. In fact, this is a crucial question: is there enough demand for new services and will it be large enough to support the necessary investment? From past experience we can learn that there is no reason at all to believe that in the immediate future a sudden explosion of demand will take place. For example, almost all initiatives so far with interactive television have failed (in the US as well as in Europe); the video-phone was a failure, and segmented pan-European television has – after many years of trial and error – attracted only a very small fraction of the market.

There is also a clear distinction between the adoption process of information media or new telecommunications services *strictu sensu* and more traditional media like broadcasting, whatever the delivery system (Burgelman, 1995). There is no reason to believe that because someone cruises on Internet, he/she will do the same in broadcasting. And especially not since, as mentioned in the previous section, cultural proximity (which includes linguistic proximity) largely determines viewing habits even in a situation of abundance.

Finally, in the context of problematic demand, there is no reason to believe, as the EU does when reflecting on the residential market for new services, that because new communication technologies have changed aspects of our work, people are willing to accept them at home too. As recent research into the adoption and use of communication technologies in the residential sphere clearly indicates, there are completely different rationalities at work with regard to the way people adopt or do not adopt communication technologies in the home or in the office (Jouet, 1993; Silverstone and Hirsch, 1992, Miles, 1988). And moreover there does not exist one typical European home, which means that this element has to be added to the existing heterogeneity and complexity of the European market.[11]

Fourth, radical new communication technologies or practices, that is, those which do not directly replace an existing way of communication, need much more time, social experimentation and careful organizational planning than others (Flichy, 1980,1991). If this is lacking they tend to fail. If one studies, in this respect, two of the most successful initiatives with regard to the information society since the early 1980s (the Internet and Minitel) one will find that they are the product of a strong central commitment, a coordinated and long-term dedicated financial effort (enabling cross-subsidy), a stable regulatory environment to encourage a chosen direction of technological evolution and almost unlimited room for users to experiment with it (free access) to kick the service off. Or to put it differently: to promote Minitel and make it a relative success (it is still mainly used for the substitution of printed telephone directories) France did everything the EU, looking for the most perfect of all markets, considers a barrier to innovation.

A fifth, final and more specific problematic area with regard to the building of the European information highway, is related to the assumption that there is a huge potential demand for new broadcasting services on a pan-European level.

Most policy-makers and actors expect a lot from this because broadcasting is already a market that does exist. Video-on-demand, especially, is often seen as essential and it is hoped that it will provide the locomotive for the trans-European networks – the killer application. From what has been said in the previous sections, a more cautious approach to this explosion should be taken.

First of all, research shows that over the last few years the total amount of television consumption has stabilized in Europe to between three and four hours a day. This implies that whatever new broadcasting services are offered, they will have to replace existing viewing habits. However viewing habits at the present moment are very well established and are pursued at almost no cost to the viewer. This raises the question of why consumers would pay for new broadcasting services given the fact that they already have a range of free choice. Related to this is the question of who is going to finance a segmentation of broadcasting in Europe, given the fact that it took CNN, for example, more than ten years to break even. Indeed, one can ask if there is enough advertising revenue to support a segmented broadcasting system given the fact that the largest television advertisers are of the Procter and Gamble type whose range of consumer goods needs broad and non-segmented audiences.

Some believe that the answer is subscription television. But here too one can ask if the European market is large enough to allow specialized television on a subscriber basis. Or more precisely: is it homogeneous enough? The analogy, in terms of such specialized offers with the written press clearly does not work, since press economics is not at all comparable with broadcasting economies. One has also to bear in mind that the extent of watching cross-border television, essential to allow a segmented pan-European broadcasting offer, is very low in Europe.

Finally, one can ask if the viewer will be able to manage an explosion in the supply of broadcast channels. The answer one reads is that someone will offer the audience a technology to make a choice for them (navigator systems pre-selecting, for example, half an hour of soap, 15 minutes of news, a movie and so on). Although possible, is not this exactly the same as what the general channels already offer?

Building the Euro-information highway on convergent policy-making?

To what degree is the EU capable of handling these policy problems? In short, the answer is that, due to its internal contradictions, present-day EU policy seems handicapped in this regard and that only a convergent approach to policy-making will satisfactorily resolve the issues.

First of all, it will be necessary for the different regulatory worlds and policies of the EU to join. Recalling the analogy with some of the main problems of the earlier RACE programme it seems essential to solve the conflict between the desire of the EU to install fair competition, open the market, abolish monopolies and so on (the ambition of the EU with regard to competition and located in Directorate-General IV) and the need for at least a stable environment with guaranteed revenues to attract the necessary investment in trans-European networks (the ambition of Directorate-General XIII).

This problem is accentuated by the fact that most national authorities think in the first place of promoting and defending, by any means, the interests of their own telecommunications operator instead of thinking and acting 'European'. Hence there is a constant tension between them and the EU (Hulsink, 1994; Mansell, 1993a). They do this by trying to hold their respective monopolies as long as possible or, which is just another way of keeping their market as close as possible, by cartellization at the national level and window-dressing with regard to liberalization. Small nations, especially, or the so called 'less-favoured regions' having, just as in broadcasting, a smaller market to build on, seem to be less inclined to follow the road of perfect liberalization (Preston, 1993). The question here is whether these countries have another choice anyway and if, given their specific economic and infrastructural situation, EU policy should not adopt specific strategies at this level (Constantelou and Mansell, 1994)

Here it is important to recall that national governments have never acted differently anyway, since telecommunications in Europe has always been regarded by the nation-states as a strategic resource for their economic and social welfare and has therefore always been regulated in a way to optimize national economic and industrial profits with national social and political objectives (Joosten, 1993).

Although large-scale comparative analysis of the regulatory concept of universal service is lacking, what is available (Garnham, 1988b; Burgelman and Verhoest, 1994) demonstrates that, just as with public service in broadcasting, it has been a compromise between all these interests (and the fact that business users and residential users had no other choice than to use the same network), differing from country to country and not a god-given concept that has a regulatory dynamic of its own. This means that 'solving' the present problems of equal distribution and access to telecommunications in Europe, in a fully liberalized market, by imposing a concept like universal service – or by proposing regulatory concepts in which infrastructure, platform services and applications are seen as separate entities[12] – without negotiating this with industry, political authorities and so on, will tend to fail. This needs to be negotiated on a pan-European level, given the heterogeneity and conflicting interests of business and residential users in the European context.

These arguments put one of the most debated questions in west European telecommunications policy in another perspective. Indeed, even if the key question is how universal service is to be guaranteed in a competitive environment (assuming that it was a 'natural' thing in a monopolistic environment) given the 'bargained' and to a minor extent, technically determined nature of that universal service, the more fundamental question then arises as to whether universal service is still on the policy agenda (or more pointedly whether solidarity is still on the political agenda). Just as in broadcasting, the key question is not how to implement public service but rather whether public service is still an issue, given the changed regulatory philosophy in cultural matters.

Nevertheless, there is no reason at all to think that, though no longer scarce, telecommunications has lost its strategic value and significance for the different nation-states or that most of these national authorities will simply accept, as the oligopolistic analysis of the market predicts, that these strategic issues will at best be controlled by two or three strong European operators. It is indeed hard to imagine that the small European states will rely on France Telecom, BT or Deutsche Bundespost Telekom for all their telecommunications needs even though these three operators will most likely be able to operate at a cheaper rate than the small states themselves.

The same protectionist attitude of national governments might be expected in relation to their media systems. Given the non-organic growth of the EU and the history of Europe as such, it is very hard to imagine that governments will allow a majority of their media, especially broadcasting, to be owned by a few multinational multimedia groups from outside their borders.

In sum: three worlds of EU regulation need to be tuned into each other: competition policy, telecommunications policy, media policy.

Second, with regard to the inadequacy of EU regulatory policy, one could point to the Green Paper on pluralism and the media (1992). However, this does not address most of the issues mentioned since it only looks at cross-ownership between broadcasting and the press. Vertical integration, cross-ownership with telecommunications operators, software companies, electricity providers, and so on are not taken into account. This implies that, looking at it from the cultural side of the mass media, EU policy is completely inadequate to tackle what, if one recalls the problems around the importing of American broadcasting, has always been a major concern in media policy: the promotion of diversity.

Finally, one of the major obstacles to overcome is the fact that the concept of the EIH is an infrastructure concept whereas the services to be provided on that network are content based. The latter, as explained, is a very sensitive issue for the member states in which they want as much subsidiarity as possible. This means that there are two competing policies at work: a centralist hardware policy and a decentralizing case for subsidiarity in what will be offered to that infrastructure.

It is therefore extremely difficult, given the utmost importance for good regulation in a privatized environment (Mansell, 1993b) to imagine how a European FCC could work, folowing a suggestion made more and more often with regard to the implementation of the Bangemann report.[13] First of all the FCC is a very American thing, rooted in their unique tradition of judicial power (Simon, 1991). But more importantly a European FCC would mean even more power and bureaucracy to Brussels. And that is clearly not on the agenda of most of the member states.

To summarize, one can ask how it is that so many problems and conflicting interests tend to be overlooked. Many reasons can be put forward, for example technocratic ideology, or technological determinism but, from a communication science point of view, two specific assumptions, both related to the concept of the European citizen, should be identified. On the one hand, it is assumed that cultural and linguistic diversity – which is a huge problem in terms of standardization but also hinders the development of pan-European information and/or media services – is a problem which must or should be solved. Audience studies and failures like uni-lingual pan-European television, indicate how difficult it is to make public taste 'uniform'. And if something can be learned from the debate on the new world information order in this respect, then it is that these processes of 'uniformization' tend to be slow-moving, if they move at all. Up until now, in Europe, there is every indication that this is also true for the EU. Indeed 25 per cent of the budget of the EU is estimated to go on translation costs.

This assumption about the possible making of some European Esperanto man is linked to a more fundamental one: that the essence of European citizenship and citizens' behaviour in this domain can be reduced to the rational consumption of communication services (Hills, 1993). This assumption might explain why policy and research seems to side-step these problems. Underlying the approach is the belief in rational considerations: in that everyone wants cheaper communication services and will therefore accept its necessary consequence of 'Europeanization'. The picture of the European information society, as drawn in all kinds of policy documents is therefore one of the perfect market in which rational consumers shop around and take what is best for them to maximize their personal profits.

CONVERGENCE OF BROADCASTING AND TELECOMMUNICATIONS RESEARCH ISSUES AND APPROACHES?

Following from the earlier analysis, some strikingly similar points of theoretical concern for broadcasting as well as telecommunications policy research can be identified.

A first point in which the study of changes in broadcasting and telecommunications converge is the need to discuss whether public service or universal service is still a valuable regulatory concept and if so, how it should be implemented. Though both concepts do not exactly mean the same – historically, universal service is an economic concept and therefore measurable, whereas public service has a more political and cultural dimension and is not measurable – it is clear that they have become more and more intertwined. If the type of the network is no longer relevant to the type of service being offered on it, as used to be the case, then it is vital to know what type of service what concept should be applied. It is therefore necessary to have precise ideas on what both concepts mean. Here, research tends to be formalistic and almost idealistic. Public service and universal service are, as shown in the previous sections, too often used as if they are operational concepts in their own right.

Historical research nevertheless shows that these concepts are not only the result of some technological factors but that they are also the result of political and economic conflict, that they differ between nations and cultures and not least, that they came into play in a very elitist environment. Indeed, one tends to forget that when public service and universal service were accepted as regulatory devices in broadcasting and telecommunications, the use of the radio and of the telephone was restricted to the then elites and the then bourgeoisie. Public service broadcasting was a service for the well-to-do who could afford to buy a radio set and for whom the market was *their* market. And universal service was universal for those who could, in the first place, afford a telephone (mainly business people in the beginning).

It is therefore a mistake to take both concepts for granted, assuming that they refer to a perfect policy or real 'publics' and real 'universals' that existed once upon a time, and then to transpose them to the present day situation which is so radically different and much more complex.[14] What is important then is to see what public service and universal service can mean in present day society (Garnham, 1993). It follows from this that in discussions of universal service – as in discussions of democracy – the particularities of the different countries will have to be taken into account.

Specifically with regard to this implementation of public service and universal service, one notices that in both fields exactly the same questions with regard to accountability arise. In public broadcasting this problem manifests itself in relation to the question of how a board of governors can be made as responsible as possible towards the general public. In telecommunications this question arises when the increasingly important role of the regulators is discussed. Given the experiences of the past and the foreseeable problems of the future it is difficult to imagine, even in the most liberal system, that no regulator will be needed. This problem is an acute one because it touches upon a more fundamental problem of representation and the prioritizing of societal values: two elements of policy-making which in the individualizing culture of postmodernity are not very fashionable at all.

A second point of research convergence is the simplistic or naive use of the categories 'market' and 'state' in policy debates on broadcasting and telecommunications. Most debates tend to use this as a dichotomous analytical pair: there is a market route to regulation and a non-market one, inevitably the state. According to the orientation of the author, this is then judged good or bad. Here too historical research and detailed analysis has shown that it has never been the one nor the other and that to regulate the market or the state was never an end in itself, but a means to an end. Indeed, public broadcasting was a compromise between a hesitating electro-technical industry in Europe (wanting to go for private broadcasting) and a dynamic political will to control the new means of communication. When then, later on, traditional industry went to look for new markets and most governments in Europe seemed to prefer more uncritical or impartial broadcasting than the public one, the road was open for liberalization. In other words, it is again an idealistic assumption that market models and state models exist in their pure form as ends in themselves. Moreover, both have advantages and disadvantages depending on what criteria are chosen to evaluate them (efficiency, innovative power, social dimensions and so on). And again, this differs from nation to nation. What is certainly clear, however, is that both need a lot of regulation. They are not self-regulating.

A third area of convergence in research is the question concerning the user or the viewer. Given the convergence of services, there is no reason why both should not be studied as one (Jouet, 1993; Moores, 1993a; Silverstone and Hirsch, 1992). It is indeed evident that insights from research on the complexity of use of communication technologies should be related to the knowledge of viewing habits (in which the same complexity is also evident). Indeed, even from an analytical point of view there is a possibility of considerable convergence in both fields. The so called SCOT approach in technology studies[15] – which emphasizes that different uses can be constructed for different technologies according to the different backgrounds of the actors involved – is indeed very similar to the encoding/decoding analysis of television texts. New approaches to the understanding of television are directly related to the growing importance of information and telecommunication technologies in the organization of daily life. It is indeed precisely because new technologies create different time and space relationships (Castells, 1989) – in which social identity formation is no longer tied to a certain social and economic space (we can work and live so to speak in different countries) – that 'new identities' can be formed via satellite television, creating new forms of cultural proximity (the MTV generation) and so on (Moores, 1993c). In turn, this reinforces time–space distanciation even more (Giddens, 1990) increasing the need for television as an 'ontological securer' (Silverstone, 1993).

In other words, the way society develops makes it almost impossible to study the impact and significance of broadcasting, at the level of the citizen, without looking at what happens in telecommunications and vice versa.

Finally, a last area of convergence between broadcasting and telecommunications research might be the study of the tension between the local and the global, which in Europe receives its specificity by the fact that the local (the nation-state) has been there far longer than the global (the EU). As argued throughout this article, there is nothing specific about European media policy. In fact, the main issues at stake are the same in other industrialized countries, but the context in Europe makes them unique. This uniqueness is the fact that Europe is a market, without having the necessary homogeneity to behave like a real market for communication services, and that it is a political unity, without any normal, bottom up, political legitimacy such a unity normally requires.

This tension between local and global reality creates a situation in which it is not just technology which is problematic for a pan-European communication policy. There are indeed many more differences than similarities at work in Europe (Miège, 1990, 1993). And it is very doubtful that these historically determined differences can be side stepped by some kind of Open Network Provision.[16] Precisely because communication policy is not only a technical thing, one can expect great problems in the long run as a result of the rising conflict between the 'nature' of the market and the ambitions of the different nation-states not to lose control over their cultural identities and/or their strategic resources in an increasingly information based economy.

EUROPEAN MEDIA POLICY RESEARCH: FROM MEDIA-CENTRISM TO GRAND THEORY?

Once it is accepted, as this chapter has hopefully made clear, that at the policy level European broadcasting and telecommunications face the same basic question with regard to the quality of public communication for the individual and for society as a whole – be it privately organized or not – there is no reason why a scientific convergence should not also be accepted. In order to come to such a 'scientific convergence', which is in fact a plea for the search for a 'grand theory' of communication, it is necessary that present research overcomes the following pitfalls.

First of all there is a large degree of tautological reasoning and analysing going on. Changes in media and telecommunications (e.g. liberalization) tend to be explained by reference to observations about, for example, the 'spirit of the time'. The question of why such changes take place is seldom posed. This is, second, due to the fact that much research in western Europe tends to be too media centred (Garnham, 1992) and by consequence adopts a technology driven perspective. This is in itself a result of a mechanistic view of causality whereby media and society are perceived as being more or less autonomous *vis-à-vis* each other (Burgelman, 1990). Such an implicit perspective makes the question 'why' hard to answer. The Green Papers of the EU on the media and on telecommunications are not the starting point for the deregulation and privatization of the sector or the result of sudden technological discoveries, as a media centred approach would suggest, but are a formalized outcome of a larger economic restructuring process in West European industry which started after the economic crisis of 1973 as well as technological discoveries in media and telecommunications.

These media centred approaches might explain, third, why so much manicheistic thinking occurs in Western European policy debates. Public versus private, market versus state, control versus freedom, regulation versus deregulation, are all used in a manicheistic way, assuming that only one or the other is possible and desirable and that each has a dynamic of its own. The main assumption here is that a pure and natural state of things is possible; accepting, for example, that it is sufficient to regulate the market but that it is hindered in doing so by a demonic state (overlooking the fact that in many cases 'the market' has asked the state to intervene in broadcasting and telecommunications).

One has to point out here that, due to an often simplistic, expressive use of causality in critical thinking – everything is seen as a function of capitalism; hence an alternative can only be real if no trace of capitalism is found in it – the same kind of manicheistic thinking (see Burgelman, 1990) can be found: for example in discussions of radical alternatives to media policy which would be free from all kind of economic, political and social constraints (for an overview see Curran,

1992, 1993). In turn this brings some authors to try to find the alchemist's stone: a policy model mediating between market and state, where the empowered citizen constitutes the beginning and the end of all societal action. Not only is this again based on the assumption that at a certain point in time a utopia existed (*in casu* the public sphere), but it also assumes that this was then violated by 'the' market and 'the' state. Moreover, such thinking assumes the capacity of people to be continuously politicized (since this is a precondition for radical and direct democracy).

Manicheistic thinking clearly overlooks the empirical reality and the constant and dynamic uncertainties and contradictions of everyday life. But more importantly, it overlooks history itself. Indeed, as pointed out on different occasions in this chapter, there never has been a situation where only one category was at work and not another one. The state has never been and never is absent, not even in the most liberal regimes; public service and universal service are time-specific and context-specific compromises between different actors and not idealistic categories; control of communications was always on the agenda even if it appeared as the lack of control; deregulation can be an instrument for left wing governments (see France) as well as for right-wing governments; and so on. This almost complete but nevertheless quite astonishing lack of historical analysis in recent European media and telecommunications policy debates, is the fourth problem we perceive in current research.

This is the case not only because historical analysis would clarify the simplistic nature of present day debates, but also because it would put things in perspective. A short study of communications in the nineteenth and twentieth century would have taught policy-makers and analysts that what is technologically possible nevertheless has to fit into a set of time and context specific parameters. This goes equally for broadcasting and film technologies (Flichy, 1980) as it does for telecommunications (Flichy, 1991). Such a historical study would also teach them that patterns of media consumption change very slowly and that there is almost never a total substitution of one medium by another (Van Kaam, 1991); that telework will most likely have no impact at all on rural development since the capacity to pursue this type of work is linked to the city and the entrepreneurs that live in it (Castells, 1989); that most people tend to value stability rather than mobility in the organization of their lives (Lange, 1991); that the availability of abundant capacity in itself does not imply the use of it – (why else would 80 per cent of Europe spend its holidays within Europe given the possibility to go worldwide at more or less comparable prices); that most of the time industrial actors are willing to risk investment in new technologies only if there is something close to guaranteed revenue (Griset, 1991; Mattelart, 1991). In other words: most of the hype surrounding the information society is based on assumptions which, looking back in time, may well be very shaky.

That does not mean, of course, that nothing changes or will change. It only points out that the drives for change do not come from technology alone and that if the information society becomes a reality it will take much more time than expected, it may be not in the best interests of those most expected and that the whole process will not be radical, but will emerge gradually, depending, as it does, on the surrounding economic and sociocultural contexts.

A more historical approach, then, would also put the whole debate of the local versus the national and supranational (Europe) into perspective, as well as the whole discourse on Europe versus US/Pacific. What is indeed disturbing here is that all arguments on the preservation of European culture and on the need to strengthen European competitiveness, tend to overlook the fact that European culture is the result of openness and interchange and that Europe was at the height of its power when it imported innovations and knowledge. Of course the situation today is different, but the balance between arguments in favour of cultural specificity and of fortress Europe can very quickly switch into some kind of Euro-specific isolationism and cultural integrism. At least it should be clear that European history itself does not give grounds for such isolationism.

Given the strong and long tradition in Europe of critical research (Beaud, 1984) one must, to conclude, ask why these media-centred approaches are so popular.

Amongst the many possible reasons – the desperate need for communication studies to establish itself as a respectable scientific field? – we believe the most important one to be the fact that west European communication science seemed to have accepted that 'the world (of the media) as it is, is how it is meant to be '. Or to put it another way, west European media and communication studies seems to have abandoned, as a social science, the larger societal projects which gave social sciences its dynamics: human liberation and the supremacy of quality over quantity (Garnham 1990a: 1–19, 1992, 1993; Keane, 1991; Lemaire, 1990).[17]

In fact, I would like to suggest that important parts of western European communication science have gone even beyond the 'new revisionism' Curran (1990) had detected in this field a few years ago. Present day communication thinking seems indeed to accept uncritically the market as the most perfect organizing principle for freedom of communication (as a reaction to the totalizing explanatory frameworks of Marxist media thinking); it also seems to accept unconditionally the autonomy of the audience and the user (as a reaction to the extremely vulnerable position critical thinking gave the audience before); and it seems to promote (and in the meantime legitimate) the unproblematic individual aesthetic pleasure in the consumption of media and information as the most important goal and effect of media culture (as a result of the shift in attention away from politics). Or to put it another way: as a reaction to the very radical schools of thinking of the 1960s and 1970s in Europe – which were based on unrealistic, over-rationalistic assumptions of the nature of man – one can see that European media studies are now moving towards extreme relativism. Since all media products are equal in their effect, because it is the user/viewer who determines the effect, questions of power or dominance in the media are no longer relevant.

It seems to me that to overcome these pitfalls, media research needs a fundamental rethinking of the Enlightenment project. Given what we have witnessed every day happening in the heart of Europe (for example, in Yugoslavia) where this project is given up or ridiculed, this rethinking is no academic luxury, but an existential necessity.

NOTES

1 Even at this point, and with respect to the fact that the economics of broadcasting and telecommunications are different, it remains the case that both sectors are dealing to a great extent with 'public goods' (programmes or information services): no incremental costs are incurred to serve additional customers. This means that, to a certain extent, the basic economic problems for both are the same: they do not apply to normal price mechanisms (viewing a programme or using an information service does not prohibit someone else from viewing or using it).

2 However, it is important to bear in mind that, though a minor factor, the 'dead weight' of history of monopolistic broadcasting (judged as slow, bureaucratic, middle-of-the-road, paternalistic, and so on) and telecommunications (judged as inefficient and bureaucratic) made these organizations a vulnerable target for the winds of change that blew in communications policy since the early 1980s.

3 However, pan-European media policy issues are mainly addressed by French and British researchers. German communication science, for example, although developed in the country where media studies is best institutionalized, seems, apart from the broadcasting debate, only marginally interested in these issues (see Becker, 1993).

4 Though since 1993 the EC has supported, mainly through its limited HCM programme, the establishment of trans-European research networks for this type of research, it must be remarked that research in this area is very dependent on the main actors in this field (television companies, telecom operators, etc.). Hence the lack of independent trans-European communication research platforms (Garnham, 1988a). And where they do exist, like the UK PICT programme, policy questions are not always the central concern (Garnham, 1994b; Mansell, 1994).

5 Research mainly concentrates on entertainment and drama. No work is being done on how the European information and news programming market is affected by this transnationalization. Nevertheless, this seems more and more the case as is illustrated by the plans of CLT to pool the information provision of all its commercial channels (RTL 2, 4, 5, M6 and RTL-TVi) and to offer this service to the market. One of the consequences here, for example, would be that the most important channel in the French-speaking part of Belgium is provided with a Euro-made information service, with some Belgian features added on. In other words, it loses its informational autonomy.

6 To some degree, an exception can be made with regard to the study of new services, like video-text or audio-text (for overviews, see Bouwman and Christoffersen, 1992; Latzer and Thomas, 1993).

7 It is indicative of the degree with which the EC still believes in the hype on the information society, that this extremely important report looks more like a promotional leaflet than a well researched and documented policy paper.

8 Long-term historical research of the Belgian case (Verhoest et al. 1994) showed that Belgium would nowadays have most certainly no R&D in this sector at all if the old PTT had not been forced to develop 'nationally' the technology needed. Consequently Belgium would nowadays not have one single industry of relevance active in the information society.

9 A heuristic research problem needs mentioning here with regard to the accuracy and reliability of cross-national and cross-sectional data. The real (instead of potential) European audience reach of pan-European satellite televisions, for example, is impossible to give. For Belgium, the viewing audience of these channels is,

cumulatively speaking, considered to be less than 5 per cent (whereas their reach is more than 50 per cent). Given the fact that up till now these specialized pan-European channels are the only successful applications of narrow-casting and that they are considered vital for the concept of the EIH (since the assumption goes that the demand for narrow-casting will rise dramatically) it is important to have the right figures at hand.

10 For an excellent analysis of this crucial problem see Joosten, 1993: 115–46.

11 It is surprising that on a topic where the residential user is so important, to the extent that some analysts state that the only black hole in the trans-European information networks is his demand, so little research is available. This pinpoints the popularity of technologically deterministic assumptions – what technology makes possible, will also happen.

12 Though interesting as a heuristical device, it is difficult to imagine how these distinct categories can be used as a regulatory and operational system for the whole communication sector, as the 'Dutch' school of regulation tends to propose (see Arnbak et al., 1990; Leyten et al., 1991; Mediaraad, 1993; Slaa, 1991; Van Cuilenburg and Slaa, 1993).

13 This proposition was, curiously enough given the consistent anti-federalist stance taken by conservative UK, first made by the chairman of BT (*Financial Times*, 13 July 1994).

14 In this respect, it is necessary to point, as Dahlgren (1991) does, to the same decontextual use that is made of Habermas's work on the public sphere. Habermas's public sphere was indeed an idealized construction as it was in reality an elitist thing which worked only within a specific context and social class.

15 The Social Construction of Technology (cf. Bijker et al., 1987).

16 It is therefore interesting to note that, the more power goes to the European parliament, which is constituted by those who have a legitimacy to defend their own constituencies, the more problems arise which make top-down imposed measures by the commission unacceptable. When the Bangemann report was debated in this parliament, it was indeed first rejected because it was judged to rely too much on an infrastructural project and to pay not enough attention to what will be offered on that infrastructure (which will be what will be visible to the European voter) (*Le Monde*, 21 July 1994).

17 One only has to look at the dozens of flow studies on European and American television in which 'Dallasification', American hegemony and so on is being criticized and which are in fact decontextualized 'output' studies, based on the intellectually dangerous assumption that what is made in Europe, preferably in public broadcasting, is therefore Euro-typical, non-commercial and thus of good quality. Such an approach is also non-productive since it assumes present day policy-making on the basis of time and context specific categories. The same can be said of the many normative approaches to communication policy-making that flourish in west European communication policy thinking (see McQuail, 1992).

REFERENCES

Achille, Y. and Miège, B. (1994) 'The limits to the adaptation strategies of European public service television', *Media Culture and Society* 16(1): 31–46. This article is a synthesis of a much larger, but as yet unpublished, analysis of the survival strategies of public broadcasting in Europe. Discusses the different scenarios public broadcasters can adopt and their expected outcome in the long term.

Arnbak, J.C., Van Cuilenburg, J.J. and Dommering, E.J. (1990) (m.m.v. N.A.N.M. van Eijk, L.G. Portielje en P. Slaa) Verbinding en ontvlechting in de communicatie. Een studie naar toekomstig overheidsbeleid voor de openbare elektronische informatievoorziening, Amsterdam: O. Cramwinckel. This book reflects the work of the influential Dutch 'school' of communications regulation in which infrastructure and services are seen as separate entities and where a classification of communication services and subsequent regulation is proposed on the basis of the communication patterns (see also Leyten *et al.*, 1991; Slaa, 1991; Mediaraad, 1993; Van Cuilenburg and Slaa, 1993). Though it is questionable if operational regulatory models can be built on the basis of their classifications, this work is interesting from an analytical and heuristic point of view.

Béaud P. (1984) *La société de la connivence. Médias, méditations et classes sociales*, Paris: Aubier. Overview of critical thinking in Europe and its significance for communications research. What is particularly valuable in this book, is that it tries to adapt Habermas's general concepts to the reality of European society and its specific social compositions.

Becker, J. (1993) 'Communications research in Germany: a collection of reviews of important new publications', *European Journal of Communication* 8(3): 257–71. Extremely comprehensive overview of the main present issues in German communications research.

Bijker, W., Hughes, T. and Pinch, T. (eds) (1987) *The Social Construction of Technical Systems*: Cambridge, MA: MIT Press.

Biltereyst, D. (1992) 'Europäische Fictionsproduktion – nur begrenzt exportfähig in Europa. Eine vergleichende Analyse über Herkunft, Konsum und Poularität von Fictionsendungen in kleinen europäischen Ländern', *Media Perspektiven* 5: 316–26.

Biltereyst, D. (1993) 'Televisiekijkers tussen culturele identiteit en imperialisme: een ge ïntegreerde receptie-analyse benadering van de cross-culturele impact van VS televisie-fictie', unpublished D.phil. thesis, University of Brussels. This works concentrates on demystifying the simplicity of the American dominance (in audiovisual matters) thesis by looking at flow studies from an audience's point of view. Develops the notion of 'cultural proximity' in order to understand the popularity of fiction programmes.

Blumler, J. (ed.) (1992a) *Television and the Public Interest*, London: Sage.

Blumler, J. (1992b) *Broadcasting Financing in Transition*, Oxford: Oxford University Press. Blumler's work provides excellent descriptions and useful overviews of the changing nature of broadcasting in Europe. Of the same nature is the work of Charon (1991) and the more functionalist pan-European analysis offered by the Euromedia group (see Euromedia Research Group, 1992; McQuail, 1990, 1991; Siune, and Trutzschler, 1992) or the European Institute of the Media (see Sanchez-Tabernero, 1993)

Bouwman, H. and Christoffersen, M. (eds) (1992) *Relaunching Videotex*, Dordrecht: Kluwer.

Burgelman, J.C. (1986) 'The future of public service broadcasting: a case study for a "new" communications policy', *European Journal of Communication* 1(2): 173–201.

Burgelman, J.C. (1990) 'Politics and the media: how relative can the autonomy be? Some theoretical remarks concerning the dominant concepts on the relationship between media and society', in J. Hochheimer, K. Jakubowski and S. Splichal (eds) *Democratization and Media: an East–West Dialogue*. Ljubljana: CCC.

Burgelman, J.C. (1995) 'Assessing information technologies in the information society: the possible relevance of communication science and research', in A. Calabrese, S. Splichal and C. Sparks (eds) *Information Society and Civil Society: Contemporary Perspectives on the Changing World Order*, West Lafayette: Purdue University Press.

Burgelman, J.C. and Pauwels, C. (1991) 'Growing convergence between broadcasting and telecommunication: policy problems at the level of the Commission of the European Communities', *Telematics and Informatics* 8(3): 135–41.

Burgelman, J.C. and Pauwels, C. (1992) 'Audio-visual and cultural policies in the small European countries: the challenge of a unified European television market', *Media, Culture and Society* 14(2): 169–83.

Burgelman, J.C and Verhoest, P. (1994) 'Les services publics de communication en Belgique (1830–1994)', *Réseaux* 66: 67–98.

Bustamente, E., Garnham, N. and Salaun, J.M. (eds) (1993) *Téléphone et télévision, enquête sur une convergence européenne*, Paris: CNET/Réseaux. See Slaa and Burgelman (1994).

Castells, M. (1989) *The Informational City. Information Technology, Economic Restructuring and the Urban–Regional Process*, Oxford: Blackwell.

Chamoux, J.P. (ed.) (1991) *Deregulating Regulators? Communications Policies for the 90's*, Amsterdam: IOS press. This is one of the volumes (see also Garnham, 1989; Christoffersen and Henten, 1993; Klaver and Slaa, 1992) in the important and well documented Euro CPR series which is one of the most independent European fora for research and debate between economists, lawyers, policy analysts, informatics people and, to a lesser degree, engineers in telecommunications. Contributions relate mainly to economic analysis of telecommunications, new services and European policy matters relevant to it.

Charon, J.M. (1991) *L 'Etat des médias*, Paris: La Découverte. See Blumler.

Christoffersen, M. and Henten, A. (ed.) (1993) *Telecommunication. Limits to Deregulation?*, Amsterdam: IOS Press. See Chamoux.

Collins, R (1994) *Broadcasting and Audiovisual Policy in the European Single Market*, London: J. Libbey. One of the most comprehensive and accurate overviews of EU regulation in broadcasting.

Collins, R., Garnham, N., and Locksley, G. (1988) *The Economics of Television*, London: Sage. A well researched and documented political economy of broadcasting explaining why television economies are public goods and hence not subject to the same industrial logic as other goods.

Commission of the European Communities (1984) *Television without Frontiers*, Green Paper on the establishment of the Common Market for broadcasting especially by satellite and cable, COM (84) 300 final, Brussels.

Commission of the European Communities (1987) *Towards a Dynamic European Community*, Green Paper on the development of the Common Market for telecommunication services and equipment, COM (87) 290 final, Brussels.

Commission of the European Communities (1992) *Green Paper on Pluralism and Concentration in the Media*, COM (92) 480 final, Brussels.

Commission of the European Communities (1993) *White Paper. Growth, Competitiveness, Employment. The Challenges and Ways Forward into the 21st Century*, Brussels.

Commission of the European Communities (1994) *Europe and the Global Information Society. Recommendations to the European Council* (High-level group on the information society – Bangemann report) EU, Brussels. These five documents constitute the core official EU documents relevant to communications policy.

Constantelou, N. and Mansell, R. (1994) 'On the road to competition in telecommunication: "catching up" in the European Union less favoured regions', Montpellier: Encip, unpublished paper.

Curran, J. (1990) 'The new revisionism in mass communication research: a reappraisal' *European Journal of Communication* 3(2/3): 135–64.

Curran, J. (1992) 'Mass media and democracy: a reappraisal', in J. Curran and M. Gurevitch (eds) *Mass Media and Society*, London: Edward Arnold.

Curran, J. (1993) 'Rethinking the media as a public sphere', in P. Dahlgren and C. Sparks (eds) *Communication and Citizenship. Journalism and the Public Sphere*, London: Routledge.

Dahlgren, P. (1991) 'Introduction', in P. Dahlgren and C. Sparks (ed.) *Communication and Citizenship. Journalism and the Public Sphere*, London: Routledge. Short but extremely accurate analysis of the use and abuse of Habermas's work in present day critical thinking in communications.

De Bens, E. and Knoche, M. (1987) *Impact of New Communication Technologies on media*

Industry in the EU countries, final report, CEE internal paper no. 160, occasional paper. This is one of the first forecasts (using Delphi methods) undertaken by communication scholars with regard to telecommunications (and one of the few the EU funded). The study has been criticized (Mettler-Meiboom, 1988) as a typical example of research in the 1980s in which technology-push thinking, user-acceptance fantasies and an idealized view of the market are taken for granted.

Dyson, K. and Humphreys, P. (1990) *The Political Economy of Communications: International and European Dimensions*, London: Routledge. Discusses deregulation, liberalization, globalization, internationalization and how this is shaped in Europe.

Euromedia Research Group (1992) *The Media in Western Europe*, London: Sage. See Blumler.

Flichy, P. (1980) *Les industries de l'imaginaire*, Grenoble: PUG. Flichy's work is one of those rare attempts to offer an historical sociology of nineteenth- and twentieth-century communications. Flichy demonstrates that the outcome of a technological invention in communications is never pre-set, but depends on a specific 'genealogy' of communications as the result of the economic, social, political and technical forces that surround it and make it country specific. Interesting in his work is his focus on the user and the shaping of usage.

Flichy, P. (1991) *Une histoire de la communication moderne. Espace public et vie privé*, Paris: La Découverte.

Fuchs, G. (1992) 'ISDN – the telecommunications highway for Europe after 1992', *Telecommunications Policy* 12: 635–45.

Garbe, D. and Lange, K. (1991) (hrsg.) *Technikfolgenabschätzung in der Telekommunikation*, Berlin: Springer. Together with other German work used in this article (Fuchs, 1992; Kubicek and Rolf, 1986; Kubicek, 1992) this book is representative of (critical) German research, mostly presented as technology assessment, in telecommunications where there is much concern over the social aspects of informatics especially with regard to privacy and individual freedom. Germany has also a very strong, and at the policy level, very influential economic research school in telecommunications research, called WIK.

Garnham, N. (1988a) 'European research in communications', in Babel-Communications, proceedings SFSIC conference.

Garnham, N. (1988b) 'Universal service in Western European Telecommunications', in N. Garnham (ed.) *European Telecommunications Policy Research Conference*, Amsterdam: IOS Press.

Garnham, N. (ed.) (1989) *European Telecommunications Policy Research Conference*, Amsterdam: IOS Press.

Garnham, N.(1990a) *Capitalism and Communication*, London: Sage.

Garnham, N. (1990b) 'The convergence of broadcasting and telecommunications', in Mediaraad (ed.) *Wat is er van uw dienst*, Den Haag: Mediaraad, 10–16.

Garnham, N. (1992) 'The media and the public sphere', in G. Calhoun (ed.) *Habermas and the Public Sphere*, Boston: MIT Press.

Garnham, N. (1993) 'The mass media, cultural identity, and the public sphere in the modern world', *Public Culture* 5: 251–65.

Garnham, N. (1994a) 'The broadcasting market and the future of the BBC', *The Political Quarterly* 1: 11–19.

Garnham, N. (1994b) 'Whatever happened to the information society?', in R. Mansell (ed.) *Management of Information and Communication Technologies. Emerging Patterns of Control*, London: ASLIB. Garnham's work is one of the most influential and rigorous, but non-dogmatic, political economic analyses of European communications. The remarkable strength of his work is that it encompasses broadcasting as well as telecommunications, offering detailed and historically grounded empirical and theoretical analysis.

Garnham, N. and Mulgan, G. (1991) 'Broadband and the barriers to convergence in the European Community', *Telecommunications Policy* 3: 182–208. See Slaa and Burgelman (1994).

Giddens, A. (1990) *The Consequences of Modernity*, London: Polity Press

Griset, P. (1991) *Les révolutions de la communication*, Paris: Hachette.

Hills, J. (1986) *Deregulating Telecommunications. Competition and Control in the US, Japan and Britain*, London: Frances Pinter. One of the first studies to take a critical look at telecommunications in Europe and to draw attention to the user.

Hills, J. (1993) 'Universal service: connectivity and consumer rights', in M. Christoffersen and A. Henten (eds) *Telecommunication. Limits to Deregulation?*, Amsterdam: IOS Press.

Hulsink, W. (1994) 'The single European Telecoms Market: from state monopolies and national champions to an oligopoly of Euro-nationals and global alliances', Tilburg: WORC paper.

Jouet, J. (1993) 'Pratiques de communication et figures de la médiation', *Réseaux*, 60: 101–20. Similar to the work of Silverstone, but in French. It should be noted that there is a much larger French school, not mentioned in this bibliography, working on users and viewer dynamics in relation to new services.

Joosten M. (1991) 'The race programme: backgrounds and problems of integration and convergence', London: CCIS/PCL.

Joosten, M. (1993) 'Restructuring telecommunications tariffs in Europe. An historical analysis of the politico-economics of tariffs in 4 member states', unpublished D.phil. thesis, City University of London. Excellent PhD which analyses European telecommunications from the point of view of the restructuring of the economics of capitalism and which points at the myth of cost based pricing.

Joosten, M. (1994) 'De verloren integratie. Opkomst en neergang van het RACE programma', in P. Slaa and J.C. Burgelman (eds) *Verglaasde steden*. Amsterdam: O. Cramwinkel, 75–88. One of the best analyses of the large and very ambitious European broad band research programmes.

Kayzer, H.J. (1993) *Controlling für Rundfunkanstalten*, Baden-Baden: Nomos.

Keane, J. (1991) *The media and democracy*, Cambridge: Polity Press. Historical grounded analysis of the public sphere in communications in Europe and its meanings for the future.

Klawer, F. and Slaa, P. (1993) *Telecommunication. New Signposts to Old Roads*, Amsterdam: IOS Press. See Chamoux (1991).

Kubicek, H. (1992) 'Von der Technikfolgenabschatzung zur Regulierungsforschung. Stand und Perspektiven sozialorientierter Telekommunikationsforschung', in H. Kubicek (hrsg.) *Telekommunikation und Gesellschaft. Kritisches Jahrbuch der Telekommunikation*, Frankfurt: C.F. Miller.

Kubicek, H. and Rolf, A. (1986) *Mikropolis. Mit Computernetzen in die 'Informationsgesellschaft'*, Hamburg: Verlag.

Lange, K. (1991) 'Zur Ambivalenz des Mobiltelefons', in D. Garbe and K. Lange (hrsg.) *Technikfolgenabschätzung in der Telekommunikation*, Berlin: Springer.

Latzer, M. and G. Thomas, (1993) *Cash Lines. The Development and Regulation of Auditex in Europe*, Amsterdam: Het spinhuis.

Lemaire, T. (1990) *Twijfel aan Europa. Zijn de intellectuelen de vijanden van de Europese cultuur?*, Baarn: Ambo. This book is an extremely interesting analysis – it was his academic testament before leaving university in disillusion – on the origins and consequences of the abandonment of the Enlightenment project in critical European thinking. His analysis states that, being disillusioned by the non-fulfilment of the ideals of the Enlightenment (as its aberrations in the Third World in matters of ecology and so on made clear) many intellectuals have shifted towards positions of relativism as an intellectual perspective, scepticism as an attitude and individualistic hedonism as a societal project.

Leyten, J., Weijgers, T. and Schaffers, H. (1991) *Informatie- en communicatiediensten en de communicatieinfrastructuur: opties voor beleid*, Apeldoorn: TNO-STB. See Arnbak *et al.*

McQuail, D. (1990) 'Caging the beast: constructing a framework for the analysis of media change in Western Europe', *European Journal of Communication* 5/4: 313–31.

McQuail, D. (1991) *Broadcasting and Electronic Media Policies in Western Europe*, London: Sage.

McQuail, D. (1992) 'Mass media in the public interest: towards a framework of norms for media performance', in J. Curran and M. Gurevitch (eds) *Mass Media and Society*, London: Edward Arnold. See Blumler.

Mansell, R.E. (1993a) *The New Telecommunications. A Political Economy of Network Evolution*, London: Sage. Exhaustive overview of telecommunications strategies in Western Europe and stringent analysis of the rationales behind it (oligopolistic rivalry versus idealistic competition).

Mansell, R.E. (1993b) 'From telephony to telematics services: equity, efficiency and regulatory innovation', PICT (paper).

Mansell, R.E. (1994) 'Negotiating the management of ICTs – emerging patterns of control', in R. Mansell (ed.) *Management of Information and Communication Technologies. Emerging Patterns of Control*, London: ASLIB. Both articles offer a well organized argument in favour of a strong regulation of telecommunications in a deregulated market.

Mattelart, A. (1991) *La communication monde. Histoire des idées et des stratégies*, Paris: Découverte. Similar to, but not so sophisticated as the work of Flichy.

Mediaraad (1993) *Informatie tot (w)elke prijs?*, Den Haag: Mediaraad. See Arnbak.

Mettler-Meiboon, B. (1986) *Breitbandtechnologie. Über die Chancen sozialer Vernunft in technologiepolitischen Entscheidungsprozessen*, Opladen: Westdeutcher Verlag.

Mettler-Meiboon, B. (1987) *Soziale Kosten in der Informationsgesellschaft. Uberlegungen zur einer Kommunikationsekologie*, Frankfurt am Main: Fischer. Both works of this German scholar are similar to that of Kubicek. They look at the problems of the information society mainly from an individual point of view (privacy; state control versus individual freedom and so on). Her work is also representative of what can be considered as a distinct German school of thinking, namely communication ecology which looks at the problems of all media and communication channels in an integrated way.

Mettler-Meiboon, B. (1988) 'Communication at stake?', in F. van Rijn (ed.) *Concerning Home Telematics*, North Holland: Elsevier.

Miège, B. (ed.) (1990) *Médias et communication en Europe*, Grenoble: PUG. This book is, to my knowledge the first that looks in an integrated (broadcasting and tele-communications, users and policy) way at the problems discussed in this chapter and offers a non-media centred, convergent, analysis. Also interesting because it contains contributions from most of the main French scholars in this field.

Miège, B. (1993) 'Les mouvements de longue durée de la communication en Europe de l'Ouest', *Quaderni*, 19: 45–57.

Miles, I. (1988) *Home Informatics? Information Technology and the Transformation of Everyday Life*, London: Frances Pinter.

Missaka, J.-L. and Wolton, D. (1983) *La folle du logis. La télévision dans les sociétés démocratiques*, Paris: Gallimard. Intelligent plea for a strong generalistic public broadcasting system (like Wolton, 1990 and Witte, 1994).

Moores, S. (1993a) *Interpreting Audience. The Ethnography of Media Consumption*, London: Sage.

Moores, S. (1993b) 'Television, geography and "mobile privatization"', *European Journal of Communication* 8/4: 365–79.

Moores, S. (1993c) 'Satellite television as cultural sign: consumption, embedding and articulation', *Media, Culture and Society* 15: 621–39. Moores's work is, together with that of Silverstone, (but see also Miles) exemplary for the type of research (considering media and telecommunications technologies as a whole and studying them as such in relation to consumption) which this chapter has argued is necessary. Though research into the way people use information and communication services is only just beginning, it is remarkable that research of this type frequently states that more and more sophisticated research on how people struggle with communication technologies is needed, that the autonomy of the household is important and so on. Though it is much too soon to see this as a sign of a 'new revisionism' in relation to more technologically oriented communication studies, one should keep in mind, that after all, how the market responds to communication technologies is determined by how communication technologies come on the market (determined by the factors outlined throughout this chapter). It therefore seems just as important to study, in a historical sociological perspective, the dialectic between supply and use, as to concentrate on usage only (see Flichy).

Mulgan, G.J. (ed.) (1990) *The Questions of Quality (the Broadcasting Debate)*, London: BFI.

Mulgan, G.J. (1991) *Communication and Control. Networks and the New Economies of Communication*, London: Polity Press.

Noam, E. and Kramer, R. (1994) 'Telecommunications strategies in the developed world: a hundred flowers blooming or old wine in new bottles', in C. Steinfield, J.M. Bauer and L. Caby (1994) *Telecommunications in Transition. Policies, Services and Technologies in the European Community*, London: Sage.

Pauwels, C. (1995) 'Grenzen en mogelijkheden van een kwalitatief cultuur- en communicatiebeleid in een economisch geïntegreerd Europa. Een kritische analyse en prospectieve evaluatie aan de hand van het gevoerde en te voeren Europese omroepbeleid', unpublished D.phil thesis, University of Brussels. Stringent analysis of the discourse of the EU on its broadcasting policy and its philosophical underpinnings.

Preston, P. (1993) 'Some limits to neo-liberal regulation: a materialistic and institutionalist perspective', Aberdeen: CPR conference, unpublished paper.

Sanchez-Tabernero, A. (1993) *Media Concentration in Europe. Commercial Enterprise and Public Interest*, Manchester: European Institute for the Media.

Schlesinger, P. (1992) *Media, State and Nation. Political Violence and Collective Identities*, London: Sage.

Schlesinger, P. (1994) 'Europe's contradictory communicative space', *Daedalus* 123/2: 25–52. In his work Schlesinger combines a critique of European broadcasting policy with a search for a legitimacy for a European policy based on the necessity of identity formation and democracy.

Silverstone, R. (1993) 'Television, ontological security and the transitional object', *Media, Culture and Society* 15/4: 573–98.

Silverstone, R. and Hirsch, E. (1992) *Consuming Technologies. Media and Information in Domestic Space*, London: Routledge.

Simon, J.P. (1991) *L'Esprit des regles resaux et reglementation aux etats unies: cable, electricité, telecommunications*, Paris: L'Harmattan.

Siune, K. and Trutzschler, W. (eds) (1992) *Dynamics of Media Politics*, London: Sage.

Slaa, P. (1991) 'Integration and segmentation in telecommunications', in J.P. Chamoux (ed.) *Deregulating Regulators? Communications Policies for the 90's*, Amsterdam: IOS Press.

Slaa, P. and Burgelman, J.C. (eds) (1994) *Verglaasde steden*. Amsterdam: Cramwinckel. This book is the Dutch version of a pan-European research project on the state of the art of convergence in selected European countries (Belgium, Germany, France, the Netherlands,, Spain, UK) and the EU. It was directed by N. Garnham who provided the analytical framework (see Garnham and Mulgan, 1991). Parts of it have been published in French (see E. Bustamente *et al.*, 1993).

Steinfield, C., Bauer J.M. and Caby, L. (1994) *Telecommunications in Transition. Policies, Services and Technologies in the European Community*, London: Sage. Comprehensive overview of the complex set of rules, Green Papers and so on that govern European telecommunications.

Van Cuilenburg, J. and Slaa, P. (1993) 'From media policy towards a national communications policy: broadening the scope', *European Journal of Communications* 8/2: 149–76.

Van Kaam, B. (1991) *Het taaie leven van de dooie letter*, Amsterdam: O. Cramwinckel.

Verhoest, P., Punie, Y. and Vercruysse, J.P. (1994) *La politique des télécommunications en Belgique 1830–1991*, Bruxelles: Synedi.

Witte, E. (1994) *De breedte van het scherm. Pleidooi voor de openbare televisie*, Brussels: Icarus.

Wolton, D. (1990) *Eloge du grand public*, Paris: Flammarion.

Wolton, D. (1992) *La dernière utopie. Naissance de l'Europe démocratique*, Paris: Flammarion. See Schlesinger.

7

MEDIA POLICY IN NORTH AMERICA[1]

Vincent Mosco and Vanda Rideout

INTRODUCTION

Due partly to the growing significance of the mass media in social life, media policy research has grown substantially over the past two decades. This chapter provides a map of the research on media policy in North America. However, no single review can do justice to the enormous body of research on policy issues dealing with the US and Canadian media industries. Acknowledging this limitation, the chapter focuses on the perspectives that guide and organize media policy research and on central trends and issues in the relationship between the state and the major participants in the policy process in these countries. Specifically, the chapter aims to introduce some balance into the discussion of media policy research by remedying the tendency in the literature to respond primarily to the demands of the industries affected by media policy and of the governments responsible for setting media policy and regulation. It also seeks to balance the tendency to assess media policy on largely economic grounds (Picard, 1989), for instance, on the relationship between specific policies and economic growth, by concentrating on the *political* dimension of media policy, particularly the relationship of media policy to democracy.

Because the research literature tends to respond to industry and government demand for research, it tends to be more descriptive than theoretically grounded and more likely to mount an argument in favour of a specific business or government interest than to explain a set of actions by situating them within their social, political, economic and cultural contexts. Moreover, this research is likely to be produced in private or government-funded institutions and directed to influencing a pending issue. In the United States and Canada, private companies, including large media providers, new media challengers and large corporate communication users, along with large government bodies, such as the US Defense Department, significantly structure the policy research agenda. Nevertheless, although these characteristics constitute a frame of reference for the research agenda, they do not determine it. Media policy research is also informed by work that is theoretically grounded, critical, oppositional, and linked to public interest and social movement organizations, though such work tends to be marginalized.

This chapter is also informed by a concern to identify the political features of media policy, particularly to expand the discussion of media policy and the question of democracy. The chapter takes a broad view of democracy to encompass the fullest public participation in decisions that affect social life. According to this view, democracy refers to both the process of *participation* in decisions and the value of moving towards *equality*. Moreover, it takes the view that participatory democracy is not limited to the political arena. A fully democratic society is one in which citizens actively create economic, socio-cultural and political participation and equality. Additionally, this conception of democracy underlines its public character. Democracy means more than the sum total of votes taken among isolated individuals. In fact, it flourishes only when individuals can transcend their private selves and constitute themselves, in part through communication, in public groups, organizations, and institutions (Keane, 1984).

PERSPECTIVES ON THE STATE AND MEDIA POLICY

The map of media policy research can be sorted according to three perspectives – pluralist, managerial and class power – which numerous social scientists identify as central ways of thinking about the role of the state in developed capitalist societies (Alford and Friedland, 1985).

Pluralism

The pluralist perspective develops from the view that power is *situational*, that it operates in specific circumstances over *specific* issues. The pluralist sees the state as the independent arbiter of interest clashes among the range of societal organizations, including businesses, trade unions, civic organizations, and others, none of which is powerful enough to consistently shape state action. According to this view, the state itself is held together by a legal structure and an organizational culture that reflect widely held values which the state acts on to impartially manage the preferences of competing interests (Dahl, 1956)

Pluralist analyses of media policy begin with the study of social values and particularly concentrate on what they conclude is a shift from support for government protection of the public interest through public ownership and regulation to support for the operation of private, competitive markets (Derthick and Quirk, 1985). In essence, from this vantage point, the state oversees a marketplace of competing political interests, with no particular interest capable of determining decision-making on its own. The range of competing participants marshal political, economic, and intellectual resources to back their preferred policy positions. An interest succeeds to the extent that it can convince state policy-makers that it has power and that it conforms to leading social value preferences (Krasnow, Longley and Terry, 1982).

Pluralist analysis of media policy is also congruent with a general *functionalist* approach to social analysis. Hence, pluralists support the view that the widespread

155

introduction of deregulatory policies results from value shifts that favour reliance on private markets for settling claims. In the US and Canada, according to the pluralist view, from the post-war period until the early 1980s, societal values and public support for media policies facilitated the operation of the market by monopoly and oligopoly media providers. Pluralist research maintains that communication providers, particularly in broadcasting and telecommunications services, were regulated to meet broad public interest goals linked to democratically based principles of fairness and equity. In telephony, for the US and Canada, these goals included universal service at fair and reasonable rates. In Canadian broadcasting, this meant that the airwaves would be public property with service provided by public (CBC and Radio Canada) and private institutions. In the US, broadcasting would be provided by licensed private institutions but the airwaves would remain a public resource. Consequently, the issuing of private broadcasting licences carried public trust obligations such as freedom of speech and of ideas, requirements for providing public information, limits to advertising, fairness in programming, and equal time for political candidates. According to the pluralist view, these practices proved increasingly dysfunctional as new participants, some taking advantage of new technologies, began to tip the balance of power in favour of competition and market power over regulation. Media policy and regulation changed from concern over the public interest to facilitating the operation of private competitive markets (Crandall, 1991; Janisch, 1986). In the US, pluralists maintain, disillusion over regulatory protection of communication monopoly providers, particularly in telecommunications and broadcasting, unleashed forces that undercut the connections between these communications providers and the notion of the public interest. Two very different coalitions, conservatives advocating free markets and anti-monopoly liberal populist interest groups, came together to support broadcasting and telecommunication deregulation (Horwitz, 1989). Liberals and public interest groups perceived that deregulation would provide a solution to entrenched corporate power. Moreover, new technologies, particularly cable television, would concurrently transcend commercial network broadcasting and create a 'wired democracy'.

Pluralist research tends to identify technology as a major source of changing values. The growth of 'smaller, faster, cheaper, better' means of communication broadens the range of choice in communications services, making it increasingly unlikely that government monopolies or regulated industries can deliver the goods better than an open marketplace of numerous suppliers (Ernst et al., 1993; Noam, 1987; Woodrow and Woodside, 1986). For example, in a standard work on the economics of media, Owen and Wildman (1992) maintain that technological advances in broadcasting services have resulted in a surge of new entrants which have lowered prices, expanded services, and sped up the process of innovation. For them, as for other pluralists, this provides *prima facie* evidence for a shift from reliance on state regulated cartels (e.g. the three major US television networks) or state owned broadcasting entities (e.g. the Canadian Broadcasting Corporation) for the provision of broadcasting services. Similar arguments are made about telecommunications to defend the introduction of competition in US (Crandall, 1991) and Canadian (Globerman with Carter, 1988; Stanbury, 1986) markets.

For pluralists, the turn to market principles benefits the *process of policy-making* as well. Pluralists have traditionally noted that, however salutary the public interest standard may have been for maintaining a sense of inclusiveness in the media system, the principle multiplied the number of claims that could be legitimately made on the system thereby overloading government with unmanageable demands. This problem is compounded by the tendency of regulators to use regulations to their own benefit, permitting what Wilson (1980) called 'staff capture' of a regulatory agency. For the pluralist, the shift to market principles streamlines the process of settling claims, eliminates many as illegitimate, and undermines the power of regulatory and policy bureaucrats, thereby creating literal technologies of freedom (Pool, 1983).

The shift to the market does not please all pluralists. It worries some, like Dahl (1982), who has moved from his now classic position in defence of pluralism (1956) to a fear that pluralism no longer explains American politics because the balance of interests has become distorted in favour of corporate power with no substantial countervailing force. In place of reliance on the market, Dahl offers an alternative, what Held (1987) describes as a *neo-pluralist position* that calls for greater representativeness, for explicit state measures to ensure fuller equality and participation from groups that would otherwise be submerged beneath the marketplace power of business. This prescription grows out of a more general concern that pluralists have tended to identify the pressures of business and a rightward shift in the intellectual climate with a *general* shift in societal values. Furthermore, pluralists have tended to place considerable stock in the capacity for social differences to even out over the range of decisions with no single institutional force capable of seizing the policy agenda for a long duration. Finally, pluralists rely on a view of the state as the chief locus of ultimate authority in policy matters and as an independent arbiter of conflicting claims, and minimize the potential for capture or contamination by any specific interest.

Managerial theory

Managerialism acknowledges the shortcomings of a pluralist view and replaces it with a vision of *limited, elite-guided democracy* (Crozier, Huntington and Watanuki, 1975). Unlike the pluralist, who views power as situational, linked to specific events and networks, the managerial theorist sees it as *structural*, embodied in the rules governing the operation of organizations and institutions. A pluralist looks for power in the constellation of interests whose balance of pressures results in a policy decision, such as the agreement between the US courts and AT&T to restructure the company or the similar reorganization that led to the creation of Bell Canada Enterprises, the chief provider of Canadian telecommunication services. Managerial theory sees power in elites whose actions constitute the policy *agenda* which frames the pluralist's discrete decisions. Whereas the pluralist perspective focuses on the individual case, with change resulting from shifts in values and technology, managerial approaches concentrate on changes in the control of power over the policy agenda.

According to this view, the fundamental driving force across all political regimes is the need to manage growing societal complexity brought about by technological change and the division of labour. Managerial theory draws its inspiration from Weber (1978) and Schumpeter (1942) whose emphasis on the constraining influence of bureaucratic rationalization marks a significant departure from pluralism, which warrants the inherent tendency to power dispersal. Managerial theory starts from the view that the twentieth century is marked by the ascendancy of bureaucratic elites who play an increasingly central role in political and technological management, including intellectual technologies, which prompted Daniel Bell (1973) to advance the conception of a post-industrial society led by knowledge workers.

Managerial research concludes that the quantitative increase in services has led to qualitative changes in the structure of media industries (Beniger, 1986). According to this view, old regulatory approaches based on distinct technologies and distinct services and industries do not work in an era of increasingly integrated and convergent technologies, services, and markets. Managerial theory maintains that the experience of regulatory agencies, such as the Federal Communications Commission in the United States and of the Canadian Radio-television and Telecommunications Commission (CRTC), have shown that it is impossible to apply traditional regulatory categories to a new communication area where the distinctions between print, entertainment, information, broadcasting and tele-communications are being eroded. From this vantage point, several discrete, manageable technologies and industry sectors have merged into an increasingly integrated, but more difficult to manage electronic services arena (Bruce, Cunard and Director, 1986).

Managerialists maintain that an absence of fundamental structural change will result in the more powerful media interests resisting challenges from competitors and using the regulatory apparatus to maintain their power. This is the managerial version of the 'staff capture' thesis which sees the major telephone companies building alliances with regulators and other government departments to shape and influence changes in these arenas to their advantage (Babe, 1990; Noam, 1987). According to this view, changes to media ownership restrictions and deregulation stem from the development of coalitions including conservative governments, large corporate users, and cable television firms which are powerful enough to overcome old powers. New groups win out because they are able to apply their economic, political and technological resources more effectively. But as Aufderheide (1987, 1991, 1992) points out, much of the cost of these conflicts shifts to other groups in society that lack the resources to successfully oppose.

The major concern within managerial research is that the market may not be the best long-term vehicle for the effective management of the media sector.

Deregulation and privatization certainly provide the necessary impetus to re-organize media industries which were characterized by both rapid technological change and stagnating regulation. But as managerial research points out, de-regulating the cable television industry in the US resulted in little or no guidance in planning or coordination (Atkin and Starr, 1990). In fact, the 1984 Cable Communication Policy Act created an uncontrolled and unregulated monopoly situation in the United States which enabled the industry to increase rates, diminish service quality and participate in other non-competitive activities. Deregulation led to continued complaints by cable subscribers, among others, which resulted in the re-regulation in 1992 of basic cable rates and reduced cable market power *vis-à-vis* other communication sectors (Coustel, 1993; Atkin, 1994).

Additionally, former supporters of reorganization in the US telecommunication industry (e.g. the breakup of AT&T and subsequent deregulation) now admit that the original decision was, in the words of one, 'a monumental mistake' (Huber, 1993). Competition in the long-distance market is now viewed as an illusion, dominated by oligopolistic players, AT&T, MCI and Sprint, and regulated by FCC price-capping. The other mistake was reinforcing another powerful monopoly force, comprised of the seven regional Bell companies, in telephone local exchange. Concerns in telecommunications have also been raised about the economic arguments used to advance deregulation and divestiture. Oettinger (1988) describes these arguments as 'fairy tales' to support political forces and the goals of large business users (see also Denious, 1986). Critics of the managerial perspective argue that the telecommunication policy shift is not a response to a managerial control problem, but reflects the growing power of large corporate users and of new communication providers and that as telecommunications takes on greater strategic global significance, domestic and international policies must be changed, integrated and exported to meet the needs of these powerful interests (D. Schiller, 1982).

Class power theory

Class power theory sees power as *systemic* and calls for comprehending more than its manifestation in situation and structure. According to this view, understanding communication policy requires expanding the focus beyond a specific case such as how the US decided to roll back cable television rates in 1993 and beyond the agenda of decision-making which bears the label deregulation. Class theory sees control over decisions and agendas as expressions of dynamic processes and power relations in the class system of capitalist societies. This research sees the policy field as class divided and makes the case that democracy can only be sustained by overcoming these divisions.

Two major strands of class power theory, instrumental and structural research, attempt to explain how Canada and the United States developed their systems of corporate-controlled media, how the state works with the dominant class to

159

advance these interests, and why it is important to examine the complex relations involved in media policy and regulation.

Instrumental research identifies and analyses the ways the media industries use economic and political power to ensure that their interests and those of the larger capitalist class are met. It examines how media industries use technologies as instruments for capital accumulation and social control influencing all aspects of social life from work to entertainment. Additionally, it identifies and investigates the significance of class power by examining the dense web of connections between media entrepreneurs and the rest of the elite class through their connections on corporate boards, professional associations and lobbying groups, and through their ties to state elites (Domhoff, 1978).

US instrumental research takes up ownership concentration, the integration of media elites with other power elites, and the instrumental role the state has played in exporting deregulation policies and a private media model to other countries to benefit multinational business. This research concludes that massive consolidation and concentration of media ownership has taken place in two stages since the early 1980s. The first stage of domestic concentration occurred within specific sectors such as daily newspaper, magazine and book publishing industries, among others. The second stage involved concentration and consolidation across media industries creating media conglomerates like Time Warner with interests in print and publishing, film and video, music and cable television, etc. Activities like those of Time Warner and other media businesses have resulted in less than 25 businesses controlling more than 50 per cent of the industry (Bagdikian, 1992). Concentration and conglomeration have also been accompanied by integration between the media, big business generally and government elites. Reliance on advertising revenues and interlocking directorates with oil companies, banks, insurance and retail firms, among others, creates a commonality and flow of interests and of personnel (Akhavan-Majid and Wolf, 1991). Examples include personnel flows between the media and government and overlaps of personnel from broadcasting and telecommunications. Other examples include the mass media's reliance on the government for news information (press releases and press conferences) (Herman and Chomsky, 1988). In addition, powerful lobby groups such as the American Newspaper Publishers Association (ANPA), the Motion Picture Association of America (MPAA), the National Association of Broadcasters (NAB), the National Cable Television Association (NCTA) all exact their influence on anti-trust, media ownership and deregulation policy decisions.

Instrumental research on US radio broadcasting reveals the early influence of the Rockefeller Foundation and of communication research conducted by Lazarsfeld and others with the financial support of broadcasters and advertisers (Buxton, 1994). Research in this tradition reveals that telecommunication deregulation and the AT&T divestiture occurred because large corporate users banded together forming powerful industry and lobby organizations to demand new services and lower rates (D. Schiller, 1982).

Other studies highlight how the US government has been an important

160

instrument in exporting its policies of privatization and deregulation to advance US-based multinational corporations in the communication and culture sectors. Policy changes have not only permitted further global expansion, they have also allowed these businesses to appropriate more of the public sphere into the private arena. Examples include the selling-off of public radio spectrum and proposals to commodify the major national electronic network, the Internet. Private corporate activity also includes promoting consumerism and the reorganization of state policy to accommodate it. Invariably these activities limit cultural diversity, social information dissemination and democracy (H. Schiller, 1989).

Canadian instrumental research has identified the major elites in print, broadcasting, telecommunications and the cable industry showing that they have secured their positions of power through an interlocked network of directorships tied to other elites in finance, resources and retail (Clement, 1975). Recent instrumental research has documented the continued ownership concentration in the cable industry. Extensive domestic monopolies in this industry grew with state approval permitting corporate expansion through cross-media ownership in radio and television stations, periodicals and newspapers as well as telecommunications and non-media businesses. Fitting the characteristics and profile of multimedia conglomerates, the largest cable operators, Groupe Videotron and Rogers Communications, have expanded into the US, the UK and France (Hannigan, 1991; Winter and Hassanpour, 1994). Domestic concentration prevails with Rogers Communications' 1994 acquisition of Maclean Hunter, giving Rogers close to half the cable market and significant holdings in newspapers and magazines, to add to its already strong position in broadcasting and telecommunication.

Instrumental research explains *how* systems of corporate-controlled media and telecommunications develop and *how* the state works with the dominant class to advance its interests. This approach differs from pluralism because it concludes that power is not equally distributed among all participants in the policy process and that the state is not the independent arbiter of differences among these participants. In fact, by examining the process of policy-making, from think tanks to largely private policy formation bodies through lobbying and media influence, this approach decentres the formal state decision-making process to open room for the full range of players and arenas that constitute the multilayered process of policy determination and implementation. Nevertheless, critics point out that instrumentalism tends to neglect conflict and contradiction in the process of elite rule, much of which grows out of the oppositional struggles of classes and movements. *Structural* media policy research deepens and expands instrumental analysis by taking up these lacunae and by shifting from the how to the *why* of class rule. This research considers that the primary function of the state in capitalist societies is to serve the interests of dominant class fractions by advancing capital accumulation to produce and reproduce material resources and by promoting legitimation to ensure the maintenance of some degree of general popular belief in the system.

161

In addition, a structural approach acknowledges the contradictions in a capitalist society that arise from the state's often conflicting functions and from struggles connected to class, gender, race and other divisions in civil society. In an attempt to constrain and control structural contradictions among classes, and between classes and civil society, a structural approach maintains that the state plays an important role to ensure the survival and growth of the system. In order to create and maintain conditions of social harmony, the state produces policies and regulations to legitimize capitalist social relations. The state is an important site of struggle and of contradictions which also affect the policy formation process (Aglietta, 1979; Jessop, 1990). Concurrently the state's regulatory agencies, the FCC in the US and the CRTC in Canada are, in the structural view, best seen as 'unequal structures of representation' (Mahon, 1980).

One finds a substantial literature on the structural analysis of media and telecommunication. Structural studies of the US film industry examine the relationships among producers, distributors, and exhibitors within the industry and their links to the banking industry focusing on how and why these relationships have translated into control over finance and content (Aksoy and Robins, 1992) that extends from independent film producers to the cable television industry (Wasko, 1994). Moreover, as McChesney (1993) demonstrates, the US commercial broadcasting system grew out of considerable conflict and opposition. From 1928 to 1935 the broadcasting reform movement vociferously opposed the commercial model. Representatives from education, labour, religious organizations, the press, intellectuals and civil society groups, fought to have a portion of the system allocated for non-commercial and non-profit use. Pitted against powerful adversaries from the commercial broadcasting industry, their lobbyists and the America Bar Association, the 1934 Communication Act supported the commercial system. With only a vague public service mandate, the Act has continued to incite conflicts, struggle and resistance. Recent activism includes the American Civil Liberties Union and public television viewers' resistance to federal funding cutbacks to public broadcasting (Aufderheide, 1991). Other pressure groups have continued to engage in what Montgomery (1989) calls 'negotiated struggles' over broadcasting policies that affect television programming. The activism of complex pressure groups has resulted in policy changes dealing with an array of issues ranging from fundamentalism in morality, to violence on prime-time television, to the inaccurate and unfair representations of women, blacks, hispanics, indigenous peoples, unions, gays, seniors and the physically challenged.

Parallelling this view, Kellner (1990) concludes that the social relations involved in broadcasting deregulation in the 1980s were the result of a 'new conservative hegemony'. Until the 1980s the broadcasting system was guided by a public service mandate. The drive to deregulate resulted in the commercialization of many public services and ended regulation in other areas. Deregulation included changing rules to eliminate the fairness doctrine, lift the commercial advertising limits for prime-time and children's programmes, loosen ownership concentration regulations, and do away with previously required and publicly accessible reports on the performance of broadcasting outlets, despite strong and widespread resistance.

Structural analysis also shows that deregulation, pro-competition, rate re-balancing and re-regulation are not just about policy changes. They are also forms of corporate restructuring that eliminate jobs, accelerate deskilling, and reduce the bargaining power of communication unions. Recently some government agencies such as the Office of Technology Assessment (1990, 1991) and the National Telecommunication and Information Administration (1991) have begun to reflect on the meaning of a communication infrastructure and universality in a changing communication system. Nonetheless, much of this concern is couched in the language of economic competitiveness and consumer rights rather than the rights of citizens in a political democracy. Consequently, instead of broadening the definitions of the public interest (Aufderheide, 1992) or of universality (Calabrese and Jung, 1992) there has been a narrowing of the notion or concept of 'the public' to that of 'consumer'. To ensure that a market form of universality (US telephone universality is approximately 93 per cent) was maintained, targeted telephone subsidization was introduced through a federal 'Life Line' and state 'Link Up America' programmes, which, euphemisms aside, are modelled after traditional welfare programmes with means tests and policing (Aufderheide, 1987; US, FCC, 1991).

For structuralists, US government intervention in telecommunications to advance the interests of dominant class fractions has been an ongoing process beginning with financial and land grant assistance in the days of the private telegraph monopoly (DuBoff, 1984). Government assistance and regulation also helped companies like AT&T and RCA to achieve market dominance (Hills, 1986) and, during the Cold War, gave the Communications Satellite Corporation (Comsat) its backing to defeat the Soviet Union in global communication satellite development (Mosco, 1990).

Exemplars of Canadian structural analysis are to be found in film, broadcasting and telecommunication analysis (Smythe, 1981). The work on film and broadcasting policy emphasizes the complex relations involved in implementing and changing media policy. Direct government intervention established a film production industry (Magder, 1993) and the Cineplex theatre chain (Pendakur, 1990). The state's intervention into film exhibition also led the way for Cineplex's expansion into the United States and into the multinational film distribution system. The federal government's Telefilm and tax incentive policies helped to further integrate the Canadian film production industry into the US market. Broadcasting policy changes (The Broadcasting Act, 1988), and government support for new technologies, which include the potential for increasing US programming, have been contested by a number of organizations and civic groups such as the Friends of Canadian Broadcasting (Raboy, 1990; Ellis, 1992).

Structural research in telecommunications concentrates on the process by which *class rule* takes place in policy-making and regulation. The struggle for competition and deregulation in the Canadian telecommunications business, particularly in public long-distance services, was led by large business users and new providers. These groups, organized into large cross-cutting national and international associations, such as Canadians for Competitive Telecommunications (1986), the Canadian Business Telecommunications Alliance (1992), and the Information Technology Association of Canada (1989) among others, lobbied for policy liberalization and competition to bring business users lower cost and customized services. The public long-distance telephone competition hearings culminated with the CRTC approving open competition (Telecom Decision CRTC 92–12) because Canada had entered a new era of 'consumer friendly competition' (CRTC, 1992). This research reveals that competition in long-distance phone service and other deregulation decisions affecting enhanced services, resale and sharing, interconnection, etc., did not occur without resistance from industry trade unions, anti-poverty, public interest advocacy, rural dignity associations and civic participation by seniors, the disabled and native peoples. These groups and organizations also fought to make sure policy principles of universality and affordability were not lost or sacrificed. One of the more significant stages in the evolution of this case is the shift in allegiance of the organization claiming to represent all Canadian residential subscribers, the Consumer Association of Canada. Won over to the consumerist view that residential subscribers are nothing more than customers, not unlike business customers, the CAC concluded that residential subscribers would benefit from competition, even if that meant increases in local rates and an end to a longstanding social contract that linked affordable rates to Bell Canada's monopoly in the marketplace (Mosco, 1990; Coulter, 1992; Rideout, 1993; Winseck, 1993).

Much of the recent class power research aims to widen the debate about transformations in the communication sector by addressing why this has become a central priority of governments in almost every society. This research addresses the growth of communication to a central position in the capital accumulation process. Under the shaping influence of capital, with considerable state involvement, technology has been used to deepen and extend the ability to turn communication and information into marketable commodities. The communication/information commodity also enhances the value of more traditional goods and services (D. Schiller, 1994).

According to a class analysis, state policies have accelerated the process of commodification by rupturing longstanding relationships among business, the state, and labour. These provided a workable regulatory solution during a period of steady economic growth, national markets, and a strong labour movement. A primary US example was the relationship that linked the three commercial television networks, the Congress, the Federal Communications Commission, unions such as the National Association of Broadcasting Engineers and Technicians, and television viewers. Another linked AT&T, the FCC, state Public Utility Commissions, the Communication Workers of America, and telephone subscribers and, in Canada, Bell Canada, the CRTC, the Communication Workers of Canada and telephone customers. From a class power point of view, these relationships are diminished, when not eliminated, by the growing reliance on media and telecommunications for economic growth, the rise of global markets, and the decline of trade unions.

Nevertheless, this stress on growth, on capital accumulation risks an overly economistic view. Media policy is also directed to the more political interest of unleashing new instruments of social control by promoting the capacity to use the means of communication to measure and monitor information transactions (Gandy, 1993). In addition to refining the process of commodification by increasing opportunities for the economic use of information contained in and about media use, this also extends the process of *social control* by increasing opportunities for detailed surveillance of individual and group behaviour at work, at home, in the marketplace and in public life.

Structural approaches are also distinguished by their acknowledgement of the contradictions, tensions, and outright class struggles that arise from political economic tendencies in communication. Specifically, they suggest that the use of communication and media to advance commodification and control creates substantial problems including breakdowns in the ability to manage markets that are subject to regular upheavals, the decline of collective purpose in societies increasingly organized around individual consumption, reduced purchasing power among growing numbers of people whose jobs are lost or downscaled, and the likelihood of new oppositional coalitions to resist these tendencies.

In a changing communication and information environment questions are being raised and activism continues as new progressive movements struggle for democratic communication systems. Efforts to secure public democratic space on the 'information highway', referred to in the US as the 'National Information Infrastructure' (NII), are being fought by a number of groups and organizations including the Centre for Media Eduction, the American Civil Liberties Union, the Media Access Project, the Consumer Federation of America, Computer Professionals for Social Responsibility, the Electronic Frontier Foundation, and the Telecommunications Policy Roundtable. These groups have had some success in building the 'open platform' universalist principle into proposals for new legislation, specifically *The National Communication and Information Infrastructure Act of 1994*, to protect and realize the democratic potential of the information highway. The open platform's principles include universal service (a minimum level of affordable information and communication service), free speech and common carriage, privacy, and the development of non-commercial public interest applications and services.

Canadian social groups are also working to preserve public space and democratic principles for the information highway. These include the Coalition for Public information, the Canadian Library Association, provincial library associations, FreeNets, the Telecommunication Workers Union, anti-poverty organizations (Rural Dignity, National Anti-poverty Association, Public Interest Advocacy Centre), and the Inuit Broadcasting Corporation. Their goals and principles include broadening the definition of universality (to include equal access, local and affordable service on non-commercial networks), ensuring the diversity of socially useful information, creating public space for public and non-commercial needs, guaranteeing privacy, and developing a programme for communication competence (electronic literacy) for all Canadians.

Research from a social class perspective includes numerous areas that require more attention. One includes the history of media policy, involving the connection between policy history and general history. An example is McChesney's (1993) history of US broadcasting policy. This traces the American Federation of Labour (AFL) affiliate, the Chicago Federation of Labour's participation in the movement from the 1920s to the 1930s for public service broadcasting. WCFL, the Farmer–Labour non-profit radio station, provided additional support for the reform movement by favouring a public broadcasting model, to be government controlled and operated. Winseck (1993) starts the process of tracing the history of labour's continual involvement in Canadian telecommunication policy. Similarly Coulter's (1992) history of corporate and state power in Canadian communication systems reveals that universal service grew out of the lack of public confidence in Bell Canada's rate structure and limited service to urban centres at the beginning of the twentieth century.

Rethinking media policy research (Mosco, 1996) also includes paying attention to cultural diversity. Influences that affect policy, in addition to social class, include gender, race ethnicity and other broadly defined social movements. These dimensions of cultural diversity may complement or conflict with a class analysis. Examples include examinations of labour hierarchies in the business of producing and distributing media and information and addressing the presence of significant gender divisions within an overall class divided system (Gallagher, 1992; Martin, 1991). Additionally, communication research that speaks to racial and ethnic divisions reveals differential access to communication. It includes research on access to ownership and control of communication companies (Tabor, 1991), to jobs in the media, communication and informational technology industries (Honig, 1984), and to the consequences of ignoring the social and cultural use and needs of indigenous people (Koebberling, 1990).

Convergence: towards a new revisionism?

The rise of positions such as neo-pluralism warrant consideration of a convergence among major perspectives on media policy. Specifically, recent thinking about the state of mass communication research, including social class analysis within the political economy tradition, has raised questions about a 'new revisionism' (Curran, 1990; Curran, in Curran and Gurevitch, 1991). Although Curran claims this warrant carefully and with reference to important exceptions, he nevertheless concludes (1990: 157–8), referring to the general discipline of communication studies, that 'a sea change has occurred in the field':

The most important and significant overall shift has been the steady advance of pluralist themes within the radical tradition: in particular, the repudiation of the totalizing, explanatory frameworks of Marxism, the reconceptualization of the audience as creative and active and the shift from the political to a popular aesthetic.

(Curran, 1990: 157–8)

Although each of these areas is of concern to theoretical perspectives on policy research, it is Curran's view of 'revisionist accounts of media organizations' that touches most directly. Here Curran charges that 'disenchantment with the class conflict model of society', influenced by the widespread impact of Foucault, led to a 'retreat from former positions'. Although these developments influenced most radical accounts in mass media research, 'the political economy approach . . . was the first to buckle' (Curran, 1990: 142). Specifically, he claims that in the 1980s leading political economists such as Golding, Murdock, and Curran himself 'began to back off'. Golding did so by stressing ideological management and the individual values of reporters, rather than press ownership, to account for tabloid attacks on welfare recipients. Furthermore, Curran charges that Murdock did so by turning to the analysis of sources and discourses over and above ownership and management pressure to explain coverage of 1981 race riots in Britain.

In addition to raising critical points about the political economy perspective, Curran is interested in suggesting a convergence trend. Pluralist scholars, he contends, are shifting away from an emphasis on the individual autonomy of journalists to take up issues of structural constraint and power. They are also departing from a traditional interest in defending market neutrality to take up market deficiencies and failures. He maintains that the outcome of these reciprocal shifts is not full convergence because pluralists and class power theorists continue to differ in how they theorize economic and political power. Nevertheless, 'an intermediate perspective situated between these two positions has emerged as dominant' (Curran, 1990).

Some, including Golding and Murdock, take issue with Curran's interpretation. Golding and Murdock disagree fundamentally with Curran's interpretation of the field of communication studies, including political economy. Murdock summarizes their view by asserting that 'this is not a map of the field I inhabit' (interviews with Peter Golding and Graham Murdock, April 1992). Specifically, both contend that the suggestion of revisionism, buckling, or back-tracking fails to take into account the range of their work which has consistently taken a broad view of Marxian theory that incorporates ideological critique, semiotics, social policy analysis, and a concern for the complete circuit of communicative activity, including production, distribution and reception. Both note that, along with their earliest defining statements in political economy, they worked on a broad range of problems, following particularly Golding's interest in social policy and Murdock's in semiotics and discourse analysis. Curran, they maintain, mistakenly focuses on one piece of their early work, which set an agenda for political economy, and compares it to the wider range of problems they address today to conclude that they are back-tracking. Golding and Murdock conclude that, though their current work responds to new political and intellectual problems, it is consistent with their broad range of interests. Hence, even as their research leads them to address Thatcherite social welfare ideology and audience reception, they return (Golding and Murdock, 1991) to the essential principles of their political economy approach.[2]

However one responds to Curran's critique, it is important because it opens opportunities for serious debate that has been lacking in, among others, the theoretical foundations of policy analysis. Though Curran's work addresses more than class power theory, it raises questions that are particularly central to it, including its relationship to cultural studies, to Marxian theory, and to the broader range of approaches to communication studies. Nevertheless, it also reminds us that testing a revisionist thesis is no simple matter. It requires a clear sense of what constitutes revision, what constituted the original vision or conceptual position, and it requires an understanding of the history that comes between original vision and the hypothesized revision.

RECENT TRENDS IN MEDIA POLICY RESEARCH

Conceptual maps provide one means of understanding the state of media policy research. Another is to examine recent trends in state media policy that have attracted the attention of the policy research community. Currently, four processes stand out: commercialization, liberalization, privatization and internationalization.

Commercialization

Commercialization takes place when the state replaces forms of regulation based on public interest, public service and related standards, such as universality, with market standards that establish *market regulation*. Commercialization applies to both public and private sector organizations, though it is more significant in the former because it can serve as a step towards privatization. In communications, this has meant greater emphasis on market position and profitability, even among state and public service broadcasting and telecommunications firms. Specifically, it leads to greater emphasis in broadcasting on audience size, advertising revenue, producing programming that anticipates an international market and linkages to other revenue generating media. In telecommunication, commercialization means building and organizing networks and services with a greater concern for those customers, principally businesses, likely to increase revenue, even if that means greater attention to linking metropolitan centres in global networks, rather than to extending networks into rural and generally under-served regions (Calabrese and Jung, 1992). Commercialization has led state communications authorities to separate telecommunications and other revenue-generating activities from postal and other services, which are mandated by constitution or legislation. Defenders of commercialization argue that it does not preclude and may even enhance public service goals, such as universality (Noam, 1987; Crandall, 1991). Conversely, opponents contend that it is a means of transforming the space of communication flows which, in a world of limited resources, inevitably means supporting one class of users over others and relying on 'trickle down' economics to overcome class divisions (Castells, 1989).

Extensive US broadcasting deregulation began in the 1980s with the removal of most major structural constraints on broadcasting ownership, licences and business practices. Examples include: increases in television station ownership limits, from 7 to 12; relaxed anti-trust legislation governing multimedia ownership; the elimination of most aspects of the financial and syndication rules governing network control of the lucrative re-run market; the elimination of the Fairness Doctrine; as well as the lifting of most advertising restrictions and requirements to meet community programming needs in television (Kellner, 1990).

The cable industry was also deregulated, partly as a response to neo-conservative practices which treated broadcasting and cable operations solely along commercial business lines. Passage of the *1984 Cable Act* effectively eliminated basic cable rate regulation (only 3 per cent of the industry remained regulated after the Act was passed). It also constrained the rights of state and local governments to control the franchising process. FCC cross-ownership rules were established to prohibit broadcasters and local telephone companies from owning a local cable system. These policy changes established a virtual monopoly for basic cable providers. In addition 'must carry rules', the setting aside of channels for public, educational and government use, were eliminated. Moreover the Act exempted cable systems from regulations applicable to common carriers, i.e. telephone companies, or those governing public utilities, which weakened what little authority the FCC had over the industry (Coustel, 1993; Aufderheide, 1992). These changes strengthened the concentration of power among leading broadcasting and cable providers, and gave broadcasting licences and cable franchises near private property status. Broadcasting deregulation and the Cable Act became mechanisms to redefine the 1934 Communication Act by eroding its important public trust and public service dimensions. What the US deregulation story reveals is that deregulation does not eliminate government involvement. Rather it directs the government to oversee market rules rather than to protect public service concerns.

Further changes, some would refer to these as 'reregulation', in the US cable policy resulted from substantial rate increases that predictably followed in the wake of deregulation, specifically the lifting of local rate regulation. Over the period 1984 to 1992, basic cable rates increased by four times the consumer price index. One result was a levelling off of cable penetration to about 60 per cent of American households. In the light of broadcast deregulation which permitted profit conscious network executives to trim costly news and public affairs at ABC, CBS and NBC, cable television, led by CNN, became the primary source of such programming.

Hence 4 out of 10 American households were deprived access to the network of record for electronic news and public affairs (Auletta, 1991). Cable companies were satisfied with lower penetration rates because they would rather earn monopoly profits from basic and discretionary cable services than build systems in lower- and working-class neighborhoods. According to Aufderheide (1992) and Coustel (1993), citizens organizations took up the fight for regulation, particularly directed at the concentration of power in four of the largest operators – TCI, Viacom, Time Warner and Cablevision – with control of over 50 per cent of the US cable market. Television broadcasters and the local telephone companies also joined the fray with complaints of outdated and unfair constraints (cross-ownership prohibitions) which prevented them from entering the cable and video business.

In 1992 *The Cable Television Consumer Protection and Competition Act* was passed despite strong resistance from the cable industry and a veto from then president Bush. The Act restored franchising and basic rate regulation power to local authorities. However, it also required local authorities to promote competition by granting several franchises in a given area. Additionally the act lifts the cross-ownership prohibition between cable and broadcasting, and between cable and local telephone companies. Although the telephone companies cannot yet directly offer cable television services, they are now permitted to deliver video services on their networks and more importantly to invest in cable businesses. By lifting these restrictions the new cable act has served as a catalyst for further concentration across media paving the way for the recent telephone company investments in cable businesses, e.g. Bell Atlantic's proposed takeover of Tele-Communication Inc.; Bell South's investment in QVC home shopping and Prime Management (cable); NYNEX's share in Viacom; and USWest's investment in Time Warner cable operations (Andrews, 1993). Nevertheless, when the FCC responded to mounting public and congressional pressure by rolling back basic rates, the bloom came off the rose of large cable firms and the interest in big mergers between telephone and cable firms dampened throughout 1994.

Canadian government actions also reveal the persistence of government interest to commercialize broadcasting (the Canadian Broadcasting Act (1988)) and telecommunication (the Canadian Telecommunication Act (1993)). Both acts share two major characteristics. They neutralize the perceived pluralist autonomous regulator, the CRTC, permitting the federal Cabinet to override broadcast and telecommunication decisions. This increases the potential for direct political intervention. Furthermore, they emphasize competition and commercial concerns over public service aspects of communication policy. Consequently, these legislative changes reflect the overt ideology of market forces.

Liberalization

Liberalization is a process of state intervention to expand the number of participants in the market, typically by creating, or easing the creation of, competing providers of communication services. Usually, this involves establishing a private competitor in a public or private monopoly marketplace. Unlike commercialization, which aims to make business practices the standard for the communication industry, with or without competition, liberalization aims specifically to increase market competition. Since the 1970s, governments have liberalized the communication industry in most parts of the world by introducing private competitors in broadcasting and telecommunications. Supporters contend that liberalization lowers prices, expands services, and generally speeds up the process of innovation (Owen and Wildman, 1992). Critics counter that it substitutes private oligopoly regulation for state regulation, carrying out price, service, and innovation mandates that advance the interests of an oligopoly cartel and its more privileged customers (Mosco, 1989).

Liberalization of the mass media includes changing legislation by opening up once monopoly areas to competition. Historically, the United States government has liberalized the media through the federal court system and through changes to anti-trust legislation (Compaine, 1982). For example, in an effort to curtail domestic concentration, anti-trust legislation was used to separate the vertically integrated film industry's theatres holdings from production and distribution. Anti-trust legislation and the courts were also used to break up and separate AT&T's long-distance service and manufacturing operations from local telephone service. Local telephone operations were reorganized into seven regional Bell operating companies (RBOCs) and long-distance services offered by the new providers, MCI and US Sprint, provided a more competitive environment for long-distance users. Additionally anti-competitive charges have also been levelled at the computer software corporation, Microsoft. Through its best selling products, the DOS and Windows operating systems, Microsoft has established a virtual monopoly in the personal computer software industry gaining over three-quarters of the market.

In the US, cross-ownership rules were implemented to limit the degree of domestic vertical integration and horizontal concentration among media firms. FCC rulings and NTIA (1993) policy recommendations hold the view that these policies are too restrictive and that media firms need to be flexible and to diversify into other media activities in order to compete globally. The FCC has provided temporary and permanent waivers to overturn restrictions on broadcast–newspaper combinations. Moreover the NTIA recommends further modification to this cross-ownership policy in order to give the FCC broader waiver authority. Similarly, national multiple ownership rules, which prior to 1984 limited radio and television station ownership to seven stations, were weakened to expand that number to 12 outlets. This policy change has resulted in increasing station sale activity, with an expansion in 1993 alone of 44 per cent (Zier, 1994). Moreover, cross-ownership restrictions on telco-cable linkages were eliminated in 1991. Lifting this restriction has resulted in aggressive investment activity by the RBOCs in domestic and international media, for instance in telephone and satellite systems in Australia and New Zealand, cellular systems and cable companies in European and Latin American countries (Andrews, 1993). In 1992 the FCC also modified its network–cable rule, so that networks or cable companies can invest in each others' systems to compete in larger markets. Taking advantage of these liberalized rules, CapCities/ABC combines a cable system with a major network. The corporation's subsequent global expansion includes investments in three European television production and distribution companies, major interests in Worldwide Television News and, through ESPN, a 50 per cent ownership in European Television News (NTIA, 1993). To be successful in a highly competitive global arena, it is the view of the US government and communication businesses that policies must accommodate business activity over a wide range of media products by permitting cross-ownership concentration and expansion into international markets. It therefore favoured the 1995 purchase of the CapCities/ABC combine by the Disney Corporation, thereby creating a fully integrated global media giant.

A number of pending Senate and congressional bills are also aimed at liberalizing US communication policy. For example, *The National Communication and Informational Infrastructure Act of 1994* (Bill HR 3636, 1994), which received 1994 approval in one arm of the US Congress, combined democratic access to the newly developing National Information Infrastructure (NII or information highway) with a free market policy approach. The Electronic Frontier Foundation succeeded in having an 'open platform service' clause included in the bill. Open platform service in the NII ensures that residential and commercial subscribers have access to voice, data, and video services over digital lines in a switched end-to-end basis at a low cost (EFFector Online, 1994). Nevertheless, while the bill created the potential of democratic access to a delivery system which is still in its infancy, at the same time it removed the few remaining restrictions which prevented local telephone companies from providing full multi-media services. *The Antitrust and Communications Reform Act of 1993* (Bill HR 3626, 1994), which passed the House of Representatives, proposed to lift the limitations placed on the Bell Companies (RBOCs) by the courts in the AT&T case. In essence, the bill would permit local telephone monopolies to re-enter the long-distance market and deliver information services.

The 1994 congressional elections gave the Republicans control for the first time in over forty years and with it a significant push to the generally rightward movement of US government policy in communication. Following intense lobbying by the major corporate players, both houses of Congress passed legislation that would substantially liberalize communication markets by ending decades-old consumer protections. The bills differ in some respects but agree on the need to end most limits on the number of media outlets one company can own and to weaken remaining controls on cross-ownership concentration, permitting one company to own broadcast television, cable, radio, and newspaper properties in the same market. Some markets would add telephone services to the list. They also deregulate the rates that mainly monopoly cable television companies charge to their subscribers. According to the media critic of the *Washington Post* (in Irving, 1995),

There's something for everybody in the package, with the notable exception of you and me. Broadcasters, cablecasters, telephone companies, and gigantic media conglomerates all get fabulous prizes. Congress is parcelling out the future among the communications superpowers, which stand to get more and more powerful, and certainly more profitable, as a result.

Other legislation calls for the gradual elimination of government agencies which, while certainly not uniformly supportive of protecting democratic uses of the communication technology, have provided some balance in an area largely shaped by a few big companies. One cannot say with any certainty which specific piece of legislation will become law, and, even as law, which will survive court challenges and efforts to reverse particular items. However, the direction of change is clearly towards unprecedented liberalization of US communications markets.

Finally, after considerable political manoeuvring, in February 1996 President Clinton signed into law a Telecommunications Act which approved unprecedented liberalization of the communications industry, opening the door to massive consolidation across all sectors.

Privatization

Privatization is a process of state intervention that literally sells off a state enterprise such as a public broadcaster or a state telephone company. Privatization takes many forms, depending on the percentage of shares to be sold off, the extent to which any foreign ownership is permitted, the length, if any, of a phase-in period, and the specific form of continuing state involvement, typically constituted in a regulatory body, in the aftermath of privatization (Duch, 1991). This process has accelerated for several reasons, including the rise of governments ideologically committed to private control over economic activity, the attraction, if for one time only, of fresh revenues for government coffers, and the pressures of transnational businesses and governmental organizations, such as the International Monetary Fund and the World Bank. For its supporters, privatization is necessary because commercialization is, at best, an inadequate first step towards market control. Critics see in privatization the elimination of the principle alternative to complete market regulation, the loss of sovereignty for nations selling off to foreign firms, and the consequent loss of local control over national policy.

Canadian public communication institutions, or crown corporations, in its mixed public/private system, experienced substantial financial cutbacks or outright privatization in the 1980s and 1990s. Privatization examples include the international telecommunications carrier, Teleglobe, and the sale of the remaining government shares (50 per cent) of Telesat Canada, the satellite communication carrier. Both Teleglobe and Telesat are now controlled by Bell Canada Enterprises, which has used government policy to expand its national dominance in telecommunications. In addition, one of the three remaining provincial publicly owned and operated telephone companies, Alberta Government Telephone (AGT) was also privatized (Canada, 1989). Privatizing these crown corporations or public enterprises has changed them from instruments of public policy, which advanced national or provincial goals such as serving rural and other under-served regions, to private monopolies whose aim it is to meet the needs of continental and international business.

Internationalization

Finally, states are also creating their own wide range of teaming arrangements or strategic alliances that integrate them in different degrees of internationalization. These include regional trade alliances, such as the North American Free Trade Agreement, 'trade plus' arrangements like the EC, as well as institutionalized planning organizations, exemplified in the Group of Seven. Internationalization also brings about specific state organizations, such as the GATT, World Bank, and International Monetary Fund which, though not new to the global political economy, have taken on increasingly powerful roles in managing relations among the most developed nations and negotiating the terms of development (and underdevelopment) in the rest of the world.

This process has been particularly important in the communication arena because the transnationalization of communication networks requires some degree of interstate coordination. Again, this is not new to the industry – the International Telecommunication Union (ITU) began to bring together governments to co-ordinate telegraph policy in the 1860s. In recent years, states have developed new arrangements that enable the richest nations to exert tighter control over global communications policy. These have brought about significant changes in international policy-making, including the decline of Unesco, site of the major support for the NWICO, and the opening of the ITU to considerably greater private sector participation (Preston, Herman and Schiller, 1989; Roach, 1993; Sussman and Lent, 1991). These organizations are either less powerful or are transformed to reflect new power balances that all but eradicate equal representation among the world's nations. It has also meant the growth of short-term, function- or technology-specific sites for meeting and planning that bring together government and corporate decision-makers who, largely outside the formal and publicly accessible traditional sites of regulatory activity, coordinate technologies, services and pricing. The rise of associations representing large business and government users, such as INTUG, the International Users' Group, has provided one important opportunity for such activity.

Internationalization shifts communication responses from national policy applications to ones where bilateral, trilateral and multinational trade agreements require structural policy changes. Two trade agreements, *The Canada–U.S. Free Trade Agreement* (FTA) (Canada, 1988) and *The North American Free Trade Agreement* (NAFTA) (Canada, 1992) are significant documents which affect communications policies in Canada, the United States, and Mexico. Both advance a *de facto* new constitution for North America, one which institutionalizes the power of markets and multinational firms over the national public sphere (Warnock, 1988). The FTA is important because it is the first trade document to extend free trade to services and investments. The agreement also identifies telecommunications as a key industry and facilitator for the service sector, particularly through the provision of enhanced or new computerized data, audio, video, and other information services. Section 1408 opens free trade in enhanced and information services. Articles 105 and Section 1402 ensures that these are given a right-of-establishment or *national treatment* which requires the CRTC or FCC to treat communication businesses of the other country as if they were nationals and cannot require such businesses to establish a physical point of presence within the country (Canada, 1988). This stipulation is particularly important in the communications sector because most of its products can be moved electronically back and forth across borders permitting, for example, a US firm with all of its employees based in the US to process and distribute messages across Canada.

The NAFTA gives substantial treatment to telecommunications (Shefrin, 1993). The rules on trade in telecommunications services are broadened from those of the FTA to include investments, intellectual property licensing, standards and transparency of rules and regulations. One of the most important aspects of the document is the right it gives to companies to use public networks to move information freely across North American borders through their own privately secured data bases. Examples include: the guarantee of private corporate networks and value added network services (VANs); rights to build, interconnect and operate private leased lines, the use of dial-up access to interconnect to public networks; the ability to perform switching, signalling and processing functions; the use of communication products of their choosing; and, the ability to lease lines at flat-rate prices (Canada, 1992; Shefrin, 1993).

The Uruguay Round of the General Agreement on Tariffs and Trade is also in the process of adding trade rules for the service sector. Trade in services will be covered under the General Agreement on Trade in Services (GATS). In this new agreement telecommunications also receives special attention in the Telecommunications Services Annex because of the importance telecommunication networks play in the trading of most service industries. The Annex is modelled on the NAFTA chapter on telecommunication services.

COMMUNICATION POLICY AND NATIONAL IDENTITY

The renegotiation of trade agreements and the implementation of new ones, prompted by economic and political restructuring and reliance on new communications technologies, challenge national sovereignty and raise questions about national identity.[3] According to some, the globalization of communication policy formation largely in the interests of transnational media and telecommunications businesses, diminishes opportunities for national policy formation, specifically to meet the political and cultural needs of citizens (Nordenstreng and Schiller, 1993). For these, communication policy increasingly flows from the boardrooms of a handful of global companies, overseen by coordinating bodies such as the World Trade Organization, with little opportunity for genuine public intervention to meet national and local needs. As a result, all countries, but particularly those whose markets are too small to sustain substantial indigenous production for the local market, are faced with a declining capacity for independent governance and cultural formation. These critics maintain that without a major reversal in recent policy trends, the centres of transnational cultural production will replace the vestiges of national and local identity with the marks of global business – the products, the advertising and the media programmes that celebrate a triumphant capitalism.

Such a turnaround is not likely in the near future. Even Canada, which led the world in fashioning policies to support indigenous cultural industries, has embraced the new global trading order and, though not without considerable political conflict, is dismantling national cultural protections. As a result, critics contend that Canada is increasingly awash in American media products, from television to computer software, which threaten what remains of Canadian national identity (Ellis, 1992). Others agree that the threat is real, but question the accomplishments of a national state apparatus which equated identity with the nation-state. Institutions like the Canadian Broadcasting Corporation and the National Film Board defended Canadian cultural producers as well as Canadian product, but from the specific standpoint of the Canadian federal state. These institutions, as Raboy demonstrates (1990), consistently missed opportunities to advance local identities, oppositional cultures, and those elements of civil society that question the centrality of the nation state. The result was cultural protection, but of a specific variety: largely elite, white, male, Anglo-Canadian, and supportive of the Canadian federal system. Still others call into question the connection between ownership of cultural resources and the preservation of national identity (Collins, 1990). Writing about the Canadian experience, though largely limiting his analysis to television drama, Collins argues that Canadian media culture bears little relationship to its political culture. According to him, the preservation of a national cultural apparatus is unnecessary and, in fact, counterproductive to the development of flourishing political culture. At best, media products have little impact on politics, at worse they constrain the development of a democratic political culture because they confine it to the rules set by government bureaucrats.

CONCLUSION

This chapter has examined the state of communication policy in North America through the lens of principal theoretical perspectives and substantive tendencies. Specifically, it first described how pluralist, managerial and class power theories differ in their approach to examining and explaining communication policy. The pluralist perspective, true to its functionalist roots, concludes that communication policy results from trade-offs among interest groups, none of which dominates the policy arena. Pluralism functions to maintain order in a complex policy arena with the direction and guidance of government policy and regulatory authorities. The managerial view maps a different terrain, one that is led by an elite of dominant powers who, with government support, maintain order in the face of complexity by steering policy decisions to advance major corporate interests. However admirable pluralism may be, concentrated corporate power makes it unsustainable. Nevertheless, managerialism advances the long-run economic interests of society by favouring its most productive interests. Finally, a class power perspective sees the policy arena as fundamentally class divided with control concentrated in the hands of a dominant, increasingly transnational, class which advances its own interests against those of subaltern classes. From this perspective, communication policy is forged out of the power of dominant class fractions, but also out of the contradictions and conflicts that arise from a class-divided society. In addition to debates about the appropriate theoretical position, the literature increasingly reflects differences of view about the extent of convergence among these positions.

The chapter also addressed central tendencies in contemporary communication policy. Commercialization is the process of reshaping public communication institutions, such as the Corporation for Public Broadcasting in the United States and the Canadian Broadcasting Corporation in Canada, to operate along private business lines. Liberalization diminishes or entirely eliminates public interest requirements, such as universality in telephony and fairness in broadcasting, to permit private communication firms to more explicitly pursue their market interests. Privatization completely eliminates a public communication organization by selling it to private interests. Finally, internationalization promotes the development of transnational media markets by eliminating restrictions on corporate expansion and by establishing a global regulatory apparatus to manage the transition from national to global markets. The development of transnational media businesses and of supranational policy organs contributes to debates about the relationship among media policy, media content and national identity. Each of these four processes suggests the value of a class power perspective and also challenges the potential to create the conditions for democratic communication.

NOTES

1 Vincent Mosco acknowledges the assistance of a grant from the Canadian Social Sciences and Humanities Research Council.

2 Curran appears to be of two minds about their recent map of the field. On the one hand he considers it simply a 're-presentation of a political economy perspective', on the other an effort 'to distance themselves from simple instrumentalist and structural views of Marxist political economy, and define "economic determination" as an initial limitation and constraint' (Curran, in Curran and Gurevitch, 1991: 10–11). Golding and Murdock maintain that they have consistently positioned themselves against simplistic political economic readings and argued for limiting economic determination to the 'first instance'. In their view, Curran's interpretation lives up to the popular caricature of the rigid early Marxist transformed into a more flexible, indeed revisionist, scholar, but it does not match the evidence.

3 For insights into the troublesome concept of identity, see Ahmad, 1992 and Schlesinger, 1991.

PRIMARY SOURCES

Babe, R.(1990) *Telecommunications in Canada*, Toronto: University of Toronto Press. Concentrating on the rise of the Bell Canada monopoly, Babe provides the standard history of telecommunications in Canada. It critiques technicism in standard interpretations of telecommunication history and applies the tools of institutional political economy to assess the consequences of monopoly power in the Canadian marketplace.

Bagdikian, B.H. (1992) *The Media Monopoly*, fourth revised edition, Boston: Beacon Press. Bagdikian documents the extent and impact of corporate concentration of ownership and control in the US media. Although this book is anchored in the analysis of print media, this edition reflects the growth of cross-media concentration and of international media markets.

Collins, R. (1990) *Culture, Communication, and National Identity: the Case of Canadian Television*, Toronto: University of Toronto Press. Collins's work has attracted attention because it challenges standard interpretations of the impact of US media, particularly of television, on Canadian national identity. Collins contends that government policies to defend Canadian cultural industries have done little more than support a privileged cultural elite with little interest in providing people with what they want or in addressing the genuine need for democratic communication.

Crandall, R.W. (1991) *After the Breakup: U.S. Telecommunications in a More Competitive Era*, Washington, DC: The Brookings Institution. This is a representative pluralist analysis of telecommunications policy in the United States. Crandall explains the breakup of AT&T and the subsequent growth of competition in the American marketplace as the response to a shift in the balance of power in the political arena, away from AT&T, organized labour and regulatory bureaucrats to new service providers and diverse classes of users.

Derthick, M. and Quirk, P.J. (1985) *The Politics of Deregulation*, Washington, DC: The Brookings Institution. Defending a pluralist perspective on power, the authors produce a comparative case analysis that includes the rise of deregulation in American media policy.

Gandy, O.H. Jr (1993) *The Panoptic Sort: the Political Economy of Personal Information*, Boulder, CO: Westview. Gandy addresses policy issues arising from the application of new communication and information technologies. The specific interest is the erosion of personal privacy and the rise of a Panoptic society. The book assesses the policy debate on what, if anything, can and should be done about the threat to privacy.

Horwitz, R. (1989) *The Irony of Regulatory Reform*, New York: Oxford. This book examines the history of broadcasting and telecommunications policy largely from a managerial perspective. Horwitz maintains that the media reform movement was so intent on unseating the monopoly power of AT&T and the major television networks that it contributed to the dismantling of consumer and public interest protections that these groups were established to defend.

Kellner, D. (1990) *Television and the Crisis of Democracy*, Boulder, CO: Westview. Kellner draws on structuralist theories of the state and critical theories of cultural practice to assess television in the United States. The book focuses on policy changes that transformed television in the 1980s and measures the impact of these against a broad view of democracy that, in the media context, refers to the ability of people to produce and distribute, as well as to consume, media products.

Nordenstreng, K. and Schiller, H. (eds) (1993) *Beyond National Sovereignty: International Communication in the 1990s*, Norwood, NJ: Ablex. This collection provides a wide range of largely class power perspectives on national and international communication policy. Chapters address a variety of national experiences and assess the growing globalization of media and telecommunication policy in trade agreements, new

178

transnational policy organs, and through increased corporate control over traditional global fora.

Raboy, M. (1990) *Missed Opportunities*, Montreal: McGill-Queen's Press. Raboy surveys the history of communication policy in Canada and argues that an emphasis on state-directed solutions has resulted in a brittle system that defines cultural sovereignty and identity with the federal state system. This has precluded genuinely democratic alternatives which would use communication policy to support a wide range of local, regional, alternative, and oppositional sources of media and communication.

Wasko, J., Mosco V. and Pendakur, M. (1993) *Illuminating the Blindspots: Essays in Honor of Dallas Smythe*, Norwood, NJ: Ablex. The chapters in this collection address the legacy of Dallas Smythe, one of the foremost scholars in communication studies, particularly in the analysis of US and Canadian communication policy. Chapters provide a critical assessment of policy research in both countries and apply a variety of theoretical and methodological perspectives to recent developments in international communication.

REFERENCES

Aglietta, M. (1979) *A Theory of Capitalist Regulation: the US Experience*, trans. by David Fernbach, London: New Left Books.

Ahmad, A. (1992) *In Theory: Classes, Nations, Literatures*, London: Verso.

Akhavan-Majid, R. and Wolf, G. (1991) 'American mass media and the myth of libertarianism: toward an elite power group theory', *Critical Studies in Mass Communication* 8: 139–51.

Aksoy, A. and Robins, K. (1992) 'Hollywood for the 21st century: global competition for critical mass in image markets', *Cambridge Journal of Economics* 16(1): 1–22.

Alford, R.R. and Friedland, R. (1985) *Powers of Theory*, Cambridge: Cambridge University Press.

Andrews, E. (1993) 'From sibling rivalry to civil war', *The New York Times*, section 3: 1–6, 28 November.

Atkin, D.J. (1994) 'Cable exhibition in the USA: ownership trends and implications of the 1992 Cable Act', *Telecommunications Policy*, 18(4): 331–41.

Atkin, D.J. and Starr M. (1990) 'The US Cable Communications Act reconsidered', *Telecommunications Policy* 14(4): 315–23.

Aufderheide, P. (1987) 'Universal service: telephone policy in the public interest', *Journal of Communication* 37(1): 81–96.

—— (1991) 'Public television and the public sphere', *Critical Studies in Mass Communication* 8: 168–83.

—— (1992) 'Cable television and the public interest', *Journal of Communication* 42(1): 52–65.

Auletta, K. (1991), *Three Blind Mice: How the TV Networks Lost Their Way*, New York: Random House.

Babe, R.(1990) *Telecommunications in Canada*, Toronto: University of Toronto Press.

Bagdikian, B.H. (1992) *The Media Monopoly*, fourth revised edition, Boston: Beacon Press.

Bell, D. (1973) *The Coming of Post-Industrial Society*, New York: Basic Books.

Beniger, J.R. (1986), *The Control Revolution*, Cambridge, MA: Harvard University Press.

Bruce, R.R., Cunard, J.P. and Director, M.D. (1986) *From Telecommunications to Electronic Services*, Toronto: Butterworths.

Buxton, W. (1994) 'The political economy of communications research: the Rockefeller Foundation, the 'Radio Wars' and the Princeton Radio Research Project', in R. Babe *Economy and Communications*, Boston: Kluwar, 147–75.

Calabrese, A. and Jung, D. (1992) 'Broadband telecommunications in rural America: an analysis of emerging infrastructures', *Telecommunications Policy* 16(3): 225–36.

Canada, (1988) *The Canada – U.S. Free Trade Agreement*, Ottawa: Ministry of Supply and Services.

—— (1989), *Alberta Government Telephone and the CRTC and CNCP Telecommunications and the Attorney General of Canada and the Attorneys General of Quebec, Nova Scotia, New Brunswick, Manitoba, British Columbia, Prince Edward Island, Saskatchewan, Alberta, and Newfoundland*, Ottawa: Supreme Court of Canada, no. 19731.

—— (1992) *North America Free Trade Agreement*, Ottawa: Government of Canada.

Canadian Business Telecommunications Alliance (1992) 'Making the connections: the CBTA's new approach', Toronto: CBTA.

Canadians for Competitive Telecommunications (1986) 'The crisis for Canadian business: telecommunications rates and the public interest', Toronto: CCT.

Castells, M. (1989) *The Informational City: Information Technology, Economic Restructuring, and the Urban–Regional Process*. Oxford: Basil Blackwell.

Clement, W. (1975) *The Canadian Corporate Elite: an Analysis of Economic Power*, Toronto: McClelland and Stewart.

Collins, R. (1990) *Culture, Communication, and National Identity: the Case of Canadian Television*, Toronto: University of Toronto Press.

Compaine, B. M. (1982) *Who Owns the Media?: Concentration of Ownership in the Mass Communications Industry*, second revised edition, White Plains, NY: Knowledge Industry Publications.

Coulter, B.G. (1992) 'A new social contract for Canadian telecommunication policy', unpublished Ph.D. thesis, Carleton University.

Coustel, J.P. (1993) 'New rules for cable television in the USA', *Telecommunications Policy* 3: 200–20.

Crandall, R. W. (1991) *After the Breakup: U.S. Telecommunications in a More Competitive Era*, Washington, DC: The Brookings Institution.

Crozier, M.J., Huntington, S.P. and Watanuki, J. (1975) *The Crisis of Democracy*, New York University Press.

CRTC (1992) *Competition in the Provision of Public Long Distance Voice Telephone Services and Related Resale and Sharing Issues*, Telecom Decision CRTC 92–12, Ottawa, 12 June.

—— (1992) *Consumer Friendly Competition: the Facts*, CRTC News Release, 12 June.

Curran, J. (1990) 'The new revisionism in mass communication research: a reappraisal', *European Journal of Communication* 5: 135–64.

Curran, J. and Gurevitch, M. (1991) 'Introduction', in J. Curran and M. Gurevitch (eds) *Mass Media and Society*, London: Edward Arnold, 7–11.

Dahl, R.A. (1956) *A Preface to Democratic Theory*, Chicago: University of Chicago Press.

—— (1982) *Dilemmas of Pluralist Democracy*, New Haven: Yale University Press.

Denious, R.D. (1986) 'The subsidy myth: who pays for the local loop?', *Telecommunications Policy* September: 259–67.

Derthick, M. and Quirk, P. J. (1985) *The Politics of Deregulation*, Washington, DC: The Brookings Institution.

Domhoff, G.W. (1978) *The Powers That Be: Processes of Ruling Class Domination in America*, New York: Vintage.

DuBoff, R. (1984) 'The rise of communications regulation: the telegraph industry, 1844–1880', *Journal of Communication* 34(3): 52–66.

Duch, R. (1991) *Privatizing the Economy: Telecommunications Policy in Comparative Perspective*, Ann Arbor: The University of Michigan Press.

Ellis, D. (1992) *Split Screen: Home Entertainment and the New Technologies*, Toronto: Friends of Canadian Broadcasting.

Ernst, M.L., Oettinger, A.G., Branscomb, A.W., Rubin, J.S. and Wikler, J. (1993), *Mastering the Changing Information World*, Norwood, NJ: Ablex.

Fortune Magazine (1994) 'Microsoft's antitrust blues', 18 April: 1.

Gallagher, Margaret (1992) 'Women and men in the media', *Communication Research Trends* 12(1): 1–36.

Gandy, O.H. Jr (1993) *The Panoptic Sort: the Political Economy of Personal Information*, Boulder, CO: Westview.

Globerman, S. with Carter, D. (1988) *Telecommunications in Canada: an Analysis of Outlook and Trends*, Vancouver, BC: Fraser Institute.

Golding, P. and Murdock, G. (1991) 'Culture, communications and political economy', in J. Curran and M. Gurevitch (eds) *Mass Media and Society*, London: Edward Arnold, 15–32.

Hannigan, J. (1991) 'Canadian media ownership and control in an age of global megamedia empires', in B. Singer (ed.) *Communications in Canadian Society*, Scarborough, Ontario: Nelson Canada, 257–75.

Held, D. (1987) *Models of Democracy*, Stanford, CA: Stanford University Press.

Herman, E.S. and Chomsky, N. (1988) *Manufacturing Consent: the Political Economy of the Mass Media*, New York: Pantheon.

Hills, J. (1986) *Deregulating Telecoms: Competition and Control in the United States, Japan and Britain*, London: Frances Pinter.

Honig, D. (1984) 'The FCC and its fluctuating commitment to minority ownership of broadcast facilities', *Howard Law Journal* 27(3): 859–77.

Horwitz, R. (1989) *The Irony of Regulatory Reform*, New York: Oxford.

Huber, P. (1993) 'Telephones, competition, and the candice-coated monopoly', *Regulation* 2: 34–43.

Information Technology Association of Canada (1989) *Telecommunications Regulation in Canada: a Patch-work of Policies*, Toronto: ITAC.

'Interviews with P. Golding and G. Murdock' (1992) Loughborough, UK, April.

Irving, L. (1995) 'Telecom policy reform: end of an era or policy errors?', remarks presented to the Annual Meeting of the Federal Communications Bar Association, Washington, DC, 22 June.

Janisch, H. N. (1986) 'Winners and losers: the challenges facing telecommunications regulation', in W.T. Stanbury (ed.) *Telecommunications Policy and Regulation*, Montreal: The Institute for Research on Public Policy, 307–400

Jessop, B. (1990) *State Theory: Putting Capitalist States in their Place*, University Park, PA: Pennsylvania State University Press.

Keane, J. (1984) *Public Life and Late Capitalism: toward a Socialist Theory of Democracy*, Cambridge: Cambridge University Press.

Kellner, D. (1990) *Television and the Crisis of Democracy*, Boulder, CO: Westview.

Koebberling, U. (1990) 'Extending telephone service to Canada's north: experiences with service availability, quality and rates', *Canadian Journal of Communication* 15(2): 16–32.

Krasnow, E.G., Longley, L.D. and Terry, H.A. (1982) *The Politics of Broadcast Regulation*, New York: St Martin's Press.

McChesney, R.W. (1993) *Telecommunications, Mass Media and Democracy: the Battle for the Control of U.S. Broadcasting*, New York: Oxford.

Magder, T. (1993) *Canada's Hollywood: the Canadian State and Feature Films*, Toronto: University of Toronto Press.

Mahon, R. (1980) 'Regulatory agencies: captive agents or hegemonic apparatuses', in J. P. Grayson (ed.) *Class, State Ideology, and Change*, Toronto: Holt, Rinehart & Winston, 154–68.

Martin, M. (1991) *'Hello, Central?' Gender, Technology, and Culture in the Formation of Telephone Systems*, Montreal and Kingston: McGill–Queen's University Press.

Montgomery, K.C. (1989) *Target: Prime Time-Advocacy Groups and the Struggle over Entertainment Television*, New York: Oxford.

181

Mosco, V. (1989) *The Pay-per Society: Computers and Communication in the Information Age*, Toronto: Garamond; Norwood, NJ: Ablex.

—— (1990) 'Toward a transnational world information order,' *Canadian Journal of Communication* 15(2): 46–63.

—— (1992) 'Une drôle de guerre', *The Media Studies Journal* 6(2): 47–60.

—— (1996) *The Political Economy of Communication: Rethinking and Renewal*, London: Sage.

Noam, E. (1987) 'The public telecommunications network: a concept in transition', *Journal of Communication* 37(1): 30–48.

Nordenstreng, K. and Schiller, H. (eds) (1993) *Beyond National Sovereignty: International Communication in the 1990s*, Norwood, NJ: Ablex.

Oettinger, A.G. (1988) *The Formula is Everything: Costing and Pricing in the Tele-communications Industry*, Cambridge, MA: Harvard University Program on Information Resources Policy.

Owen, B.M. and Wildman, S.S. (1992) *Video Economics*, Cambridge, MA: Harvard University Press.

Pendakur, M. (1990) *Canadian Dreams & American Control: the Political Economy of the Canadian Film Industry*, Detroit: Wayne State University Press.

Picard, R. (1989) *Media Economics: Concepts and Issues*, Newbury Park: Sage.

Pool, I. (1983). *Technologies of Freedom*, Cambridge, MA: Harvard University Press.

Preston, W. Jr, Herman, E.S. and Schiller, H.I. (1989) *Hope and Folly: the United States and Unesco 1945–1985*, Minneapolis: University of Minnesota Press.

Raboy, M. (1990) *Missed Opportunities*, Montreal: McGill–Queen's Press.

Rideout, V. (1993) 'Telecommunication policy for whom?: an analysis of recent CRTC decisions', *Alternate Routes* 10: 27–56.

Roach, C. (ed.) (1993) *Communication and Culture in War and Peace*, Newbury Park, CA: Sage.

Schiller, D. (1982) *Telematics and Government*, Norwood, NJ: Ablex.

—— (1994) 'From culture to information and back again: commoditization as a route to knowledge', *Critical Studies in Mass Communication*, 11: 92–115.

Schiller, H.I. (1989) *Culture,Inc.*, New York: Oxford.

Schlesinger, P. (1991) *Media, State and Nation*, London: Sage.

Schumpeter, J. (1942) *Capitalism, Socialism, and Democracy*, New York: Harper and Brothers.

Shefrin, Ivan H. (1993) 'The North American Free Trade Agreement: telecommunications in perspective', *Telecommunications Policy* 17(1): 14–26.

Smythe, D. W. (1981) *Dependency Road: Communication, Capitalism, Consciousness and Canada*, Norwood, NJ: Ablex.

Stanbury, W.T. (1986) 'Decision making in telecommunications: the interplay of distributional and efficiency considerations', *Telecommunications Policy and Regulation*, Montreal: The Institute for Research on Public Policy, 481–509.

Sussman, G. and Lent, J. (eds) (1991) *Transnational Communications: Wiring the Third World*, Newbury Park: Sage.

Tabor, M. (1991) 'Encouraging "Those who would speak out with fresh voice" through FCC minority ownership policies', *Iowa Law Review* 76: 609–39.

US, Congress, Office of Technology Assessment (1990) *Critical Connections: Communication for the Future*, Washington, DC: Government Printing Office.

—— (1991) *Rural America at the Crossroads: Networking for the Future*, Washington, DC: Government Printing Office.

US Department of Commerce, NTIA (1993) *Globalization of the Mass Media*, Washington, DC: US Department of Commerce.

—— (1991) *The NTIA Infrastructure Report: Telecommunications in the Age of Information*, Washington, DC: US Department of Commerce.

US, FCC (1991) *Monitoring Report*, CC Docket No. 87–339, Prepared by the Staff of the Federal-State Joint Board in CC Docket No. 80–286, Washington, DC: Government Printing Office.

US House of Representatives (1994) *The Antitrust and Communication Reform Act of 1993*, Bill HR 3626.

—— (1994) *The National Communication and Informational Infrastructure Act of 1994*, Bill HR 3636.

US Senate (1993) *The National Public Telecommunications Infrastructure Act of 1994*, Bill S2195.

Warnock, J.W. (1988) *Free Trade and the New Right Agenda*, Vancouver: New Star Books.

Wasko, J. (1994) *Hollywood in the Information Age: Beyond the Silver Screen*, London: Polity.

Weber, M. (1978) *Economy and Society*, Berkeley: University of California Press.

Wilson, J.Q. (ed.) (1980) *The Politics of Regulation*, New York: Basic Books.

Winseck, D. (1993) 'A study of regulatory change and the deregulatory process in Canadian telecommunications with particular emphasis on telecommunications labor unions', unpublished doctoral thesis, University of Oregon.

Winter, J. and Hassanpour, Amir (1994) 'Building babel', *The Canadian Forum* 10–17.

Woodrow, R.B. and Woodside, K. (1986) 'Players, stakes and politics in the future of telecommunications regulation in Canada', in W.T. Stanbury (ed.) *Telecommunications Policy and Regulation: the Impact of Competition and Technological Change*, Montreal: The Institute for Research on Public Policy, 101–249.

Zier, J. (1994) 'Station sales rebound in '93', *Broadcasting & Cable* 9 March: 33.

8

MEDIA AND CULTURE IN LATIN AMERICA

Elizabeth Fox

In some ways, Latin American media research since the 1950s has shown a remarkably consistent commitment to critical analysis, rising to meet the demands of the political circumstances of each period. In other ways, it has come full circle, from the applied media development research of the 1950s and 1960s to the applied media development research of the 1990s. Surveying Latin American communication research trends, I want to argue that these two tendencies, the ability to engage in political activism and the ultimate return to a more applied discipline are results of the way the media developed in the region and the changing relationship between the media and the Latin American state, rather than of some special critical insight of Latin American intellectuals.

The relation between the state and media in Latin America moved from the state's initial support and encouragement of the private commercial media until the 1960s, at which point it became one of confrontation and conflict between media owners and reformist governments. This relation changed again to control over the media by authoritarian regimes, and, finally, with the return of democratic regimes, to privatization and the freedom of the market. These stages for the most part were present in all countries of the region, although not at the same time, or even necessarily in the same order. Media research took on a different approach at each stage in this relationship.

During the first stage of harmonious, generally mutually beneficial relationship between the private media and Latin American governments, media research was basically non-critical and applied, exploring the development potential of radio and television and the impact of their messages on traditional attitudes and beliefs, in other words, development communication research. When the development model began to show cracks, states felt the need to take a more direct role in the media. Leaders began to look more critically at the increasingly powerful media and attempt to decrease private control, increase national content, and establish some form of state control over broadcasting and even the press. Herein were the roots of critical communication studies, with researchers often working within reform movements, closely allied with reformist regimes, or in the international sphere in efforts to bring about a new international information order. In both cases research efforts were centred on an increased domestic or international role of the state in media and culture.

The failure of reformist regimes to achieve their wider social and political aims and the wave of authoritarian regimes that washed across the region, often staying for decades, ushered in a new school of communication research. Dictatorships imposed harsh political censorship on individual journalists, but largely allowed the private media industry to develop commercially, as long as it supported the regime. Critical researchers now worked side by side with alternative communication efforts, or from their places of exile, against authoritarian regimes. They spoke out against the state on issues like media and democracy, political communication and alternative communication. Research began to examine the role of the state more closely in terms of past cultural policies and the relationship between the state and popular culture.

The gradual return of democratically elected regimes and more open markets brought with it a more pragmatic form of media research, largely driven by profits and markets or centred on issues like state regulation, rather than control, of the private media. The media were increasingly autonomous from the state, but not antagonists, as they had been in the earlier period of state-directed media reform, and the role of the critical intellectual became increasingly marginalized. The return of applied communication research in areas like health and education, and the growth of cultural studies were less confrontational with the state and more attuned to the rebirth of democracy and the building of democratic institutions. A style of research emerged in many ways more functional to the everyday workings of the media in societies and to the state's use of media in its communication programmes. Communication researchers ran political campaigns, presided over national broadcasting councils, directed public television stations, and worked on issues like the regulation of the media in a free market.

The intense, often fiercely critical dialogue of the Latin American research community with media and culture in their societies reflects this changing relationship between the state and the media. It also accounts for the relative insularity of the Latin American research community, which largely has followed its own path, taking from outside intellectual currents what it needs to fuel its arguments, but usually returning to its internal dialogue, shaped principally by the evolving relationship between the media and the state.

As the relationship between the state and the media changed from one of confrontation to collaboration, some say research and theory on media and culture in Latin America has lost its former direction and conviction. Others find the new approaches like the studies of popular culture a welcome relief from what to them were the ideological certainties and reductionisms of the past. Still others applaud what they see as the move towards greater intellectual modesty and pluralism aimed at providing answers to issues like media regulation, communication for health and education, violence and media, and financing cultural resources. Regardless of how the role of the intellectual has been judged in the past, it will surely continue to evolve as the growing riches and poverty of the new communication age generate new areas of tension between the state and those who control the resources of information and culture.

BACKGROUND

In the last two decades, Latin America has gone from a continent ruled by authoritarian, non-democratically elected regimes to a region of largely democratically elected governments. In 1976 Argentina, Bolivia, Brazil, Chile, Ecuador, Paraguay, Peru, Uruguay, and all of Central America (with the exception of Costa Rica) were under dictatorships. By 1995 only Cuba remained undemocratic. At the same time, during the decade of the 1980s and into the 1990s, the region suffered its worst economic and social crisis since the Depression. Between 1981 and 1991, according to the United Nations Economic Commission for Latin America and the Caribbean, per capita gross domestic product dropped over eight per cent. People lost jobs and moved into poverty on a scale never before seen in the region. In 1980, 136 million Latin Americans – about two-fifths of the population – lived in poverty. By 1986 their ranks had swelled to 170 million, and by the end of the decade they had topped 200 million.

Government spending and public assistance did not alleviate the growing poverty. The foreign debt crisis in Latin America, combined with the introduction of neo-liberal economic policies and structural adjustment guidelines, led to a reduction in public spending on education, health, and housing. As poverty increased, the gap between the rich and the poor widened, reversing many of the gains of the 1950s and 1960s.

Despite economic difficulties in other sectors of the economy, the last two decades witnessed an explosion of the commercial media, especially broadcasting, throughout Latin America. Today, Latin American broadcasting is well developed, overwhelmingly commercial, and highly competitive. In almost all countries, about 9 in 10 people have access to radio and television. Elite audiences are targeted with a wide range of news and information programming from home and abroad. Large mass audiences are segmented by types of radio and TV stations, with news and entertainment tailored to different markets. Mexico and Brazil now have two of the largest media monopolies in the world –Televisa and TV Globo. These giants, wielding enormous political power in the selection and even removal of national leaders, have practically monopolistic control of their national markets. The Televisa and Globo empires encompass television, radio, film, video, and much of publishing in their respective countries, including, in the case of Televisa, part ownership of one of the world's largest private satellite companies and the largest Hispanic TV network in the United States.

Venezuela has followed the Mexican and Brazilian model of strong domestic media monopolies, integrating all aspects of the broadcasting industry and wielding independent political power. Peru, Colombia, and Argentina have more fragmented broadcasting industries, all three of which are in transition towards increased private control, greater monopolization, and growing political influence.

Uruguay and Chile, emerging from authoritarian control of the media under military dictatorships, are redefining state–media relations in the direction of privatization and deregulation under elected governments.

The relationship between the state and the media in Latin America is changing in the direction of the increased autonomy and political power of the private broadcasting industries. The failed efforts of Latin American states in the 1960s and 1970s to institutionalize a redistributive or social development role for the domestic media and increase the role of civil society in their regulation led the way to the virtual autonomy of the commercial media industries from government oversight. This autonomy often came in exchange for the media's political docility and even active support for authoritarian, non-democratic regimes. It allowed private media industries to grow stronger, eventually permitting their virtual independence from the government.

Today, few Latin American leaders would advocate policies of state control or of cultural nationalism for domestic broadcasting industries. There is no need. Domestic media are competing strongly and successfully in international export markets, and Latin American broadcasters have become significant exporters of entertainment as well as news. Latin American soap operas – telenovelas – garner huge audiences in Poland, China, Russia, Spain and scores of other countries. Mexico's ECO news service and Galavision are seen in countries of Europe and North America. On a smaller scale, Brazil, Argentina, Venezuela, Peru, Chile and Colombia have become cultural exporters, their radio and television industries filling time on satellite services, cable systems, and radio networks in the region and targeting the large hispanic audiences in the United States.

In addition to domestic broadcasters, the region is served by a host of Latin American, North American and European satellite-delivered news and entertainment channels, distributed domestically on cable and pay-TV. The 1990s saw an explosion of satellite growth as ageing systems of the mid-1980s give way to new satellites with digital compression, direct-to-home capabilities, and longer expected lifespans.

The commercially successful, politically powerful private media of late twentieth-century Latin America, however, were not always the norm. Although radio and television throughout Latin America had been privately owned and commercially operated since the early 1920s, when critical communication research began in the 1960s, the relationship between the media and the state was more problematic. Much of the impetus for the first critical, policy-oriented research arose from the tension between the state and private media owners.

A CRITICAL LOOK AT DEVELOPMENT COMMUNICATION

In the late 1950s and early 1960s, Latin American countries were buffeted by severe economic problems and mounting social pressures, in the case of Cuba resulting in revolution. In the search for a solution to these pressures, along with other reforms like land tenure and tax reform, earlier efforts from the 1920s and 1930s for national communication and cultural policies came back into vogue. The emphasis was on the use of audiovisual technologies to provide education, information and modern values to the 'traditional masses'.[1] International development programmes like the Alliance for Progress, the World Bank, and the Organization of American States made funds available for communication equipment and campaigns to use the mass media in health, education, rural development, and family planning, usually within government agencies. For the most part, states saw these efforts as independent from the commercial broadcasting industries and the press, which continued to operate in the same way as they had in the past. Much of the early communication research in and on Latin America was related in some way to the planning, implementation or evaluation of these development communication efforts.

In some countries the relationship between the state and the established private commercial media, however, was beginning to sour. Development communication efforts as a separate or parallel effort set up by the state were not achieving their goals. In addition to wanting to harness the development potential of the media, governments in power were feeling the need to control the private media or to set up their own media to communicate directly with the growing masses of voters, increasingly exposed to radio and television. Political leaders like Eduardo Frei and Salvador Allende in Chile, Juan Velasco in Peru, and Carlos Andrés Pérez in Venezuela began to argue for state-run or public media and for national communication policies. In response, the private media became increasingly defensive and hostile towards the state.

An implicit assumption of development communication had been that the private media were willing partners of development, even if their motives were commercial. The private and commercial orientation of the Latin American mass media had been firmly established for decades, along with a high percentage of foreign content, financing and control. Never before had the state viewed their operations as a threat. They became a threat, however, with the failure of development to solve social problems. Why, asked political leaders, should one naively believe that the media in Latin America would promote pro-development behaviour when their owners mainly were interested in personal profit?

In 1976, Luís Ramiro Beltrán, a former employee of the main state-run agricultural extension agency in Latin America, presented a paper at the International Association of Mass Communication Research (IAMCR) Conference in Leipzig. His paper, 'Alien premises, objects and methods in Latin American communication research', later published throughout the world (Beltrán, 1976 and 1979), summarized the main criticisms of over ten years of development communications research in Latin America. It contained the objections of Latin American political leaders and intellectuals who were beginning to look critically at the role of the media in their societies. Beltrán and his colleagues in development communications had managed agricultural extension programmes, overseen health and family planning campaigns, and cooperated in distance education and learning exercises. They now questioned the objectivity of the 'science' of communications, its ability to measure behavioural changes among the inhabitants of the region, and the need to refocus research towards the private media.

Research focusing on the individual and on individual behaviour rather than on the constraints of the social structure, they believed, was by nature conservative. The questionnaires, sample surveys, interviews, and statistical analyses used to direct and evaluate media effects and audiences could not capture the complexities and cultural diversity of the inhabitants of the vast continent. The results of this research served to maintain the status quo and fix blame for underdevelopment on the individual rather than on economic or political constraints. (Ironically, twenty years later, these same questionnaires, sample surveys, interviews, and statistical analyses would come back into vogue, this time employed by communication researchers for election polling: see Muraro, 1994; Consejo Nacional de Televisión, 1994.)

Researchers raised doubts about the role of the private commercial media and suggested examining the messages contained in the mass media, usually financed by alcohol and tobacco advertising, and the types of behaviour they encouraged – consumerism, elitism and racism. In 1973, a meeting organized by the International Centre for Education and Communication for Latin America (CIESPAL), held in Costa Rica, recommended as the principal focus of communication research:

The critical analysis of the role of communication at every level of operation in relation to class domination internally as well as external domination, and the study of new channels, messages, situations of communication, etc., that contribute to the process of social transformation.
(*Lenguajes* 1, April 1974, cited in Sánchez Ruíz, 1992: 21–2)

The questions raised as a result of the failure of development and development communications opened different avenues of research and activism in the field of media and culture. One avenue, encouraged by the new-found interest of many states in creating their own media, was the critical analysis of national media structures – a tradition of Latin American media research that continues today. This body of often emotionally charged descriptions of national broadcasting structures and content occupies a significant portion of the literature. (See, for example: Fernández, 1982; Herrán, 1991; Hurtado, 1989; Gargurevich, 1987; Lira, 1987; Mayobre, 1986; Moreira, 1989; Sodre, 1981; Rivadeneira and Tirado, 1986.)

Much of this research was directed at documenting private broadcasters' monopolistic control, excessive commercialism, and socially unproductive content. Often, it was coupled with a nationalist defence against foreign domination of the media and culture. Initially, this type of research stopped short of recommending specific changes in media ownership or control. Later, many of

189

the authors worked directly with national media reform movements in the region – Antonio Pasquali and Olwaldo Capriles in Venezuela, Luís Peirano and Rafael Roncagliolo in Peru, and Fátima Fernández in Mexico.

This first wave of critical research problematized the media and its relationship with the state. The media were no longer perceived as neutral in the development process and became part of a wider criticism of the modernization paradigm. If the media were supposed to be serving development and they were not, then there was something wrong with the media, and the state should do something about it.

DEPENDENCY

One of the main actions the state could take *vis-à-vis* the media was to encourage national content and reduce dependency on foreign news, entertainment and capital. The perceived failures of development and modernization pushed studies of media and culture into the range of dependency theories, perhaps the most original critical theory to come from Latin America. Dependency analysis was born from the crisis of the theories of development, including import substitution, and from the realization that dependency was a key explanatory element of the region's economic woes and inability to prosper. Underdevelopment, according to dependency theory, was not a rudimentary phase of development or the result of traditional attitudes and cultures, as development theorists would maintain. It was the result of the form in which these societies and economies were inserted in world markets. The Latin American theories of dependency reconceptualized Marxist theories of imperialism and the dysfunctional nature of capitalism from the perspective of the periphery. In the area of media and culture, dependency was expressed in terms of cultural domination. Oppressed cultures were suffocated by the cultures of their foreign masters, at times with the assistance of national facilitators.

Cultural dependency theory, derived from Marxist analysis, focused on the material base of the international media industries. According to Marxist theories, including imperialism and dependency, the investment of the mainly US advertisers, programme distributors, and broadcasters in Latin America and the role of the US government in supporting their overseas operations were the determinant factors in the evolution of the Latin American media. Some of the earliest work carried out within this framework had come from the United States (Schiller, 1969). The influential journal *Comunicación y Cultura en América Latina*, edited first (1973) in Santiago de Chile and later in Buenos Aires and Mexico City, moving with the succession of military coups in the region, contains much of the most representative literature of this approach from the region and from critical researchers from North America and Europe working with Latin Americans (for example, Dorfman and Mattelart, 1970; Mattelart, 1970).

Dependency analysis and subsequent studies on world systems and transnationalization in the 1970s provided the intellectual framework for many studies on Latin American media and culture. The Instituto de Estudios Latinoamericanos, ILET, in Mexico City, Santiago and Buenos Aires, and the Instituto para América Latina, IPAL, in Lima, Peru, brought together the efforts of researchers, working in their own countries, or, while in exile, under the support of ILET and IPAL. (See, for example, Arriaga, 1980; Beltrán and Fox, 1980; Esteinou, 1983; García Canclini and Roncagliolo, 1988; Portales, 1981 and 1987; Reyes Matta, 1983; Roncagliolo, 1986; and Selser and Roncagliolo, 1979.)

Studies described the foreign ownership and control of domestic media and the increasingly transnational and multinational nature of investment, programming, audiences and advertising in Latin America. This research coincided with the increasingly nationalist positions taken in international fora by Latin American states in relation to cultural autonomy, the international flow of news and information, as well as foreign investment in the cultural industries.

State-directed policies related to the research on cultural dependency and imperialism contained measures such as quotas for national production and limits on foreign investment in domestic media, advertising, and cultural institutions. Dependency theories provided little explanation, however, for understanding the institutions through which foreign influence was mediated and received by the dependent society and culture – the diversity, differences and conflicts at work within the receiving society.

NATIONAL COMMUNICATION POLICIES AND REFORM

As mentioned earlier, another avenue of critical, policy-oriented communication research that emerged from the region was closely connected with movements for domestic political and social reform. From the 1970s and into the mid-1980s, national communication policies efforts were undertaken throughout the region, notably Chile, Venezuela, Peru, Mexico, and briefly in Argentina. These efforts, ostensibly focusing on the private media's lack of role in social and economic development and popular participation, generally were initiated by governments as parts of broader political and economic reforms, and usually resulted in a wider state role in broadcasting. These policies, almost uniformly, were enacted in the face of an active and vocal opposition from the private media.

Despite significant differences in the parties and political ideologies that motivated the media reforms, they shared some common characteristics. All the reforms were concerned in one way or another with introducing public-service functions into the media, preserving cultural and creative traditions, and formulating policies for the large, disadvantaged sectors of society. In their own ways they were concerned with devising democratic structures and financial and management arrangements that would be representative, participatory and workable. And, none, with the exception of Cuba, proposed exclusive state or party control of the media as the only alternative to private commercial media.

191

In Chile (1966–73), media reform movements were involved in setting up a government-controlled national television network. In Venezuela (1970–5), the reform movement, supported by the president and led by leading Venezuelan intellectuals, attempted to increase the role of the public sector in broadcasting, including setting up a 'mixed' public–private broadcasting system. In Peru (1968–75) reforms went even further, expropriating controlling interests in private radio and television stations and nationalizing the leading newspapers, placing these under government control with the plan, never implemented, to hand them over to organized sectors of the population. In Mexico (during the1970s), the 'right to communicate' was written into the Mexican Constitution, and the Mexican government made significant inroads into the private broadcasting monopoly, including legalizing the government's right to employ 12.5 per cent of private commercial television broadcasting time for government use and setting up a national educational television network. In Argentina, President Juan Perón (1973–4) re-nationalized television and expropriated the studios of the private channels.

With worsening economic conditions, by the early 1980s most Latin American governments had backed away from their attempts at state control and national cultural policies and had made their peace with the private domestic broadcasting industries. Latin American governments, however, continued to play an active role in movements for international media reform and a new international information order through organizations like the Andean Pact, the Third World Bloc at the United Nations, the Movement of Non-Aligned Countries, the MacBride Commission, and the different activities under the aegis of Unesco. Latin American political leaders and intellectuals joined the demands of African and Asian countries for political, economic and cultural sovereignty.

Communication researchers were protagonists in many of the national media reform movements, supplying information and planning and often participating directly in their implementation. A large portion of the research from this period in those countries where reforms occurred was connected in some way with justifying, planning, evaluating or carrying out programmes to limit the private media, increase national content, widen popular participation, and increase the scope of government media. Communication researchers Antonio Pasquali, Luís Ramiro Beltrán, Carlos Ortega, Luís Peirano, Luis Anibal Gómez, Oswaldo Capriles, Elizabeth Safar and many others worked directly in the reform movements in their countries. Later, Latin American researchers, many of whom were exiled from their countries because of political repression under the military, continued to play a major role in the international debates on cultural imperialism, protesting the growing role of the transnational corporations in the worldwide control of media and culture. The contribution of ILET was especially important in this field, working first from Mexico under the direction of exiled Chilean intellectuals Juan Somavía and Fernando Reyes Matta with the collaboration of Héctor Schmucler from Argentina, Rafael Roncagliolo from Peru, Diego Portales from Chile, and Mexican and Latin American researchers.

THE MEDIA, AUTHORITARIANISM AND DEMOCRATIZATION

In many countries, the development programmes and social and economic reforms of the 1960s and 1970s did not fulfil their promise of political democracy, economic growth, and political security. Social inequalities and structural rigidities seemed to be increasing. Critics from the right challenged the role of civilian governments both as sources of economic leadership and planning and as vehicles for the redistribution of power and wealth. Revolutionary movements and pressures for wider political participation were growing, and the traditional social and political structures seemed incapable of containing them. To some, the military appeared to offer the only solution.

The new breed of military regimes that swept Latin America hoped to obtain economic development by an autocratic state employing technocrats in increasingly close association with transnational corporations. The military regimes that overthrew civilian governments throughout the region (Brazil 1964, Chile 1973, Uruguay 1973, Argentina 1976, Bolivia 1980) manipulated formal education and symbols of nationalism and modernization, using the mass media to control public and private information and communication. The military placed private broadcasting under their political control, censored newspapers and magazines, and arrested and killed journalists. At the same time, the new ideology of economic growth under political authoritarianism gave a free hand to the commercial and transnational growth of the mass media. The military's large investments in new communication technologies and national infrastructure and extensive use of advertising further boosted the commercial development of broadcasting.

The mirage of state reform of the media faded in the face of the military dictatorships that tenaciously held on to power across the continent, in the case of Chile into the 1990s. If research and policy on media and culture during the 1970s had been concerned with working with the state to reform its communication resources, a perverse fascination with the authoritarian state and its manipulation and control of these same resources by and large occupied the analysis of the 1980s. Given the inability of researchers to work within the state or for state-driven reforms, a concern with popular opposition and resistance to authoritarian control occupied their attention.

The rich and varied research produced in some countries under authoritarian states includes critical analyses of the military's manipulation of media and ravages of personal freedoms – for example the work of Giselle Munizaga and Paulina Gutiérrez in Chile and of Patricia Terrero in Argentina. Other studies examined the use of media by authoritarian regimes, resistance and 'alternative media' under dictatorships, and the limits and difficulties of 'redemocratizing' national media systems (Portales, 1981). Private research institutions such as CENECA in Chile, and CEDES and CLACSO in Argentina, and universities like the Universities of Campinas and São Paulo in Brazil played key roles in keeping critical enquiry alive, often under difficult circumstances. In some countries, for example Paraguay, the lack of intellectual freedom and the minimum conditions for scholarship under the military left little room for research or analysis of communication and culture. In others, research continued, albeit with minimal support, for example, in Bolivia (Rivadeneira Prado, 1982) and Uruguay (Gabay, 1988).

ALTERNATIVE MEDIA

During the long years of military dictatorship and non-democratic regimes, people and organizations deprived of access to the mass media and eager to keep alive a cultural and political resistance to the dictatorships turned to other media like community radio and newspapers, local video production, and neighbourhood theatre. These experiences came to be known as 'alternative' media and were a form of expression or protest in societies where having an opinion or expressing an idea were often dangerous, and access to the mainstream or commercial media was impossible.

Alternative media were not new to Latin America. Historically the region harboured thousands of diverse and varied forms of expression, often ways of keeping alive the alternative values and expressions of a group that was politically, economically, ethnically or culturally excluded or removed from power. Some alternative uses of the media, for example the Radio Mineras of the Bolivian tin miners, began soon after World War II. Other alternative media were led by the Catholic Church after Vatican II announced the Church's preferential option for the poor and support for many of the components of liberation theology. As a result, as part of its pastoral activities the Church developed different group and popular 'alternative' communication media.

In some cases the alternative media were both an authentic alternative to the government-controlled, alienating mass media and a form of democratic and participatory communication. In others they served as filters that decoded, interpreted and helped people resist the monolithic message disseminated by the mass media under the dictatorships. In still others, the alternative media served a specific role of popular organization and education. Much of the Latin American research on alternative communication was closely connected with action programmes, and many researchers also were protagonists in alternative communication media and processes. Some of the experiences of alternative communication are analysed in Festa and Lins da Silva (1986).

POPULAR CULTURE

During the years of dictatorship, and deprived of access to the state and to state-directed reforms of the media, some Latin American researchers changed their focus from the authoritarian control of the media to the study of popular culture. Research on popular culture is among the most insightful and theoretically challenging to come out of Latin America, and it profoundly shook the foundations of theories of alternative communication. This 'theoretical earthquake' is most clearly exemplified in the work of Jesús Martín-Barbero and Néstor García

Canclini, whose studies of popular culture challenged research (and policy) on development, dependency, and reform and questioned the very existence of alternative communication.

Many of the theories of alternative communication are premised on the purity and absence of contamination from mass media of popular communication processes and actors. Research on popular culture and reception (Fuenzalida and Hermosilla, 1989; Fuenzalida *et al.*, 1990; García Canclini, 1990; Martín-Barbero, 1987) disputed this premise. As Huesca and Dervin observe: 'The lines between oppressor and oppressed – assumed to be demarcated clearly in much of the alternative communication work – were seen as blurred and moving' (1994: 12).

Studies of popular culture revealed the contradictions, mixtures and syncretism that make up the supposedly 'traditional' attitudes of the peasant, the Indian and the poor in Latin America, the main targets of modernization and development communication efforts. They showed that cultural identity is not only or simply the product of the imposition of the strong on the weak or the foreign on the national, but a mixture of acceptance, rejection and re-elaboration, continually under negotiation. They revealed the mixture within the alternative of submission, complicity, resistance and reconversion.[2]

Theories of popular culture, like those of Jesús Martín-Barbero and Néstor García Canclini, questioned theories of dependency and domination as well as the possibility of state-driven policy reform. These concepts, the authors affirmed, had been constructed on a simplistic and mechanical view of culture and of the state that ignored their historical formation and the transactions that take place continuously at all levels. As Martín-Barbero explains:

> people came out of the world of academia and government planning and had to confront the cultural reality of these countries: the new combinations and syntheses – the *mestizajes* – that reveal not just the racial mixture that we come from but the interweaving of modernity and the residues of various cultural periods, the mixture of social structure and sentiments. We became aware of the memories and images that blend together the indigenous Indian roots with a *campesino* culture, the rural with the urban, the folkloric with popular culture, and the popular with the new mass culture.
>
> (Martín-Barbero, 1993: 2)

The awareness of popular culture as that 'dense variety of strong, living, popular cultures which provide a space for profound conflict and unstoppable cultural dynamism' (Martín-Barbero, 1993: 2), enabled Latin American research to break out of the circle of false logic which made it appear that capitalistic homogenization was the only meaning of contemporary modernity. Research was invited to study the processes creating mass culture without transforming these into processes of cultural degradation – to study these processes from the perspective of mediations and the protagonists of culture.

Néstor García Canclini's work concerned how communication researchers should study the hybrid cultures constituting modernity in Latin America. How, he asked, can the partial knowledge of the different disciplines that are concerned with culture be brought together to elaborate a more plausible explanation of the contradictions and failures of modernization? What are the tools to capture the hybrids of culture and make them understandable in the context of often less than transparent cultural policies (García Canclini, 1989). This challenge was met in the work on popular radio by Rosa María Alfaro *et al.* (1990), popular humour by Peirano and Sánchez León (1984), and by Argentine cultural historians' studies of the sub-genres of detective novels, children's stories, magazines, radio theatre, and journalism (Ford, Rivera and Romano, 1985). Other researchers carried out studies of specific programmes and popular TV entertainers (Altamirano, 1987), and of the relation of popular and transnational cultural products (García Canclini and Roncagliolo, 1988). As the prospect of redemocratization began to appear more likely, however, other researchers turned again to policy analysis, attempting to understand cultural policy and the possibility of future policy formulation within the new democratic states.

NEW CULTURAL POLICIES AND POLITICS

The Latin American Council on Social Sciences, CLACSO, formed a research group on cultural policies, including García Canclini, Guillermo Bonfíl, Sergio Miceli, Oscar Landi, Luís Peirano, and José Joaquin Brunner. Their studies took cultural policies beyond the state-directed cultural policies of the previous decades to include transnationals, the domestic private sector, and grassroots organizations. This shifting of research emphasis away from the state was the logical result of the privatization of public services, the shift towards unregulated market economies, and the increased role of the private media in the formation of political subjects and the definition of a political culture. The CLACSO group brought together researchers to study the cultural basis of popular and revolutionary movements and the role of culture in the construction of hegemony and consensus (García Canclini, 1987; Landi, 1984; Brunner, 1985; Miceli, 1984; CLACSO, 1989).

Research examined the role of media and culture in the construction of hegemony and consensus in the new political arena. Roberto Amaral and Cesar Guimarães studied the relationship between television (Globo) and politics in Brazil (1986 and 1990); Lins da Silva (1990) looked at the media in the 1989 Brazilian elections; Javier Protzel (1991) examined media and political marketing in the Peruvian elections between Várgas Llosa and Fujimori; and Oscar Landi analysed the role of television in setting the scenario, agenda and language of politics in Argentina (1992).

NO UNIFYING THEME

The gradual return to democracy in Latin America, coupled with the introduction of free-market economic policies, deregulation and the privatization of state-owned enterprises formed a new relationship between the state and the media and

196

introduced some new issues in media research. Studies that had been carried out on movements for communication and development, national communication policies and reform, and in the struggles against dictatorship gave way to myriad different projects. None of these focused the collective energies of the research community in quite the same way as those of the past. Enrique Sánchez Ruíz speaks of the movement away from the intellectually authoritarian style of the past, with a monopoly on the absolute truth, towards a greater intellectual modesty and pluralism (Sánchez Ruíz, 1992: 16). José Marques de Melo (1993: 218) interprets the change in research as the preservation of a critical attitude in the formulation of hypotheses and the initial assumptions of research, but notes the use of both qualitative and quantitative measures to describe and diagnose the processes of media and culture.

Rather than grand designs and theories about the state and the media, research and policy on media and culture in Latin America has begun to focus on those spaces in which media and culture have a distinct social, economic or political impact, be this in education, election campaigns, the market, or new development efforts. These spaces are predominantly spaces within elected democracies and free-market utopias; research is more administrative and less critical. Signs of what to some can be called a coming of age and to others a growing pragmatism or conformity of the Latin American research community (Faraone, 1992), are provided by the upsurge of interest in studies on media education and on the relationship between media and formal schooling.

This shift makes research coming from Latin America appear less critical, or perhaps more resigned, than that coming from Europe or even the United States. Indeed, as Sinclair (1994: 27) observes, most of the current literature on globalization or internationalization is concerned with the Americanization of Europe, probably because these issues continue to be of interest to the state in these societies. There is little of this research coming from Latin America. Latin American political leaders and governments have by and large abandoned nationalist concerns for protecting cultural identity as well as measures for underpinning the role of state media. The European Union's demands for quotas for nationally-produced programming, or debates over the shrinking public broadcasting sphere sound passé in Latin America where states fought these battles some twenty years ago, and where the private sector is now so strong that it exports national programming. Today, state concerns are in the fields of health, education, economic growth and political stability. States are also for the first time beginning to address some of the regulatory issues that come with the democratic oversight of the private media sector. Research reflects this interest.

CHANGING ROLE OF REGULATION

In a recent study of television, Vizcaíno (1992), in a clear departure from the more critical research of the past, analyses issues of public versus private interest in

Colombian broadcasting, including questions of regionalization, the financial base of television, and specific proposals for producers and politicians. The work of the Division of Research, Supervision and Development of the National Television Council of Chile, the public body charged with overseeing the content of commercial and state television in Chile under the new democratic regime, provides another example of a new interest in regulation as part of the changing relationship between the state and the media. The Council studies programming trends in Chilean television and their degree of conformity with the legislation regulating television content. The Council uses content analyses, focus groups, people meters, and participant observation to analyse and measure television programming and the perceptions and opinions of television audiences (Consejo Nacional de Televisión, 1994).

Yet another example of the new context of research on media and culture in Latin America is contained in Guillermo Sunkel's reflections on mass media and violence in the Chilean transition, and in debates on media and violence in Colombia (Arizola *et al.*, 1988). Sunkel's conclusions place the debate on the media in Chile squarely within the parameters of ongoing discussions on media and violence in Europe or North America, in other words, how the state can regulate market forces:

> Presently, the media operate within a framework of the market in which two principles predominate – freedom and responsibility. Within this framework it is clear that the media are free to do their 'business' in the field of information. There is, however, no consensus regarding the limits of the media's activity of informing, with the possible exception of questions of libel, slander and privacy. The debate over the media and violence can be a starting point to define what exactly is meant by 'responsibility' in the field of information and when the 'business' of the media crosses the line into illegitimacy.
>
> (Sunkel, 1994: 39)

The growing pragmatism of media research does not mean that studies on the effects of 'globalization' and 'transnationalization' are no longer carried out in Latin America. There continues to be a significant amount of this research conducted, especially in graduate and undergraduate communication schools throughout the region. It tends to be descriptive, however, and its links with domestic policy again are tied to issues of trade and regulation, for example, the role of the state in new regional economic trade agreements. An example of this is the research carried out in Mexico on the cultural impact of the North American Free Trade Agreement (Esteinou, 1992, among many others).

TELENOVELAS AND AUDIENCES

Within the current space of Latin American research, the Latin American soap opera, enormously popular and economically successful both domestically and as an export, has inspired a large amount of research. In 1993, Ana María Fadul published *Serial Fiction in TV: the Latin American Telenovelas*. Her volume stresses the need to go beyond an ideological analysis of the manipulative and commercial role of the soap opera. The soap opera, Fadul argues, should be understood as a richer and more complex phenomenon and its positive contribution in behaviour change should be recognized, as in Brazil and Mexico where the soap opera has been used as a vehicle for family planning and health programmes.

Researchers, however, do not ignore the social and political context within which the phenomenal success of the Latin American soap opera occurred. Martín-Barbero and Sonia Muñoz in their volume *Televisión y Melodrama* (1992: 11) ask, 'What is the importance of studying soap operas in a country so painfully torn apart by suffering and violence as is Colombia today? What guarantee do we have that this study will not end up legitimizing the escapism of some and the profits of others?' The studies these authors bring together from researchers in Argentina, Brazil, Colombia, Chile, Mexico and Peru, however, ask less about the impact and influence of the technologies, channels and codes of the media and more about communication itself, understood as 'the web of words and desires, memories and structures of feelings, social divisions and cultural discontinuities, appropriations and resistances that the media mediate and with which the people knit together their everyday lives' (Martín-Barbero and Muñoz, 1992: 6). In an attempt to comprehend communication processes, the studies examine the contexts in which soap operas are viewed and the modes of soap opera viewing by women and youth from different social groups. The work on Mexican soap operas by Jorge González (1994) and Jesús Galindo (1985) also is descriptive and interpretive of the production processes, 'texts' and audience viewings or 'readings' of Latin American soap operas.

The research of Fuenzalida and Hermosilla, who carried out pioneering studies on television reception analysis and audiences in Chile in the 1980s, has continued in other countries. Guillermo Orózco in Mexico, for example, examines audience segmentation and the different appropriations of messages of audiences. Orózco has developed the concept of the multiple identity of the audience, with a methodology that captures traditional audience categories as well as the manner in which the audience mediates the message for their own use (Orózco, 1993 and 1994). All these efforts attempt to understand the specificity of the Latin American communication experience and audience.

TECHNOLOGY

The rapid spread of new technologies of communication throughout the region since the 1970s should have led to far more research on technology policy and impact than has so far occurred. A 1983 survey by Mattelart and Schmucler, *América Latina en la encrucijada telemática* was an early attempt to link state policies and technological options with social and political impacts. There was little follow-up to this study, although the recent privatization of telephone companies in the region have inspired some analysis, especially in those countries where state-owned telephone companies were sold to private companies from Europe and North America. This paucity of critical research on technology is probably the result of the lack of national technology policies in the region and the absence of state support for research on the social costs and benefits of adopting different technology options.

In Brazil and Mexico, the presence of a strong state role in national technology policies made these the countries where the most research has been done on communications technology. This was aided by the strong public university structure in both countries and the existence in Mexico of two international research centres: the Centro de Estudios Económicos y Sociales del Tercer Mundo (CEESTEM) and the Instituto Latinoaméricano de Estudios Transnacionales (ILET). These institutions attracted significant national and international funding for research on communication technology within the broader context of social and political changes. There was also significant support for research on communication technologies from Mexican universities, as shown for example in the work of Ligia María Fadul (1984) and Carmen Gómez Mont (1992).

FINAL NOTE

The challenge facing Latin America today in the relationship between the state and the media – to construct truly democratic media within largely free-market economies – is more pragmatic and diffused than it has been at any time in the last quarter of a century. It requires an examination of the rights and obligations of the individual, the organizations of civil society and the increasingly autonomous, powerful, and transnational, media and culture industries. Among many other tasks it involves the design and implementation of regulatory regimes, the organization of direct and indirect state assistance, and the formulation of trade policy for media and cultural organizations.

So far these wider considerations of rights and obligations, political representation and accountability have been largely missing from the research agendas of the region. The long absence of democratic systems made some topics largely academic, and most state-oriented reforms fortified governmental and private commercial broadcasting industries rather than democratic structures. Today, however, Latin American researchers are contributing to the construction of democratic communication in areas like communication and regional integration (Kunsch, 1993), communication rights and the rule of law (Rama, 1992) and communication and health (Beltrán, 1993).

The challenge of constructing truly democratic media within largely free-market economies, however, is complicated by the need for a new image of the relationship between the state and the institutions of media and culture, be these private or public, individual or collective. In the words of Pasquali, it calls for 'a new socio-political and ethical foundation of inter-subjectivity, community, privacy and power' (1991: 8). The images of the past – communication and development; communication and democracy, alternative communication – do not fit the technological, social and political complexities of today's communication industries. And, the futurist image of an information economy that solves all problems and satisfies all demands by the magic of the unfettered market, what Schmucler (1994) calls the 'utopía mediática', ignores basic questions of access and distribution.

Regardless of how the role of the intellectual has been judged in the past in the study of media and culture in Latin America, it will continue to evolve, often critically and productively, as the communication age generates new areas of tension between the state and those who control the resources of information and culture.

NOTES

1 Latin America's tradition of activism in media and culture began even earlier in this century. In the 1920s, following the Mexican Revolution, Education Secretary and intellectual José Vasconcellos encouraged the growth of national literature, art, and other forms of expression and used culture to promote a sense of national unity and identity, integrating Mexico's Indian populations in the national market and new society. The government set up the country's principal film studies, most movie theatres, a bank to finance national film production, and commissioned the Mexican muralists – Rivera, Siqueiros, Orōzco – to paint the walls of government buildings. In the 1930s Mexican President Lázaro Cárdenas donated a radio receiver to every agricultural and workers' community so they could listen to the courses, book reviews, and concerts transmitted by the state radio station. José Carlos Mariátigui founded the Peruvian Socialist Party in the 1930s with a programme for Peruvian culture, recognizing the central role of indigenous cultural forms in national development and identity. And, by 1930, as part of national educational and cultural policies led by intellectuals, the Uruguayan state had set up a public broadcasting service, a symphony orchestra, a national ballet and a film club.

2 While perhaps these findings were similar to North American and European studies on reception analysis and ethnography of the audience, within the political context of Latin America the impact of the studies on popular culture was qualitatively different. Earlier studies of alternative communication had tended to paint civil society – all that is separate from the state – as truly autonomous. Yet, as one analyst observes, 'The fact was that most of the movements that burgeoned throughout Latin America during the sixties and seventies only appeared to be exterior to the state because the states they faced were typically authoritarian ones, in contrast to previous movements that had been totally incorporated by the state' (Castañeda, 1993: 199).

This appearance of autonomy, according to the same analyst, was the result of the fact that the struggle against the dictatorships in Latin America had indeed taken place outside previously existing state structures and within the multiple new forms of grassroots and alternative movements. It also responded to the failure of the state to achieve reform and development aims, especially the progressive state, and the perhaps wishful thinking that a new form of power, coming from the popular movements, could succeed where the state had failed. These sentiments were especially evident in the literature on alternative communication that tended to romanticize the experiences of grassroots communication and attribute to them far greater staying power in setting national cultural policies than they actually could muster with the return of democracy.

REFERENCES

Alfáro, R. M., *et al.* (1990) *Cultura de masas y cultura popular en la radio peruana*, Lima: Tarea.

Altamirano, J. C. (1987) *Así así se mueve Don Francisco*, Santiago: ILET.

Alvárez, L. (1990) *Medios de comunicación y trampas a la democracía: Ensayos sobre comunicación y democracía*, Montevideo: CLEAH.

Amaral, R. and Guimarães, C. (1986) 'A televisão brasiliera na transição (un caso de conversão rapido a nova ordem)', *Comunicação y Política* 6(1/86) 11–29.

—— 1990 'Medios de masa y elecciones: Un experimento Brasilero', *Telos* 19: 131–9.

Arizola, P. *et al.* (1988) *Television y violencia*, Bogotá: Colciencias

Arriaga, P. (1980) *Publicidad, economía y comunicación masiva: México los Estados Unidos*, Mexico City: ILET/Nueva Imagen.

—— Beltrán, L. R. (1976) 'Alien premises, objects and methods in Latin American communication research', in E. Rogers (ed.) *Communication and Development: Critical Perspectives*, Beverly Hills: Sage.

—— (1979) 'Premisas, objetos y métodos foráneos en la investigación sobre comunicación en América Latina', in M. de Moragas (ed.) *Sociología de la comunicación de masas*, Barcelona: Gustavo Gili.

—— (1993) 'La salud y la comunicación en Latinoamérica: Políticas, estrategías y planes', working document for the Reunión del Comité Asesor sobre Políticas de Comunicación para la Promoción de la Salud, Organización Panaméricana de la Salud/UNESCO, Quito, Ecuador, 6–7 Septiembre 1993.

Beltrán, L. R. and Fox, E. (1980) *Comunicación dominada: Los Estados Unidos en los medios de América Latina*, Mexico City: ILET/Nueva Imagen.

Brunner, J. J. (1985) 'Cultura y crisis de hegemonías', in J.J. Brunner and G. Catalán, *Cinco estudios sobre cultura y sociedad*, Santiago de Chile: FLACSO.

Brunner, J. J. (1988) *Un espejo trizado: Ensayos sobre cultura y políticas culturales*, Santiago: FLACSO.

Capriles, O. (1976) *Estado y politica de la comunicación en Venezuela*, Caracas: ININCO.

Castañeda, C. (1993) *Utopia Unarmed, the Latin American Left after the Cold War*, New York: Alfred Knopf.

Catalán, C. (1988) 'Mass media and the collapse of a democratic tradition in Chile', in E. Fox (ed.) *Media and Politics in Latin America: The Struggle for Democracy*, London: Sage, 45–55.

CLACSO (1989) *Innovación cultural y actores socio-culturales*, (vol. 33/34) Buenos Aires: CLACSO.

Comisión de Estudios sobre Televisión y Violencia (1988) *Televisión y violencia*, Bogotá: Colciencias.

Consejo Nacional de Televisión (1994) *Estudios de tendencias de la programación en la televisión chilena*, Santiago: Consejo Nacional de Televisión.

Dorfman, A. and Mattelart, A.(1970) *Para leer el Paso Donald: comunicación de masas y colonialismo*, Buenos Aires: Siglo XXI.

Esteinou, J. (1983) *Medios de comunicación y construcción de la hegemonía*, México: ILET/Nueva Imagen.

—— (1992) *Los medios de comunicación ante el tratado de Libre Comercio*, México: PCF.

Fadul, A. M. (1993) *Ficção seriada na TV as telenovelas Latinoamericanas/Serial Fiction in TV: the Latin American telenovelas*, Sâo Paulo, ECA-USP.

Fadul, L.M. (1984) 'Las comunicaciones vía satélite en América Latina', *Cuadernos de Ticom* 13, UAM-X. México.

Faraone, R. (1992) *Reflexiones sobre comunicación social*, Montevideo: Universidad de la República/FHCE.

Fernández, F. (1982) *Los medios de difusión en México*, México: Juan Pablo.

Festa, R. and Lins da Silva, C.E. (eds) (1986) *Comunicación popular y alternativa*, Buenos Aires: Ediciones Paulinas.

Ford, A., Rivera, J.B. and Romano, E. (1985) *Medios de comunicación y cultura popular*, Buenos Aires: Legasa.

Fox, E. (1988) *Politics and Mass Media in Latin America: the Struggle for Democracy*, London: Sage.

—— (1989) *Medios de comunicación y politica en América Latina: la lucha por la democracia*, Barcelona, Gili .

Fox, E. Schmucler, H, Terrero, P. *et al.* 1982. *Comunicación y democracía en América Latina*, Lima: DESCO.

Fuenzalida, V. and Hermosilla, M.E. with Eduards, P. (1989) *Visiones y ambiciones del televidente: estudios de recepción televisiva*, Santiago: CENECA.

Fuenzalida, V. (1990) *La televisión en los '90*, Santiago: CPU.

Gabay, M. (1988) *Política, Información y sociedad, represión en el Uruguay contra la libertad de información de Expresión y Critica*, Montevideo: Centro Uruguay Independiente.

Galindo, J. (1985) 'Vivir y sentir la telenovela', *Chasqui* 16, Quito: CIESPAL.

García Canclini, N. (1982) *Las culturas populares en el capitalismo*, México: ILET/Nueva Imagen.

—— (ed.) (1987) *Políticas culturales en América Latina*, México: Grijalbo/Enlace.

—— (1989) *Culturas híbridas: estrategias para entrar y salir de la modernidad*, México: Grijalbo.

García Canclini, N. and Roncagliolo, R. (eds) (1988) *Culturas transnacionales y culturas populares*, Lima: IPAL.

Gargurevich, J. (1991) *Historia de la prensa peruana, 1594–1990*, Lima: La Voz.

—— (1987) *Prensa, Radio y TV: Historia Crítica*, Lima: Horizonte.

González, J. (1994) 'Las estructuras del encanto: Ideas para analizar la producción social de las telenovelas', in C. Cervantes Barba and E. Sánchez Ruíz (eds) *Investigar la comunicación: propuestas iberoamericanas*, Guadalajara: Universidad de Guadalajara/ Centro de Estudios de la Información y la Comunicación, 105–34.

Herrán, M. T. (1991) *La industria de los medios masivos de comunicación en Colombia*, Bogotá: FESCOL.

Huesca, R. and Dervin, D. (1994) 'Toward communication theories of and for practice: the past/future of Latin American alternative communication research', *Journal of Communication* 44(4): 53–73.

Hurtado, M. de la L. (1989) *Historia de la TV en Chile, 1958–1973*, Santiago: CENECA.

Kunsch Drohling, M. (ed.) (1993) *Industrias culturais e os desafios da Integração Latino-Americana*, São Paulo: Intercom.

Landi, O. (1984) 'Cultura política en la transición democrática', in O. Oszlak *et al.*, *Proceso, crisis y transición democrática*, Buenos Aires: CEDAL.

—— (ed.) (1987) *Medios, transformaciones culturales y política*, Buenos Aires: Legasa.

—— (1992) *Devorame otra vez: Que hizo la televisión con la gente que hace la gente con la televisión*, Buenos Aires: Planeta.

Lins da Silva, C. E. (1990) 'Industria da comunicação: personagem principal das eleições Presidenciais Brasileiras de 1989', *Intercom: Revista Brasileira de Comunicação* 62/3.

Lira, J. P. (1987) *Televisión en Chile: un desafío nacional*, Santiago: CED/CENECA.

Martín-Barbero, J. (1987) *De los medios a las mediaciones: comunicación, cultura y hegemonía*, Barcelona: G. Gili.

—— (1989). *Procesos de comunicación y matrices de cultura: Itinerario para salir de la razón dualista*, México: G. Gili.

—— (1993) *Communication, Culture and Hegemony From Media to Mediations*, London: Sage.

Martín-Barbero, J. and Muñoz, S. (eds) (1992) *Televisión y mélodrama*, Bogotá: Tercer Mundo.

Marques de Melo, J. (1993) 'Investigación en comunicación: tendencias de la escuela Latinoaméricana', *Anuario del Departamento de Historia*, 5, Editorial Complutense, Madrid, 201–23.

Mattelart, A. (1970) 'Estructura del poder informativo y dependencia: la dependencia del medio de comunicación de masas', *Cuadernos de la Realidad Nacional* 3.

Mattelart, A. and Mattelart, M. (1986) *Le carneval des images*, Paris, INA/La Documentation Française.

Mattelart, A. and Schmucler, H. (1983) *América Latina en la encrucijada telemática*, Buenos Aires: Paidos.

Mattelart, M. and Piccini, M. (1974) 'La televisión y los sectores populares', *Comunicación y Cultura*, 2

Mayobre, J. A. (1986) *Las políticas de televisión en Venezuela*, Lima: IPAL.

Miceli, S. (1984) *Estado e cultura no Brasil*, São Paulo: DIFEL.

Mont, C. G. (1992) *El desafío de los nuevos medios de comunicación en México*, México: AMIC/Diana.

Moreira, S. V. (1991) *O radio no Brasil*, Rio de Janeiro: Rio Fundo Editora.

Muraro, H. (1994) 'Intenciones de voto por el partido oficial y ajuste económico', *Contratexto*, 7, Universidad de Lima.

Orózco, G. (1993) 'Dialéctica de la mediación televisiva: estructuración de estrategias de recepción por los televidentes,' *Análisi*, 15, Barcelona: Universitat Autònoma de Barcelona.

—— (1994) 'Autonomía relativa de la audiencia: implicaciones metodológicas para el análisis de la recepción', in C. Cervantes Barba and E. Sánchez Ruíz (eds) *Investigar la comunicación*, Guadalajara: Universidad de Guadalajara, Centro de Estudios de la Información y la Comunicación/ALAIC, 183–95.

Pasquali, A. (1991) *El ordén reina: escritos sobre comunicaciones*, Caracas: Monte Avila.

Peirano, L. Ballon, E., Bartlet, I. *et al.* (1978) *Prensa: apertura y límites*, Lima: DESCO.

Peirano, L. and Sánchez León, A. (1984) *Risa y cultura en la televisión peruana*, Lima: DESCO/YUNTA.

Portales, D. (1981) *Poder económico y libertad de expresión: la industria de la comunicación Chilena en la democracía y el autoritarismo*, México: ILET/Nueva Imagen.

—— (1987) *La dificultad de innovar*, Santiago: ILET.

Protzel, J. (1991) 'Vargas Llosa y Fujimori: de una modernidad a otra: crisis del marketing político en el Perú', *Diálogos de la Comunicación*, 29.

Reyes Matta, F. (1983) *Comunicación alternativa y búsquedas democráticas*, México: ILET/FES.

Rama, C. (ed.) (1992) *Industrias culturales en el Uruguay*, Montevideo: ARCA.

Rivadeneira Prado, R. and Tirado, N. (1986) *La televisión en Bolivia*, La Paz: Quipus.

Rivadenera Prado, R. (1982) *Resistencia y coexistencia*, La Paz: Editores Gilbert.

Robina, S. (1986) *Bancos de informaciones nacionales: la búsqueda de la soberanía informativa*, México: ILET.

—— *et al.* (1986) *Informática y educación*, México: ILET.

Roncagliolo, R. (1986) 'Transnational communication and culture', in R. Atwood and E. McAnany (eds) *Communication and Latin American Society*, Madison: University of Wisconsin, 79–88.

Sánchez Ruíz, E. (1992) *Medios de difusión y sociedad*, Guadalajara: Centro de Estudios de la Información y la Comunicación.

Sardoli, L. C. and Moriera, S. V. (1988) (second edition) *Radio Nacional!: Brasil em Sintonia*, Rio de Janeiro: Martin Fontes Funarte.

Schiller, H. (1969) *Mass Communications and American Empire*, Boston: Beacon.

Schnitman, J. (1984) *Film Industries in Latin America: Dependency and Development*, Norwood: Ablex.

Selser, G. and Roncagliolo, R. (1979) *Trampas de la información y neocolonialismo: las agencias de noticias frente a los países no alineados*, México: ILET.

Simpson, M. (1981) *Comunicación alternativa y cambio social*, México: Universidad Nacional Autónoma de México.

Sinclair, J. (1994) 'Culture and trade: some theoretical and practical considerations on cultural industries', paper presented to the 19th conference of the International Association of Mass Communication Research, Seoul, Korea, 3–8 July.

Schmucler, H. (1994) 'El regreso de las palabras o los límites de la utopia mediática', paper presented at the II Congreso Latinoaméricano de Investigadores de la Comunicación, Guadalajara, México, 27–30 June.

Sodre, M. (1981) *O monopolio da fala: função e linguagem da televisão no Brasil*, Petropolis: Vozes.

Sunkel, G. (1994) 'Medios de comunicación y violencia en la transición Chilena', *Contratexto*, 7, Universidad de Lima, 9–39.

Vizcaíno, M. (1992) *Los falsos dilemas de nuestra televisión: una mirada tras la pantalla*, Bogotá: ACOTV/CEREC.

9

THE MEDIA AND WAR

Daniel C. Hallin

War has been a central fact of social life at least since the agricultural revolution, some ten thousand years ago, deeply involved in many of the most important changes in technology, culture and social and political organization. But the study of war has for the most part remained outside the mainstream of social investigation (Shaw, 1991; Giddens, 1985). In media studies a similar tale can be told. Despite the fact that empirical media research originated to a significant extent in response to the mobilization of communication for war during the First World War (Lippmann and Merz, 1920; Lasswell, 1927), the literature was until recently very thin both in volume and in intellectual scope.

This is now beginning to change. Researchers began to turn their attention to the subject after Vietnam; the trend accelerated in Britain with the Falklands/ Malvinas War, and became an intellectual 'rage' in many countries with the Gulf War – which had enough advance warning to permit some scholars to plan research before the onset of the war. A substantial body of research has also developed in Israel.

This research has produced many important conclusions, which I will try to outline in the course of the discussion. At the same time, it has many weaknesses and much room for development. Much of it has been topical or polemical in approach: it has been concerned, for example, with whether the media really 'lost Vietnam', or to denounce censorship or 'cheerleading' in the Falklands/Malvinas War or the Gulf War. These can be important issues to address, but their centrality has sometimes led to distortions – for example, to exaggeration of the effect of censorship – or to neglect of broader intellectual questions. Much of the work, even the best work, lacks connection to general social theory: it does not address, or only begins to address, the impact of war and wartime communication on the relation of state and civil society, the structure of the public sphere, or political culture and social ideology, though it seems likely that war plays a profound role in shaping all of these (Marwick, 1977, 1988). The field in its present state also lacks coherence: much of the work makes little reference to other literature on the media and war or to the broader literature on war and society. One important manifestation of the fragmented state of the field is the fact that very few works deal in any systematic way with more than one war.

206

I have organized my discussion into three sections. In the first section I attempt to pull together what is known about the media and war from the mid-nineteenth century – when war reporting in the modern sense began – to the Second World War. The literature on this period is surprisingly thin. Nevertheless, it seems to me crucial to examine this period in some detail, for several reasons. This period – the era of total war – involved profound changes in the social organization of warfare, including the role of the media and public opinion. It is therefore particularly easy to see the macro-social significance of research on the media and war. It also provides a crucial baseline for assessing changes in the media's role. Finally, the cultural and organizational models established shape the course of subsequent conflicts so profoundly that the latter are really unintelligible without understanding these models. The lack of reference to this historical context seems to me one of the greatest weaknesses of the field.

In the second section, I examine research on the three wars which have been the primary focus of scholarship: Vietnam, the Falklands/Malvinas War and the Gulf War. I have attempted in this section to review what we know concretely about the role of the media in each of these wars, saving theoretical and methodological issues for the most part for the following section. In the final section, I review what seem to me the three major approaches or domains within the literature on the media and war: (1) research on the media and public opinion; (2) research on the sociology of the media in wartime – research, that is, on the nature of journalistic routines in war coverage, the relations between the media and the military, government, and other social actors during war, and the economic context of war reporting; and (3) the small but growing literature on war as culture.

In surveying this literature I have limited the field in a number of ways. I have chosen to focus primarily on the news media, and on international military conflicts. I therefore deal only tangentially with a variety of related literatures: on fictional representations of war, propaganda, the role of telecommunications and information technology in war, on terrorism, internal war and the Cold War and arms race. Finally, I deal here mainly with the Anglo-American literature; I have tried to broaden the scope of the discussion at least a little, but it is largely limited to the literature on US and west European media. Even with these limitations, space does not allow discussion of every relevant work; the bibliography includes a number of works not discussed in the text.

THE MEDIA IN THE ERA OF TOTAL WAR

The literature on the history of the media and war prior to Vietnam is remarkably thin. The only broad overview is provided by Philip Knightly's *The First Casualty* (1975), a delightful and useful book, but not in any sense a scholarly study. Major histories of journalism will often have useful if brief discussions of war reporting. But monographs dealing in any detail with the early history of media and war are rare, and many of those that exist belong to an era when journalism history was extremely personalized, telling stories about 'the great reporters and their times'

DANIEL C. HALLIN

(Hohenberg, 1964; Crozier, 1959) without connecting them to any theoretical framework for understanding the relations among the press, the state, the public and popular culture.

From the fragments of research that exist, the early history of media–military relations in the US and Britain from 1850 to 1950 might be outlined something like this. It is generally agreed that modern war reporting, based on professional journalists reporting from the battlefield, began with the Crimean War. It was in the American Civil War, however, that the institutional structures of war reporting which have carried down to the present began to emerge, particularly the dual system of censorship and accreditation which gave the press access to the battlefield and the military substantial control over its activities. This system continued to be refined in subsequent wars.

The emergence of the accreditation/censorship system was connected with the development of 'total war'. In the general literature on war and society, the concept of 'total war' is essential to understanding the modern period (Shaw, 1988; Dyer, 1985; Howard, 1975; Marwick, 1977, 1988), and research on the media and war needs to situate itself in relation to this framework much more fully than it has done. The age of total war began with the *levée en masse* of the French Revolution and the accompanying idea of the citizen army. The French Revolution involved an unprecedented mobilization of society as a whole for war and an accompanying ideology that attached participation in war to citizenship in a national state. Other European states were forced to follow the French model to a significant degree. The American Civil War carried the process a step further in its mobilization of the industrial economy for war. In the First World War it reached its full flowering. The armies sent into the field were vast as a percentage of the population – as much as 20 per cent in the French case. They were fighting a technological conflict that required staggering quantities of industrial production. This meant that the 'home front' became crucial for military success, and had to be treated as an integral part of the war effort. Total war required unprecedented central co-ordination of the economy, and unprecedented concern with civilian 'morale', since civilians had to be mobilized as a force of economic production, a source of 'manpower' and a political constituency for a tremendously costly enterprise. Civilian morale would also increasingly become a target of hostile military action, particularly with the development of air power. So military planners naturally began to concern themselves with the systematic management of public opinion and of the media.

Several characteristics of the system that emerged in the US and Britain in the era of total war are notable. First, strategies for managing public opinion were developed which involved a philosophy of positive action to mould public opinion, emphasizing publicity rather than censorship (Kennedy, 1980). Second, the mobilization of the 'home front' also involved considerable volunteer action – the emerging culture of total war was a participatory culture, though one which involved a deep passion for unity which resulted in considerable curtailment of political pluralism and civil liberties, especially during the First World War

208

(Kennedy, 1980). Third, a wartime relation between the state and civil society developed which involved not primarily suppression of civil society by the state, but cooperation, co-optation and blurring of the lines, in which state functions were often taken on by institutions like the press, and vice versa. This was manifested, for example, in the Office of Censorship established in the US during the Second World War, which was headed by a journalist and which relied on voluntary cooperation by the press. Similar understandings and institutional arrangements affected the role of entertainment media (Doherty, 1993; Koppes, 1987). Finally, the press in the US and Britain developed a style of war reporting which combined strategic reporting heavily dependent on official sources, viewing the world from the centralized perspective of those who managed the global war apparatus, with a populist perspective which concentrated on and often glorified the 'GI' or the 'Tommy' and the ordinary family on the 'home front'.

After the Second World War, with total war rendered impractical by the advent of nuclear weapons, a new age of 'limited war' began, manifested first in Korea and in the Suez crisis.[1] Nevertheless, the understandings of war which prevail today are still derived to a large extent from the age of total war; indeed subsequent wars have typically been presented to the public in their initial stages as replays of the Second World War, and many of the conflicts over wartime communication arise from the clash between expectations based in the culture of total war and the political reality of limited war.

The changes in the state, in journalism, and in public opinion and culture produced by the era of total war clearly need to be studied in much greater detail, and the subsequent history understood in relation to them.

RESEARCH ON VIETNAM, THE FALKLANDS/MALVINAS WAR AND THE GULF WAR

Vietnam

Vietnam marks the turn towards limited war. Policy-makers did not attempt to mobilize all of American society for war; indeed, the Johnson administration tried hard to keep the war from eclipsing other political priorities. This had two crucial consequences for media–military and media–state relations. First, it meant that censorship was not instituted (Hammond, 1988; Wyatt, 1993: 159; Twentieth Century Fund, 1985: 66). Instead, reporters had to agree as a condition of accreditation to a set of guidelines for the protection of military security. Vietnam was thus the first war in which reporters were accredited to accompany military forces but not subject to censorship. Second, and probably more important, political consensus was never complete, and eventually gave way to polarization. This meant that journalists shifted to some degree away from the Second World War attitude that they were part of a national war effort and applied more 'normal' standards of political reporting.

For many years the conventional wisdom has held that the media were primarily responsible for the collapse of public support for the war, and thus were decisive in its outcome. This view has been shared across the political spectrum in the US: conservatives have portrayed the media as the villains of the war, causing a collapse of the national will, while liberals, including many journalists, have seen the press as heroes, telling the people the truth the government preferred to conceal. A similar view is also widely shared abroad. Many in the British military assumed at the time of the Falklands War that the case of Vietnam showed that media coverage was inherently harmful to a military operation. Television is often considered decisive. Vietnam was the first televised war, the argument goes; through television, the public saw the 'literal horror of war' in a way it never had before, and therefore lost its stomach for continued fighting.

The research literature, however, has never provided support for this view. Braestrup (1977) has been cited in its defence. His argument is that the media misinterpreted the outcome of the Tet offensive of 1968, portraying it as a success for the North Vietnamese and NLF when in fact it was a failure. But Braestrup has distanced himself from the wider claims that the media took a generally oppositional stance towards the war or were the prime mover in the shift of public opinion against it.[2] His book includes an analysis by Burns W. Roper which suggests that Tet had relatively little influence on public opinion, which shifted gradually away from support for the war beginning early in 1966.

Other studies have consistently rejected the thesis that the media took an anti-war stance and led the shift of policy and opinion against the war. Hammond (1988), prepared for the Center of Military History as part of the US Army's general study of the war, gives a detailed account of media–military relations, based on Army documents and an analysis of press accounts archived by the Army. It paints a picture of relatively respectful relations between the military and the media, relations which, however, became strained as the political contradictions of a protracted limited war made themselves felt. Hammond's study also found that the system of voluntary ground rules worked well for protecting military security (see also Twentieth Century Fund, 1985).

Hallin (1986, 1994b) examines coverage by *The New York Times* from 1960 to 1965, and by the three television networks from 1965 to 1973. He shows that in the early years the media strongly supported American involvement in Vietnam, which they interpreted in a Cold War framework similar to the geopolitical framework of the Second World War, and that the Kennedy and Johnson administrations were generally successful in 'managing' news content. Later, he argues, the media became more critical, though they were at least as much followers as leaders in the process of political change, responding to changes in elite and mass opinion and to the decline of morale among troops in the field after withdrawal began. As for television, Hallin argues that it presented not the 'literal horror of war', but a relatively sanitized, and indeed in the early days often a romanticized view, based on the nation's collective memory of the Second World War. And television was particularly prone to following rather than leading political change, lagging behind other media and other segments of society in moving towards a more critical stance.

A detailed content analysis of television coverage by Lichty (1984) similarly found that most was bland and routine, with little heavy combat or blood and gore, and Patterson (1984) reports similar findings.

Wyatt (1993) gives an overview of press coverage from 1955 to the end of the war, based to a large extent on archives and oral histories of participants, both in the media and in government. Wyatt, like others, finds that relations between the media and government were more cooperative than confrontational through the peak years of the war. He stresses the government's information-supplying apparatus, which was extremely convenient for journalists and provided the basis for the bulk of their coverage.

Zaller (1992) reports a content analysis of magazine coverage, showing a strongly pro-war slant in the early years and a later shift towards a more critical balance. Herman and Chomsky (1988) analyse the ideological assumptions of Vietnam coverage, and also look at retellings of the war in subsequent years.

Mueller's (1973) study of public opinion and the Vietnam war argues that the decline of support for the war was essentially a reaction to the mounting casualty toll, and was not determined by the nature of news coverage. Research on public opinion and the Vietnam war will be discussed more fully below.

There is also a significant literature on the media and the anti-war movement (Gitlin, 1980; Hallin, 1986; Small, 1994; Halloran, Elliott and Murdock, 1970). This research generally finds that the media were hostile to the anti-war movement in the early part of the war, presenting it in a way that reinforced its marginalization; later, as the movement began to enter the mainstream, coverage became more extensive and more neutral.

Despite a broad consensus among researchers on the basic outlines of the story, there are important holes in our knowledge of the media's role in the Vietnam War. Most significant is the lack of research on the print media. Hallin examines the coverage of one newspaper over a period of several years early in the war. Wyatt's *Paper Soldiers* is, as its jacket says, a 'readable study of the Vietnam press corps'; it does not, however, attempt systematically to analyse the content of press coverage, a content which presumably has considerable variation by region and type of publication.

The Falklands/Malvinas War

The Falklands/Malvinas War was also a limited war, but several circumstances made it very different from Vietnam. The first was the unusual geography: the war took place in a part of the world where transportation and communication are extremely difficult, which meant that the media were even more than normally dependent on the military to get to and transmit the story. Second, it was largely a naval war until the end, which also contributed to tight military control of journalists. Third, it was a short, successful war, with relatively little dissent at home. Censorship of field dispatches was instituted, with dispatches vetted both before transmission from the task force and upon arrival in London. These circumstances combined to produce a media environment not so different in many ways from the Second World War.

The major studies of the media and the Falklands conflict include Harris (1983), an early and useful account by a journalist, and Adams (1986). Mercer, Mungham and Williams (1987) give a detailed account of the government and military public relations apparatus and policies. This study includes considerable discussion of the demands wartime PR must balance: there is pressure, on the one hand, to minimize the information flow, in order to protect security and minimize potentially controversial revelations. On the other hand, the government's publicity apparatus must have credibility if it hopes to influence public opinion, and this requires providing a flow of reasonably accurate information. Even in the unusual case of the Falklands/Malvinas War, the British government did not have a monopoly on information, and often had to respond to information released by the Argentinians or in Washington. Publicity is both a threat to governments at war and a necessary political tool, and they often have difficulty managing this contradiction.

The practices and attitudes of the journalists are examined in Morrison and Tumber (1988), who reproduce extensive parts of interviews with them, and also include results of a content analysis of television coverage and an analysis of audience response. A study by the Glasgow University Media Group (1985) focuses on news content, and gives evidence of a strong slant towards official views. Taylor (1991) deals with the popular press, particularly its use of photography. Aulich (1992) includes discussions of the Falklands/Malvinas in a variety of media, focusing on visual representations. It includes a chapter on Argentine press coverage.

In general, these studies suggest the following conclusions:

1 The flow of information from the war zone was limited by a number of factors, including wariness of publicity on the part of the military and government, particularly the Navy and technical factors related to geography and to the hasty departure of the fleet and the lack of planning for the logistics of media coverage.

2 MoD public relations policy was in many ways poorly coordinated, leading to tension with the press and sometimes resentment between field commanders and London over the handling of the media and the release of particular information.

3 Journalists with the task force, though they were often furious with the conditions under which they worked, also generally came to identify with military personnel they covered, particularly once they went ashore with ground troops, and portrayed them favourably.

4 Overall the media coverage was highly favourable to the British military operation, ranging from the extreme jingoism of the popular press, to the more

detached but still essentially supportive coverage of the quality press and television.

One interesting case that emerges in a number of the studies provides a particularly good overview of the forces at work: the case of still photographs of British casualties. No such pictures appeared in the British press – the image of war it portrayed was in that sense highly sanitized (Taylor, 1991: 110). There seems to be a series of factors that contributed to this outcome. Inadequate transmission facilities and a small number of photojournalists with the operation meant that only 202 photographs altogether were transmitted from the war zone. The MoD seems to have held back some photos that were considered to be bad news. The Press Association apparently failed to transmit some casualty photos. And editors, finally, chose not to use what photos reached them (Morrison and Tumber, 1988: 181–2).

The most systematic work on the Falklands War focuses on journalistic practices and the interaction between journalists and the military. One important limitation of this work is that it focuses mainly on journalists accompanying the task force, and there is relatively little research on editors at home – an ironic set of research priorities, given that special circumstances of this war meant that the reporters in the field were less central than in most wars, and the editors at home more so. As with Vietnam, there is much more research on the content of television than of print news.

The Persian Gulf War

The Persian Gulf War continued the trend begun with the Falklands War and then adopted by the US military in the Panama and Grenada invasions[3] towards relatively close control of the media. Field censorship was instituted, the first time since Vietnam that the US military had imposed it. And a pool system was established which restricted journalists' freedom of movement and access to the war zone. Like the Falklands War, too, the nature of the war itself hindered media access to the fighting, and enhanced military control of information. Most of the war was fought from the air, which meant that, except on a few occasions when journalists in Iraq were present to witness the aftermath, it could be covered only second-hand, through military briefings and at the bases and ships from which strikes were launched. Once ground combat began military control of information was weakened, as many reporters went 'unilateral' and the pool system began to break down. But the ground war was too short and successful for this erosion of military control to change dramatically the nature of the war reporting. The Gulf War was also the first war which could be covered by live television around the world; much of the writing about its significance revolves around these two facts of military control and live global television.

The Gulf War captured the imagination of media scholars as probably no event ever has, and the literature is too large and diverse to be reviewed in a completely comprehensive way here. Fialka (1991: 2) provides an account of the difficulties faced by the working journalist in reporting the war. He emphasizes military control of access to front-line units, which he considers much more important than censorship in affecting the coverage, and paints a picture of a war 'the great majority of journalists saw from the vantage point of the briefing rooms of posh hotels in Riyadh and Dhahran or from grey metal chairs in the broadcasting studio on the E-Ring of the Pentagon'. MacArthur (1992) is a journalistic account of media–military relations and propaganda efforts before and during the war. Kellner (1992) provides a political critique of television coverage of the war, comparing it with other accounts of events. Taylor (1992) examines the propaganda activities of both the allies and Iraqis, showing that the allies were vastly more skilled at manipulating the world media. He points out that one of the most important changes introduced by the new media environment of the Gulf War was the fact that military officials could address the public directly through television, rather than relying on the mediation of journalists. Hackett (1993) examines coverage of anti-war activists in the US press. He shows that these voices were in many ways marginalized, but also argues that they did succeed in capturing a voice in the news, particularly in local newspapers.

Much of the scholarly work appears in anthologies. This includes Bennett and Paletz (1994) which brings to bear on the case of the Gulf War a variety of perspectives drawn from the literature on media, public opinion and foreign policy, and emphasizes the role of the media in the political debate leading up to the Gulf War. Denton (1993) is an eclectic volume whose essays cover everything from military ground rules to war themes in advertising. Greenberg and Gantz (1993) includes many studies of public opinion and the Gulf War, as well as content analyses, an analysis of wartime public relations, and a section on the reactions of children to the war. Jeffords and Rabinovitz (1994) focuses on the war in popular culture, and makes considerable use of feminist and post-structural theory. Specific articles in a number of these anthologies will be discussed at greater length in section 3.

The Gulf War was of course an international war, with UN sanctions and participation by a number of countries. And it took place in a media environment that is becoming increasingly globalized. This means, for one thing, that the national character of news organizations may be weakened to a degree:[4] CNN's presence in Baghdad is hard to imagine in an earlier era, even during a limited war. There was very limited US reporting from Hanoi during the Vietnam War. And it means that the war has a global audience, receiving news from a combination of national and international channels. A number of works deal with the global character of the Gulf War. Gustadt (1993) examines the CNN audience worldwide. An anthology edited by Mowlana, Gerbner and Schiller (1992) includes work on Gulf War coverage in a wide range of countries. Much is impressionistic, but some studies are more research-based, including Nain's analysis of the Malaysian press. Swanson and Smith (1993) compare television coverage in seven countries, finding that globalization did not produce uniform narratives across national boundaries. A similar argument is made about news-paper coverage by Kaid *et al.* (1993). A special issue of *The Nordicom Review* (1992) examines coverage in Scandinavian media. Shulman (1994) examines allied control of the channels of news in the Gulf War. Savarese (1992; 1993) compares press coverage in Italy, Britain Germany, France and Spain. Wolton (1991) examines French coverage, and includes an interesting discussion of reaction in the Arab world, where the information produced by Western media was often seen as gloating over Arab defeat.

In general, these studies find Gulf War coverage, like Falklands coverage, to be sanitized, heavily dominated by official sources and perspectives, and highly favourable to the military operation. There is more diversity, and more ambiguity, about how this news content is to be explained, and what impact it had on public opinion – questions which will be considered in the sections which follow. There is also considerable ambiguity – this of course is inevitable – about what the Gulf War may mean for the future of media–military relations. Many early accounts assumed that it would mark the beginning of an era of extremely tight military control of the reporting of war. But this is too simple, and indeed in some ways precisely wrong. Vietnam, much to the surprise of many, was followed by a period of tight military control, from the Falklands to the Gulf War. In the wake of the Gulf War, however, military attitudes about the media seem to be changing, returning to something like the Second World War view that the media are a useful part of the war effort (Brown, 1992). This could lead to a period of active military PR without the suspicion and restriction that have characterized recent wars.

MAJOR DOMAINS IN THE STUDY OF MEDIA AND WAR

Public opinion

Research on the media and war has always been motivated to a large extent by a concern with effects on public opinion, particularly the role of the media in either mobilizing or eroding public support for the use of military force. In the late 1980s and early 1990s a number of quite sophisticated studies were published which produced important findings particularly about the relations among elite opinion leadership, media coverage, and public support for war. The greatest weakness of research on war and public opinion is probably the absence of ethnographic studies: public opinion on war has been studied through survey methods which define it essentially in terms of binary attitudes of support or opposition, and reveal relatively little about what war means to members of the mass public.

The most widely cited work on war and public opinion is probably Mueller (1973), which examines the trends in US public support for the wars in Korea and Vietnam. Each is characterized by an initial 'rallying' of support followed by a decline. The decline, Mueller argues, can be accounted for primarily as a response to the rising cumulative toll of American casualties. Mueller does not deal directly with the role of the media, except to observe that fragmentary survey evidence seems to indicate that TV increased rather than diminished support for the war, and that the similarity of the patterns of decline in Korea and Vietnam contradicts the notion that TV turned the public against the Vietnam War. The cumulative casualty explanation for declining support is not fully satisfying: casualties increase with time, but so do many other things, for which Mueller did not have measures, but which might account for the change in public opinion – the balance of elite opinion, news about troop withdrawals, or public perceptions of the probability of winning. Mueller does present evidence suggesting that public opinion often follows shifts in official policy. And he summarizes research which suggests that anti-war protest was not responsible for declining support for the war, and indeed could even have produced a backlash, since even those opposed to the war were often hostile to anti-war protest.

One of the concepts introduced by Mueller was the notion of the 'rally effect', which has been developed further by Brody and Shapiro (1989). The 'rally effect' is the tendency for public support for political leadership to shoot up with an international crisis, often defying the normal expectation that the public will respond to perceived success or failure of political policies. Thus Kennedy's popularity shot up following the Bay of Pigs invasion, despite the obvious failure of the policy. Mueller conceives of the rally effect essentially as an expression of patriotism. Brody and Shapiro reconceptualize it as a response to elite opinion leadership: a rally occurs when political elites unite in support of the president – or decline to express criticisms publicly. This change in elite behaviour results in news coverage heavily favourable to the president, and public opinion responds to that information environment. Brody (1994) tested this model in the Gulf War, and found that during the initial crisis period, from August to October 1991, trends in public opinion towards the president were accounted for largely by the balance of elite comment represented in the media. After the rally phase, public opinion responded primarily to the mix of favourable or unfavourable news about policy outcomes.

Zaller (1992) has developed a theory of opinion formation that focuses primarily on elite opinion leadership and the role of the media in communicating it. Members of the mass public, according to Zaller, generally form opinions by following the lead of elites they trust. The main function of the media in this process is to communicate to the public information about what positions elites are taking. The effect of the media on public opinion towards a war, therefore, depends on whether elites are united or divided. In the case of Vietnam, Zaller's research shows that the effect of exposure to the media was different in the early and later periods of the war. In the early period, when elites were generally unified, the media had a 'mainstreaming effect': those who were most intensively exposed to the media were most likely to support the consensus position, which was at that time pro-war. In the later period, post-1968, the effect of media exposure was polarizing. Liberal and conservative elites diverged in this period, and those most

216

exposed to the media were most likely to reflect the position of 'their own' elites: conservatives to support and liberals to oppose the war. In research on the Gulf crisis, Zaller (1994) found a mainstreaming effect of the media where elites agreed (for instance, on sending troops to Saudi Arabia) and polarizing effects where they disagreed (on whether there should be an early start to the war). The media are important, in Zaller's model, but as an intervening variable, and it is specifically the partisan cues in news content that shape attitudes towards wars as towards other political events.

Morgan, Lewis and Jhally (1992: 225) is a widely cited study of the influence of TV on public knowledge about the Gulf War. As with most studies of knowledge about political affairs, the authors found that the level of knowledge was low. They also found that heavy television viewers knew less about the war than lighter viewers, leading them to conclude that 'television seemed to confuse more than clarify', and that heavy viewers were more likely to support the war. Many of the findings are intriguing, for example the fact that, on average, heavy television viewers, and specifically heavy TV news viewers, gave lower estimates of Iraqi casualties than light viewers. But the study suffers from problems common to most 'cultivation analysis': it does not adequately control for the differences between heavy and light viewers, and it does not seriously address the question of the direction of causality – the possibility that supporters of the war might choose to watch it more on TV. It also seems problematic that, for the most part, heavy and light viewers of TV *in general* differed in their knowledge, while differences in *news* exposure were not associated with differences in knowledge on most measures. Oliver, Mares and Cantor (1993: 153–4) did find an association between TV news viewing and support for the war, though they also found evidence consistent with the possibility that selective exposure might account for it.[5]

Shaw and Carr-Hill explore the impact of newspapers on Gulf War attitudes, arguing that while TV is clearly the main source of *information* for most viewers, newspapers, which in Britain clearly vary in political orientation, might play an important role in forming *opinions*. They found a fairly strong tendency for readers of the more jingoistic tabloids to express more hawkish, aggressive views, with a variety of controls for demographics and general political orientation. The results are extremely interesting, though of course the problem of direction of causality remains; it would be useful to see an analysis like this done over time, looking at changes in the attitudes of readers of different newspapers as those papers developed their interpretation of an international crisis, perhaps using a methodology similar to that developed by Fan (1993).

Shaw and Carr-Hill also make the point that although some have argued the public relates to a mass-mediated war as a spectator sport and is screened from any consciousness of its violence, their data show a fairly widespread sense of anxiety about the violence of the war. The studies on children and the war in Greenberg and Gantz (1993) also suggest that the war was not universally experienced as a spectacular game.

217

There are a number of studies on public attitudes towards the media during the Gulf War (Pan *et al.*, 1993; Milavsky and Galceran, 1993; Dennis *et al.*, 1991). They generally show high public satisfaction with the media, support for military censorship, support also for reporting from Iraq, and in some cases hostility to reporting on anti-war protest. Shaw and Carr-Hill (1991) found in their data on British public reactions some evidence of resistance to media messages: about 40 per cent of the public agreed that TV 'glorified war too much' in the period before the story of the Amirya shelter bombing, and significant numbers of newspaper readers, especially of the tabloids, also felt this.

Peled and Katz (1974) address the question of the functions the media serve for the audience during wartime, based on a study of the Israeli public during the 1973 war. They find that in addition to information and interpretation, the audience seeks release from tension and reinforcement of social solidarity. Television was particularly valued for release from tension. McLeod, Eveland and Signorielli (1994) apply this framework to the Gulf War, and like Peled and Katz, find that the audience desires for tension release and solidarity enhancement are high during wartime and decay afterwards. These studies suggest a broader understanding of the rally effect, as it is manifested in times of actual warfare, than that put forward by Brody. Drawing on Durkheim and Coser, they see it as a general increase in the priority given to social integration, involving increased support for political authorities and increased hostility towards enemies and dissenters, as well as changes in expectations about the functions of the media. Both studies present data showing that these sentiments fade once the war is over.

There is relatively little research in the 'reception analysis' tradition looking at how audiences decode war news, nor, in general, is there much in the way of ethnographic study examining the way members of the public gather information about war and give meaning to it, or the way war affects the routines of their lives. An exception is research by Liebes and Ribak (1994) and Liebes (1992a) which examines the way Israeli families negotiate the meaning of news reports about the *intifada*. Much traditional public opinion research is based on an assumption that public responses to political events are in fact very thin. Zaller (1994), for instance, argues that members of the mass public are best understood as lazy information processors, responding to partisan cues in the news, but not to any of the more subtle aspects of framing or narration that interest many who analyse news content. It seems likely, however, that the 'lazy organism' hypothesis would apply much less to an actual war than to a more 'routine' foreign policy crisis, and if this is correct the need for ethnographic methods would be particularly important to the study of public opinion and war.

This example raises a distinction that can be drawn between research which assumes that war is essentially continuous with other political processes, and research which assumes that war is in some way special, and involves distinct processes of opinion formation, distinct journalistic practices, and so on. Which of these views is right is obviously an empirical question, and the answer may shift depending on which process and what situations one examines.

Media sociology

This section deals with media sociology in the broad sense: it is concerned with the ways in which research on the media and war has drawn from and contributed to the literature on the structure and function of the media and their interaction with other social institutions. It will be useful at the outset to summarize the range of forces involved. If, for example, we want to explain the strongly pro-war balance of Gulf War coverage in the US and Britain, the factors involved might include:

1 The exercise of state power through censorship, control of access, control of information, or pressure.
2 Political elites, who may, for example, be relied upon for information or to set the terms of debate.
3 The attitudes and culture of journalists.
4 The working routines of journalism.
5 Economic pressures on the media, including ratings competition and advertising sales.
6 Management or ownership.
7 Public opinion, which we considered as a 'dependent variable' in the previous section, but which may have an influence of its own on the production of news content; a special case of this might be the influence on military morale of the tone of reports from the field.

It is clear that all of these factors are involved to some extent in the determination of news content. Most studies deal with one or two of them, sometimes looking at the interaction, for example, between journalistic routines and elite influence, or economic imperatives and response to public opinion. Few try to consider in a broader way which are most consequential under what circumstances. Debates over the significance of military restrictions during the Gulf War illustrate what is at stake here. Some accounts suggest that these restrictions decisively shaped news content. Other accounts suggest that, because of the elite consensus at home, or because of filtering mechanisms within news organizations, military restrictions may in the end have made little difference. A number of studies, for example, have found that editors and television producers are reluctant to use graphic war footage or photos even when it is available (Morrison and Tumber, 1988; Taylor, 1992; Hallin and Gitlin, 1993), an editorial preference rooted in their relations with the audience, advertisers, and military families and personnel, as well as cultural norms.

Bennett and Paletz (1994) includes a number of studies which examine media coverage of the debate preceding the Gulf War in light of previous research on media and foreign policy. The main conclusion that emerges from these studies is strong confirmation of what Bennett (1990) and Bennett and Manheim (1993) call the 'indexing' hypothesis, according to which news coverage of a political controversy is 'indexed' or 'cued' to elite debate: how much criticism appears in the news, and what issues are discussed, reflects the degree and focus of elite debate. Entman and Page (1994) examine coverage of the debate in *The New York Times*, *The Washington Post*, and ABC news, finding that media content indeed varied with the parameters of elite debate. They also argue that even in this period of intense elite divisions, administration views got a privileged hearing. Cook (1994) shows that the reporting of the Gulf crisis, though it was taking place in the Middle East, was largely structured by the system of domestic news beats in Washington. What Bennett calls the 'indexing' or 'cueing' hypothesis is also developed in Hallin (1986, 1994a, 1994b), Solomon (1992) and Nacos (1990). Nacos examines newspaper coverage of crises, both domestic and foreign, the latter including the Cuban missile crisis, the Dominican invasion of 1965 and the Grenada invasion of 1983, and confirms the hypothesis that elites will 'rally' around the president during a crisis, producing a strongly supportive balance of news commentary.

Steele (1992) looks at the use of experts by the US television networks during the Gulf War, noting the preference of TV producers for 'players' connected with the policy-making community, and arguing that this produces an 'operational' bias towards interpreting war in terms of tactics and efficiency: How is the bombing carried out? How effective has it been? What will be Hussein's next move? This 'technical' bias in war coverage is also discussed in Hallin (1986).

There are many studies of the press corps in Washington or London and its relations with officials. What about war correspondents in the field? Morrison and Tumber (1988) provides a roughly comparable study. They found considerable tensions between journalists and the military during the Falklands War, based in part on conflicts over access to communication, transportation, and information, and in part on cultural differences. The latter arose not so much from political views as from the contrast between the competitive individualism of journalists and the hierarchy and collectivism of military culture. On the other hand, they found a strong tendency for journalists, whatever their political attitudes, to identify with the troops as they lived and shared dangers with them, to want to be accepted by them, to take on their ways of thinking – in short to report the war 'as participants rather than observers' (1988: 121). Mercer, Mungham and Williams (1987) report similar findings. This is not unlike the process often described with beat or lobby correspondents in Washington or London, who become in some sense insiders, though it perhaps occurs in a particularly strong way given the life-and-death situation reporters share with the troops. Morrison and Tumber's findings seems consistent with research on other wars. Mercer, Mungham and Williams (1987: 282) quote a senior Israeli officer as saying 'the best propaganda we have is the Israeli soldier'.

Hallin (1986, 1994a) makes the argument that war involves a different set of journalistic routines from those addressed in most media sociology. He distinguishes among three spheres of social reality, which involve different norms of journalistic practice: the spheres of consensus, legitimate controversy and deviance. Most media sociology concerns reporting within the sphere of legitimate controversy, where professional standards of balance and 'objectivity' prevail. But in wartime, Hallin argues, even in a limited war, another model of journalism comes into play, sometimes prevailing over and sometimes coexisting uncomfortably with the standard routines of political reporting. This is a model in which the journalist is expected not to stand back as an observer, but to participate actively in the reaffirmation of consensus norms. Hallin and Gitlin (1994) extend this work, looking at local news coverage in the Gulf War, and arguing that it performed a 'ritual' function of celebrating community consensus, a function frequently performed by local news, though usually in 'non-political' contexts. This finding clearly dovetails with the work of Peled and Katz (1974) and McLeod, Eveland and Signorielli (1993) on audience expectations of media performance during wartime. Hallin and Gitlin also explore the relation of local journalists to military families, around whom much of the local news was structured, and the influence of public opinion on local TV news. Reese and Bucklaw (1995), also focusing on local TV news, reached similar conclusions.

Morrison and Tumber (1988) found considerable ambivalence among journalists, both in the field and in London, about whether the journalist's proper role was as observer or patriot. Liebes (1992b) looks at patriotism in US and Israeli war coverage, stressing the differences in news conventions when journalists are covering 'their own' war, or that of another country, including, for example, the tendency to personalize 'our' side but not 'their' side. Many accounts of the Falklands/Malvinas War describe the controversy over whether the BBC was sufficiently patriotic, and the delicate balancing act the Corporation itself tried to perform, the Chairman of its Board of Governors saying that it could not be 'neutral as between our country and an aggressor', and endeavouring at the same time to emphasize the importance of protecting its national and international reputation for professional independence (Mercer, Mungham and Williams, 1987: 229).

Glasser and Liebes (forthcoming) explores the operation of censorship in Israel. Censorship, as they demonstrate, is not a unilateral exercise of state power, but involves negotiation and manoeuvring between journalists and censors, as well as cooperation between them, based upon a common background, a long-term working relationship and shared cultural assumptions, though the latter may be weakening.

Pedelty (1995) is based on an ethnographic study of the international press corps in El Salvador in 1991. The situation he describes is different from that in most of the literature on media and war in that these journalists were covering a foreign military, not the military of their own country. Pedelty explores the culture of the foreign correspondents (their attitudes, for example, to violence and their relation to it) and the working routines of war reporting. Among his most useful contributions are analyses of the means of social control constraining journalists, including controls exercised by the local military, for instance, through threats of violence, and through editors at home. Pedelty offers a kind of modern update, and an application to war reporting, of Warren Breed's classic article, 'Social control in the newsroom'.

221

The Gulf War involved a strong shift towards live television reporting, and has inspired a number of analysts to reflect on what this might mean for the profession of journalism. Katz (1992) has referred to this shift towards live coverage as the 'end of journalism', since it makes it very difficult for journalists to gather background information or to reflect upon and interpret what they and the audience are witnessing. They have the prestige of 'being there', and often will be cast as important characters in the televised drama, as they don their gas masks or refuse to take cover; but they have no more information than what the audience can see and hear, and in that sense become superfluous (Banks, 1992; Katz, 1992; White, 1994; Wolton, 1991; Zelizer, 1992). This is perhaps especially important when they are reporting televised press conferences, where military officials, in effect, take over the function of reporting the news.

There is unfortunately not much of a literature on the media and war within the political economy tradition, aside from critiques of the ideological content of war news: there is little, that is, that focuses on the influence of media ownership or economics on war coverage. Many discussions of the media and the Gulf War mention the support of 'corporate media' for the war, but the connection between corporate ownership and support for the war is not really examined systematically.

War as culture

One of the greatest weaknesses in the literature on the media and war – already suggested above in relation to the limitations of research on public opinion – is the absence of research into the nature of war as a cultural system, research, that is, which analyses war as meaningful social activity, and which connects media representations of war to larger structures of meaning in society.

The general literature on the war as a cultural phenomenon is neither large nor integrated into a coherent field, though it contains many fine works. These include Dyer (1985), Fussell (1975, 1989), Howard (1976), Marwick, (1977), Slotkin (1973), Vagts (1981), Franklin (1994, 1988), Trachtenberg (1989) and a number of feminist works cited below. Even the literature on nationalism, a subject which itself has only recently begun to attract the scholarly attention it deserves, deals surprisingly little with war. In this area, there is a particular need for cross-fertilization between studies of fictional representation of war, often developed within literary theory, and social science research on the news media and war.

Just in the past few years, mostly since the Gulf War, a number of scholars have begun to apply a cultural studies approach, broadly understood, to the study of media and war, and this seems a promising area for future research.

Hallin and Gitlin (1993) argue for understanding war as a form of popular culture. War is different from other political events, the argument goes, both because it has such extraordinary appeal to the cultural imagination, and because in wartime ordinary people become actors on the stage of history in a way that is normally not possible: their lives are at stake, of course; and they are also offered the opportunity, both soldiers and families on the home front, to become heroes in the media's narratives of war. The mass public, and the media which address that public, present war not primarily as a political policy, but as a form of individual and national self-expression. This cultural expression has two primary faces. War is understood, first of all, as a contest in which individuals and the nation can display mastery, professionalism, potency – the ability to overcome an enemy and accomplish a task. Second, war is understood as a ritual of solidarity, a celebration of community unity unattainable in ordinary times. These cultural understandings of war, according to Hallin and Gitlin, are rooted in war as a social activity and do not need to be created from scratch by state or media propaganda. The onset of the war triggers them across much of the society as, for example, soldiers set aside political doubts to focus on the 'job' they are trained to do and on which their lives depend. And they generally prove irresistible to the media, both because they provide excellent stories and images, and because standing back from them would leave journalists socially isolated. Hallin (1986) also develops the notion of war as expressive activity, looking at images of war over the course of the Vietnam conflict.

Taylor (1991) looks at the use of photographs in the British popular press from the First World War through the Falklands and Northern Ireland. The work is wide ranging, but is especially valuable for its discussions of the populist search for individual heroes and of the representation of patriotism. His work dramatizes the way common citizens become elevated in wartime to the status of patriotic symbols. The literature on nationalism has noted that the latter involves a 'symbolic elevation of the populace' (Greenfield and Chirot, 1994: 82) to a place of honour in political culture, and wartime news reporting is clearly an important site for this elevation. In the British and American tradition a populist style of news reporting serves to give the mass public a feeling of participation in the war effort, by cementing the bonds of sentiment between soldiers in the field and those at home, and by presenting war as an activity of ordinary people. In part, Taylor argues, this is done through idealized images of family life, which dominate much of the reporting in the popular press. This imagery of family life serves both to make war emotionally accessible to the mass public and to project an image of the nation itself as a family so that sentiments of caring can be mobilized in support of the war. Taylor also makes interesting observations about the way images of the English countryside serve as symbols of patriotism.

A significant new literature on war is also beginning to emerge out of feminist theory and gender studies. This literature includes Cooke and Woollacott (1993); Cooper, Munich and Squier (1989); Elshtain and Tobias (1990); Jeffords (1989, 1993), Sturken (1991) and Theweleit (1987, 1989). It is concerned, first of all, with the role of women in war, an important issue for media analysis, since women make up the majority of the audience for the popular media in wartime, and wartime communication is in large part directed towards securing their support. And it is concerned with the gendered character of representations or discourses concerning war. As Boose (1993: 69) puts it, 'A key observation that the feminist perspective has contributed to the critique of culture is the recognition that every public power arrangement depends on the control of femininity and masculinity as concepts, from which notions the control of individual, sexed subjects becomes possible', and through this, one could add, the mobilization of populations for the collective enterprise of war.

One particularly developed example of the feminist approach is Jeffords' *The Remasculinization of America* (1989). Jeffords argues that representations of Vietnam in American film and novels are motivated primarily by a concern to restore the 'masculinity' of a culture threatened with 'feminization' by defeat in Vietnam, the women's movement, and other social changes. In making this argument, she tries to show how the imagery of warfare reflected in these retellings is rooted in a conception of male self-sufficiency, centred around the male community of warriors, and the spectacle of the male body, a body 'reunified' and empowered through technology. This suggests one way of understanding the appeal of war – the tremendous emotional enthusiasm it can generate in participants and spectators. It also suggests one way in which the spectacle of war, both in fiction and in news, may have a cultural significance that goes beyond public attitudes specifically towards the use of military force.

A number of examples of feminist and gender studies approaches applied to the Gulf War can be found in Jeffords and Rabinowitz (1994). Wiegman, for example, argues that the Gulf War involved a kind of domestication of the soldier, who is now presented as having subjectivity and interiority of a sort he did not have in earlier representations, a reworking of masculinity that, she believes, stems from Vietnam and the women's movement. The old, 'hard' masculinity, meanwhile, is preserved in the image of technology. And Cloud argues that television coverage of the Gulf War channelled political concerns into a kind of therapeutic discourse of 'doing something for the emotional end of it'. Her work extends the analysis of family themes raised by Taylor, and points out, probably correctly, that these themes were particularly prominent in the Gulf War. This analysis makes an interesting contrast to Jeffords, suggesting that femininity as well as masculinity can be used to mobilize support for war.

Some of the feminist literature is prone to reductionism. 'As long as there is gender, there will be war', Jeffords claims (1989: 73), a view which seems as dubious as earlier claims that 'as long as there is property there will be war', and which at any rate could hardly be established by studying movies. But the feminist literature seems a particularly powerful and promising example of what a cultural analysis of war might look like.

Finally, there is surprisingly little literature on images of the enemy, though this theme comes up in most discussions of propaganda. And this would seem another fruitful area for further research, especially since there is a growing literature on the cultural constructions of race and 'orientalism'. Among the works that do deal with representations of the enemy or other in wartime are Dower (1986); McNair (1988) which deals with the Cold War, Saliba (1994), Taylor (1991) and Liebes (1992b).

CONCLUSION

I will conclude with a few broad recommendations for advancing the study of the media and war, some introduced above and some not.

1 First, there is a need for greater integration of the field, for greater awareness of the range of approaches that have been applied to the study of the media and war, often in isolation from one another.
2 Second, research on the media and war needs to be connected to broader questions of social theory: it needs to address the role of wartime communication in shaping the relation of state and society, the structure of the public sphere, including the political role of journalism, and the wider culture, including conceptions of citizenship, national identity and gender.
3 There is also a need for greater attention to historical background, in part because this is one way to move beyond topical critiques of the media's coverage of particular wars, towards research that would contribute more fully to social theory. The point here is not that we need more descriptive studies of past wars, though certainly there is a tremendous amount that could be done on journalistic practices and content in earlier wars. What is most needed, however, is greater sensitivity in any study, including a study of a contemporary war, to the long-term evolution of wartime communication.
4 Another way to give intellectual depth to the field would be to introduce more comparative research. Again, the point is not simply to produce descriptive studies of war coverage in different countries, but to connect differences in war reporting to relevant general characteristics of the societies involved: their political structure, their journalistic traditions and structures, their place in the world system, their political culture, and their historical experience of war.
5 Finally, a somewhat different kind of recommendation: there is clearly a need for research on a new form of military action emerging in the post-Cold War world: international 'peace-keeping' operations, which, with multinational command and the absence of much of the nationalist culture of earlier wars, as well as the absence of an 'enemy', may involve significantly different dynamics of media coverage and opinion-formation.

NOTES

1 The literature on the media and Korea is especially thin. See Knightly, 1975; Twentieth Century Fund, 1985; Aronson, 1970; Adams, 1986: 25–30.
2 Braestrup was rapporteur for the Twentieth Century Fund Task Force on the Military on the Media, whose report (1985) rejected this view of the media and Vietnam.
3 There is not a great deal of scholarly research on the media in these operations, but Sharkey (1991), Twentieth Century Fund (1985) and Mercer, Mungham and Williams (1987) give the basics of media–military relations, Herstgaard (1988) gives a journalistic account of the White House news management on Grenada, and Nacos (1990) includes a study of Grenada as a political story.
4 Mercer, Mungham and Williams (1987: 173) recount that a British Admiral called

Reuters during the Falklands War to ask the news agency to withhold information on British shipping movements around Ascension Island. He was told by the German who answered the phone that Reuters was an international agency, and couldn't be responsible for any particular national interest.

5 The main focus of their article is on the connection of authoritarianism as a personality trait with support for the war.

REFERENCES

Adams, V. (1986) *The Media and the Falklands Campaign*, London: MacMillan.

Aronson, J. (1970) *The Press and the Cold War*, Indianapolis, IN: Bobbs-Merrill.

Aulich, J. (1992) *Framing the Falklands War: Nationhood, Culture and Identity*, Milton Keynes: Open University Press.

Banks, A. (1992) 'Frontstage/backstage: loss of control in real-time coverage of the war in the Gulf', *Communication* 13: 111–19.

Bennett, W.L. (1990) 'Toward a theory of press–state relations in the United States', *Journal of Communication* 40: 103–25.

Bennett, W.L. and Manheim, J. (1993) 'Taking the public by storm: information, cueing and the democratic process in the Gulf conflict', *Political Communication* 10: 331–51.

Bennett, W.L. and Paletz, D. (eds) (1994) *Taken by Storm: the Media, Public Opinion and U.S. Foreign Policy in the Gulf War*, Chicago: University of Chicago Press.

Boose, L.E. (1993) 'Techno-muscularity and the "boy eternal": from the quagmire to the Gulf', in M. Cooke and A. Woollacott (eds) *Gendering War Talk*, Princeton: Princeton University Press.

Braestrup, P. (1977) *Big Story: How the American Press and Television Reported and Interpreted the Crisis of Tet 1968 in Vietnam and Washington*, Boulder, CO: Westview Press, 2 vols.

Brody, R.A. (1994) 'Crisis, war and public opinion: the media and public support for the president', in W.L. Bennett, and D. Paletz (eds) *Taken by Storm: the Media, Public Opinion and U.S. Foreign Policy in the Gulf War*, Chicago: University of Chicago Press.

Brody, R.A. and Shapiro, C.R. 'A reconsideration of the rally phenomenon in public opinion', in S. Long (ed.) *Political Behavior Annual*, vol. 2, Boulder, CO: Westview Press.

Brown, J.B. (1992) 'Media access to the battlefield', *Military Review* 72 (July): 10–20.

Cloud, D. (1994) 'Operation desert comfort', in S. Jeffords and L. Rabinowitz (eds) *Seeing Through the Media: the Persian Gulf War*, New Brunswick, NJ: Rutgers University Press.

Cook, T. (1994), 'Washington newsbeats and network news after the Iraq invasion of Kuwait', in W.L. Bennett, and D. Paletz (eds) *Taken by Storm: the Media, Public Opinion and U.S. Foreign Policy in the Gulf War*, Chicago: University of Chicago Press.

Cooke, M. and Woollacott, A. (1993) *Gendering War Talk*, Princeton: Princeton University Press.

Cooper, H.M., Munich, A.A. and Squier, S.M. (1989) *Arms and the Woman: War, Gender and Literary Representation*, Chapel Hill: University of North Carolina Press.

Crozier, E. (1959) *American Reporters on the Western Front*, New York: Oxford University Press.

Dennis, E. *et al.* (1991) *The Media At War: the Press and the Persian Gulf Conflict*, New York: Gannett Foundation Media Center.

Denton, R.E. Jr (ed.) (1993) *The Media and the Persian Gulf War*, Westport, CT: Praeger.

Dobkin, B. (1993) 'Constructing news narratives: ABC and CNN cover the Gulf war', in R.E. Denton, Jr (ed.) *The Media and the Persian Gulf War*, Westport, CT: Praeger.

Doherty, T. (1993) *Projections of War: Hollywood, American Culture and World War II*, New York: Columbia University Press.

Dower, J.W. (1986) *War Without Mercy: Race and Power in the Pacific War*, New York: Pantheon.

Dyer, G. (1985) *War*, New York: Crown Publishing.

Elshtain, J. B. and Tobias, S. (eds) (1990) *Women, Militarism and War*, Savage, MD: Rowman & Littlefield.

Entman, R.M. and Page, B.I. (1994) 'The news before the storm: the Iraq war debate and the limits to media independence', in W.L. Bennett and D. Paletz (eds) *Taken by Storm: the Media, Public Opinion and U.S. Foreign Policy in the Gulf War*, Chicago: University of Chicago Press.

Ettema, J.S. (1994) 'Discourse that is closer to silence than to talk: the politics and possibilities of reporting on victims of war', *Critical Studies in Mass Communication* 11: 1–21.

Fan, D.P. (1993) 'Media coverage and U.S. public opinion on the Persian Gulf', in B.S. Greenberg and W. Gantz (eds) *Desert Storm and the Mass Media*, Creeskill, NJ: Hampton Press.

Fialka, J. (1991) *Hotel Warriors: Covering the Gulf*, Washington, DC: The Woodrow Wilson Center.

Fussell, P. (1975) *The Great War and Modern Memory*, New York: Oxford University Press.

—— (1989) *Wartime: Understanding and Behavior in the Second World War*, New York: Oxford University Press.

Franklin, H.B. (1988) *War Stars: the Superweapon and the American Imagination*, New York: Oxford University Press.

—— (1994) 'From realism to virtual reality: images of America's wars', in S. Jeffords and L. Rabinowitz (eds) *Seeing Through the Media: The Persian Gulf War*, New Brunswick, NJ: Rutgers University Press.

Giddens, A. (1985) *The Nation-State and Violence*, Berkeley: University of California Press.

Gitlin, T. (1980) *The Whole World is Watching: The Mass Media in the Making and Unmaking of the New Left*, Berkeley: University of California Press.

Glasgow University Media Group (1985) *War and Peace News*, Milton Keynes: Open University Press.

Glasser, T. and Liebes, T. (forthcoming) 'Negotiated censorship: how the Israeli press manoeuvres between 'responsible' and 'watchdog' journalism', unpublished paper.

Greenberg, B.S. and Gantz, W. (eds) (1993) *Desert Storm and the Mass Media*, Creeskill, NJ: Hampton Press.

Greenfield, L. and Chirot, D. (1994) 'Nationalism and aggression', *Theory and Society* 23: 79–130.

The Gulf War in the Media (1992), *The Nordicom Review* 2.

Gunter, B. and Wober, M. (1993) 'The Gulf crisis and television: the public response in Britain', in B.S. Greenberg and W. Gantz (eds) *Desert Storm and the Mass Media*, Creeskill, NJ: Hampton Press.

Gustadt, L.E. (1993) 'Taking the pulse of the CNN audience: a case study of the Gulf War', *Political Communication* 10: 389–409.

Hackett, R.A. (1993) 'Engulfed: peace protest and America's press during the Gulf War', New York: Center for War Peace and the News Media, New York University, Occasional Paper.

—— (1991) *News and Dissent: The Press and the Politics of Peace in Canada*, Norwood, NJ: Ablex.

Hallin, D.C. (1986) *The 'Uncensored War': the Media and Vietnam*, New York: Oxford University Press.

—— (1994a) 'From Vietnam to El Salvador: hegemony and ideological change', in *We*

227

Keep America on Top of the World: Television Journalism and the Public Sphere, London: Routledge.

—— (1994b) 'The media, the war in Vietnam and political support: a critique of the thesis of an oppositional media', in *We Keep America on Top of the World: Television Journalism and the Public Sphere*, London: Routledge.

Hallin, D.C. and Gitlin, T. (1993) 'Agon and ritual: the Gulf war as popular culture and as television drama', *Political Communication* 10: 411–24.

Halloran, J.D., Elliott, P. and Murdock, G. (1970) *Demonstrations and Communication*, Harmondsworth: Penguin.

Hammond, W.M. (1988) *Public Affairs: the Media and the Military*, Washington, DC: US Government Printing Office.

Harris, R. (1983) *GOTCHA! The Media, the Government and the Falklands Crisis*, London: Faber and Faber.

Herman, E. and Chomsky, N. (1988) *Manufacturing Consent: the Political Economy of the Mass Media*, New York: Pantheon.

Herstgaard, M. (1988), *On Bended Knee: The Press and the Reagan Presidency*, New York: Farar Straus Giroux.

Hohenberg, J. (1964) *Foreign Correspondence: the Great Reporters and Their Times*, New York: Columbia University Press.

Hooper, A. (1982) *The Military and the Media*, Aldershot: Gower.

Hopkin, D. (1970) 'Domestic censorship in the first world war', *Journal of Contemporary History* 5: 151–70.

Howard, M. (1975) 'Total war in the twentieth century: participation and consensus in the Second World War', in B. Bond and I. Roy (eds) *War and Society: a Yearbook of Military History*, London: Croom Helm.

—— (1976) *War in European Society*, New York: Oxford University Press.

Jeffords, S. (1989) *The Remasculinization of America: Gender and the Vietnam War*, Bloomington: Indiana University Press.

Jeffords, S. and Rabinowitz, L. (eds) (1994) *Seeing Through the Media: the Persian Gulf War*, New Brunswick, NJ: Rutgers University Press.

Jensen, R. (1992) 'Fighting objectivity: the illusion of journalistic neutrality in coverage of the Persian Gulf war', *Journal of Communication Inquiry* 16: 20–32.

Kaid, L.L. *et al.* (1993) 'Telling the Gulf war story: coverage in five papers', in B.S. Greenberg and W. Gantz (eds) *Desert Storm and the Mass Media*, Creeskill, NJ: Hampton Press.

Kasza, G. (1988) *The State and the Mass Media in Japan, 1918–1945*, Berkeley: University of California Press.

Katz, E. (1992) 'The end of journalism? Notes on watching the Persian Gulf war', *Journal of Communication* 42: 26–41.

Kellner, D. (1992) *The Persian Gulf TV War*, Boulder, CO: Westview.

Kennedy, D.M. (1980) *Over Here: the First World War and American Society*, New York: Oxford.

Knightly, P. (1975)*The First Casualty*, New York: Harcourt, Brace, Jovanovich.

Koppes, C.R. (1987) *Hollywood Goes to War: How Politics, Profits, and Propaganda Shaped Second World War Movies*, New York: Free Press.

Lasswell, H. (1927) *Propaganda Technique in the World War*, New York: Knopf.

Lichty, L.W. (1984) 'Comments on the influence of television on public opinion', in P. Braestrup (ed.) *Vietnam as History*, Washington, DC: University Press of America.

Liebes, T. (1992a) 'Decoding television news: the political discourse of Israeli hawks and doves', *Theory and Society* 21: 357–81.

—— (1992b) 'Our war/their war: comparing the *Intifadeah* and the Gulf war on U.S. and Israeli television', *Critical Studies in Mass Communication* 9: 44–55.

Liebes, T. and Ribak, R. (1994), 'In defense of negotiated readings: how moderates on each side of the conflict interpret Intifada news', *Journal of Communication* 44: 108–24.

Lippmann, W. and Merz, C. (1920) 'A test of the news', *The New Republic*, 4 August.

MacArthur, J.R. (1992) *Second Front: Censorship and Propaganda in the Gulf War*, New York: Hill and Wang.

McLeod, D.M., Eveland, W.P. and Signorielli, N. (1994) 'Conflict and public opinion: rallying effects of the Persian Gulf war', *Journalism Quarterly* 71: 20–31.

McNair, B. (1988) *Images of the Enemy: Reporting the New Cold War*, London: Routledge.

Marwick, A. (1977) *War and Social Change in the Twentieth Century*, New York: Oxford University Press.

—— (1988) *Total War and Social Change*, London: Macmillan.

Mercer, D., Mungham, G. and Williams, K. (1987) *The Fog of War: the Media on the Battlefield*, London: Heinemann.

Milavsky, J.R. and Galceran, I. (1993), 'The public's response to a mediated war', in B.S. Greenberg and W. Gantz (eds) *Desert Storm and the Mass Media*, Creeskill, NJ: Hampton Press.

Miller, M. (1992) *Spectacle: Operation Desert Storm and the Triumph of Illusion*, New York: Simon & Schuster.

Moeller, S.D. (1989) *Shooting War: Photography and the American Experience of Combat*, New York: Basic Books.

Morgan, M., Lewis, J. and Jhally, S. (1992), 'More viewing, less knowledge', in H. Mowlana, G. Gerbner, and H.I. Schiller (eds) *Triumph of the Image: The Media's War in the Gulf, a Global Perspective*, Boulder, CO: Westview Press.

Morrison, D. E. and Tumber, H. (1988) *Journalists at War: the Dynamics of News Reporting During the Falklands Conflict*, London: Sage.

Mowlana, H., Gerbner, G. and Schiller, H. I. (eds) (1992) *Triumph of the Image: the Media's War in the Gulf, a Global Perspective*, Boulder, CO: Westview Press.

Mueller, J.E. (1973) *War, Presidents and Public Opinion*, New York: Wiley.

—— (1994) *Policy and Opinion in the Gulf War*, Chicago: University of Chicago Press.

Nacos, B.L. (1990) *The Press, Presidents and Crises*, New York: Columbia University Press.

Oliver, M.B., Mares, M.-L. and Cantor, J. (1993) 'News viewing, authoritarianism and attitudes toward the Gulf war', in R.E. Denton, Jr (ed.) *The Media and the Persian Gulf War*, Westport, CT: Praeger.

Pan, Z., Ostman, R.E., Moy, P. and Reynolds, P. (1993) 'Public perceptions and evaluations of U.S. news media performance in the Gulf war', in B.S. Greenberg and W. Gantz (eds) *Desert Storm and the Mass Media*, Creeskill, NJ: Hampton Press.

Patterson, O. (1984) 'An analysis of television coverage of the Vietnam war,' *Journal of Broadcasting* 28: 397–404.

Pedelty, M.H. (1995) *War Stories: the Culture of Foreign Correspondents*, London: Routledge.

Peled, T. and Katz, E. (1974) 'Media functions in wartime: the Israel homefront in October 1973', in J.G. Blumler and E. Katz (eds) *The Uses of Mass Communications: Current Perspectives on Gratifications Research*, Beverly Hills, CA: Sage.

Reese, S.D. and Bucklaw, B. (1995) 'The militarism of local television: the routine framing of the Persian Gulf war', *Critical Studies in Mass Communication* 12: 40–59.

Regan, P.M. (1994) *Organizing Societies for War: the Process and Consequences of Societal Militarization*, Westport, CN: Praeger.

Richardson, L.F. (1948) 'War-moods', *Psychometrika* 13: 147–74, 197–232.

Saliba, T. (1994) 'Military presences and absences: Arab women and the Persian Gulf war', in S. Jeffords and L. Rabinowitz (eds) *Seeing Through the Media: The Persian Gulf War*, New Brunswick, NJ: Rutgers University Press.

229

Savarese, R. (1992) *Guerre intelligenti: Stampa, radio, tv informatica: la comunicazione politica dalla Crimea al Golfo Persico*, Milano: FrancoAngeli.
—— (1993) 'The European press and Saladin the fierce', *European Journal of Communication* 8: 53–75.
Schuman, H. and Rieger, C. (1992) 'Historical analogies, generational effects and attitudes toward war', *American Sociological Review* 57: 315–26.
Sharkey, J.E. (1991) *Under Fire: U.S. Military Restrictions on the Media from Grenada to the Persian Gulf*, Washington, DC: Center for Public Integrity.
Shaw, M. (1988) *The Dialectics of War: an Essay in the Social Theory of Total War and Peace*, London: Pluto Press.
—— (1991) *Post-military Society: Militarism, Demilitarization and War at the End of the Twentieth Century*, Philadelphia: Temple University Press.
Shaw, M. and Carr-Hill, R. (1991), 'Mass media and violence: attitudes to the Gulf war in Britain', in M. Morgan (ed.) *The Media and the Gulf War, The Electronic Journal of Communication/La Revue Electronique de La Communication* (special issue) 1(4), Montreal.
Shulman, H.C. (1994) 'The international media and the Persian Gulf war: the importance of the flow of news', in S. Jeffords and L. Rabinowitz (eds) *Seeing Through the Media: the Persian Gulf War*, New Brunswick, NJ: Rutgers University Press.
Sigelman, L. *et al.* (1993), 'As time goes by: daily opinion change during the Persian Gulf crisis', *Political Communication* 10: 353–68.
Slotkin, R. (1973) *Regeneration Through Violence: the Mythology of the American Frontier, 1600–1860*, Middletown, CN: Wesleyan University Press.
Small, M. (1994) *Covering Dissent: the Media and the Anti-Vietnam War Movement*, New Brunswick, NJ: Rutgers University Press.
Solomon, W.S. (1992) 'News frames and media packages: covering El Salvador', *Critical Studies in Mass Communication* 9: 56–74.
Steele, J.E. (1992), 'Enlisting experts: objectivity and the operational bias in television news analysis of the Persian Gulf war', Washington, DC: Woodrow Wilson Center Media Studies Project, occasional paper no. 12.
Sturken, M. (1991) 'The wall, the screen, and the image: the Vietnam veterans' memorial', *Representations* 35: 118–42.
Swanson, D.L. and Smith, L.D. (1993) 'War in the global village: a seven-country comparison of television news coverage of the beginning of the Gulf War', in R.E. Denton, Jr (ed.) *The Media and the Persian Gulf War*, Westport, CT: Praeger.
Taylor, J. (1991) *War Photography: Realism in the Press*, London: Routledge.
Taylor, P.M. (1990) *Munitions of the Mind: War Propaganda from the Ancient World to the Nuclear Age*, Wellingborough: Patrick Stephens.
—— (1992) *War and the Media: Propaganda and Persuasion in the Gulf War*, Manchester: Manchester University Press.
Thewelweit, K. (1987, 1989) *Male Fantasies*, 2 vols, Minneapolis: University of Minnesota Press.
Towle, P. (1975) 'The debate on wartime censorship in Britain 1902–14', in B. Bond and I. Roy (eds) *War and Society: a Yearbook of Military History*, London: Croom Helm.
Trachtenberg, A. (1989) 'Albums of war', in *Reading American Photographs: Images as History from Matthew Brady to Walker Evans*, New York: Hill and Wang.
Twentieth Century Fund (1985) *Battle Lines: Report of the Twentieth Century Fund Task Force on the Military and the Media*, New York: Priority Press Publications.
Vagts, A. (1981) *A History of Militarism*, Westport, CN: Greenwood Press.
White, M. (1994) 'Site unseen: an analysis of CNN's war in the gulf', in S. Jeffords and L. Rabinowitz (eds) *Seeing Through the Media: the Persian Gulf War*, New Brunswick, NJ: Rutgers University Press.

Wiegman, R. 'Missiles and melodrama (masculinity and the televisual war)', in S. Jeffords and L. Rabinowitz (eds) *Seeing Through the Media: the Persian Gulf War*, New Brunswick, NJ: Rutgers University Press.

Wolton, D. (1991) *War Game: L'information et la guerre*, Paris: Flammarion.

Wyatt, C.R. (1993) *Paper Soldiers: the American Press and the Vietnam War*, New York: W.W. Norton.

Zaller, J.R. (1992) *The Nature and Origins of Mass Opinion*, Cambridge: Cambridge University Press.

—— (1994), 'Elite leadership of public opinion: new evidence from the Vietnam war', in W.L. Bennett and D. Paletz (eds) *Taken by Storm: the Media, Public Opinion and U.S. Foreign Policy in the Gulf War*, Chicago: University of Chicago Press.

Zelizer, B. (1992) 'CNN, the Gulf war and journalistic practice', *Journal of Communication* 42: 66–81.

INDEX